Media Theories and Approaches

A Global Perspective

Mark Balnaves
Stephanie Hemelryk Donald
Brian Shoesmith

palgrave
macmillan

First published 2009 by
PALGRAVE MACMILLAN

Palgrave Macmillan in the UK is an imprint of Macmillan Publishers Limited, registered in England, company number 785998, of Houndmills, Basingstoke, Hampshire RG21 6XS.

Palgrave Macmillan in the US is a division of St Martin's Press LLC, 175 Fifth Avenue, New York, NY 10010.

Palgrave Macmillan is the global academic imprint of the above companies and has companies and representatives throughout the world.

Palgrave® and Macmillan® are registered trademarks in the United States, the United Kingdom, Europe and other countries.

ISBN-13: 978–0–230–55161–9 hardback
ISBN-10: 0–230–55161–0 hardback
ISBN-13: 978–0–230–55162–6 paperback
ISBN-10: 0–230–55162–9 paperback

This book is printed on paper suitable for recycling and made from fully managed and sustained forest sources. Logging, pulping and manufacturing processes are expected to conform to the environmental regulations of the country of origin.

A catalogue record for this book is available from the British Library.

Library of Congress Cataloging-in-Publication Data

Balnaves, Mark.
  Media theories and approaches : a global perspective / Mark
  Balnaves, Stephanie Donald, Brian Shoesmith.
      p. cm.
  Includes bibliographical references and index.
  ISBN 978–0–230–55161–9
  1. Mass media. I. Donald, Stephanie. II. Shoesmith, Brian. III.
  Title.
  P90.B273 2009
  302.23—dc22

2008037818

10 9 8 7 6 5 4 3 2 1
18 17 16 15 14 13 12 11 10 09

Printed and bound in China

Mary Claire, Gerard, Dash and Xavier
Morag and Ellen
Vivien, Francesca, Patrick, Gavin and Briony

Contents

List of figures

List of tables

Foreword

China in March 2008 represented the biggest web market by users of any other country in the world. It had an estimated 230 million users, adding a staggering 73 million users in 2007 alone. For companies like Google (who represent only 15 per cent of the market share – the largest market share is held by Baidu at about 75 per cent), this market will be worth US$3.5 billion by 2012. Such a scenario, wherein China challenges US pre-eminence in usage and delivery, indicates how market, growth and politics define the grounds of media debate today.

It was only in the 1920s, as Briggs and Burke (2002) point out in their book *A Social History of the Media*, that the *Oxford English Dictionary* first picked up that people spoke about the media as an important part of their lives, or indeed as a collective 'thing' at all. This book is about 'the media' but it is also about 'global media studies'. When the first astronauts who landed on the moon toured the world they were universally greeted with the phrase 'We did it!' 'We' may have meant the US, but many viewers around the world took it to include them as well, part of the audience. 'We' uttered at the climax of a major media event gave the impression of an interdependent, interconnected, world. The landing on the moon, though, was a Cold War event when nuclear war was on the horizon. Interconnections were, then as now, determined by power and money. There was an East–West split (Soviet bloc–Allies) and a North–South (rich–poor) divide (the latter still continues). The wealthy nations' description of other, less advantaged, nations also reflected the ethnocentric view of international affairs dominated by the powerful. 'Third World countries' or 'developing nations' were phrases used to describe nations struggling to feed their own people. Even recently, with events like the tragedy in Rwanda, 'First World' nations were slow to put the massacres of the Tutsi people as a top news agenda item while the arguably parochial O.J. Simpson drama was unfolding in Los Angeles. September 11, 2001, however, has changed the mediascape, and the sense of space in which important events occur. Commentators like Tom Pyszczynski proclaimed, for example, that the event for the average US citizen was equivalent to the cultural trauma that many indigenous peoples experienced in response to colonization by European and American countries (cited in Prewitt et al., 2004). You may or may not accept that assessment, but it is the case that something enormous happened to the mediation of global events after that date. The aftermath of 9/11 brought with it psychological shock for wealthy nations together with a rhetoric of 'axis of evil' and terror as an all-encompassing and everywhere threat. The 9/11 tragedy also brought with it, though, a recognition of the basic fact that we are physically connected in our future. Climate change, similarly, has heightened this awareness of interconnectedness, in terms of overall human survival. Most recently to the writing of this book, the 2008 natural disasters in Sichuan, China and in Myanmar have prompted great media interest, and profound international empathy. The sense that natural disasters are part of a global experience and are not localized to 'other people' is travelling through the intimacy of immediate media reportage.

A genuine global media studies programme, therefore, is not just about the rich, North, view of the world. Globalization is about the networks – of media, goods, people – that cross national boundaries and can vary in their extent, intensity, tempo and influence. Global media studies as a discipline involves studying the complexity of the media process, locally and globally. The media networks and flows are not all unidirectional, originating from Hollywood or from monopolized news agencies. The modern global mediascape is rich and complex and often contradictory. The authors have tried to capture some of this complexity in looking at different phenomena within this global mediascape – including theories, structures and organizations, content, audience and effects.

Acknowledgements

The authors are grateful for colleagues' permission to reproduce material and to relatives and colleagues for their ideas and contributions to the formation of the book.

- Kim Balnaves, doctoral student at Charles Sturt University, for her insights into children, education and digital games;
- John and Charles Balnaves and Harrison for their insights;
- Ulla Carlsson, Dr, Professor, Director, NORDICOM, Göteborg University, for permission to reproduce work from *The Rise and Fall of NWICO – and Then? From a Vision of International Regulation to a Reality of Multilevel Governance*. NORDICOM;
- Miguel Centeno, Princeton University, for his permission to reproduce global flows maps from his unpublished paper 'McDonalds, Wienerwald, and the Corner Deli';
- Maurice Dunlevy for his insights into modern journalism and his generous permission to use his unpublished work on news; some of which was done jointly with Mark Balnaves in the Canberra days;
- John G. Gammack for his permission to cite and include sections of his co-authored book with S.H. Donald on tourism and the branded city;
- Chris Harrison, Human-Computer Interaction Institute, Carnegie Mellon University, for permission to reproduce his Internet maps;
- Dylan Horrocks for his insights into world-building and comics;
- The International Federation of the Phonographic Industry (IFPI) for permission to reproduce its data and information from its reports on digital piracy;
- Nick Jankowski and the *Electronic Journal of Communication* (2004) **14**(3/4) for permission to reproduce or adapt from the essay 'Digital Culture and the Digital Divide: A Theoretical Framework';
- Anne McLaren, University of Melbourne, for permission to use work from her paper *Targeting Chinese women: constructing a female cyberspace*;
- Debra Mayrhofer, Edith Cowan University, Mark Gibson and the editorial collective at *Continuum*, and Taylor & Francis, for permission to reproduce parts of 'The Media Professions and the New Humanism' in *Continuum: Journal of Media and Cultural Studies* (2004) 18(2), http://www.informaworld.com;
- Laura Nelson for permission to reproduce work from her project *Looking for Love in Cyberspace*;

- Erika Pearson, for her permission to reproduce work from her Honours thesis *The Digital is Political* and other works;
- Madanmohan Rao and Eastern Universities Press for permission to reproduce or adapt material from the chapter 'Push, Pull, Layering, and Blogs: user behaviour in the online medium' from *News Media and New Media* (2003);
- Tom O'Regan, University of Queensland, for his permission to use work from the joint Australian Research Council (ARC) study on the history of audience ratings;
- Ian Saunders, University of Western Australia, for his ideas on 'dome logic';
- Greg Smith, for permission to reproduce his work on the Berbers;
- Glen Spoors, Edith Cowan University, for his provision of extensive references and insights to work on games culture;
- Damien Spry, University of Technology Sydney, for his written contribution to the section on mobile cultures in Chapter 3;
- David Tham, for his assistance with compiling the online atlas;
- John and Glenda Tomlinson and Madeline Lambert for their support and access to family archives on the history of cinema in Albany;
- John Yunker, president and chief analyst at bytelevel/research and Fellow of the Society for New Communications Research, for permission to reproduce for students his country code map.

The authors are also grateful to students and colleagues at Edith Cowan University and University of Liberal Arts Bangladesh (ULAB), colleagues in Chinese media, especially in Guangzhou and Hong Kong, and Leicia Petersen and Ming Liang for their various contributions.

A very special thanks from the authors to Emily Salz, Commissioning Editor at Palgrave Macmillan, for her ideas and extensive and insightful summaries of reviews that helped to shape the text intellectually as well as in format. Thank you also to Sheree Keep and Anna Reeve at Palgrave for their assistance and good humour. The authors are grateful to the reviewers of the initial manuscript for this book. The comments were much appreciated and the suggestions followed up.

Finally, Bryony Allen's copy editing – thorough and witty – and the work of Linda Norris and colleagues at Aardvark Editorial were much appreciated.

Convergences

part

1

Media studies involves tracing the media through the ways in which they participate in contemporary social and cultural life. It deals with various components of that process, including structures and organization of media, content, audience and effects.

In this book the authors will explore in detail each of the components of the mediation process in a global context. The book will introduce you to the world of media studies in an era where nations are becoming more interconnected through modern media networks.

This section is called 'convergences' because the authors, like many of our peers, have learned to recognize that convergence did not arrive with the computer and that all previous communications are moments of convergence. Convergence is the transformation of older media, like print, into new cultural or new technology forms, like online news. Different societies and cultures are dealing with convergence and globalization in different ways.

Globalization at the minimum involves networks – of media, goods, people – that cross national boundaries and can vary in their extent, intensity, tempo and influence. In this section the authors will introduce you to some of the key issues in media studies and globalization, and provide you with background to the history of convergence of media and the current global context.

Chapter 1, Introduction, introduces the discipline of media studies and the ideas of globalization and convergence.

Chapter 2, Technologizing the Word, looks at the historical context of convergence, including:
- writing and the alphabet, an early technologization of the word;
- the printing press, enabling standardization of languages, grammars and spelling;
- broadcast media, introducing instantaneous worldwide and mass audience communication;
- computers and social media, combining the one-to-many possibilities of mass media with the many-to-many capability of personal networks.

Chapter 3, A Global View, puts convergence in a contemporary context and outlines:
- the terminology used to describe some of these global changes, and their implications for globalization;
- the problem of autonomy versus interconnectedness of cultures and the idea of a digital divide;
- the rise of mobile cultures as a global phenomenon.

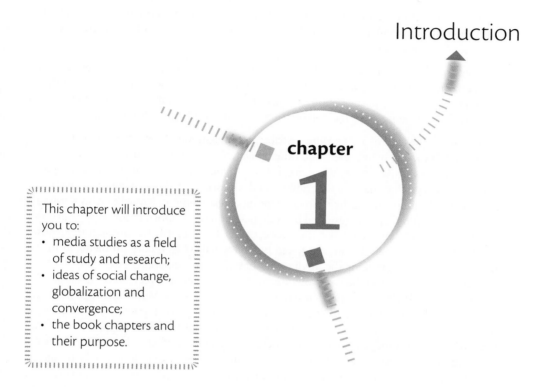

Introduction

chapter

1

This chapter will introduce you to:
- media studies as a field of study and research;
- ideas of social change, globalization and convergence;
- the book chapters and their purpose.

Four-year-old Madeleine McCann disappeared from an apartment in Praia da Luz, in the Algarve, Portugal, on Thursday 3 May 2007. Madeleine, from Rothley in Leicestershire, United Kingdom, had, her parents said, been taken from her bed while they were eating at a restaurant in the same complex, close to the apartment. Kate and Gerry McCann told police that they had regularly checked on Madeleine and their two-year-old twins.

Madeleine was never found and the story went global. The parents soon became 'media' suspects in the disappearance and debate about their innocence or guilt became passionate and prurient conversation among those who did or did not support them. Meanwhile the parents set up a website, http://www.findmadeleine.com, to seek help in finding Madeleine and received contributions of millions of dollars to the cause.

The McCann story has all the elements of interest to media studies and this book. There is a global system that distributes the story. There are interpersonal Internet networks, such as blogs, where the story becomes a hotly discussed topic. There are complex cultural and intercultural interpretations of the symbolic content. Chinese and British reactions for example were different. There are issues of social class and media agenda setting. Did the McCanns receive overly supportive reporting and coverage or overly negative reporting? Was the emphasis on their story to the detriment of other more deserving stories?

Roger Silverstone famously asked 'Why Study the Media?' (1999). And so we echo him. Why study the media and processes of mediation of symbolic content? Why study the McCann tragedy? Because media are central to our everyday lives. And every day people ask questions about the media. Who mediates the media? And how? And what are the consequences? Indeed, what are the aspects of the media that are 'invisibly ideological' (Silverstone, 1999)?

> How do we assess the ways in which the struggles over and within the media are played out: struggles over the ownership and control of both institutions and meanings; struggles over access and participation, struggles over representation; struggles which inform and affect our sense of each other, our sense of ourselves? (Silverstone, 1999, 5)

Research into the media and the distribution of symbolic content helps us to better understand how our own society and other societies work. But it can also provide organizations and policymakers with key insights into planning for the future. For example, it was not long ago that many demographics and minorities in western countries were not represented in simple things like audience ratings measurement. Knowing who is missing from and who should be represented by audience ratings is important for equity purposes and fairness. Such knowledge is not esoteric, nor is it necessarily the product of idealism or of commercial greed. It can be applied by policymakers to rectify problems in measuring audiences, and making the media work better for more people.

Dennis McQuail (McQuail, in Downing et al., 2004, 1) in his overview of media studies says that media studies is a field that has 'uncertain boundaries'. Valdivia (2003, 3) further argues that defining the media studies field 'remains a project fraught with difficulty'. While this may or may not be true, we know, as Thompson (1997, 30) points out, that cultural forms in modern society have increasingly been mediated by the mechanisms and institutions of mass media or mass communication. For example, a mobile phone, as a cultural form, may signify wealth in one society and be a symbol of fashion in another. Now, you might say that a mobile phone is not a mass medium. Mass media and mass communication are often associated with newspapers, radio, television and other media that are one-to-many. Interestingly, a mobile phone can be a personal communication technology at one moment and, potentially, a receiver of broadcast advertisements at another. Either way though, it is possible to argue that whether operating as a personal or mass technology, a mobile phone is part of a process of mediating symbolic content. In all cultures we attach meanings to things, people and to practices as well as to our physical environment. The media are an intimate part of this process of distributing symbolic content and meanings. In media studies, this mediation, or technologizing of the word, has a long history and starts, at least in alphabetic writing systems, with the alphabet. Language is a medium as are speech, writing, print and audio-visual representation.

Technologizing of the word. Describes the move to media – such as writing and the alphabet – as major revolutions in human evolution.

We can therefore perhaps again quote Silverstone and usefully describe media studies as *tracing the media through the ways in which they participate in social and cultural life* (Silverstone, 1999, 4).

In media studies, the technologization of the word – using media to convey meaning – is often discussed from different components of the process of distributing symbolic content. Traditionally, this includes theories, structures and organizations, audiences, content and effects.

- *Theories:* Theories are explanations. Media theorists or writers try to explain different phenomena in the process of mediation. For example, the question 'Does showing violence in movies lead to violent people?' raises causal questions about the effects of the media in society. There may be competing theories that come up with competing conclusions.

- *Structures and organizations:* Media, political and social systems all affect the process of mediation of symbolic content. Ownership and control of the media, media economics, and of course the media professions themselves, are all part of the structures and organization of media.
- *Content:* What we see, hear or read, whether today's news in a newspaper or an SMS (text) message, are a part of the symbolic content of media. The symbolic content is what lies behind the actual content – the relationship between reader, sociocultural context and information that creates the symbolic 'ness' of the mediated information transfer. The distribution of symbolic content can, of course, be affected by the structures and organization of media as well as the culture within which we live. The construction of meaning from media content, or media texts, and ideological conflicts involved in these constructions are a major area of research in media studies.
- *Audiences:* Early media researchers had an intense interest in the behaviour of audiences or in fact what constituted 'an audience'. The study of audiences can be at individual, group or societal level.
- *Effects:* The process of mediation of symbolic content has effects. For example, in the United Kingdom advertising junk food to children who are watching television is considered harmful and, indeed, is banned. Effects research has an empirical tradition, also called administrative research in the United States. Early empirical or administrative research took a commercial interest in how public opinion was being shaped by media or how audiences were using media or advertising in their buying behaviour. Critical research in contrast, dealt with power and ideology and how culture had itself become an industry.

Empirical research. Observations about the world using systematic quantitative or qualitative research methods.

Administrative research. Refers to early US media research tied to commercial or governmental interests in audience behaviour and persuasion.

Critical research. Refers to early European theorizing about media, ideology and culture.

to recap...

Media studies involves tracing the media through the ways in which they participate in contemporary social and cultural life. It deals with various components of that process, including structures and organization of media, content, audience and effects.

Social and global change

If media studies involves tracing the media through the ways in which they participate in contemporary social and cultural life, then we cannot ignore the global nature of this enterprise. The technology of digital media is expanding into complex networks. Indeed, the virtual world of multiplayer, globally accessed online worlds such as *Second Life* and *World of Warcraft* now involves hundreds of thousands of people. Massively multiplayer online role playing game groups (MMORPG) such as *World of Warcraft* now have budgets the size of the Gross Domestic Product of small nation states. They also set up new regional bases, with Korea, the US and increasingly China becoming centres of participation in these trends.

The modern discourse on the technology of media often uses statistics and comparisons to show the scale of technological change. In 1996, the 'The Hitch-hiker's Guide to Cybernomics' in *The Economist* said:

Twenty-five years ago only about 50,000 computers existed in the whole wide world; now the number has rocketed to an estimated 140m. And that does not include any of the chips inside cars, washing machines or even talking greeting cards. A typical car today has more computer-processing power than the first lunar landing-craft had in 1969. In 1844 Samuel Morse launched the era of instant communication by telegraphing the prophetic words: 'What hath God wrought!' In 1960 a transatlantic telephone cable could carry only 138 conversations simultaneously. Now a fibre-optic cable can carry 1.5m conversations. (*The Economist*, 1996, S3–7)

The discourses on changes in the technology of media include discourses on changes in how media professions operate. Friedland and Webb (1996) describe how they set up *Online Wisconsin*, an online journal as part of their journalism course at the University of Wisconsin, beginning in 1993. They were driven to it by the realization that news was already being delivered in new ways. 'The rapid pace of acceptance of new technologies means the vision of the "multimedia journalist" carrying a tape recorder, small format video camera, and notebook becomes less futuristic every day ... we can now define multimedia journalism as the combined application of hypertext, graphics audio, and video in a single journalistic publication on the Internet' (Friedland and Webb, 1996, 55). As they point out, the move was already happening and was being led partly by traditional media organizations and partly by computer-based organizations.

Convergence. The transformation of older media, like print, into new cultural or new technology forms, like online news. Different societies and cultures are dealing with convergence and globalization in different ways.

The process of bringing together different media into one activity or one medium is called convergence. The Internet is a convergence technology because it brings together video, sound and text. Convergence can also mean new service types or corporate restructuring, for example telecommunications companies also becoming broadcasting companies and publishing companies. Convergence raises obvious questions about whether society has changed as a result of the introduction of new media. There are two main positions on the issue of social change in this world of global media. Webster (1995) distinguishes between those social theorists who think that contemporary society is a new kind of society, different from hitherto existing societies, and those for whom it is a continuation of established social relationships but with an intensified role of information and media.

The supporters of continuity over change tend to be *pessimistic* about the future. The supporters of contemporary society as a new kind of society tend to be *optimistic*. Those who support the idea of continuity in social and technological change tend to have ideology and issues of power, ownership and control as their predominant concern. Those who support the idea of radical change tend to have pluralism and issues of free flow of information, diversity and competing power bases as their predominant concern.

Influential to discussions on emerging technologies has been the work of Manuel Castells (1996; 1997; 1998) who introduced several ideas concerning the networked realm of globalization. 'The rise of the network society calls into question the processes of construction of identity... thus inducing new forms of social change. This is because the network society is based on the systemic disjunction between the local and the global for most individuals and social groups' (Castells, 1997).

Technology is, without a doubt, one of the most important contributory factors underlying the internationalization and globalization of economic activity (Dicken, 1998, 145) Since the development and expansion of telecommunication networks brought the concept of the 'shrinking world' to public knowledge, an idea derived from McLuhan's (1962) concept of global village, the convergence of technologies such as the telephone, fax, and computer, has inspired debate about issues of societal transformation toward an information society. Manuel Castells in his early work motivated discussion on themes concerning the philosophical and theoretical basis of the information society. Works such as *Postmodern Geographies* (Soja, 1989) and *Collapsing Space and Time* (Brunn and Leinbach, 1991) heralded ideas that emphasized diversity and increased freedoms.

It was not, however, until the expansion of the Internet in the mid-90s and the analysis of experiences of networks, their meaning to users, their operability and other qualitative issues related to the communicational information systems, that critical debate on the subject really took off. The development of data-transaction speed and the enormous increase in users resulted in the Internet being known variously as the *information highway*, the *electronic frontier* or the *virtual land of expression* (Adams, 1998). Graham crystallizes the main argument as follows:

> Human life becomes liberated from the constraint of space and frictional effects of distance. Anything becomes possible anywhere and at any time. All information becomes accessible everywhere and anywhere. (Graham, 1998, 168)

Concomitant to the debates surrounding globalization and the new economy is the emerging interest in the politics of networks. This relates to the ideas of surveillance, political regulation, civic influence and their ensuing developments. With the convergence of the mobile phone, computer and GPS (global positioning system) it is now possible to track the geographical location and past time-paths of individuals. Currently there are attempts to legislate to protect the rights of the individual and, most recently, discussions on the Fourth Amendment in the United States.

In this book, the authors will provide examples to you that show both radical change and continuity. For example, in Figures 1.1 and 1.2 it is possible to see globally the extent and tempo of Internet exchanges as well as the density of Internet connections. North America and Europe have extensive contact with each other and much of the population has access to the Internet. But, as media studies thinkers, can we say more about these global interconnections? Is this a case of rich nations controlling technology and media flows? Or is there more to it?

Figure 1.1 Map of density of Internet connections

Source: Reproduced with permission from Chris Harrison, Human-Computer Interaction Institute, Carnegie Mellon University.

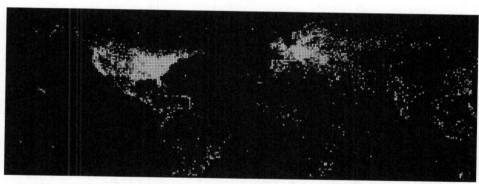

Figure 1.2 City to city Internet connections

Source: Reproduced with permission from Chris Harrison, Human-Computer Interaction Institute, Carnegie Mellon University.

For example, Carlin is an Australian diver and salvage operator who has 'discovered' the wrecks of HMAS *Perth* and USN *Houston* in the Sunda Straits, Indonesia. Carlin was assisted in his search by a local Indonesian fisherman, who gave him a surprise:

As the fisherman pushed off, the Australian noticed he had a bucket sitting between his legs. Inside he was amazed to see a GPS. How a seemingly impoverished fisherman happened to have such a sophisticated device – and knew how to use it – still baffles him. (McBeth, 2002, 51)

A quantitative view of media diffusion, as in the Internet map above, does not tell us the full impact of digital media worldwide. There is also debate about the benefits of globalization and what it means for nations and cultures. For example, globalization according to Mittelman is a 'coalescence of varied transnational processes and domestic structures, allowing the economy, politics, culture and ideology of one country to penetrate another' (1996, 3). Note that Mittelman's definition hints at control of one nation or country over another. Hjarvard's (2003) definition of globalization, though, has a softer touch. He says that we can think about global connections and *globalization* in terms of:

- the extent and intensity of the global media links and networks (the distance and area covered, the complexity of the networks, how finely meshed they are);
- the tempo of media exchanges and the influence of the global media links (the degree of activity and interaction over long distances and the impact of that activity and interaction, including the volumes of goods, people, and communication flows).

How we think about globalization obviously affects how we analyse what we see. In this book the authors will present you with global examples that show the extent and intensity of the global media links as well as their impact. It will be up to you to decide whether societies and cultures are radically changing or if they are becoming more free or less free in a globalized, media, world.

Part I, Convergences, provides you with background to the history of convergence of media and the current global context. Chapter 2 investigates the first revolution in media, the rise of the alphabet, and the second major revolution before the broadcast era, the printing press. Chapter 3 provides background to the modern global, digital, media world.

Part II, Theories, gives you a detailed overview of the theoretical origins of administrative research (media effects), critical research (ideology and its impact) and the concepts of information and communication in the disciplinary literature. Chapter 4 summarizes the different empirical perspectives on diffusion, agenda setting, uses and gratifications, constructivism and assumptions about how influential the media, in fact, are. Chapter 5 looks at how the idea of ideology has been developed and used in the media studies field, especially notions like hegemony. Chapter 6 looks in detail at how concepts of information and, by extension, communication, have been defined by different theories, many in the communication and media fields. How we conceive of information as a phenomenon has a dramatic effect on how we think about communication and human interaction.

Part III, Content, Audiences and Effects, looks at the rise of information warfare as a specialist area of persuasion, how cultures are being transformed in a global media world, and games audiences. Chapter 7 will outline the concept of information warfare and the concept of propaganda. Chapter 8 discusses the concept of culture and intercultural communication and issues in cultural change created by globalization. Chapter 9 uses India and China as case studies of change.

Part IV, Structures and Organization, looks at key debates in media and democracy, digital identity, the media professions, media economics and research. Chapter 10

to recap...

Globalization at the minimum involves networks – of media, goods, people – that cross national boundaries and can vary in their extent, intensity, tempo and influence.

introduces the idea of e-democracy and the pressures on governmental and other organizations created by new media, including radical and rebellious media. Chapter 11 discusses how journalism and public relations have been affected by social media. Chapter 12 provides an overview of changes to media economics, especially the impact on ideas of currency in advertising. Chapter 13 studies the online and multimedia games phenomenon. Chapter 14 gives an insight into how research methods and ways of studying the audience and media are adapting to new media environments. Chapter 15 provides a summary of key issues that arise from discussion of the components of the mediation process.

Media Theories and Approaches complements the text with an online World Media Atlas. The Atlas maps media ownership, usage, and diffusion statistics, from newspapers to the Internet, together with an overview of trends in regulation.

Summary

The study of media involves more than mass media and, in a world increasingly characterized by global networks and links, can usefully be described as global media studies. In this book the authors aim to introduce you to some of the studies that have had a significant impact on the way media studies is studied but the authors have also tried to keep in mind that media studies is more than a field of study. The text will try to remind you that the concepts we write about are not remote theorizing but something you can see or apply at every moment of your waking life. The authors also try to relate them to your possible future careers. Much of this book is about newspapers, radio and television and the careers associated with them. The authors write about journalism, journalists and newsgathering, about the nature of news and about important fields from which much of it is drawn, such as politics. Moreover, the authors have diverse backgrounds with one a specialist in professional education, another a specialist in Chinese media and the other in South Asian media. It is their collective interest in the effects of the media in diverse cultures and situations that link them. The authors hope that the concepts in this book will prove to be not only part of your broad liberal education but also a useful adjunct to what you are practising as students of journalism, public relations, advertising and marketing.

At the conclusion of this chapter you should now be able to:
- think critically about what makes up the field of media studies;
- start thinking on the ideas of globalization and convergence and their impact.

Key themes

Defining the media studies field. Media studies differs from disciplines such as psychology or history. It draws on psychology, history and other disciplines but its boundaries are defined by the processes involved in the distribution of symbolic content in societies. The early debates about the impact of media in society or the influence of media on audiences drew on administrative research (media effects) and critical research (culture, ideology and media).

Globalization and social change. Analyses about media and social change and globalization tend to be either optimistic or pessimistic about the future. Some theorists see the global networks leading to greater interdependence and dependence on more powerful cultures. Others see the networks and links offering new possibilities for communication and global cooperation. There can be no doubt, however, that there are now global media networks and links and that convergence characterizes media at national and international levels. Understanding the extent and intensity of those networks and links and their impact requires analysis of the quantitative and qualitative dimensions of national and global media.

*Discussion
questions*

1   If you were limited to only three aspects of the media, what would they be? What does this tell you about yourself? How do you use media? Is it a form of communication? A channel for information? A way of making yourself fit into society? If you were asked to specify a certain medium and describe its most important uses for you in everyday life, what would that be and what would be the constraints of having to choose only one medium to manage your needs?

2   Find a news story that has global impact, such as the McCanns' tragedy. See if you can get different national views on that story. Bring it to class and see if you can show how the different components of the process of mediation might come into play.

3   The immediacy of media in our lives may cause us to question our own sense of security and our chance of happiness. Do you agree with this? Bring to the class for discussion two contrasting examples from the media that affect your sense of security or happiness.

4   Look up the media table in the online World Media Atlas. What conclusions can you draw about how media technologies differ country by country, region by region?

Further reading

Silverstone, R. (1999). *Why study the media?* London: Sage.

Peer review

The Internet provides significant resources for the media studies discipline. However, you have to be careful in how you approach them. Traditionally, journals in the field are peer reviewed. When a media scholar submits an article to a particular journal for publication then a panel of experts reviews that article and checks that it meets best practice for the field. Peer review often involves a blind refereeing process where the author does not know the names of the reviewers and the reviewers do not know the name of the author of the paper. This helps to reduce bias and preserve independence in review. Not all sources on the Internet are peer reviewed. For example, Wikipedia sites can be useful but often they are not peer reviewed. The weblinks provided to you in this book, such as Voice of the Shuttle, are good first stops for you to gain an idea on what scholars and others are putting up as reference sites, but be careful in their use.

World Media Atlas

The online World Media Atlas, constructed by the authors, will provide yearly updates of statistics and regulation trends in the following areas:

1. Ownership and control
2. Newspapers online
3. Radio
4. Cinema
5. TV ratings
6. Internet use
7. Kids
8. Music
9. Expenditure (advertising in all media)
10. Regulation
11. Media table

Voice of the Shuttle
http://vos.ucsb.edu

Other sites that may be of interest:
http://www.mediaknowall.com/
http://www.intute.ac.uk/artsandhumanities/communications/
http://www.cultsock.ndirect.co.uk/index7.html

Technologizing the word

chapter

2

This chapter explores the four major revolutions in media and convergence:
- writing and the alphabet, an early technologization of the word;
- the printing press, enabling standardization

of languages, grammars and spelling;
- broadcast media, introducing instantaneous worldwide and mass audience communication;
- computers and social media, combining the one-to-many possibilities of mass media with the many-to-many capability of personal networks.

In each age where a new medium has been introduced humans have had experiences of convergence – the transformation of older media into new cultural forms. In this chapter the authors will explore those experiences and provide a historical overview of the development of media. This chapter will explore the four major revolutions in media and convergence:

- writing and the alphabet, an early technologization of the word;
- the printing press, enabling standardization of languages, grammars and spelling;
- broadcast media, introducing instantaneous worldwide and mass audience communication;
- computers and social media, combining the one-to-many possibilities of mass media with the many-to-many capability of personal networks.

It was only in the 1920s – according to the *Oxford English Dictionary* – that people began to speak of 'the media', and a generation later, in the 1950s, of a 'communication revolution', but a concern with the means of communication is very much older than that. (Briggs and Burke, 2002, 1)

The authors hold that there are four distinct revolutions in the history of media that were a 'shock of the new' to the people who lived at the time. These revolutions were the creation of the Greek alphabet, the invention of the printing press, the rise of modern science and the evolution of broadcast media (telephone, radio and television) and the arrival of the computer and social media. It might seem odd to include the telephone in a broadcast list but, like radio and television, telephone networks allow communication over geographically large distances. Through their experiences of telephone networks people were therefore not altogether surprised when computer networks arrived. The Internet, though, made possible many-to-many communication with textual and visual information. The idea of convergence emerged with computer networks precisely because they combined a variety of different types of media. We, like many of our peers, have learned to recognize that convergence did not arrive with the computer and that all previous communications are moments of convergence, as we will show as the chapter unfolds.

Social media. Modern networks that make participatory forums possible.

The shock of the new involved in each of these revolutions feelings of threat and feelings of opportunity. For example, Erik Barnouw (1975) starts his book *Tube of Plenty* with a picture from the New York *Daily Graphic* 1877 titled 'Terrors of the Telephone: the orator of the future', shown below. In this picture, reproduced from the *Daily Graphic* by the authors, there is a sweating orator apparently wired up to audiences around the world (the lines connect to different cities and countries around the world). A popular song at the time, 'The Wondrous Telephone', proclaimed:

> You stay at home and listen
> To the lecture hall,
> And hear the strains of music
> From a fascinating ball!
> (Barnouw, 1975, 3)

When the telephone was introduced to Vienna and Budapest, enterprising salesmen saw the medium as a means of distributing music. Cultured Viennese were encouraged to subscribe to a telephone service in order to listen to their favourite performer and orchestras. As Carolyn Marvin points out in *When Old Technologies Were New* (1988), new media such as telephones disrupted established social relations, unsettling customary ways of dividing the private person and family from the more public setting of the community. On the lighter side, she describes how people spoke louder when calling long distance, and how they worried about catching contagious diseases over the phone. Take a moment to consider how people respond to mobiles when they use them in public spaces. First, they often speak loudly and second, they usually tell their interlocutor where they are speaking from 'I am on the bus' 'I am just at the mall', as though trying to fix themselves in place, even though they are mobile. This represents a similar anxiety about change and technology demonstrated in previous periods of developing communications.

Figure 2.1 Terrors of the telephone

Source: *New York Daily Graphic*, 15 March 1877.

There were also contemporary fears that the telephone would displace writing and replace newspapers. However, the introduction of a new medium does not necessarily remove another. Historically different media have adapted to changed circumstances, just as oral culture adapted to print culture, print culture adapted to broadcast culture, and so on. Media therefore appear to operate in what Braudel (1975) calls an ensemble of histories. Braudel says that at any given moment in history one can find different combinations of economic production coexisting at the same time – feudalism coexisting alongside capitalism, capitalism coexisting alongside socialism. At one moment one form of economic production may be the dominant form. The same principle can apply to media in society. When the printing press entered society it coexisted with scribal culture, the dominant form at the time.

Ensemble of histories.
Describes the capability of different economic and cultural phenomena to coexist, rather than one phenomenon completely displacing another.

The Greek alphabet and the written word

_____

_____

_____

_____

The four parallel lines above are not a mistake by the printer, the publisher or indeed the authors of this book. They are *grammas* – straight lines – that a teacher in ancient Greek and Roman times drew with a stilus on a writing-tablet. The pupil copied the example written by the teacher or master. Finds from Hellenistic and Roman Egypt confirm the technique (David Harvey, 1978, 65). Learning to write in the Greek and Roman world went hand in hand with learning to read as it does in other cultures. In the world we have inherited from the Greeks and Romans we have learned to place our letters on the bottom line. Languages that use the Devanagri script, Hindi and Nepali, use the top line to guide their letters. Classical Chinese was written and read from left to right and in vertical strips. But in all cases, the need for order and the management of the spoken word through a system of writing is evident. In alphabetic systems there were four stages – learning the letters of the alphabet, learning syllables, monosyllables and polysyllables and then learning sentences and this model seems to apply across all cultures with alphabetic scripts. In China, students use boxes to balance each ideogram as a character on a four-point spectrum, and learn in part by rote and in part through understanding the phonemes and root elements that make up complex characters (*hanzi*).

Writing between lines, or in boxes in China, is today of course taken for granted and is a commonplace in modern schools throughout the world. The introduction of the alphabet and writing, however, changed a way of life.

The *Iliad* and the *Odyssey* were committed to writing between 700 and 550 BC. As David Harvey (1978) says, this operation – committed to writing – is something that today seems commonplace, occurring tens of thousands of times an hour all over the literate world.

The original act was rather different; it was something like a thunder-clap in human history, which our bias of familiarity has converted into the rustle of papers on a desk. It constituted an intrusion into culture, with results that proved irreversible. It laid the basis for the destruction of the oral way of life and the oral modes of thought. This is an extreme way of putting it, intended to dramatize a fact about ourselves. We as literates, inheritors of 2500 years of experience with the written word, are removed by a great distance from the conditions under which the written word first entered Greece, and it requires some effort of the imagination to comprehend what these were and how they affected the manner in which the event took place. (David Harvey, 1978, 4)

Seneca (a Roman Stoic philosopher, statesman, dramatist and humourist, 4 BC to AD 65) took an intense interest in the techniques that writing demanded. 'Boys learn in accordance with a written model (*praescriptum*); their fingers are held, and they are guided by the hand of another through the forms (*simulacra*) of the letters' (David Harvey, 1978, 69). But the technique of writing was not the only experience of the medium. There was in Greek and Roman times the status that came with writing and therefore the motivation to ensure it was learned. In the second century the wealthy Athenian Herodes Atticus, for instance, had a son who had difficulty with reading and writing. 'When his son could not master his alphabet, the idea occurred to Herodes to bring up with him twenty-four boys of the same age named after the letters of the alphabet, so that he would be obliged to learn his letters at the same time as the names of the boys' (David Harvey, 1978, 75).

The creation of the alphabet and the Greek alphabet in particular was a revolution or a 'thunder-clap' as David Harvey says (1978). The Greek alphabet added vowels and brought the alphabet closer to sound, unlike the Semitic alphabet that works on consonants alone. Writing does not include just any semiotic marking which an individual makes and assigns meaning to. A simple scratch on a rock or a notch on a stick that is interpretable only by the one who makes it might be 'writing', but in a trivial sense, as Walter Ong (1988) points out:

> The critical and unique breakthrough into new worlds of knowledge was achieved within human consciousness not when simple semiotic marking was devised but when a coded system of visible marks was invented whereby a writer could determine the exact words that the reader would generate from the text. This is what we usually mean today by writing in its sharply focused sense. (Ong, 1988, 84)

It is remarkable that the alphabet was invented once only and late in the timeline of human history. Ong says that the explanation for this becomes clearer if we reflect on the nature of sound:

> For the alphabet operates more directly on sound as sound than the other scripts, reducing sound directly to spatial equivalents, and in smaller, more analytic, more manageable units than a syllabary: instead of one symbol for the sound *ba*, you have two, *b* plus *a*. (1988, 91)

The completely phonetic alphabet also appears to foster abstract, analytic, thought – something Ong thinks was an accidental but crucial intellectual advantage of the Greek alphabet. The phonetic alphabet and writing are also technologies, even though 'we find it difficult to consider writing to be a technology as we commonly assume printing and the computer to be' (Ong, 1988, 81). Yet writing and especially alphabetic writing is a *technology*, 'calling for the use of tools and other equipment' (1988, 81).

Rhetoric. The art of using public speaking for persuasion.

When Greece became fully literate the art of rhetoric carried over into a society of writing. Oral culture was transformed rather than replaced through writing. Rhetoric is the art of public speaking for persuasion. The Greek rhetor is from the same Latin root for orator, which means a public speaker. Rhetoric, Ong (1988) writes, has retained much of the old oral feeling for thought and expression as basically antagonistic. An orator speaks in the face of real or implied adversaries. There were three main forms of rhetoric for Aristotle – ethos, where the appeal to the audience is based on ethics and the credibility of the speaker; logos, where the appeal to the audience is based on logic and reason and pathos, where the appeal to the audience is based on emotion.

The technologizing of the word, the outcome of writing, is the first big revolution in communication, essential for all that followed. However, it would be, as Ong (1988) says, a mistake to think of a medium as a box that simply transfers units of information to another box (the box in the end being the human mind).

> Human communication, verbal and other, differs from the 'medium' model most basically in that it demands anticipated feedback in order to take place at all. In the medium model, the message is moved from sender-position to receiver-position. In real human communication, the sender has to be not only in the sender position but also in the receiver position before he or she can send anything. (Ong, 1988, 176)

There is of course a physical side to any medium of communication, whether speech or writing. The art of writing required technique and recording. Egyptian, Chinese, Indian, Greek and Roman societies, and others, found that writing made it possible to store their records for posterity, an enormously attractive feature in the eyes of tyrants, kings and priests.

Books in Egyptian, Roman and Greek times

In literate Greece and Rome literature was pursued for its own sake and money did not enter into authors' calculations. Authors were happy if their writings met with approval from peers. Writing books for profit is very much a modern phenomenon, originating at the time of the Industrial Revolution. When an author in Greek and Roman times wanted to make known their work they would invite friends around and read it to them. This reading out aloud of original compositions became in time the public lecture. But we also know that Roman audiences could be very tough on authors.

If someone liked an author's work then others copied it. This was how works were passed about and read. Wealthy people could afford slaves whose sole job was to copy books for a master's library. Booksellers in Athens and Rome employed slaves to make copies of books and sold or hired them. Authors had no voice in this process. Copyright as a word and as a practice was unknown in Greece and Rome. There was nothing to stop a person from copying another person's literary work and selling it for a profit (Rawlings, 1901, 26–36).

Collections of books in ancient Egypt, Greece and Rome did form into libraries, although it is not clear whether the libraries were archives – places where records were kept – or publicly accessible. In Egyptian history there is only one library mentioned by a single historian. According to Diodorus Siculus the library was made by Osimandyas, a king of Egypt. The entrance, he says, had the inscription: 'Place of Healing for the Soul' or 'Balsam for the Soul' or 'Dispensary of the Mind'. Egyptologists have identified the plan of the library with a hall of the great palace temple of Rameses II.

Babylonia and Assyria also had their libraries. The royal library kept cuneiform tablets. The tyrant Pissantratus, 537–527 BC, has been credited with the establishment in Athens of the first public library. The library of Alexandra, founded by Alexander the Great, is the largest and best known. Situated in Egypt, Alexandra was a Greek and not an Egyptian city. The first library was established by Ptolemy Sote, a ruler of literary tastes about 300 BC. Copyists were employed to transcribe manuscripts for the benefit of the library. It is said that under Ptolemy Euergetes all books brought into Egypt were seized and sent to the library to be transcribed. The copies were returned to the owners, whose wishes were evidently not consulted, in place of the originals (Rawlings, 1901).

The Romans, apparently accidentally, burnt the library when they destroyed Alexandria. Several scholars, however, have shown that a large number of books remained at the time of the Saracen invasion in AD 638. The libraries of this time were not part of a print culture. They were repositories for works produced in a scribal culture. Thousands of slaves worked to produce copies and preservation itself, over time, was a problem. Reproducing books was laborious and labour intensive, requiring a high degree of skill. Writing as a technology survived through to the 1400s at which time scribal culture transformed into a print culture. With print the nature of preservation of records and knowledge and its social distribution changed, irrevocably.

Preserving ancient texts, however, remains a contemporary issue. The National Library of China, for example, is the largest library in China with over one million rare books with its earliest collection from royal archives dated at AD 417. The library used to open its windows to air the books but pollution has become a significant and recognized problem. The books have also been subject to various accidents. A hot water pipe that burst in the Beijing Ethnic Cultural Palace damaged the three century-old Da Zang Jing (Chinese Buddhist Tripitaka), a complete collection of Buddhist documents with 1,675 canons and 7,240 volumes. The water also damaged more than 200,000 volumes of rare works from 56 different ethnic groups. Preserving these documents, extremely expensive at it is, has become a priority in China. A library preserves knowledge, arts, spiritual wisdom and language, but it also provides continuity, coherence, legitimacy and a sense of history – all vital components of a nation based on the idea of unity and integrated cultural belonging.

Ancient texts might be difficult to preserve but that is no guarantee that modern digital media have the problem solved for electronic media. Modern DVDs do not have a shelf life of hundreds of years and the machines that read the different media change over time, leaving materials lost or inaccessible.

activity What are the practical issues in preserving contemporary wisdom and knowledge? How stable, for instance, is the photographic film on which early cinema and documentary is recorded? How much more stable are the digital technologies that have superseded it? Can you find examples of storage methods (video systems for instance) that are now unusable because of the swift changes in domestic and public hardware systems? What might be the impact of these losses on human society and the way it comprehends its past and organizes its future? We are really asking you to consider the role of media in the preservation of thought, and how that impacts on the construction of history, on political reality and on social wisdom! Those are big questions, but try to think your way through a few small case studies to build a picture from your perspective of what is at stake.

The printing press

Elizabeth Eisenstein had a shock in the 1960s when she began to think about the consequences of the printing press for society. No one, she wrote, had truly investigated the full social consequences of the change from a scribal culture to a print culture after the invention of the printing press in the mid-1400s. How did the invention of the printing press change communication, she asked? Her conclusion, reported in a two-volume history of the print revolution, is stunning. Eisenstein found that the printing press had brought about the most radical transformation in the conditions of intellectual life in the history of western civilization. The effects of the printing press, she concluded, were sooner or later felt in every department of human life (Eisenstein, 1983).

It is debatable whether Eisenstein is right to conclude that many historians missed the printing press in Europe as a major agent of social change. If we look at Febvre and Martin's seminal work, published before Eisenstein and cited by her but not published in English until 1984, then we find in embryo form many of the ideas taken up by Eisenstein. Figure 2.2, adapted by the authors from Febvre and Martin's (1984) work shows Mainz as the cradle of the printing press. Johannes Gutenberg is credited with the invention of the printing press in 1452. We know about Gutenberg because his partners in the invention took him to court and, as far as we know, he made no money from his labours (Febvre and Martin, 1984).

Eisenstein *is* perhaps right to point to the lack of a broader appreciation in the historical literature for the role of print-as-revolution. This could be, as she suggests, due to simple human feelings. Why would a simple mechanical process – a printing press – have a revolutionary effect on all human culture, leading to the Renaissance and advanced scientific thought?

Figure 2.2 The spread of printing

Source: Adapted from Febvre and Martin (1984).

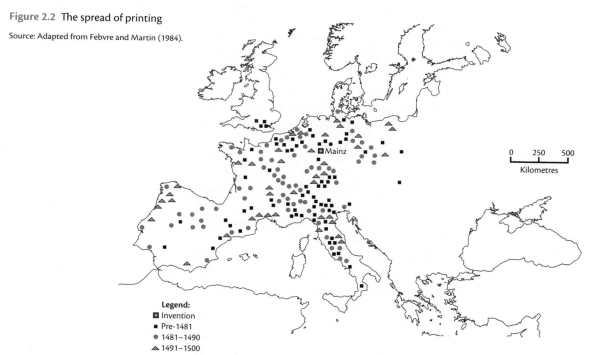

Eisenstein (1983) identified a variety of specific effects that occurred because of the printing press:

1. There was an increase in the quantity of books and a related reduction in the number of hours required to produce books. Previously, monks and scribes had spent hours writing on parchment to produce Bibles and other works. These parchments and books were preserved in a scriptorium in a monastery. The printing press enabled the copying of books on paper and the diffusion of literature outside the scriptorium.

2. Identical words and images could now be simultaneously mass-reproduced. In scribal culture each reproduced work was individual and there could be variations in spelling and form. People in geographically dispersed locations could, with print, read the same ideas and see the same images, whether maps, drawings or pictures. Standardization of languages, grammars and spelling was possible.

3. New occupations were created, from those who handled the machines to those who edited and translated texts, marketed products and promoted authors. New business models for communication emerged to deal with the economics of the print industry.

4. An industry developed where authors could become celebrities and where intellectual copyright became important. The ideas of society's interest in the ownership and distribution of knowledge through public libraries and individual rights into knowledge as property emerged. As we saw in the discussion of Egypt, Greece and Rome there was in their time no idea of copyright and differing notions of libraries.

5. A whole range of texts became available in the vernacular (the spoken language of the culture) together with calendars and maps. Previously Latin had been the written language of knowledge. People could, with print, read the Bible in their own language. This dramatically affected the Roman Catholic Church's monopoly on knowledge and stirred the Protestant political classes to link the vernacular versions of the Protestant faith to issues in grammar and standardization:

> In England, the Crown put its stamp of approval, not only on a vernacular Bible and Book of Common Prayer but also on the grammars and primers that paved the way for lay reading. Education and religion were cast in the same uniform vernacular mold.
>
>> 'And as his majesty purposeth to establyshe his people in one consent and harmony of pure & true religion: so his tender goodness toward the youth & chyldhode of his realme, entendeth to have it brought up under one absolute and uniforme sorte of lernynge … conseryng the great encombrance and confusion of the young and tender wittes … by reason of the diversity of grammar rules and teachinges.'
>
> Thus ran the introduction to the 1542 edition of William Lily's celebrated grammar: 'An Introduction of the Eyght Partes of Speche'. Three years later in 1545 came the authorized Primer, published by Grafton 'for avoyding of the dyversitie of primer bookes that are now abroade … and to have one uniform ordre of al suche bokes through out all our dominions'. This small and cheap authorized Primer placed in the hands of English readers a guidebook that served the cause of uniformity, the Anglican religion and popular education all at once. (Eisenstein, 1983, 350)

It would be simplistic to say that the Protestants loved knowledge and freedom of the press and the Catholic Church did not. Catholics did print in the vernacular. The Catholic Church, however, was particularly concerned with heretical or unorthodox texts and set up an Index of banned books. The demand from ordinary people for the vernacular – own language – versions of what they were reading evolved regardless of political or religious affiliations. Protestant royalty disliked criticism as much as Catholic clergy.

6. The increased range of works in different fields enabled readers to see different ideas and to compare them, leading to new ideas and innovations. In just three years, between 1517 and 1520, the Protestant reformer Martin Luther's 30 publications generated more than 300,000 copies. Many Reformer presses ran even when the Catholic Church either banned books or insisted on Catholic Church approval before publication. Printing presses, like the Internet, provided the opportunity to spread quickly alternative sources of knowledge and even radical and revolutionary ideas.

7. The preservation of knowledge was enhanced by mass-reproducibility.

Thomas Jefferson is an example of the last point when he wrote:

> Very early in the course of my researches into the laws of Virginia, I observed that many of them were already lost, and many more on the point of being lost, as existing only in single copies in the hands of careful or curious individuals, on whose deaths they would probably be used for waste paper. I set myself therefore to work to collect all which were then existing … In searching after these remains, I spared neither time, trouble, nor expence … But … the question is What means will be the most effectual for preserving these remains from future loss? All the care I can take of them, will not preserve them from the worm, from the natural decay of the paper, from the accident of fire, or those of removal when it is necessary for any public purpose … Our experience has proved to us that a single copy, or a few, deposited in MS in the public offices cannot be relied on for any great length of time. The ravages of fire and of ferocious enemies have had but too much part in producing the very loss we now deplore. How many of the precious works of antiquity were lost while they existed only in manuscript? Has there ever been one lost since the art of printing has rendered it practicable to multiply and disperse copies? This leads us then to the only means of preserving those remains of our laws now under consideration, that is, a multiplication of printed copies. (cited in Eisenstein, 1983, 115–16)

Preservation and control of knowledge are important in all human societies, whether orally based, scribal based or print based. Jefferson's point is that knowledge can be better preserved in a print environment where mass-reproducibility reduces the risk of loss of unique works. Private interest in preservation and collection of works grew quickly within the first centuries of printing.

> What kind of people had private libraries? Of 377 such libraries in the late 15th and the 16th centuries of which we have catalogues, 105 belonged to churchmen (53 to ecclesiastical dignitaries, i.e. archbishops, bishops, canons and abbots, 18 to university teachers and students, 35 to parish priests), and a rather large number (126) were owned by lawyers, of whom 25 were members of the Parliaments or of one of the courts of appeal, 6 were local government officials, 45 were barristers, 10 public prosecutors, 15 notaries. (Febvre and Martin, 1984, 263)

Religious works dominated publication in the rise of the printing press but professional fields outside the Church steadily increased their collections (Febvre and Martin, 1984, 324).

	Lawyers	Churchmen
1480–1500	1	24
1501–1550	54	60
1551–1600	71	21

Lawyers and printers were also interested in the uniformity and standardization of the national and local languages that they were using. The spoken languages of the different nations and cultures started to take on uniform styles, including spelling (Febvre and Martin, 1984, 324).

Manuscript	Printed Text
bee	be
on	one
greef	grief
thease	these
swoord	sword
noorse	nurse
skolding	scolding
servaunt	servant

Eisenstein saw standardization, reproducibility of identical works on a large scale, the capacity for preservation of knowledge and the speed of diffusion of knowledge as the key elements of the major changes in European society that followed the invention of printing presses. Eisenstein in her work says that printing was a force for change but sometimes she appears to be saying that printing was the primary – indeed only – agent of change that led to the Reformation and the rise of modern science. The idea that technology at all times drives social and cultural change is a form of technological determinism. It is unlikely that Eisenstein has taken this position even though a print culture clearly displaced a scribal culture.

Technological determinism. Assumes that technology is the main cause of social change.

In many respects the conditions described above prefigure the conditions that distinguished the Industrial Revolution. Further, many of the key elements of the print revolution can be found in the broadcasting and computing revolutions. Broadcasting and computing networks, like print, increase the speed of diffusion of knowledge and potentially democratize the social distribution of knowledge. Similar tensions also occur with each new medium. In the case of print, queens, kings, princes and religions sought regulation and control. The tension between media as a way of enhancing access to knowledge and social forces that want to control that access has continued into the 21st century.

It is important to remember that literacy and the book still count. Indeed the attainment of literacy has probably never been so important. The United Nations Education Cultural and Scientific Organization (UNESCO) decided in 1948 that universal literacy was a goal it would pursue through funded campaigns in the developing world. These campaigns have had some success. For example, it was quickly recognized that making women literate was the quickest path to ensuring social change, thus in terms of gender equality literacy campaigns have assumed a significant role in Africa and Asia. Moreover, as the world moves quickly towards a computerized and digital future, literacy has acquired even greater importance. The whole notion of the alphabet can also become intensely politicized. Take for example Azerbaijan, a small oil-rich nation on the Caspian Sea that had been a Soviet republic. In 1990 it gained its independence and decided to follow in the footsteps of the Turkish reformer Mustafa Kemal Attaturk and reform its system of writing. It converted from the Cyrillic script (the script of the Soviet Union) to the Roman script – to convey a language related to Turkish and Arabic in a predominantly Muslim country. Clearly the alphabet, literacy and the book still matter.

Print and the people

We do not have many reliable statistics on the reading publics up to the late 1800s, whether in China, Korea, England, Germany, India or any other country. We do know that there was significant demand for news from the everyday person. By 1785 there were 124 letterpress printers in London, 316 by 1824 and 500 by the mid-1800s. Wooden printing presses produced at most a hundred impressions. Iron frame presses produced double this figure. Power presses created 12,000 sheets of *The Times* in an hour. 'Between 1801 and 1831, when heavy taxation on newspapers held production back, the production of officially stamped copies alone more than trebled from 16,085,000 to 54,769,000 a year' (James, 1976, 17).

Between 1780 and 1830 the population of England doubled from 7 to 14 million and readers quintrupled from one and a half to between 7 and 8 million. In 1832 the Society for the Promotion of Christian Knowledge (SPCK) said that England was 'for the first time become a reading population, actuated by tastes and habits unknown to preceding generations, and particularly susceptible to such an influence as that of the press' (James, 1976, 18).

But who was 'the press'? The iron frame press could be bought new for 30 pounds. Before 1850 only 20 per cent of printers employed more than three people. Printers also sold other goods including medicines, tooth-picks, silver cases, together with circulating libraries, which were basically posters, newsletters, and leaflets stuck up and read in the streets.

Presses were rarely installed in specially built premises: printers moved into whatever rooms they could find in vacant shops and premises, reinforced where necessary to bear the weight of the machines. They were therefore in close physical contact with other activities, even sometimes those of household life. When the officers came to take the printing press of the Radical printer Richard Carlile in 1819, they caused great inconvenience to Mrs Carlile lying in labour in the room above. (James, 1976).

It was not only the big steam and power presses that had an impact. The hand press also led to a massive expansion of posters and pamphlets. The 'fat face' types allowed printers to create large print posters. These posters and pamphlets were called the 'circulating libraries of the poor' or the 'language of the walls' – the blogs of the street. People would post their news and commentaries on walls and expect replies. The circulating libraries were also a means to learn to read. 'Harriet Martineau described a boy learning to read from them. Posters and leaflets played a central part in all the social, political and religious movements of the time. They were produced often within hours of each other as answer and reply. As J.D. Burn noted, "the walls afford an excellent battle field for polemical combatants, whereon they frequently wage war to the death for their respective dogma"' (James, 1976). And of course, anyone with familiarity of Chinese cities will think of the shared newspapers still stuck up on notice-boards in residential quarters and in public areas, or the big character posters that defined political disquiet in the late 1960s and again in 1978. The latter have been superseded by blogs, but the connections between reading news and places of study, work or residency, persist.

Printers around Britain celebrated reforms that allowed a more open press environment. Indeed, mock presses were paraded in streets with printers singing:

'The Press!' all lands shall sing;
The Press, the Press we bring,
All lands to bless:
O pallid Want! O Labour stark!
Behold we bring the second ark!
The Press! The Press! The Press!

'Worker scholars' and a radical (pauper) press also emerged from this rapid rise of small print shops. Maids, dustmen and butchers became the butt of cartoons and comic songs, though the ridicule was edged with apprehension as to the social consequences of educating the labouring classes (James, 1976, 21).

But worse of all, our lab'ring folks,
that toiled in their vocations
'Thro all the week contendedly,
as did become their stations.
Distracted now with learned things,
home, wife and work neglect Sir,
And slyly call their laziness,
this march of intellect Sir.

'Two under fifty for a fardy!'

Figure 2.3 Long song seller

Source: Mayhew (1861, 222).

The March of the Intellect among the working classes – a saying of the day – led to barbed comments from the wealthy about the aspirations of the poor. 'I am out of all patience with this march of mind. Here has my house been nearly burnt down, by my cook taking it in her head to study hydrostatics, in a sixpenny tract, published by the Steam Intellect Society' (quoted in James, 1976, 21). *The Penny Magazine*, sold by the Society for the Diffusion of Useful Knowledge with a sizeable circulation of 200,000, had as its purpose a non-critical approach to political affairs as a counter to the radical press emerging from the working class. Taxes on newspapers were also designed to limit the expansion and distribution of the working class press. While the radical press declined the rise of the Fourth Estate continued.

English historian Thomas Carlyle in 1840 attributed the term 'Fourth Estate' to Edmund Burke. Burke, he wrote, said there were Three Estates in Parliament; but, in the Reporters' Gallery yonder, there sat a *Fourth Estate* more important far than they all. It is not a figure of speech, or a witty saying; it is a literal fact, – very momentous to us in these times. ... Whoever can speak, speaking now to the whole nation, becomes a power, a branch of government, with inalienable weight in law-making, in all acts of authority. (Carlyle, 1904)

The three estates in Parliament were the nobles and clergy (House of Lords) and the House of Commons. The introduction of the printing press into England by William Caxton in 1476 did not though automatically bring with it freedom of the press and a Fourth Estate. The rise of a popular press in England was held back by severe restrictions on printers and editors. The Star Chamber, created in 1586, provided death penalties for printers who defied those in power. William Carter, for example, was arrested and tortured in 1580 and hanged in 1584 for printing Catholic pamphlets. Three hundred years later political satire and criticism of the government of day were not hanging offences. What had happened in between was a steady expansion of the means of becoming informed, from the creation of corantos, primitive newsheets used on the streets written by intelligencers (forerunners of journalists), through to the circulating libraries of the poor (Emery, 1969).

Fourth Estate. Refers to the media as key in the Fourth Estate's critical role and in affecting public opinion – in addition to nobles and clergy (House of Lords) and the House of Commons.

Corantos. Primitive newsheets used on the streets written by intelligencers.

Intelligencers. Forerunners of journalists.

The French Revolution and the American Revolution also heralded the rise of the mass reading public. Over 40,000 American homes read revolutionary papers. Many Americans first learned of the Declaration of Independence through the *Pennsylvania Evening Post* on July 6, 1776 with other newspapers following. The *Connecticut Courant*, one of the best printed papers of its time using its own paper mill, in 1781 had a circulation of 8,000 subscribes for each issue, amazing for its time and larger than any equivalent British publication (Emery, 1969, 121). With news came advertising. Advertising in daily newspapers and magazines was US$39 million in 1880 and US$200 million by 1910.

Not everything, though, is a 'newspaper'. For Emery (1969) the modern newspaper had several important characteristics in the age of mass readership. A true newspaper
- must be published at least once a week;
- must be produced by mechanical means (to distinguish it is from the handwritten 'news letters');
- must be available to anyone willing to pay the price, regardless of class or special interests;
- must print anything of interest to the general public, as contrasted with some of the religious and business publications;
- must have an appeal to a public of ordinary literary skill;
- must be timely, or at least relatively so, in the light of technical development;
- must have stability, as contrasted to the fly by night publications of more primitive times (Emery, 1969, 5).

activity Create a list with categories similar to the one above, describing what constitutes (a) a blog (b) a wiki and (c) news online. Pay attention to the factors of frequency, literacy, content, access or subscription, and form.

The accessibility of newspapers to everyone is, as Emery (1969) points out, essential to any possibility of the operation of a Fourth Estate. However, the ethos of reporting

to recap...

The printing press
made mass-reproduc-
tion of ideas possible. It
expanded access to
knowledge by putting it
into the vernacular;
enabled the standardi-
zation of languages,
grammars and spelling
across cultures and
nations; and enhanced
the preservation of
knowledge.

for newspapers is equally important. Joseph Pulitzer embodied that ethos: 'Every issue of the paper presents an opportunity and a duty to say something courageous and true; to rise above the mediocre and conventional; to say something that will command the respect of the intelligent, the educated, the independent part of the community; to rise above fear of partisanship and fear of popular prejudice' (Pulitzer cited in Emery, 1969, 369). Pulitzer's career witnessed the birth of the modern newspaper and journalism as a fully fledged profession. Pulitzer bought the *World* in 1883 for US$346,000 and 10 years later it employed 1,300 staff with an annual profit of US$1 million.

The rise of print and the news in modern industrial democracy has been driven as much by popular movement as by commercial interests taking up innovations in mass printed media. The modern newspaper, however, did bring with it the technology of mass production, the rise of the journalist as a full-time worker and, of course, advertising.

Empire, telegraphy and news

The printing press made possible the mass-reproduction of ideas. However, it was telegraphy that provided the first modern networks that sped up communications across vast distances. Telegraphy might look like a poor cousin to radio and television, but it is an important precursor to wireless broadcast technology and computer networks.

In 1825 information by mail had taken four months to travel from Calcutta to Falmouth, but by 1906 this time had been reduced to thirty-five minutes. It meant not only that British newspapers could carry detailed reports faster to the public; in addition it facilitated the rapid implementation of an imperial grand strategy, both military and naval. It also opened up public administration more directly to the scrutiny of the government's Colonial and Foreign Office or, in the case of the 'Jewel in the crown', the India Office, for, as one historian has observed, the British empire was sustained as much by cheap pulp paper as by the gunboat. (Chapman, 2002, 67)

But it was not only the British empire that took an interest in telegraphy. For example, in 1877 the Ottoman empire had the eighth largest telegraph network and it covered over seventeen thousand miles. In the British empire the telegraph and the railway tended to develop together. In the Ottoman empire, Japan and China, the development of the telegraphy was independent of the railway.

The mysterious sight of its poles and wires excited wonder and suspicion in the lay Ottoman. Peasants and nomads had never before experienced anything like the wires that passed through their villages and by their tents in the highland wilderness, then wound off through the mountains to the sultan's palace. In the mostly barren landscape they stood as tangible monuments of new spatial and intellectual frontiers, and provided, as in the West, a vast apparatus of social and cultural experimentation. Interestingly, the pure physicality of the telegraph became a means to signal to the Sultan complaint and rebellion. Ottoman peasants and rebels destroyed telegraph lines to attract attention or to wreak havoc. Not surprisingly, the British military, also hampered by the destruction of lines in its colonies, took an intense interest in radio when it emerged precisely because telegraphy had become an accessible and destroyable symbol of empire. (Bektas, 2000, 669)

Empires also became linked through telegraph. At the beginning of the Crimean war, the fastest message from the Crimea could reach London in five days. It took two days for a message to go from the Crimea to Varna by steamer and three days on horseback from Varna to Bucharest, 'the nearest point that had been connected to the European telegraph network through the Austrian lines' (Bektas, 2000).

Britain and France joined the Ottoman empire against Russia in the Crimea. France built a line between Bucharest and Varna and Britain laid submarine lines between Varna and Balaklava in the Crimea where the British army was based. 'By late April 1855, Balaklava was in communication with Varna. Messages in cipher were received there and transmitted via the new French line to Bucharest and thence to Paris and London. The whole operation took about five hours at that time, including at least two hours for carrying messages across the Danube by boat, because the cable under the river had not yet been laid' (Bektas, 2000, 671).

At the height of telegraphy Britain owned or had an interest in 80 per cent of submarine cables (Chapman, 2002). This global network of telegraphy was not only at the service of the military or Sultans wanting to control their empire. Telegraphy fed hungry empire publics keen for news.

> For the first time, 'world politics' became possible, and in this Britain led the way, a role in leadership that was facilitated by what was later to become known as the 'All Red Route' of telegraphic cable communications that connected up all British territories with London. The result of such ambitious investment was that there was a greater volume and variety of information upon empire than had ever existed before. The demand was there, backed by public belief in the civilizing internationalism of British colonialism, epitomized by the impact of Queen Victoria's diamond Jubilee speech and by the fascination of a mass market of newspaper consumers in a world that was increasingly influenced by European imperialism and commercial domination. (Chapman, 2002, 67)

James Carey (1989) and Daniel Headrick (1981) summarized its impact. Telegraphy:

- separated communication from human and mechanical locomotion and generally sped up the processes of communication;
- promised the distribution of information everywhere;
- increased the volume of information available;
- reorganized human perceptions of time and allowed newspapers to operate in 'real time';
- led to a restructuring of journalism;
- changed the nature of language by making it sparser and its use more economical;
- divorced news from analysis, that is, changed the manner in which humans explain their world. If you receive your news quicker, then the nature of your responses changes;
- became the sinews of imperialism.

Castells (2001) not surprisingly saw the telegraph as the forerunner of the modern networked society. Telegraphy gave audiences and publics global networks together with expectations about those networks – that they were relatively fast and could bring news from the most remote communities in the world.

Radio

As we have seen, the history of the development of print is not the sole province of entrepreneurs and clever inventors. 'Amateur' interest in news – whether the poor in London or the writers for the radical press – has been as important as commercial interest in their money making potential. The modern newspaper represented a balance between commercial interests and an emerging literate population that wanted to know what was happening. The telegraph sped up the transmission of news from global sources to those newspapers.

Radio, like the modern Internet, annoyed commercial and government interests alike because it was ... messy. Like print, there was a tension between democratization of the medium and control. Like the Internet, everyone thought they could use it. By 1910 in the United States, radio amateurs outnumbered operators in the US Navy and United Wireless. Amateur equipment was often also superior to that used by the commercial operators (Douglas, 1987, 207).

The number of licensed amateurs and amateur stations increased sharply in the three years following enactment of the Radio Act: from 322 licensed amateurs in 1913 to 10,279 in 1916. Between 1915 and 1916 alone the authorities licensed 8,489 amateur stations. During the same period, only 5,202 commercial operators and fewer than 200 shore stations were licensed. In 1917, the number of licensed amateur operators totalled 13,581. Estimates placed the number of unlicensed receiving stations at 150,000 (Douglas, 1987, 293).

Douglas (1987) reported on what amateurs of the time said that they talked about. Operators would 'gossip about everything under the sun'. They would 'ask each other for the baseball or football scores, make appointments to meet the next day, compare their lessons. And they quarrel and talk back and forth by wireless in regular boy-fashion.' We can in early radio amateurs see the Internet chat rooms of the future and, before that, the popularity of Citizens' Band (CB) radio.

The radio spectrum, the 'ether', was initially accessible to all. However, radio technology was in the hands of corporations (RCA, GE, Westinghouse and AT&T). In order to remove amateurs from the spectrum and to monopolize message handling, the corporations that owned the radio technology imposed licensing fees for the millions of dollars of equipment set up throughout the US. The military, separately, had safety concerns over unfettered access to the airwaves, with the potential of chaos in reports of accidents at sea or elsewhere as well as bogus messages (Douglas, 1987, 316). Corporate and military concerns led to regulatory intervention that decided which wavelengths would be allocated to competing claimants. By 1922 the government gave premium spectrum to the commercial wireless companies and the military.

Radio, for the everyday citizen, represented access to a national and a global world, providing the means to relay news and information without intermediaries, and quickly. When *Titanic* sank, the amateur airwaves buzzed with real news and scuttlebutt alike. For the corporations and the military, this democratization of the medium represented a shock – a threat to profit and to control over how communication should proceed. The reaction by the US government to this shock has set the scene for modern online and wireless media and their contradictions. Major corporations own the technology of satellites and the Internet and, as in the days of early radio, they shape the messages we get and the physical technology we use. At the same time the 'amateurs' try to bypass the control of the messages and even the technologies that relay them.

By the late 1930s 26 million households in the US owned at least one radio and spent on average five hours daily listening to one of the three national networks or local radio stations. The most popular night-time genres were comedy and variety. *The Jack Benny Program*, *The Edgar Bergen and Charlie McCarthy Show*, *Burns and Allen*, *Fibber McGee and Molly*, *The Bob Hope Show*, among others, dominated night-time listening. 'All employed a format that combined either one male host or a male–female team with an ensemble of supporting characters' (Hilmes, 1997, 183). Radio also had a social purpose, allowing people to study the habits and emotions and fashions of people from different backgrounds. The advertising agency JWT early on recognized 'these vast new layers of people who have money to spend and who have very few media to reach them excepting the tabloids and confession magazines' (Hilmes, 1997, 117).

In the 1930s advertisers and broadcasters started crude ratings to study audiences. Often this involved calling households as they were listening to the radio to find out what was being listened to. As survey methodology became more sophisticated, however, larger scale surveys were undertaken. Paul Lazarsfeld's and Patricia Kendall's analysis of a survey done by the National Opinion Research Center supported by the National Association of Broadcasters and reported in 1948 is an example of the emergence of formal audience research using statistical sampling methods. The survey showed listening preferences as well as attitudes towards radio and its role in society. Table 2.1 gives a brief insight into how Lazarsfeld and Kendall summarized data on programme preferences and the categories used. While these tables might look commonplace to the modern reader they were in the 1940s, of course, the first steps in large-scale audience research in broadcasting. Today audience preferences can be broken into hundreds of categories and the time spent measured by the minute.

Table 2.1 **The constancy of programme preference (1947 compared with 1945)**

	Daytime preferences				Evening preferences	
	Men		Women		Total	
	1945	1947	1945	1947	1945	1947
News broadcasts	65	61	76	71	76	74
Comedy programmes					54	59
Popular and dance music	15	23	35	39	42	49
Talks on public issues	22	19	21	22	40	44
Classical music	12	11	23	20	32	30
Religious broadcasts	19	22	35	41	20	21
Serial dramas	7	6	37	33		
Talks on farming	13	16	12	13		
Homemaking programmes	5	5	44	48		
Livestock and grain reports	14	17	6	10		

Source: Lazarsfeld and Kendall (1948, 21).

If you turned on a radio set in Britain during the early years of the British Broadcasting Corporation (BBC) then you would have found a very different diet of programming, compared with the United States. In November 1923 London was broadcasting 3 hours 25 minutes of music each day to 2 hours 5 minutes of everything else (Briggs, 1985, 63). Chamber music and symphony music and sometimes a military band dominated the airwaves. As in the United States, there were in the early years many 'home constructors' who built their own radio sets. The Post Office, responsible for regulating radio licences, estimated that there were 160,000 amateur sets and 80,000 licensed sets. As the BBC took control of transmitting equipment and radio licences the spectrum ended up fully controlled by the government. The British Broadcasting Corporation (BBC) was controlled by a Royal Charter that gave the BBC the job of delivering 'education and entertainment'. At first this involved rules that there were to be no broadcasts on matters of political, industrial or religious controversy. John Reith, the first managing director of the BBC, opposed this and pushed the government to allow reporting of current events with discretion allowed on presenting controversial topics.

The United States and Britain represented two different systems of broadcasting, one dominated by commercial corporations and advertising and the other dominated by a government corporation without advertising and revenue collected through radio licences. In contemporary Britain, the BBC's radio monopoly no longer exists even though the BBC's reputation is now worldwide. The golden age of radio was also to give way to television, although we can now suggest that the Internet and streamed radio has brought back a second golden age.

to recap...

Radio, for the everyday citizen, represented access to a national and a global world, providing the means to relay news and information without intermediaries and quickly.

Film and television

Perhaps the best way to get a sense of how people reacted to cinema – film play – is to go to one of the world's most remote urban settlements at the beginning of the 20th century. Albany in Western Australia today has a population of 30,000. In the mid-1920s it had a population of about 2,000. Despite its distance from civilization and its small population, Albany had a fascination with cinema. In 1925 Henry Lambert and his wife Elizabeth opened the Regent Theatre. The picture of the opening, while slightly deteriorated, conveys the formality of the occasion for the town.

Figure 2.4 Opening of the Regent Theatre, Albany's first cinema, Western Australia, 1925

Source: From the collection of Henry Ernest and Elizabeth Lambert.

The report in the *Albany Advertiser*, the local paper, on the Regent Theatre is striking in its placement of cinema in its perceived effects and global context:

> If one remembers that about 29 years have elapsed since the birth of the Photoplay, one is amazed at its development, and at the gigantic speed with which it has made itself at home in the four corners of the earth. No art has ever spread with such rapidity as that of the Photoplay. Its popularity is so great that the industries connected with it have reached, according to some statisticians, the third place in the business affairs of the world; grain and coal occupying the two leading positions. Broadly speaking, the more a story is addressed to persons of easily stimulated imagination, the fewer pictorial aids will be needed. On the other hand, tales replete with incident and intended for the masses, more or less demand this assistance, for a reader can take in only so much as he can readily transform into mental pictures. The film play is thus pre-eminently the vehicle for stories rich in incidents and action, but much depends on the manner and the surroundings in which they are placed before audiences. (*Albany Advertiser*, 1924)

In 1894, thirty years or so before the opening of the Regent Theatre in Albany, a Kinetoscope parlour opened in New York. The first films to flicker through Thomas Eddison's coin-operated Kinetoscopes featured boxers, ballerinas and bears and ran only a fragment of a single reel (about 50 feet and less than a minute). The Panoptikon was created to cater for larger audiences. Projectors enabled vaudeville theatres to use single-reel motion pictures as top of the bill novelties or as popular chasers at the beginning of each advertised programme. Cigar stores, pawn shops and small restaurants were converted into Nickelodeons.

The largest production companies of the time – Biograph, Essanay, Kalem, Lubin, Melies, Pathe, Selig and Vitagraph – agreed in 1908 to become Edison licensees in the Motion Picture Patents Company (MPPC – also know as the 'Trust'). From then, film producers paid licence fees to the Trust in order to purchase the patented equipment. The MPPC monopoly was eroded by the formation of independent companies and anti Trust charges. In 1914 William Fox had entered film production two years before with the formation of a studio subsidiary, Box Office Attractions. D.W. Griffith left the Trust to work for Reliance-Majestic and made the $110,00 adaptation of Thomas Dixon's bestseller *The Clansman, The Birth of a Nation* in 1915. 'Wherever the film was exhibited white-robed horsemen were employed to gallop up and down the nearest street and publicise every screening' (Cook, 1985, 5). While this particular example is a disturbing reminder that technology and art do not necessarily sit on the side of inclusive politics, democracy or even good taste, it is also a striking example of the showmanship of cinema even at its roots. Roadshow releases and regional releases competed for domestic distribution and exhibitor earnings. The need for a national network of distribution emerged. In 1914 the first national network Paramount Pictures Corporation was set up releasing 104 films a year (Cook, 1985).

The corporate system of Hollywood – studio systems, stars and the national networks for distribution of films – has undergone structural change since the 1930s, most notably the vertical integration of media organizations (companies owning all forms of media). Cinema spread across the world with unerring rapidity, with major production centres in China and the United Kingdom celebrating centenaries of film in the 21st century, and more emerging to sustain the visual hunger of the global audiences for stories on screen. Television also had a dramatic impact on audience attendance, as Figure 2.2 demonstrates. After the introduction of television in the 1950s audiences shifted towards television as the dominant medium.

Figure 2.5 Decline of cinema viewing in Britain

Source: Statistics adapted from Briggs (1985).

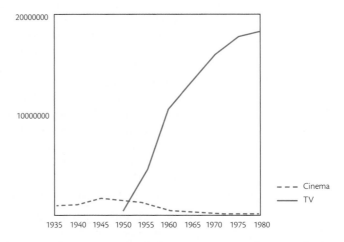

The history of cinema and television is not simply one of advertising, audiences, stars, and studios. The whole development of film and, indeed, television, has involved experimentation with different narrative forms and the ways that stories and pictures are edited and presented. There is also a whole world of theorizing film and its purpose. Pam Cook's *The Cinema Book* is an excellent resource for those looking for an intelligent and concise way into this complexity. The classic narrative system, for example, well developed by the 1920s, involved assumptions about structure, such as the linearity of cause and effect, a high degree of narrative closure, a fictional world governed by spatial and temporary verisimilitude (the appearance of being true) and the centrality of narrative agency of psychologically rounded characters (Cook, 1985, 216). This means that between the beginning and the end of a story there is a familiar ordering of events – a logic – for the viewer or the audience and characters that have motivations or personalities that assist the plot in culturally or psychologically understood ways. 'Beginning', 'middle' and 'end' indicate 'narrative closure'. The classic 'hero' for instance may be a central character whose actions lead to a resolution in the plot. Bruce Willis in the movie *Die Hard* is an action hero faced by terrorists. The cinematic codes, such as editing, set up characteristic action shots and juxtapositions of shots. Mise en scène itself refers to the practice of stage direction in the theatre in which things are 'put into the scene' (arranged on the stage). 'When applied to film, it refers to whatever appears in the film frame, including those aspects that overlap with the arts of the theatre: setting, lighting, costume, and the behaviour of the figures' (Cook, 1985, 151). The way the director stages the event for the camera has an effect on what is a scene and how it is viewed. Particular genres are also associated with film and the language of film. Genres are recognizable repertoires of conventions running across visual imagery, plot, character, setting, modes of narrative development, music and stars. Film noir is one example of a film genre that emerged in a specific period. 'Whoever went to the movies with any regularity during 1946 was caught in the midst of Hollywood's profound postwar affection for morbid drama. From January through December deep shadows, clutching hands, exploding revolvers, sadistic villains and heroines tormented with deeply rooted diseases of the mind flashed across the screen in a panting display of psychoneuroses, unsubliminated sex and murder most foul' (Cook, 1985, 93). Art cinema is often used as a

Narrative forms. The ways that stories and pictures are edited and presented.

Classic narrative system. Cinematic conventions where there is linearity of cause and effect and a high degree of narrative closure.

Mise en scène. The practice of stage direction in the theatre in which things are 'put into the scene' (arranged on the stage).

Genre. Recognizable repertoires of conventions running across visual imagery, plot, character, setting, modes of narrative development, music and stars.

Film noir. Cinema narrative with highly stylized visual expression, a circular form of narration, and often a narrative of murder and deception in love.

Art cinema. Cinematic conventions where none of the conventional links of continuity occurs.

counterpoint to classic narrative and classic cinematic conventions where none of the conventional links of continuity occurs.

The language of film theory and film practice reflects an interest in the creative and the professional role of those behind a film and the social implications of a film. Auteur theory, for instance, deals explicitly with the role of the author. The French journal *Cahiers du Cinema* introduced the idea of *politique des auteurs,* arguing that despite the commercial nature of cinema the director, like any other artist, was the sole author of the work. This idea has been fundamental over many subsequent years of adulating the director, seeing a trajectory in his/her (usually *his*) work, and indeed for mapping other histories against the ideas that have shaped a director's response to his times. Everyone might have their own example, but we would suggest Stanley Kubrick, Orson Welles and Zhang Yimou as three classic examples. Whether or not one admires their films, there is little doubt of their historical and cinematic clout.

Cinema attendance is not just about seeing a film. It is also a profoundly social experience. Scholars such as Annette Kuhn have remarked that film-going produces memories, of the places you went to see films, and the people you saw them with. This may be because the depth and intensity of information that a film provides combine with the experience of watching the film and going to a place to do so, and create a deep and lasting memory.

Auteur theory. The role of the author in the creative work.

to recap...

The rise of cinema has involved experimentation with different narrative forms and the ways that stories and pictures are edited and presented. These conventions have evolved for film whether delivered via cinema or television. Television became a dominant medium in the latter part of the 20th century but it did not completely displace the cinema experience.

Reflection

(a) Can you identify the first film you remember having seen on a big screen? Where was it? What sequences do you recall most vividly? (b) Are there films that bring back memories of your own life by association? What impact would you say they have had on how you view your surroundings, your social relationships and your own sense of the visual environment?

Creative industries. Describes the whole entertainment industry, from ballet dancer to movie producer.

Modern artists and authors are now often classified as part of the creative industries, a name that evolved to describe the whole entertainment industry, from ballet dancer to movie producer. The idea of creative economies and industries, however, had its origins in changes in the division of labour and the emergence of a society where people's lives are not dominated by physical labour.

Computers and social media

> We are witnessing the evolution of a universal interconnected network of audio, video and electronic text communications that will blur the distinction between interpersonal and mass communication and between public and private communication. (Neuman, 1991, 12)

People can spend more time watching television and using computers because the division of labour has changed since the beginning of the 20th century. The majority of the workforce is no longer needed for intensive labouring work to produce the agricultural goods or indeed the manufacturing goods for the whole of society. The expression 'information superhighway', coined as part of the Bill Clinton hi-tech ticket in the 1991 United States presidential elections, is a reflection of this societal change brought on by the information/services sector. By 2007 many homes in industrialized countries had become 'home entertainment centres' with wide screens, access to pay television and terrestrial or wireless broadband networks for the Internet.

Our interest in this chapter has been on the human experience of new media. The Internet was seen by observers as a seismic shock. Negroponte (1996, 204) said the Internet was '10.5 of the Richter scale of social change'. Castells said that the Internet is the fabric of our life (2001). Bill Gates, who has a vested interest in the technology of computing and the Internet, declared that computers and the Internet were 'rocking us the same way the discovery of the scientific method, the invention of printing, and the arrival of the industrial age did' (Gates, 1995, 273).

Interestingly, we have had for many years in the telephone, two-way media that allow connection to geographically separated areas. Telephones have also been a part of **universal service** legislation. Telephones in industrialized countries are viewed as socially and economically necessary, to the point where a household who cannot access the network might be subsidized in provision of technology and calls. City users in some countries, for example, often paid higher prices for their calls in order to subsidize rural users. Rural users who lived a long way from local exchanges often had assistance with telecommunications infrastructure to connect them with the network. Universal legislation has changed as telephone networks have become cheaper and phones more accessible through terrestrial and wireless networks. However, the principle of accessibility to networks remains an important one.

Many of the services we associate with the Internet – like real time news in online sites – have also been available via the telephone. For instance, Theodore Puskas, a collaborator with Thomas Edison, created the *Telephon Hirmondo* for Hungary where he had exclusive rights to telephone connection. Family members could listen to news simultaneously through a crude phone. Each day a programme was provided to subscribers. It included hourly news bulletins, summaries of stock exchange prices, short entertaining stories, poetry readings and even linguistic lessons (Briggs, 1977). The service operated successfully for 23 years. The modern telephone newspaper comes in the form of touch-tone phones providing access to information on news, sport, weather and so on.

The difference between the Internet and the telephone, of course, is in the combination of computing, voice and vision. The Internet also provides a one-to-many and many-to-many platform for individuals. Terrorists can self-produce videos and put them up on websites. Individuals can produce short video clips of themselves and put them up on YouTube for millions to see. The communicative, participational, side of the online and mobile media, however, has emerged as one of the most dramatic outcomes of the digital revolution. William Quick coined the term blogosphere in the *DailyPundit*.com, a conservative journal, to describe the rise of the online forums that allow conversation on any topic under the sun. Famous blog sites such as http://www.technorati.com and www.baidu.com give overviews of and access to popular blogging sites. The new participational media are called social media because they are designed to allow individuals and groups to create extensive communication networks and at the same time classify their personal interests within those discussions and collected information. Current examples (which may be outdated by the time we go to press!) are MySpace and Facebook. 'Tagging', RSS (really simple syndication) feeds, SMS, and other techniques are all a part of software tools available to the amateur to produce their own content within their own communicative space. Amateur media users, disliked by corporations and governments alike, have turned to the communicative spaces in the Internet. These are arguably the spaces that are no longer available in the traditional broadcast spectrum.

Universal service. Legislation that ensures that people have equal access to society's basic communications and media.

to recap...

The communicative, participational, side of the online and mobile media has emerged as one of the most dramatic outcomes of the digital revolution.

Summary

The examples in this chapter might seem European and North American centric. However, the authors have chosen trends that represent the trajectory of industrialization that it must be said was originally European in origin. Clearly, though, much of the development of the technology of media is international. The techniques required for paper production through to moveable type came from east and west.

There have of course been many great innovations in modern industrialized times that have nothing to do with media. However, communication and media revolutions form the foundations for how the social distribution of knowledge is organized and how the freedom to communicate may or may not be possible. A society dominated by parchment as the main means of recording knowledge has difficulties with reproduction of works on any large scale. Knowledge, indeed, is easier to make scarce in such an environment. A society dominated solely by oral techniques is limited in the scope of knowledge it can possibly create or preserve, over time. The printing press enhances reproducibility, distribution and preservation of knowledge. Knowledge is, potentially, more accessible and subversive ideas more easily distributed in a print environment. Telegraphy and broadcasting speed up what the printing press made possible by allowing real time delivery of knowledge over vast distances. The telephone and the Internet enable people to operate in two-way communicative spaces in real time. Control over what people say in such spaces is much more difficult compared with slower media.

There has been an ongoing tension in the history of our communication habitats between those who wish to control what people say and those who, simply, want to say something – whether it is gossip or subversive ideas. The different media that have emerged over time represent different challenges to democracy and to human development. They also represent challenges in entertainment and whether or not people are allowed to enjoy themselves and be social. The amateur radio users of the early 20th century were not happy when they were squeezed out of the spectrum. The modern 'bloggers', arguably their descendants, are often seen as a curse and a nuisance. As we have seen, people, corporations and governments talk about their experiences of a new medium and the coming together of older and newer media. These experiences shape how media come to be used or not used and how the social distribution of knowledge and the freedom to communicate operate from one era to the next.

At the conclusion of this chapter you should be able to:
- recognize that the introduction of a new medium often involves radical changes to structures and organizations in a culture;
- critically discuss changes to the social distribution of knowledge created by changes in the type of media used;
- apply the ideas of convergence and globalization to the history of the development of media.

Habitats. The communicative spaces that we occupy.

Key themes

Convergence. The term convergence emerged with computer networks to describe the bringing together of different types of media – text, sound and video – into one medium. Convergence, however, did not arrive with the computer. All major historical developments in media have involved transformation of older media into new cultural and mediated forms. Writing brought with it a coded system of visible marks whereby a writer could determine the exact words that the reader would generate from the text. Writing did not replace orality but transformed it. The printing press brought with it the ability to transform writing into mass-reproduced books and other literature such as posters for the circulating libraries of the poor. The ability of hundreds of thousands of people to read in their own language, the vernacular, at the same time transformed the social distribution of knowledge. The printing press, however, did not replace writing. Telegraph and radio transformed the speed by which news and other information was received and began an interconnected media world where instantaneous or near instantaneous communication became a reality. Computers, social media and mobile media in their turn have brought together oral and visual media and transformed our sense of participation in, potentially, a global community.

Social distribution of knowledge. The media of communication are directly related to the social distribution of knowledge. The circulating libraries of the poor, for example, helped those without resources to learn to read. The printing press freed knowledge from parchment and made it more accessible. Telegraph and radio opened up news and its distribution globally. There can often be a tension, however, between those who wish to contain and constrain knowledge, for political or other reasons, and those who wish to expand access.

Standardization. The printing press enabled identical words and images to be simultaneously mass-reproduced. In scribal culture each reproduced work was individual and there could be variations in spelling and form. People in geographically dispersed locations could with print read the same ideas and see the same images, whether maps, drawings or pictures. Standardization of languages, grammars and spelling was possible because of print.

Technologizing the word. Technologization of the word is the outcome of writing for Walter Ong. It is the first big revolution in communication and media, essential for all that followed. This process of mediation has become more complex as different media have emerged over time. However, it is writing that sets the scene for changes in perception of space and time and how knowledge is transmitted and preserved.

Discussion questions

1   Bring to class your own timeline of the history of media. What would you put in it? What dates did you think were crucial and heralded major change?

2   Can you find equivalents of the 'language of the walls' online?

3   Ong argues that media like writing can change/enhance the way we think and our capacity for abstract thought. Do you agree? Can you find examples that might support his case?

4   In what ways do you think that the Internet or other media have enhanced access to knowledge and its distribution? Bring to class examples that you think show dramatic changes to the social distribution of knowledge because of historical changes to media.

Further reading

Briggs, A. and Burke, P. (2002). *A social history of the media: From Gutenberg to the internet.* Cambridge: Polity.

Mayer, G. and McDonnell, B. (2007). *Encyclopaedia of film noir.* Greenwood Press.

University of Minnesota's Media History Project
http://www.mediahistory.umn.edu/

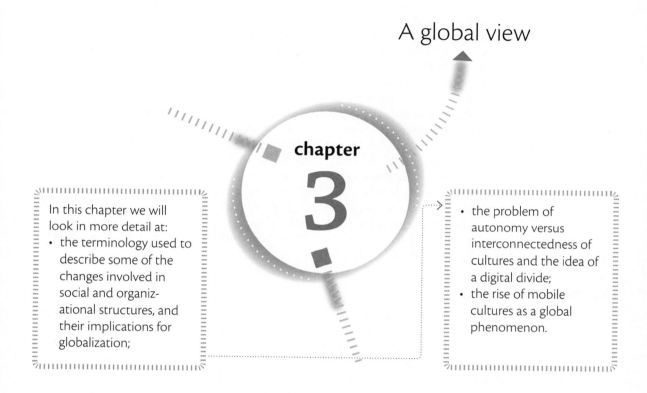

A global view

chapter

3

In this chapter we will look in more detail at:
- the terminology used to describe some of the changes involved in social and organiz-ational structures, and their implications for globalization;

- the problem of autonomy versus interconnectedness of cultures and the idea of a digital divide;
- the rise of mobile cultures as a global phenomenon.

Chapter 2 argued that major revolutions in the technology of media have also involved major changes in social and organizational structures. In particular people and societies have become increasingly interconnected through media developments. In this chapter we will look in more detail at:

- the terminology used to describe some of these changes, and their implica-tions for globalization;

- the problem of autonomy versus interconnectedness of cultures and the idea of a digital divide;

- the rise of mobile cultures as a global phenomenon.

Globalization involves a chequered process of systematic desegregation in which local cultures lose their autonomous and separate existence and become thoroughly interdependent and interconnected ... local cultures everywhere tend to reproduce themselves precisely, to a large extent, through the appropriation of global flows of mass-mediated forms and technologies. (Ang, 1996, 157)

Globalization according to Mittelman is a 'coalescence of varied transnational proc-esses and domestic structures, allowing the economy, politics, culture and ideology of one country to penetrate another' (1996, 3). Ang supports this idea of interdependence of cultures, with domination and dependency coming from the more powerful.

Ang and Mittelman set the scene for talking about globalization. These are the questions that their work suggests we need to bear in mind in this discussion:

- Are the world's cultures changing because of increased interconnectedness and interdependence?
- Are some cultures dominating and even destroying the cultures of others?
- Is this a modern phenomenon, or can we find traces of it in earlier histories of humankind?

In the previous chapter we found that there were tensions between the forces that wanted to control a medium, for profit for instance, and forces that wanted to open it up to the poor and disadvantaged, to increase literacy or perhaps to make trade more possible for remote communities. These tensions carry over into the global arena. The explanation for them lies in part in the importance of autonomy to human societies, and in part in the bare fact that changes driven by businesses and governments may or may not have the best interests of everyone affected by such change on their agenda. If you seek examples for this, look first at the challenges faced by indigenous communities and traditional societies as they attempt to make modernization and communications work for them, rather than against them. And of course all case studies show that, as in the history of the evolution of media, the way things happen in practice often differs from theory.

Describing social change

The language used to describe social change or inequality is important to our understanding of what is happening nationally and internationally. As the language changes, so we can see how people's thinking is changing with every new shift in social practices and conditions around the world. Constructing a genealogy of terms invented to describe developments in communication and cultural technologies from the mid-20th century is instructive. In each case the term becomes one among many that have been used to describe the changes in knowledge formation associated with the burgeoning of the communication environment in the period under scrutiny. Moreover, the brevity of the lifespan of the various terms is striking. Tables 3.1 and 3.2 provide an overview of some of the major concepts to describe major societal change. Have a close look and see if any of the older terms help you to understand features of the present day, or which groups of terms are most helpful to you in describing lives and situations that you observe in the world today.

Of all the terms we identify only two appear to have had longevity – McLuhan's global village and Bell's post-industrial society. The brief life of the other terms is indicative of the fact that they may have failed to actually capture and describe the conditions they purport to describe. The terms are, in short, little more than metaphors used to describe an ongoing condition of asymmetry that has characterized global economic, political and cultural relations since at least the 16th century, the beginning of European expansion on a global scale. The terms also change because of the speed with which things appear to change. Again, it is important to refer back to earlier communication 'revolutions' and the apparent speed of change (Burke, 2000), suggesting that the velocity of change is relative to the social structure of an era.

Table 3.1 **Terms used to describe revolutionary change**

Year	Term		Year	Term
1950	Lonely crowd		1971	Age of information
1953	Organizational revolution			Compunications
1957	New social class			Post-industrial society
1958	Meritocracy			Self-guiding society
1959	Education revolution			Super-industrial society
	Post-capitalist society		1972	Post-traditional society
1960	End of ideology			World without borders
	Post-maturity economy		1973	New service society
1961	Industrial society		1974	Information revolution
1962	Computer revolution		1975	Communications age
	Knowledge economy			Mediacracy
1963	New working class			Third industrial revolution
	Post-bourgeois society		1976	Industrial technological society
1964	Global village			Megacorp
	Managerial capitalism		1977	Electronics revolution
	One-dimensional man			Information economy
	Post-civilized era		1978	Network nation
	Service class society			Republic of technology
	Technological society			Telematic society
1967	New industrial state			Wired society
	Scientific-technological revolution		1979	Computer age
1968	Dual economy			Micro millennium
	Neo-capitalism		1980	Micro revolution
	Postmodern society			Microelectronics revolution
	Technocracy			Third wave
1969	Age of discontinuity		1981	Information society
	Post-collectivist society		1982	Communications revolution
	Post-ideological society			Information age
1970	Computerized society		1983	Computer state
	Personal society			Gene age
	Post-economic society		1984	Second industrial divide
	Post-liberal age			
	Pre-figurative age			
	Technetronic era			

activity   Using brainstorming techniques, work in groups of 4–5 and come up with as many contemporary terms and phrases that you think try to capture the idea of change. Then do the same exercise for terms that you remember from the past three to four years (or as far back as you can go). Now write them up on a board and talk about them. Which work best? How many and which ones do you think will be remembered or still in use in ten years? What do your discussions reveal to you about (a) the rate of change and (b) stasis in the contemporary world?

Table 3.2 **A selective description of key terms used to describe social change**

Era	Term	Source	Motivations	Conditions
1940s	Newspeak	*1984* by George Orwell	Reaction to authoritarian propaganda	Polarization of the world along ideological lines
1950s	The end of ideology	Daniel Bell (1965) *The end of ideology: On the exhaustion of political ideas in the fifties*	A US American response to the Cold War and the polarization of politics and culture	A response to living in a nuclear world
	Rise of the new information class	Milovan Djilas (1953) *The new class: An analysis of the communist regime*	A response to the Soviet state and its reliance on a compliant bureaucracy as an alternative to the capitalist states of western Europe	The new bureaucrats and their reliance on information to maintain control in a Marxist–Leninist context
	The rise of the meritocracy	Michael Young (1958) *The rise of the meritocracy 1870–2033: An essay on education and equality*	Explores post Second World War concerns with egalitarianism and the provision of the welfare state to ensure equal provision of services to citizens	The increase of information workers as a result of changing education practices in a liberal democracy
	The emergence of post-capitalist society	Ralph Dahrendorf (1959) *Class and class conflict in an industrial society*	A further reflection on the changing nature of European society and its shift from free markets to Keynesian economic control and its affect on the social composition of a society	Changes in the nature and composition of class as a sociological category in changing economic circumstances
1960s	Global village	Marshall McLuhan (1964) *Understanding media: The extensions of man*	A timely recognition of the significance of changes in communication, information and entertainment patterns based on electronic media	Recognition of emerging global contacts and their potential effect on culture
1970s	Age of information	The phrase 'information age' starts to be used, for example Helvey's 1971 *The age of information: An interdisciplinary survey of cybernetics*	Awareness of the link between the creation of knowledge, computing, and the economy and society	Increasing internationalization of production
		Jean-Francois Lyotard (1979) *The postmodern condition: A report on knowledge*	Changing patterns of social life, rise of feminism and acceptance of birth control	A major shift in perception that challenged the dominant meta-narratives of industrial society
	Information economy	Marc Uri Porat (1977) *The information economy: Definitions and measurement*	Term signifies the shift from an economy based on industrial capital to one based on transnational capital that privileges information as a product	Employment dominated by service and information industries
	Post-industrial society	Daniel Bell (1973) *The coming of post-industrial society: A venture in social forecasting*	Describing the shift in productive capacity in the industrialized world towards a knowledge-based economy	Shift from US and Europe to Japan of manufacturing heralding change in centre–margin relations
1980s	Information society	A term that has evolved over the decades and common usage emerged in the 1980s	Refinement of the notion of the Age of Information, where computers have become central convergent media	The 'me' generation where greed is good characterized by conflation of knowledge and information, with both viewed as commodities

	Third wave	Alvin Tofler (1980) *The third wave*	A term invented to signify a new industrial and social order, where mass media have been 'demassified' and decentralized. Has been very influential in China	The recognition that there had been fundamental changes in working and social relations as well as the relations of production
	Gene age	Robert Lewontin, Steve Rose and L.J. Kamin (1984) *Not in our genes: Biology, ideology and human nature*	The rise of biotechnology and emergence of sociobiology. The view that genes are the basic building blocks of life and thus contain and transmit information biologically	Fundamental change in ways society thinks about human life as a consequence of progress in biological knowledge and information. A shift in the nature versus nurture debate
	The control revolution	James R. Beniger (1986) *The control revolution: Technological and economic origins of the information age*	A detailed, essentially cybernetic account of how technologies since the 19th century have been used for social control	An influential work that is underpinned by a recognition of the unease apparent in post-industrial culture about the degree of social control the modern bureaucratic state exercises
1990s	Information superhighway	Al Gore (1994) *Building the information superhighway*	Awareness that the Internet represents a significant new medium with wide applications across cultures	Prominence of networking. Possibly the first clearly articulated political response to the 'information revolution'
	Virtual communities	Howard Rheingold (1993) *The virtual community: Homesteading on the electronic frontier*	Exploration of the link between the virtual and real community	The impact of computer networks on geographically dispersed individuals and communities
	Cybersociety	Steve Jones (1998) *Cybersociety 2.0*	The effects of the Internet are becoming apparent. Attempts to theorize the impact of e-to-e communication are undertaken in the recognition that a new sense of space has emerged along with new constructions of what comprises a community	The Internet rapidly diffuses as a medium
	Network society	Manuel Castells (1996) *The rise of network society*	Apparent bipolar opposition between the Internet and the self	How to address real transformations in society and identity created by new and global networks is well and truly on the agenda
2000s	The digital divide	National Telecommunications and Information Administration (1995) *Falling through the net: A survey of the 'have nots' in rural and urban America*	Recognition of the pervasiveness of the new technologies and the articulation of a political solution to solve a US domestic issue that became a global issue	Confirmation that communication technologies had changed and were perceived to have profound political, economic and cultural consequences
	Digital and mobile culture		The pervasive influence of digital forms on all aspects of modern life, from domestic settings to outer space	Rise of social networking and mobile cultures

Each of the terms, and the influential texts where they are elaborated, explores new ways of thinking about the world and the human condition. The terms are attempts to describe major shifts in what is conceived as 'information' and 'knowledge', the nature of the distribution of information and knowledge itself, and the centrality of information and knowledge to a new economy. Chapter 6 examines in more detail key classics in describing or explaining information as a phenomenon.

New technologies successively create new ways of thinking about the world, and the phenomena of the world. At the same time there is always tension between the new and what it challenges. These technological interventions have different impacts in developed economies and in developing regions of the world. But one should not underestimate either. The flow of the new is not one-way of course. In the digital era, and specifically since the entry of Japan, and latterly Korea, into the forefront of cybernetics and digital design, ideas of what might define the new, and the revolutionary, have come from Asia and influenced the West. Evidence is also beginning to emerge suggesting that the same trajectory applies to Africa, although the continuing inequalities and catch-up economies in Africa mean that innovations are still few.

activity   Create a table of those ideas, terms, and media 'buzzes' that have emerged in the past five to ten years. Think about computer gaming, mobile technologies, design models, fashion identities. How many have origins or key exponents in the US, Japan, China, Korea, or Europe? How do they impact your understanding of (a) yourself and (b) the world around you?

Monopolies of knowledge

How then do we make sense of this diverse terminological universe that has emerged in the past few decades? One possible direction is to turn to the ideas and concepts of Harold Innis (1894–1952), the Canadian political economist and communication historian. Innis (1951) was not satisfied with quick solutions but rather sought to explain events, not as a continuum, but in terms of interrelatedness and continuity. As Crowley and Heyer (1991, 1–2) argue, Innis virtually invented the sub-discipline of communication history, so compelling are his arguments. Innis was also a prescient thinker. As Berland says:

> the differential production of 'intellectual capital' is a necessary cornerstone of the very complex dynamic constituting modern and contemporary centre-margin relations. Innis' principal contribution to the history and theory of culture is his insistence on the central role of communications and transportation technologies in materially mediating economic, administrative, cultural and intellectual life. Shaped by their commercial and geographic context, these technologies facilitate the ongoing production of centre and margins – that is, spatially differentiated hierarchies of political-economic power. (Berland, 1999, 282)

In other words, Berland credits Innis with understanding that not only how the world is shaped by money and power, but also the ways in which geographies of power and influence are created and maintained, are very much related to technology and media know-how and control in certain places. The USA famously 'owns' the Internet, to the extent that – and every non-US citizen finds this a touch alarming – emails 'travel through' US Internet hubs. Think of the power this affords the USA. And then perhaps consider why the People's Republic of China has a separate system.

The best use of Innis, however, is Carey's essay 'Culture, Geography, and Communication: The work of Harold Innis in an American Context' (1989). Carey gives an overview of Innis's thinking and the manner in which communication technologies shape culture (or civilization, which was Innis's preferred term). Four propositions from Innis's work and Carey's overview of Innis can be discerned:

- Monopolies of knowledge develop and decline in relation to the medium of communication (for example the Catholic Church lost control of language through Latin and parchment, time-biased media, when printing diffused the vernacular, space-biased media).
- The speed of a medium has an impact on a culture. Space-biased media are light and portable. They are easily transported and disseminated and clearly space oriented, with a short lifespan unless preserved. They are associated with secular societies that occupy large territories. Time-biased media are durable and heavy and not easily transported. Their dissemination and spread is limited but they may have a long life. They are associated with hierarchical societies that are defined by sacred and moral precepts.
- All technologies have a contradictory potential – the unexpected use of technology. The mobile telephone companies at the beginning of the mobile revolution in the 1980s and 1990s did not realize for example how important texting (SMS and MMS) would become for younger users.
- Concentration on a medium of communication implies a bias in the cultural development of the civilization or culture concerned. A society dominated with space-biased media (or mass communications) will be very different from a society dominated by time-biased media.

Time-biased media are those that are so slow that they give political or religious or other leaders much more control over how knowledge is stored and distributed in the community/society. Parchment takes a lot of effort to produce and cannot be spread or diffused quickly. In the Middle Ages in Europe the language of power was Latin, a language spoken only by the educated and rich, and only written and stored by monks. This gave them a great deal of influence over access to scripture and its interpretation. Mass communications – whether the printed word or broadcast media or a wireless system – overtake time-based media and require those who would control information to reorient their strategies!

There is a tendency to see Innis as a technological determinist (Drache, 1995) although as Drache points out, it is difficult to sustain this argument once you grasp a core idea of Innis, who says quite explicitly that all technologies have a contradictory potential. Technological determinism means that a theoretical position assumes that the technology will force change of a certain type. Those who argue against this point out that it is the way technologies are used, the context in which they are used, and whether or not the situation is conducive to a particular technology in the first place, that matter more in determining what happens. That is, digital communication may create the utopia of the Electronic Frontier Foundation but equally it could induce the information dystopia described by Caleb Carr in his novel *Killing Time* (2000) where chaos and social breakdown, not to mention war and mayhem, are directly attributable to the information revolution begun in the latter part of the 20th century.

Sassen (2002), an urban theorist, has also begun to address the issue of the impact of the digital on society and culture, which for her comprises the modern city and its particular social forms. Like Castells (2001) she sees the digital as having an inherent capacity to form networks:

Monopolies of knowledge. Describes the role of communication and media in the distribution and control of knowledge.

Space-biased media. Media that are light, portable and easily transported and disseminated – associated with secular societies.

Time-biased media. Media that are durable and heavy and not easily transported – associated with hierarchical societies.

Understanding the place of these new network technologies from a sociological perspective requires avoiding a purely technological interpretation and recognition of the embeddedness and the variable outcomes of these technologies for different economic, political and social orders. They can indeed be constitutive of new social dynamics, but they can also be derivative or merely reproduce older conditions. (Sassen, 2002, 2)

The application of Innis, on the other hand, does add to our understanding. The struggle between the old and the new means of communication is central to his argument and is described in great detail in *Empire and Communications* (1950). He also has an explanation of how the new triumphs over the old. The success of a new means of communication in supplanting the old arises because it attracts a monopoly, or more specifically it creates monopolies of knowledge.

The most obvious example of monopolies of knowledge is the monks in their scriptoria in the Middle Ages. Keeping all knowledge in Latin and in monasteries enabled certain classes of society to control the production, preservation and distribution of knowledge. If the majority of the population could not read Latin and knowledge was preserved in Latin then only a small part of the population would have access to the world's knowledge. But Latin written on parchment where it takes days to produce one page also limits the speed of distribution of knowledge. Burke's *A Social History of Knowledge* (2000) explores how new monopolies of knowledge emerged in early modern Europe. Chapter 2 showed how the speed with which printing permeated European culture compelled scholars (the clerisy is Burke's preferred term) to conceptualize the world in different ways leading to new strategies for collecting, storing, cataloguing, distributing and consuming knowledge.

Textual communities. A textual community revolves around an authoritative text and designated interpreters.

In the analysis of a more recent era Marvin (1988) provides a key to this concept of monopoly. Marvin takes the notion of the textual community and uses it to explain how technologies such as electricity, telephony and phonography were introduced and successfully dispersed through Victorian society. A textual community revolves around an 'authoritative text and their designated interpreters' (Marvin, 1988, 12). Thus the medium is subordinated to certain people and certain forms of content. It is as if Hollywood film were the only way in which film could be used as a technology and that the only audiences were English speaking. This may seem quite reasonable to some readers, but imagine that your first language is not English, that you do not share US American values and that you live in a rural community in Ghana, or an indigenous community in Alaska. Does it seem sensible then, or rather strange? The technologies Marvin describes have become so normalized that it is difficult to grasp that in their day they were not only potentially revolutionary but there was no guarantee that they would be successful. Marvin's account draws upon the work of Brian Stock (1996), a Canadian medievalist, who invented the concept of the textual community to account for the impact of literacy on religious schism in 11th century Europe.

to recap...

Ideas like monopolies of knowledge and textual communities have evolved to describe how communities and societies control communication and how different media, space or time biased, affect that control.

A textual community is built upon a number of key concepts, namely the text and interpretations of the text that creates a social structure built on the principles of inclusion and exclusion. Those who are included in the interpretive framework are empowered, while those who are excluded become powerless. The convergence of these elements, in the right conditions, leads to the creation of a powerful entity, a development Marvin charts in her detailed study of the introduction of the electrical media and the activities of its proponents in the 19th century.

The digital divide

Monopolies of knowledge is a theoretical term used to describe how knowledge gets controlled and the role of communication in that control. The digital divide is a commonly used phrase to describe inequalities in the technology of media between societies and nations, at local and global levels respectively. In the past decade the term 'digital divide' has attracted a good deal of attention from politicians, analysts and critics alike. Couldry (2000) argues that the term is a convenient label used to describe a debate about access to digital technology and the asymmetrical relations of modern communicative power since the mid-1990s. In his view the term has focused on a particular debate that has exercised the imagination of both politicians and academics in this period because it highlights a particular cultural shift that seems to defy conventional explanation.

This shift, according to critics (Norris, 2001), revolves around a set of relationships between individuals, groups, regions and even nations that are linked in some way to those new forms of communication dependent on digital encoding for the distribution and consumption of information and knowledge. The relationships are perceived as essentially ones of inequality, between the 'haves' ' and 'have nots' in a globalized economy. Norris points out that the term has become 'shorthand for any and every disparity within the online community' (2001, 4). She goes on to elaborate the term by pointing out that it is not just a technological issue but rather one that has significant economic social and political dimensions as well (2001, 4). In particular Norris makes the useful distinction between 'the global divide' and 'the social divide' (2001, 3–4).

Castells also entered this debate pointing out that the digital divide 'adds a fundamental cleavage to the existing sources of inequality and social exclusion in a complex interaction that appears to increase the gap between the promise of the Information Age and its bleak reality for many people around the world. Yet, the apparent simplicity of the issue becomes complicated on closer examination' (2001, 247).

The US National Telecommunications and Information Administration (NTIA) began its discussion of digital culture in 1995 with an analysis of telephone and computer penetration of homes in the US (NTIA, 1995), which it extended in 1997 and 1999. The analyses of the data identified a number of trends that suggested the gap between the 'haves' and the 'have nots' was accelerating in a world increasingly dependent on digital communication. To emphasize the significance of their findings, the NTIA named the reports 'Falling Through the Net', evoking images of social contracts and safety nets provided by the state to protect the less endowed sections of a society.

UNESCO took up the cause in 2000 with *Bridging the Digital Divide* articulating a concern that the developing world was being excluded from a new digital era seemingly dominated by the US command of the resources. In 1998 26.3 per cent of the US population accessed the Internet and this grew to 54.3 per cent in 2000. By contrast only 2.4 per cent of the world's population accessed the Internet, the figure rising to 6.7 per cent by 2000. The discrepancies caused alarm among policymakers and social theorists for a number of complex reasons.

There is an implicit perception in both the NTIA reports and the UNESCO documents that digital communication is of a different order to previous communication 'revolutions', a view we wish to challenge. The difference, the argument seems to go, lies in the speed, volume and interactivity of the medium. Its introduction is the harbinger of a new order. Its impact is economic, political, social and cultural. Exclusion from this new order will exacerbate the already vast gap between North and South (rich and poor). Castells (2001, 246–74) and Norris (2001, 4–9) provide much richer and more insightful accounts of the global implications of the digital divide than the somewhat reductive account proposed by UNESCO.

The NTIA and UNESCO discussions on the digital divide deploy what Marvin calls essentially antifactual arguments that see the history of communication as 'the evolution of technical efficiencies in communication'. This is a form of technological determinism and also a mode of cultural determinism. The report assumes that the ways in which technologies are deployed and used in central economies such as that of the USA should be the ways in which technologies are taken up and used elsewhere. But why should this be so? Why also should we not worry about the digital divide within communities and social worlds? Is it sensible that some children should have fast broadband access to information through their school computers, and at home in their bedrooms, while others may have no access at all? This is as bad a situation as some children in one part of a city having a well-stocked library, and others having no books other than the most basic school textbooks. We suggest therefore that it is more useful to see digital deprivation as:

to recap...

The concept of a digital divide emerged in international policy debates to describe the problem of 'haves' and 'have nots' in a globalized knowledge economy.

> A series of arenas for negotiating issues crucial to the conduct of social life; among them, who is inside and outside, who may speak, who may not, and who has the authority and may be believed. Changes in the speed, capacity, and performance of communications devices tell us little about these questions. (Marvin, 1988, 4)

class discussion

In order to debate the complexity of the digital divide notion, think about what specific media bring what benefits or disadvantages to those with access. Then, take the next step of thinking through whether it is the medium in and of itself that is crucial to privilege, or whether the ability to change content in the medium matters more. Finally consider how that content is made valuable – that is, who accesses and uses it, and what effects that may have on everyday life. In this debate you are triangulating your approach, taking not just the medium, but also the content and the producer and the consumer into account.

Contradictory potential of media technology

It is worthwhile looking briefly at some country examples to see how media can change society and also how media are used to bypass traditional authority or global pressures. Indonesia, Samoa and Ghana are good examples of countries that have not been and are still not rich. They are also examples of countries where new technology certainly exposes them to outside cultures but where the technology has often been adapted to meet their own needs.

Samoa

One of the problems associated with examining the impact of media on social change in different countries is, simply, lack of data, especially for the pre-television or pre-computer era. We do have some figures on Western Samoa, a small South Pacific island nation, when it first introduced television and these provide an interesting insight into how modern media can displace traditional activities. Table 3.3 shows how social activities, such as talking, have changed dramatically after the introduction of television.

Table 3.3 **Television viewing and other evening activities in Western Samoan households, 4–10 pm**

	Per Cent of Time Spent	
	Without TV	With TV
Prayers	6	4
Eating	17	10
Talking/discussion	30	9
Story telling/singing	15	3
Visiting friends/community activities	22	4
Playing cards/weaving mats	10	0
Watching TV	0	70

Source: Adapted from Martin (1987, 3–21).

Television replaced a set of social activities that were time-biased media (weaving, story telling) with a space-biased medium, watching television. However, the data do not explain why one activity has replaced the others.

Western Samoans, by adopting television, had entered into the 'televisual' world of the US-based American culture. They had entered into a global network. As Innis (1999) points out, in the conclusion to *The Fur Trade of Canada*, the first indigenous hunter to trade a fur with a *voyageur* in the 16th century entered into a global economic network, whether they recognized it or not. We would argue the same still applies on ever more complex levels, as the Samoan experience demonstrates.

The Western Samoan experience with television is not a 'divide' or a 'gap'. It does make sense, though, to talk about potential impacts of television on its indigenous culture. It is at this level that there is genuine concern that global networks have impacts that may be terminal for some cultures.

Indonesia

In 2002, on the fourth floor of the Ciputra Shopping Mall, South Jakarta, were seven or eight Internet cafes in a row. All of them at that time were full to bursting with both young men and women occupying chairs, packed close together. Space is at a premium and demand to access the computers is high, as two universities are located immediately adjacent to the shopping mall and most of the students cannot afford to purchase their own computers. Both demand and use of computers is high in this sector of Jakarta but this is not reflected in the statistics relating to access available for Indonesia.

The computers are used for study but also for leisure, for surfing the net. The former activity is usually endorsed by society while the latter causes concern. There is evidence that pornography may be accessed in these settings and it is this sort of web surfing that alarms the authorities. Sexual indiscretion and pornography in particular have a special resonance in a predominantly Muslim country like Indonesia. Moreover, it is clear that in the urban setting access to computers through the cyber cafe is widespread among the young.

In another context, under the Suharto regime the publication of the *Jawa Pos*, one of Surabaya's (East Java) leading newspapers was strictly controlled. Its ambition to become a major regional publisher was frustrated at every turn by the New Order regulations relating to newspaper publication. Post-Suharto, it produces over 70 titles ranging from newspapers and tabloids catering for Surabaya as well as nearby towns to special interests magazines focusing on sport and motoring. All these publications are produced in a specially built complex located on the outskirts of Surabaya, and printed on very modern, computerized printing presses by a vertically and horizontally integrated company. The success of the *Jawa Pos* group of companies is replicated elsewhere in Indonesia. The increase in the volume of publications in terms of readership and titles points to an increase in literacy among the people of East Java. Warschauer (2001) explores the connection between increasing exposure to computers and literacy, suggesting that the two are linked. So, computer access and newspaper publishing must be considered as part of the same story of the growth of reading in a post-authoritarian state.

MJTV is a more recent and a good example of a local Indonesian community taking advantage of the relative cheapness of digital technology. In Yogyakarta Indonesia, September 2007, MJTV or Masjid Jogokariyan Television was launched by the *takmir* (management) of Jogokariyan Mosque in Jogokariyan village on the first day of Ramadhan. It operates on a VHF 4 channel and has a broadcasting radius of 2.5 kilometres. MJTV can reach all residents of Jogokariyan's 887 families, 4,000 people, 95 per cent of them Muslim. The Mosque invested Rupiah 20 million (euro €1,500 and US$2,200 at the time) to purchase CCTV cameras and other broadcasting equipment, transmitters, converters, VCD players, switchers and TV sets (Wahyuni, 2007).

Ghana

In the mid-1990s Bossman Dowuona-Hammond said that 'In the past, fear prevented us from getting the tools we needed. With the right tools, we can compete' (Zachary, 2002). He convinced Ghana's government that it was worthwhile controlling a satellite link that bypassed Accra's phone system. This would make it cheaper for Ghanaians to access phone services (at a time when multinationals were making money from a terrestrial network that did not work). The key to gaining appropriate access to communication technologies for Ghana was to sidestep the logic of capital characterized here as multinational profiteering, and to embrace high-end mass communication technologies, to 'leapfrog' the old and take up the new on terms favourable to their local needs.

> Ghana's telecom mess limits the utility of the Internet, raises the costs of information services – and suggests that the country is mired in the Stone Age, technologically. But the situation here, as in much of sub-Saharan Africa, defies such straightforward conclusions. There is another side to the country's technological profile, a burgeoning homegrown technology culture that explodes assumptions about the inherent backwardness of Africa and the nature of the so-called digital divide. (Zachary, 2002, 88)

In the late 1990s, luminaries such as Microsoft's Bill Gates and the UN's Kofi Annan together with the G8 group and the World Economic Forum saw the giving of computers to poor countries as an opportunity to close the digital divide. As Zachary points out, 'These plans have come to little or nothing. In the main, the rich have dropped boatloads of computers onto the poor with no awareness of the environment in which the machines will (or will not) be used' (Zachary, 2002).

If technology alone is used as an indicator of a digital divide, then the United States can be construed as 'poor' in mobile phones, as Figure 3.1 demonstrates. The US has significantly fewer mobile phones than Italy but significantly more personal computers than Italy. Perhaps the world community should be sending mobile phones to the United States and personal computers to Italy?

If we look at Ghana, one of the world's poorest countries, then we see that its mobile phone numbers are low, compared with wealthier nations. But if we examine Figure 3.2 closely, then it becomes clear how rapid mobile phone subscription growth was in Ghana from 2000 to 2005.

Figure 3.1 Mobile subscription per 100 people and PCs per 100 people

Legend: 1. Italy 2. Sweden 3. Britain 4. Germany 5. South Korea 6. France 7. Japan 8. United States 9. Ghana

Source: International Telecommunications Union data, 2005 (http://www.itu. int).

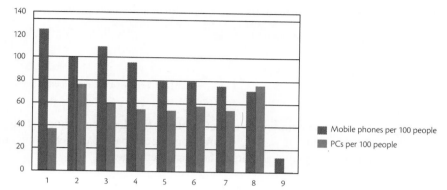

So, if we compare the US (8) with Italy (1), we find that indeed Italy has wide distribution of mobile phones compared with America but only moderate distribution of PCs. By all social and economic criteria Ghana is considered a poor country and yet the data show that there is a high penetration of PCs, and as we show in Figure 3.2 the situation in respect to mobile phones is rapidly changing in Ghana. Likewise mobile penetration in China is highly dynamic. Conventional arguments about the digital divide are challenged by these data, which augments our view that it is digital culture that should be the focus of our discussions and analysis.

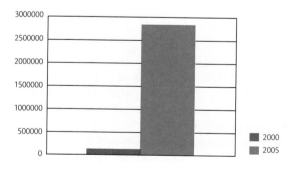

Figure 3.2 Mobile subscriptions, Ghana, 2000 and 2005

Source: International Telecommunications Union data, 2005 (http://www.itu.int).

The Ghanaian enthusiasm for the mobile phone is replicated in Nigeria (http://news. bbc.co.uk/2/hi/business/1905744.stm, accessed 10 March 2002), which suggests to us that the inclusive power of digital communications, which is the core activity of digital culture, is widely accepted by diverse social and cultural groups.

Interestingly, the Ghanaian experience can also be found in the United States. Minnesota State noted in its planning for the digital divide that Internet use was, by 2000, unequal between white populations and other ethnic groups. However, there had also been a far higher than expected increase in Internet use among ethnically different groups, especially Asian and Island populations. Table 3.4 shows the differences between the groups.

Table 3.4 **Percentage of US households with Internet access, 1998 and 2000**

	Asian and Pacific Islander	White	Hispanic	African/American
1998	36.0	29.8	12.6	11.2
2000	56.8	46.1	23.6	23.5

Source: Digital divide: beyond the infrastructure (2001).

What these data tell us is that we have to telescope very carefully any analysis of the digital divide. If we rely on only one coordinate, say technology, then a very skewed picture of the digital cultural landscape emerges.

In Chapter 1, it was said that globalization involved media, goods and people that cross national boundaries. These crossings can vary in their extent, intensity, tempo and influence across and between countries and cultures. In the discussion about Samoa, Indonesia and Ghana we have seen that modern media open up new crossings through new communicative spaces and that the effect of these crossings varies according to the culture and contexts of the people and places involved.

Modern digital media have added a new dimension to the spaces of globalization – an intensified communicative mobility. Mobile communications allow people to work outside the office, maybe because they are global cosmopolitans with a high level of privilege but limited time, or the mobile may allow you to work when you are very poor and have no office at all, but still need to maintain connection in order to find work. The meaning of technology is spatially and temporally different for people depending on their situation.

Mobile cultures and sense of place

In very different circumstances, the rise in popularity and prevalence of social networking software has made potential broadcasters of us all. YouTube provides a ready audience for anyone – or any group – with basic recording technology, a grasp of simple software, and the time and creative capacity to generate new content or compile and edit from pre-existing material. Never before have the roles of producer, director, editor and commentator been so readily exercised by so many, for so many. The local, in such circumstances, becomes simultaneously less constrained by the cultural domination of global media producers and more liberated by the access to global technologies, audiences, peers and cultural communities.

This local adoption and manipulation of media in cultures around the world has led media theorists to revise their notions of US influence on global media. Jeremy Tunstall published in 1977 the seminal *The Media Are American* and argued that the United States dominated global media. In his 2008 *The Media Were American* he has revised this argument and now puts the case for a world media structure comprised of interlocking national, regional, and cultural systems. Japan's advertising industry is one example of this. Second only to the US, although little over 20 per cent of its market size, the Japanese advertising market is dominated by Japanese advertising agencies and Japanese products.

The Japanese advertising agency Dentsu is the largest in Japan and in Asia generally and the fourth largest agency in the world. It is also the first international agency to access the rapidly growing Chinese market. In this sense, we see the national media market in Japan as being significantly resistant to global and US forces, while Japanese media players themselves emerge as important regional players that at times resemble the types of cultural intrusion elsewhere characterized as being American.

Damien Spry's work (2007) on mobile cultures in New South Wales has demonstrated issues and trends that are replicated elsewhere. He points out that mobile phones and mobile devices have made possible new communicative spaces and mobile cultures that bypass communicative limitations in traditional situations, like classrooms, the family home and other family or institutional locations.

group activity In Spry's research, young people (12–18 years) articulated widely different opinions of mobiles depending on their age, background and gender. Perhaps you can use his model to replicate your own 'local' study. Using focus group methodology (for which you need a note-taker, a facilitator and an observer in the group), bring together 8 young people of similar ages from your class (remember, you and indeed any student cannot do this without the ethical approval of the school, your colleagues and your lecturer). Discuss the uses, the abuses and the benefits of mobile phones in your lives. What are the key issues that emerge? Discuss as a group how you would investigate these further in a more substantial research project. If you have statistical expertise, think about the benefits and problems in designing a survey on the matter of the issues you have raised.

Mobile communications are not necessarily private, and there are concerns about the reach of networks into every corner of people's everyday lives. Mobiles are singular but not private. Often they are linked to work, or to large networks that impinge on both home and work life, blurring the boundaries between the two. Modern private and government corporations do not like their employees at work to use their computers for expressive or social purposes. Many corporations go to extraordinary lengths to monitor their staff's communication behaviour. However, people tend to be messy and often do not fit into neatly defined expectations from governments or corporations. Those who do not fit in to expectations of defined ways of communicating sometimes go to jail or, worse, face execution, as religious editors in the print era often did in Europe during the era of absolute monarchies, and as still happens in some authoritarian regimes today.

Tables 3.5 and 3.6 confirm the trends towards diversification of access to sources of information outside traditional media and the rise of peer-to-peer (P2P) communication and sharing of information on the Internet. Italy and China, in particular, stand out in P2P file-sharing activity.

Television, of course, already contributes to a sense of place. People are happy with their home entertainment systems or their television sets in the corner of the lounge room or bedroom or, increasingly, communication centre. Mobile communications are creating a different but also important sense of place. In the UK mobile phone text messages exceeded 35 billion in 2005 and continue to grow. The Office of Communication in the UK (Ofcom) estimates that the average number of messages sent per mobile connection rose by 17 per cent in 2005, to just fewer than 11 messages per connection per week. Table 3.7 shows the changes over time.

Table 3.5 Percentage of adults who use wireless devices to access news and information online

UK	29
France	18
Germany	18
USA	26
Japan	40
China	10

Note: Urban sample only in China.
Source: Ofcom (2006).

Table 3.6 Percentage of adults with broadband at home who are members of P2P file-sharing communities

UK	24
France	20
Germany	17
Italy	43
USA	20
Japan	26
China	72

Source: Ofcom (2006).

Table 3.7 Average messaging use per active mobile per week

2001	5.5
2002	7.2
2003	8.2
2004	9.3
2005	10.9

Source: Ofcom (2006).

Table 3.8 Average daily visitors (000) to major social networks

	June 2006	June 2007	Change
MySpace	16,764	28,786	72
Facebook	3,742	14,917	299
hi5	2,873	4,727	65
Friendster	3,037	5,966	96
Orkut	5,488	9,628	75
Bebo	1,188	4,833	307
Tagged	202	983	386

Source: comScore World Metrix.

Social networking sites have meanwhile become popular around the world. A quick look at the regional differences is suggestive as each example has certain features and these may appeal to different cultural groups. In June 2007 Orkut had the largest number of users in the Indian subcontinent and in Brazil. Facebook has grown larger than MySpace and is strong in the Middle East as well as in western countries. hi5.com operates extensively in Peru, Colombia, Central America, and areas as remote as Mongolia, Romania, and Tunisia. Friendster, one of the first social networks, can be found throughout South East Asia. Tables 3.8 and 3.9 provide an overview of the diffusion of social networks.

Table 3.9 **Total worldwide home–work locations among Internet users 15+**

	N. America	Latin America	Europe	Middle East Africa	Asia-Pacific
MySpace	62.1	3.8	24.7	1.3	8.1
Facebook	68.4	2.0	16.8	5.7	7.1
hi5	15.3	24.1	31.0	8.7	20.8
Friendster	7.7	0.4	2.5	0.8	88.7
Orkut	2.9	48.9	4.6	0.6	43.0
Bebo	21.8	0.5	62.5	1.3	13.9
Tagged	22.7	14.6	23.5	10.0	29.2

Source: comScore World Metrix.

Media theorists see these figures as signifying basic changes in our sense of place. For example Gillard, Wale and Bow (1997) suggest that social place can only be understood in terms of social situations, which, until recently, have been tied to physical place. Mobility created by wireless communication has 'changed the logic of the social order by reconstructing the relationship between physical place and social place and by altering the ways in which we transmit and receive social information' (Gillard et al., 1997). For Ling and Yttri (2002; 2005) and Green (2002; 2003) increased mobility also undermines traditional family rituals by allowing teenagers exclusive individualized access to peer groups outside parental supervision and monitoring. The comprehensive pan-European investigation *Children and Their Changing Media Environment* identified significant differences between the Nordic countries and the rest of Europe concerning the relationship between children and media (Livingstone and Bovill, 2001). Children living in Nordic countries have a well-developed peer culture. The rest of Europe tends to have a more family-oriented culture (Suoninen, 2001).

Weilemann and Larsson (2002) found in their study of Swedish youth that their phones are not just treated as personal possessions and the calls are not treated as private communications. Rather teenagers spend their time rendering their communication 'public' by ensuring several people take part in it. 'The remote communication, i.e. the phone calls they receive or make, as well as the SMS messages they receive or send, are accounted for in the ongoing local interaction. Teenagers thus share the communication they take part in with their co-present friends. Not only the communication but also the phone itself is often shared' (Weilemann and Larsson, 2002). Johnson's (2003) study of Norwegian teenagers found that the mobile phone served two (distinct but related) purposes: (1) 'gossip' and 'chat' for the maintenance of social networks and (2) gift-giving, with an emphasis on strengthening social networks. Johnson noticed the function of chatting as 'meaningless' but not 'unnecessary' and says we need to understand the 'unnecessary' as one of the most important reasons for the immense growth of mobile phone use. 'Text messages, and talking on the mobile phone gives the actors – or users – an opportunity to be part of a social network, which is disembedded from 'place' as we know it in a pre-communication sense' (2003, 167).

Japanese children may be less 'peer-based' than their Nordic counterparts, but it is not the case when it comes to highly peer-based Japanese youth/teens. Generally the trend worldwide is for children (up to the age of elevenish) to use mobiles primarily for contact with family and thereafter to use them for peer group social networks. Ito (2003), interested in theories of place in Japan, looked at the power dynamics of the home, school and street of Japanese youth. In contrast to the breakdown between personal and professional lives experienced by adult mobile users, youth, she found, tend to see mobile phones as liberating and expressive personal technologies (2003, 1). For a theory of place, Ito drew on Massey (1993) who argues that different social groups are placed in very different positions when it comes to power and communication flows. Some groups are more in charge of things than others.

Ito looked at Shibuya, a centre within Tokyo that at that time had the highest density of mobile use in the world, to see how new power relationships in Japan might be developing (Ito, 2003, 14). Mobile phones, she found, embody a fast and footloose street culture beyond the surveillance of the institutions of home and school. For example, there is a practice called *enjo kosai* that started in the nineties, where high school girls, date men in return for money or expensive gifts. While literally meaning 'compensated companionship', *enjo kosai* can lead to commercial sexual relations and the term is often preferred now by young women who engage in what might more commonly be called teenage prostitution. The role of the mobile phone here is significant as it enables young women to contact and make arrangements with clients away from the scrutiny of parental or educational supervision, and outside of the institutions of organized crime. The practice has antecedents in the phone clubs and phone pager cultures that were similarly used to arrange 'dates'; in more recent years the additional function of the mobile phone (*keitai*) as a platform for Internet browsing has led to the development of *keitai*-accessible Internet dating sites which are often considered little more than bulletin boards for *enjo kosai* (dating). Internet sites designed to be accessed by desktop computers suffer less stigma and less attention from legal authorities who attempt to crack down on *enjo kosai* (Tomita, 2005; Spry, 2007).

Ito contests the popular arguments that youth morals are being eroded or that social bonds are broken as a consequence of their mobility. 'While mobile phones have become a vehicle for youths to challenge the power-geometries of places such as the home, the classroom, and the street, they have also created new disciplines and power-geometries, the need to be continuously available to friends and lovers, and the need to always carry a functioning mobile device' (Ito, 2003, 19). Five of the ten student couples in Ito's study were in ongoing contact when they were not at school, and all these couples had established practices for indicating their absence from the shared online space. 'They invariably send a good night email to signal unavailability, and would often send status checks during the day such as "are you awake?" or "are you done with work?" We saw a few cases when they would announce their intention to take a bath, a kind of virtual locking of the door' (Ito, 2003, 20).

Plant's (2001) study for Motorola on mobile phones bears out Ito's observations. In many cases, she says, the mobile is being used to keep established relationships alive. A Bankok working girl keeps in touch with her remote family village or a Filipina cook in Hong Kong keeps in contact with her children.

> At the same time, these new networks can allow users to establish lives outside the family and its control. In Beijing, a shy 17-year old with shoulder-length hair explains that the mobile makes it possible for him to have relationships with friends of which he knows his parents disapprove. For this very reason, many Afghans living in Peshawar were horrified by the prospect of girls and boys making private calls, leading private lives and forming their own friendships and attachments without the knowledge or approval of their families. In the words of one young Afghan contrib-

utor: 'I do know some girls who have mobiles, but I think they are bad girls. They talk to boys.'(Plant, 2001, 58)

In Bangladesh a similar social trend has emerged where young people contact one another over the phone before suggesting to their parents that may have found a suitable marriage partner.

The mobile phone has revolutionized the power-geometry of space–time compression for teenagers in the home and in the street, allowing them to communicate without the surveillance of parents and siblings (Green, 2002; Ito, 2003; Skog, 2002). This democratization of the family paints a picture of a future in which children 'may become actively involved in shaping their families through negotiation and participation in decision-making processes' (Tingstad, 2003, 262).

The relatively low cost and simplicity of the mobile phone, like radio in its early days, has made its spread and reach global. Plant (2001, 77) in very optimistic voice says that the mobile phone is uniquely adaptable, capable of playing many different roles, and able to 'make itself useful in a wide variety of cultural contexts, social worlds and individual lives. As its use spreads, so it will continue to diversify'.

However, a note of caution is necessary on what happens in future to these new communicative spaces. In Chapter 2 we witnessed the closure of the radio spectrum to amateurs, not simply because of requirements for efficiency or limits on spectrum, but because corporations did not like the idea of millions of people chatting on the airwaves for free. Mobile conversations, while costs are lowering, can mount up to significant expenses, especially for younger users, and corporations make billions of dollars or pounds from encouraging people to communicate more.

Summary

Since the 1950s there has emerged a range of different concepts to describe modern social change. Concepts like global village and post-industrial society have continued to resonate because they signify the possibilities of an interconnected world and an international economy no longer based simply on manufacturing but on knowledge.

Globalization can be defined as a process where powerful or wealthy cultures dominate weaker or poorer cultures. However, the picture at the empirical level becomes a little more complex when we observe what people do. The interconnectedness created by modern media can serve local and global purposes. Mobile communications are creating a different but also important sense of place that affects family relations and patterns of autonomy and authority, especially for the young.

The authors used the Canadian theorist Harold Innis's work to talk about how the concentration on a medium of communication in a society can often bias the cultural development of the civilization or culture concerned. There is no argument with the fact that computing and the Internet are significant cultural additions that have profoundly changed cultural behaviour.

There are many instances, at an individual level as well as collectively, where audiences are taking advantage of digital technologies in ways that the digital divide argument does not acknowledge. This is not to suggest that asymmetries of access and power do not exist. On the contrary, it is abundantly clear that they do, but what the authors wish to assert is that if we ignore the contradictory potential of these digital technologies then we ignore the complexity and variety of a technologically enriched era.

At the end of this chapter you should be able to:

- take the idea of globalization introduced in Chapter 1, in its minimal definition, and expand it to ideas about what is happening with global media;
- critically discuss ideas like monopolies of knowledge and textual communities and apply them to real life examples;
- seek further examples on how media, locally and globally, create new communicative spaces and alter traditional familial or authority structures.

Key themes

Digital divide. There is an inequality of access to media between the rich and the poor within wealthy nations and between the people of rich and poor nations. The digital divide is an expression used to describe what is seen as an increasing gap between the knowledge rich and the knowledge poor in a digital world. Globalization is also often used as a term to describe how wealthier nations may dominate others. However, while there clearly are inequalities in access to the Internet in the general, for example especially in continents like Africa, the picture is very complex in the particular. Ghana bypassed its terrestrial infrastructure in order to get access to satellite and mobile technology. This idea was not a gift from western nations but a practical solution to a substandard terrestrial network. Globalization, therefore, is a complex phenomenon where the less wealthy nations develop their media and their infrastructure in ways that are not simple dependency arrangements.

Sense of place. The mobile phone has revolutionized the power-geometry of space–time compression for children and young people in the home and in the street, allowing them to communicate without the surveillance of parents and siblings. This change in 'sense of place' is important to our understanding of globalization and the possibility of a global culture. The communicative spaces that are emerging can and often are transnational, bypassing the surveillance of individual societies. The global games culture, discussed in Chapter 13, is one example of this.

Discussion questions

1   Bring to class examples that you think exemplify the contradictory potential of modern media technologies.
2   Can you find examples of media content that supports textual communities? Bring them to class and show why they support textual communities and what effects that community might have on society.
3   What are the new 'space-biased' media? Do you think that the speed of a medium does affect a culture, in Innis's sense?
4   Are there inequalities in access to and use of modern media in advanced industrial countries? Can you find contemporary examples?

Further reading

Castells, M. (1996). *The rise of network society*. Oxford: Blackwell.
Castells, M., Fernandez-Ardevol, M., Linchuan Qiu, J. and Sey, A. (2008). *Mobile communication and society: A global perspective*. Cambridge, MA: MIT.
Couldry, N. (2000). *The place of media power: Pilgrims and witnesses of the media age*. London: Routledge.
Katz, J.E. (ed.) (2008). *Handbook of mobile communication studies*. Cambridge, MA: MIT.
Ling, R. (2008). *New tech, new ties: How mobile communication is reshaping social cohesion*. Cambridge, MA: MIT.
Livingstone, S., Bober, M. and Helsper, E. (2005). *Inequalities and the digital divide in children and young people's Internet use: Findings from the UK Children Go Online project*. London: LSE. www.children-go-online.net.

Theories

part
2

Part 1 introduced the discipline of media studies and the global context in which it now operates. The authors concluded that globalization can be defined as a process where powerful or wealthy cultures dominate weaker or poorer cultures. However, the picture at the empirical level becomes a little more complex when we observe what people do. The interconnectedness created by modern media can serve local and global purposes. Mobile communications, given as an example, are creating a different but also important sense of place that affects family relations and authority relations.

In Part 2 the authors look closely at the theories that have helped to define media studies. Theories are explanations of phenomena. Several important things have happened in media studies theory that have affected out view of structures and organizations, audiences, content and effects. First, audiences are now seen as active interpreters and not passive receivers of messages or meanings. Second, the effects of media on audiences are no longer seen as direct and uniform. Third, postmodern ideas of discourse, power, ideology and hegemony have displaced traditional, deterministic, Marxist perspectives in media studies.

Chapter 4, Classics in Media and Effects, introduces you to the empirical tradition in media studies. It looks at:
- the shift from a simple model of media influence to more complex theories such as agenda setting, constructivism, diffusion of innovations and uses and gratifications;
- the emergence of the concept of the active audience to describe the complexity of how people use media.

Chapter 5, Classics in Media and Ideology, introduces you to some of the key changes in the Marxist tradition and alternative perspectives within that tradition that have emerged over time. Chapter 5 examines:
- the concepts of ideology and hegemony in media studies;
- the emergence of postmodernism as a way of thinking about discourse and language and the role of power;
- theorization about the public sphere.

Chapter 6, Classics in Reasoning about Information and Its Ownership, is a detailed overview of the concept information and how different conceptions of information have different effects. The chapter investigates:
- the major styles of reasoning about information;
- the concepts of copyright and the public domain;
- the idea of a second enclosure as a description of what is happening in the control of information;
- mechanisms, like the creative commons, that are emerging as ways of protecting rights to knowledge.

Classics in media and effects

chapter

4

This chapter will provide an overview of:
- the shift from a simple model of media influence to more complex theories such as agenda setting, constructivism, diffusion of innovations and uses

and gratifications;
- the emergence of the concept of the active audience to describe the complexity of how people use media.

The last chapters have introduced you to ideas of convergence and globalization. There are also theories that attempt to explain these phenomena and the components of the mediation process – structures and organizations, content, audiences and effects. This chapter will provide an overview of:

- the shift from a simple model of media influence to more complex theories such as agenda setting, constructivism, diffusion of innovations and uses and gratifications;
- the emergence of the concept of the active audience to describe the complexity of how people use media.

Osama bin Laden and Islamic militants actively use media in the 21st century to influence followers and opponents alike, because bin Laden thinks media have effects. Media research on effects covers personal, interpersonal, inter group, organizational, mass, cultural and intercultural communication. The early communication and media research, from psychology through to sociology, had an intense interest in the influence of the media on personal and group behaviour. This interest, as the previous chapters have shown, has continued to the present. How persuasive are modern media or messages? Much of what we know about modern persuasion comes from empirical communication research – research about what is happening in the world. We need to know the key classics in effects research because they tell us why media are considered more influential in some contexts and less influential in others.

In this chapter, much of the work we introduce pertains primarily to the US and to research ideas that have developed in the West. The authors will however, make some reference to alternative models of media influence and experience, to indicate the wide range of possibility for new ideas, new paradigms and new questions in media study.

The influence of media

The majority of the early work into creating a methodology for studying media effects was done in the United States. The effect of propaganda and advertising on the individual was one of the first preoccupations of governments, businesses and scholars after the First World War. What makes people support a cause rather than oppose it? Do advertisements influence people to buy products? In early studies, the idea that people's minds might be manipulated by powerful advertising and propaganda through newspaper and later the radio seemed to be confirmed. In 1937 Harold Gosnell, in a study about the relationship between social and economic characteristics and newspaper reading habits and election returns in Chicago, found that endorsements of newspapers could influence the way readers voted. Media messages through mass media like the newspaper and radio were conceived as being injected into the minds of the masses where they were stored in the form of changes in attitudes and behaviour. 'Eventually such feelings or attitudes produced the behaviour desired by the message source' (Kraus and Davis, 1976, 117).

Attitudes. Mental states of readiness to respond; based on experience and have an influence on behaviour.

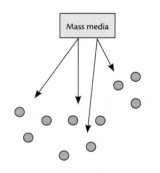

Figure 4.1, adapted from *Communication Models* (McQuail and Windahl, 1981), graphically represents this 'hypodermic', or stimulus-response, or one-step assumption about mass media. Individuals receive messages and act on them.

The received view in United States' media textbooks is that research has shifted from a conception of direct, undifferentiated, and powerful effects in the 1920s and 1930s to an understanding of psychological effects mediated by personal, group and other factors. Empirical research in social psychology quickly showed that a direct effects notion of mass communication was misleading and that the relationship between attitudes and behaviour is a complex one. For example, in 1934 Lapiere travelled with a Chinese couple to 66 hotels, automobile camps, tourist homes, and 184 restaurants and cafes in the United States. Lapiere then sent questionnaires to all the places he visited, asking them if they would accept Chinese as guests. Ninety per cent replied 'No' (Lapiere, 1938). There can be significant differences therefore between what people say they do and what they actually do. People may say in a questionnaire that they think an advertisement is effective, but behave otherwise.

Figure 4.1 One-step model of mass media influence

Source: Adapted from McQuail and Windahl (1981).

Attitude measurement is a major area of media effects research. However, just what constitutes an 'attitude' depends on (1) convention within the disciplines, (2) the user's own theoretical purposes – which may vary, and (3) the outcome of empirical investigations designed to establish similarities and differences in constructs. The construct 'attitude' is regarded as a subclass of the construct 'motive', because it embodies an affective component and an action tendency. Attitudes are not cognitions or beliefs or values or habits or opinions or beliefs. It was Paul Lazarsfeld's work in the 1940s that teased out some of the complexities of media influence on attitudes and behaviour.

Theorist snapshot: Paul Lazarsfeld

In the public mind, 'opinions' and 'attitudes' are used interchangeably. Paul Lazarsfeld, a founder of survey methodology, conducted one of the seminal survey studies on public opinion in the early 1940s, reported in *The People's Choice* (1944). In the study, Lazarsfeld and his colleagues were interested in the extent to which mass media influenced voting behaviour. An unexpected finding emerged. 'Whenever respondents were asked to report on their recent exposures to campaign communications of all kinds, political discussions were mentioned more frequently than exposure to radio or print' (Lazarsfeld, Berelson and Gaudet, 1944, 150). This recognition of the role of personal influence led to the two-step model of mass media influence, outlined in Figure 4.2.

Lazarsfeld's study introduced the idea of opinion leaders into the research literature and the communication lexicon. Opinion leaders are people who not only pass on information and points of view to others, but also act as a barrier to and mediator of effects of mass media. For example, your mother might be an opinion leader in an area of your life, say political party preference, influencing your voting choices. You in turn may be an opinion leader in an area of your mother's life, say colour of clothes, influencing her purchasing choices.

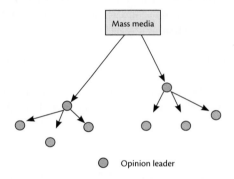

Figure 4.2 Two-step model of mass media influence

Source: Adapted from McQuail and Windahl (1981).

Paul Lazarsfeld and Robert Merton joined the Columbia Department of Sociology in 1941. Both are famous for developing survey and interview methodology. Merton became expert at interview methodology and created the focused interview and focused group methods. These qualitative methods are commonly used in modern media research. Lazarsfeld developed modern survey methodology and conducted seminal research work on public opinion and media influence.

Lazarsfeld's work transformed simplistic assumptions about the influence of modern media. His work, *The People's Choice*, demonstrated some of the limitations of modern mass media in changing attitudes and behaviour.

Theodore Adorno, the famous Jewish neo-Marxist Frankfurt School scholar, visited Lazarsfeld after he fled Nazi Germany. Adorno was interested in the conditions that lead to prejudice and persecution and drew a distinction between administrative research that served government and industry and critical research that sought to critique the whole capitalist enterprise.

Adorno was opposed to quantitative research as manipulative but conceded that it was necessary in large societies. As he said in his famous study *The Authoritarian Personality*, 'How can one say with assurance that the numerous opinions, attitudes, and values expressed by an individual actually constitute a consistent pattern of organized totality? ... There is no adequate way to proceed other than by actually measuring, in populations, a wide variety of thought contents and determining by means of standard statistical methods which ones go together' (Adorno et al., 1950, 3).

The 1940s at Columbia University is a snapshot of the US and European divide on media theory at the time – the study of power as ideology (Adorno) versus the study of influence as the result of many circumstances (Lazarsfeld). Adorno and Lazarsfeld were and remain a microcosm of the key debates in sociology, media and methodology.

There were events that appeared to give support to the one-step model of media influence. One of the most famous of these is Orson Welles's *War of the Worlds* radio broadcast on 30 October 1938. Twenty-five year old law student Henry Brylawski was on his way to pick up his girlfriend in Washington when he heard on his car radio that a huge meteorite had smashed into a New Jersey farm. New York was under attack by Martians. "'I knew it was a hoax,' said Brylawski, now 92' (Lovgen, 2005).

But many others took the broadcast literally. They had missed the introduction to the broadcast that highlighted it as a play. According to a front-page article in *The New York Times* twenty families in New Jersey rushed out of their houses with wet towels over their faces as protection from Martian poison gas. When Brylawski got to his girl-friend's apartment the girlfriend's sister was quaking in her boots. 'She thought the news was real', Brylawski said (Lovgen, 2005). Brylawski is a classic case of opinion leader effect as he was able in any conversations with his girlfriend and her sister to modify their views.

The reasons for the dramatic effect of Orson Welles's radio broadcast, however, are more complicated than they initially seem. In 1938 there was significant international tension over the rise of Hitler and the possibility of war. Radio historian Elizabeth McLeod gives a good example of reactions to that context. Some heard only that shells were falling 'and assumed they were coming from Hitler' (Lovgen, 2005). We also know now that the newspapers, in competition with radio as a medium, exaggerated the extent of the overreaction to the Welles' broadcast and the number of people who believed the broadcast was, in fact, real.

Table 4.1 provides an overview of different conceptions of audience effects against the different theoretical models. The models dealing with ideology will be addressed in Chapter 5.

Table 4.1 Theories by different conceptions of media effects

Theoretical Tradition	Concept of Audience	Individual	Societal	Key Questions
Agenda setting	Citizen	Adopts or modifies agenda	Reciprocal influence	Who influences the media agenda?
Constructivism	Hypothesis and reality testers	Personal schemata	Social schemata	Who constructs reality?
Diffusion of innovations	Active decision-maker	Adopts/rejects innovation	Diffusion	Who influences decision-making?
Knowledge gap	Informed citizen	Gains knowledge	Gap between knowledge rich and poor	Who are the major users of knowledge?
Marxism and cultural studies				
– Structural	Stratified by social class	False consciousness	Capitalism	Who owns?
– Poststructural : critical theory : semiotics : discourse	Passive and atomized Lonely voyeur Sites	False consciousness False consciousness False consciousness	Culture industry Consumerism Marginalization	Whose culture? Whose text? Which reading? Whose discourse?
Technological	Sensory	Media extend senses	Hot/Cool Time/space bias	Which medium? Time/space bias
Uses and gratifications	Personal interests	Gratification	Equilibrium	Which gratifications?

Figure 4.3, adapted from Severin and Tankard's *Communication Theories* (1988), provides an overview of major works related to effects. Modern research on effects, as we will see below, has moved from a powerful, direct and unmediated, conception of effects towards a powerful, mediated, conception with intervening factors such as opinion leadership, agenda setting and opinion formation. James Beniger's *The Control Revolution* is more concerned with the nature of information society than effects of mass media on individuals. However, the authors have included his work in Figure 4.3 because it highlights a shift of research interest in the US towards institutional factors affecting modern media and society.

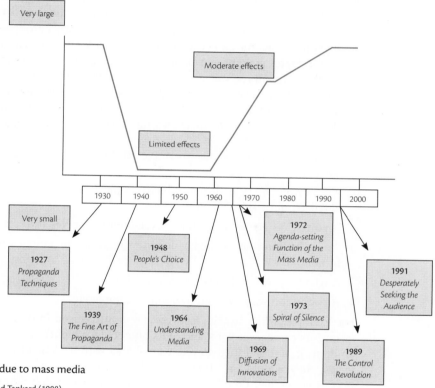

Figure 4.3 Size of effects due to mass media

Source: Adapted from Severin and Tankard (1988).

Diffusion

The concept of opinion leadership has grown into an independent field of study called diffusion research which examines issues of adoption, the mental processes a person goes through when accepting a new idea or a new product, and diffusion, the social system through which new ideas or products pass. Rogers (1983) provided a detailed review of this tradition in *Diffusion of Innovations*.

Innovations are new ideas, new technologies, new forms of behaviour, fads and fashions. Interest in the ways in which they spread goes back to the 19th century but serious empirical study of their diffusion began in the United States in the 1920s. Sociologists wanted to know how new ideas and technologies were spread through space and time, what role media played in the diffusion, and what role the innovations played in effecting social change. They noted that diffusion occurred in a definable area, over a definable period of time, that it differed in space and time for different patterns of movement. They saw that not everyone hears of – or is even interested in – every innovation and that not everyone who hears of one is interested in adopting it. Car seatbelts were available for decades before a law made them compulsory fittings in new cars and then not even a law could force everyone to use them. Television was adopted rather slowly in Britain and the United States but very rapidly in Australia after it was introduced in 1956. This was probably due to the availability of programming, and because the idea of television was already current in the UK and the US. Colour television was adopted even more rapidly, possibly for similar reasons. In the 1980s and 1990s home computers were being widely adopted, as were microwave ovens and compact disc players.

Governments and private enterprise are always concerned with the diffusion of information. They want to get messages through to target groups and to the great mass of the population. The early classic diffusion studies were concerned with the diffusion of United States government policies, with the diffusion of innovations in rural areas and with treatments among doctors. Sociologists studied the way in which information about hybrid seed corn was diffused among American farmers and the length of time they took to adopt this innovation. They studied the spread of ham radios, new teaching methods, new forms of medical treatment, rumours, knowledge of news events, and campaign messages.

Summarizing much of this work, Everett Rogers said that the adoption of an innovation occurs in five stages:

1. An awareness stage during which people learn of the innovation but get little detailed information about it.

2. An interest stage in which they develop more detailed interest.

3. An evaluation stage during which they weigh up the innovation and decide whether or not to try it.

4. A trial stage when they try it on a small scale.

5. An adoption stage when they adopt it completely.

For example, when hybrid seed corn was introduced into American farming a few farmers became aware of it and of its potential for higher crop yields. A few developed an interest in it and then sowed a small area with it. When they saw that it gave high yields, they adopted it. They told other farmers about it and these farmers were impressed by their crops. Slowly the innovation was widely adopted. Publicity in rural media helped in the adoption but a very important role was played by person-to-person communication. The few farmers who pioneered the use of the seed corn got their information from agricultural researchers and from mass media and passed it on, together with accounts of their experiences with the corn, to other farmers. Thus there was a two-step flow of communication from media to 'influentials' to other farmers.

Diffusion of innovations.
Argues that most new ideas come through the media, but are mediated by individuals, like opinion.

Many researchers have been interested in the role the mass media play in the **diffusion of innovations** and information. One classic study showed that news of a critical event can be diffused very quickly. Paul Sheatsley and Jacob Feldman studied the diffusion of news about President Kennedy's assassination and showed that within 30 minutes of his being shot, 68 per cent of the US population knew about it. Within two hours 92 per cent knew. Half the people first heard the news not from the mass media but from other people, either by face-to-face communication or by telephone. The others heard from radio or television (Sheatsley and Feldman, 1965).

A similar, global story could be told about the diffusion of awareness of the events of 11 September 2001. One of the authors of this book was in Malaysia. It was the evening in that time zone and she was coming home from a late meeting. She turned on the television in her hotel room to catch the late BBC World news. Instead, as she flicked through the channels, she saw the CNN coverage of the second plane. Within seconds she had alerted several people on her hotel corridor, telephoned friends and family in Western Australia (which is the same time zone as Malaysia), but also in eastern Australia (where some people were in bed as it was three hours later still) to alert them to the need to turn on the television. She also rang her brother in the UK, as his workplace had been named by a commentator as a likely next target, to beg him to get out of his building. This all happened within ten minutes of switching on the TV. She kept her eyes on the screen throughout her calls.

reflection   What has been a major mediated event in your lifetime? Do you remember it? Where were you? How did you find out what was happening? What media use did you access to diffuse information to others?

In closed societies with a controlled media, the diffusion effect is constrained. However, there are constant stories emerging in China, which do proliferate quickly across mobile media, the Internet and word of mouth, even if the information is withheld or played down in formal media sources. Recent examples include the child-slavery in Shaanxi scandal, and the collapse of a major underground train construction site in Beijing. However, ongoing incidents of unrest in the far west (Xinjiang) are crucial issues to China's national security, but very few in the urban conurbations on the eastern seaboard have any idea that this is happening. So, diffusion is of course dependent on the accessibility of media to the information, and to the people who can spread the story. Diffusion is very dependent on existing networks. Email lists are crucial, as are mobile phone number 'groups' and social networking sites, or special interest MSN groups. Without those pre-existing links to dispersed people, it would be much harder to get news out quickly and effectively to those who need to know and who will spread it further still, or in some cases, take direct action.

Dozens of similar studies have looked at the diffusion of information about news events, including the Soviets' launch of the first satellite, Alaska gaining statehood, America's first satellite, President Eisenhower's stroke, his decision to seek a second term, the results of a heavyweight title fight, the Pope's encyclical on birth control, and the shooting of Governor George Wallace of Alabama. Study after study has shown that when the diffusion of information is plotted against time, the graph becomes an S-shaped curve, known as a curve of diffusion. The curve shows that a few people learn about the event first, then a lot of people learn about it quickly, then the diffusion tapers off at the end of the learning period.

The intensity of people's interest is an important factor. Information about obscure events diffuses slowly and reaches few people. Information about vital events, such as the Kennedy assassination and 9/11, diffuses quickly and gets to almost everyone. In their classic Rovere study, Melvin L. DeFleur and Otto N. Larsen showed that as stimulus intensity – the repetition of a message – increases, the proportion of people who get the information will also increase but there will be diminishing proportions as the number of repetitions increases: by doubling the number of repetitions you will not get to double the number of people. They studied the impact of dropping information leaflets on communities in the event of a civil defence emergency that puts the mass media out of action (DeFleur and Larsen, 1958). The authors below provide a summary of the experiment and Defleur's comment on the experiment many years later.

Leaflets carrying a civil defence message were dropped to eight communities with similar characteristics. The media cooperated and did not publicize the event. A sample from each community was carefully polled four days after the leaflet drop. The number of people in each community that had learned the message varied with the number of leaflets dropped per inhabitant. Only about 25 per cent of the population learned the message in those communities that received only one leaflet for every four inhabitants. When the ratio was doubled, this increased to 37.4 per cent where communities received one leaflet for every two inhabitants and 44 per cent for two leaflets per inhabitant. Eighty-seven per cent of the inhabitants learned the message when thirty-two leaflets per person were dropped.

> Repetition can help diffuse information. But presenting a commercial or a political announcement over and over can be expected to have diminishing returns in terms of the percentage of the audience who learn the message. Arguably, this will also depend on the type of message involved. An important political directive, however unwelcome, is likely to be assimilated quickly, whatever the rate of repetition, as people strive to protect themselves from retribution for failing to obey.

> The Project Rovere studies had another important finding: the people in the towns played an active role in spreading the messages that were on the leaflets. Thus the study verified the importance of interpersonal channels in spreading information. In place of the two-step flow described in *The People's Choice*, however ... the study found a multistage flow. Even persons who had not seen a leaflet helped spread the message. The information presented to some people through the leaflets was passed on and on through chains of residents, much like rumor being passed from person to person (and with many of the same distortions). (DeFleur and Dennis, 1981, 320–1)

The S-curve is one common finding in diffusion studies. Another is hierarchy or neighbourhood effects. This occurs when innovations are adopted in central places that are not necessarily connected to each other. Some US states, for example, have been shown to be leaders in policy innovations. Their innovations then spill over to neighbouring states, often in gradient fashion to successively adjoining states. In his seminal study, 'The Diffusion of Innovations Among American States', Walker (1969, 63, 880–9) studied the dates at which states had adopted a wide range of policies. He computed scores of policy innovativeness for each state and then worked out which were the 'innovators' and which the 'laggards'.

Much of the diffusion research has been concerned with barriers to communication. In fact, Steven H. Chaffee has argued that 'Instead of assuming that the generic problem is that of facilitating change in political outcomes via communication, we could examine constraints on communication that affect the intervening process through which the political system operates' (Chaffee, 1975, 87). Chaffee notes a number of constraints, including topic-specific constraints: there are some topics 'nice people' won't talk about in public. There are many topics mass media will not mention. Good jokes generally travel fast in the workplace but few of the really 'dirty' ones will make the papers. Items not considered newsworthy will not be published. Items that might offend media audiences will be excluded. In 1985, the Australian Broadcasting Corporation showed a British telemovie that ended with a close-up of a lesbian enjoying a self-induced orgasm while being cuddled by a man. Even in 1980 this could not have been shown because of moral qualms. It could still not be aired in mainland China and most of South East Asia where lesbian themes are outside the mainstream of popular acceptability.

Similarly the sources of information can be constraints on diffusion. In western democracies the mass media have considerable freedom accorded to them in the expectation that they will both diffuse political information and act as watchdogs on the custodians of it – governments, departments, institutions and the like. But government is often reluctant to release information and media are sometimes reluctant to press their demands for it.

The media are selective about what they do publish. Although one of the reasons for their freedom is so that they can express the demands of individuals and pressure groups, there is not enough room for all of them and some of them are deemed un-newsworthy. Moreover, the media tend to report most items in terms of people rather than issues. Similarly, when covering the passage of legislation, they tend to concentrate on the fights between politicians or bureaucrats or pressure groups rather than the legislation. They also tend to cover public opinion inputs in rough fashion – quotes from 'representative' spokespersons rather than by commissioning polls. As Chaffee says:

> The sheer cost of monitoring support more extensively – e.g. for other levels such as the regime and the political community, or for other authorities such as the legislative and judicial branches – probably accounts for what might seem to be media-imposed constraints on the provision of this type of information. (1975, 98)

Another constraint on diffusion is political infighting inside media organizations. Chris Argyris, Leon Sigal, David Halberstam and others have shown in their studies of newspapers that fights between national, metropolitan and foreign desks, or fights by individuals over status and bylines can constrain what is reported. Then there are the constraints within the audience. In Chaffee's words:

> There is far more information to be found in the news columns and broadcasts of the media then in the minds of the audience. Surveys regularly show that only a fraction of the citizenry can identify the major authorities beyond the President and a few other chronic newsmakers. (1975, 101)

And the more ignorant a voter is, the more likely s/he is to make up her mind late in the campaign on which party to vote for (Lazarsfeld, Berelson and Gaudet, 1944; Berelson, Lazarsfeld and McPhee, 1954). Moreover, most people normally have to be 'involved' before they will act. Public information campaigns generally 'fail' to convert people who disagree with what they urge. And when offered political information, people tend to select from it only what they agree with.

Agenda setting

It was not long before ideas generated by diffusion research were extended to the media professions themselves and the processes by which they choose news or advertising. McCombs and Shaw recognized that media personnel select news and advertising and through this very process create particular kinds of emphases. Media play a role in 'setting the agenda' for the issues of the day, making some issues important and relegating others to a lower ranking. Stories placed at the beginning of a television news hour, for example, are judged to be important and worth thinking about. McCombs and Shaw called this agenda setting.

This approach is both a hypothesis and a theory. Its underlying assumption is that audiences tend to see as important those issues that the mass media see as important.

to recap...

Diffusion of innovations theory looks at how 'innovations' (new ideas, stories, products, policies) are diffused by the media through the social system and how individuals adopt those innovations. It is an attempt to combine social and psychological processes of media influence and assumes a multistage flow.

Agenda setting. Explores the transfer of salience from the media to the public.

As Jack McLeod puts it, 'an audience member exposed to a given medium agenda will adjust his or her perception of the importance of issues in the direction corresponding to the amount of attention devoted to those issues in the medium used' (1974, 137). In their pioneering paper, 'The Agenda-Setting Function of Mass Media', McCombs and Shaw predicted that 'when the media emphasize an event, they influence the audience to see it as important'. They asked a sample of undecided voters in Chapel Hill, North Carolina, to rank issues in the 1986 US presidential elections and compared the rankings with the media's emphasis on those issues. They concluded that increased salience of a topic or issue in the mass media corresponded with an increased salience of that topic or issue among undecided voters (McCombs and Shaw, 1972, 176–87). To make the comparison, they recorded the agenda of issues set by the local newspapers and by three television networks and the viewing habits, attention to issues and judgements about them made by the local audience. In their study during the 1972 election they expanded the audience to a cross-section of all voters and got similar results (see Shaw and McCombs, *The Emergence of American Political Issues*, 1977). They found that newspapers were the prime movers in defining the agenda of issues for Charlotte, North Carolina voters and that what issues the newspapers emphasized in spring and early summer influenced what the voters saw as important in autumn. But in the autumn television exerted a short-term influence on the issues agenda by spotlighting a few of the issues. The TV agenda correlated more strongly with the voters' agenda in autumn than did the newspapers' agenda. Among the other interesting findings of their first study were:

> There is a progressive increase in the use of mass communications during a presidential campaign. In fact, the major political role of the mass media may be to raise the salience of politics among the American electorate every four years.

> The influence of the media's agenda on an individual's concern with issues is directly related to how much he or she is exposed to mass communication. Those individuals most frequently exposed to mass communication show higher levels of agreement between personal agendas and mass media agendas. (McCombs and Shaw, 1972)

There have been other approaches to agenda setting. Funkhouser analysed 14 major issues of the 1960s and compared press coverage with aggregate public opinion statistics. He showed the relationship between press attention and public opinion on such issues as the Vietnam War, campus unrest and urban riots – and he showed both press interest and public opinion peaked well before the historical climax of the events (Funkhouser, 1973). Winter and Eyal (1981) examined the agenda-setting impact of the press on the civil rights issue from 1954 to 1976 and Winter, Eyal and Rogers (1980) investigated the issues of inflation, unemployment and national unity in Canada. Both studies showed significant agenda-setting effects on public opinion. In a study of the 1976 US presidential election, Weaver, Graber, McCombs and Eyal (1981) found that where the population is of low educational standard and more likely to have blue-collar jobs, the impact of newspapers and television was mixed in the early part of the year but later in the year the agenda-setting effects of newspapers gave way to television's spotlighting impact. In discussing these findings in his chapter on agenda setting in the *Handbook of Political Communication*, Maxwell E. McCombs (1981) notes that 'Over time the newspaper reader is likely to be exposed to mentions of most issues many more times than his counterpart in the TV news audience'.

McCombs also reports one of his own studies that compared what the media talked about with what students talk about:

> Many topics of great personal concern are never prominent topics of discussion with family or friends. A great deal of the content of daily conversation consists of the trivial and topics of passing moment, not the abiding and pressing issues of the time.

> The study of public opinion among college students also found that for only a single issue – Watergate – did a majority of students most frequently talk about the same issue they considered personally most important. At the other extreme, only about ten percent of the students who regarded energy and environmental issues as personally most important said it was their most frequent topic of discussion. Overall, just over half of the students most frequently discussed and considered personally most important the same public issue ... While more than two-thirds of the students talked more frequently about Watergate than any other public issue of the time, less than half considered Watergate the issue of greatest personal concern. (McCombs, 1981, 129)

McCombs has some qualifications on agenda-setting theory. He says the agenda-setting role of the press is not a universal influence: some issues are more susceptible than others to press influence. Nor does he contend that the mass media are the only influences on what issues are salient. Moreover, agenda-setting effects often have been demonstrated, but they are not of consistent and major magnitude in all circumstances. He notes that mass media not only provide cues about topics and issues but because of their selectivity, they also tend to emphasize certain aspects of people and objects involved in them: 'Not every attribute of a person, issue, idea, or event in the news is considered newsworthy' (McCombs, 1981, 134).

Finally, he notes: 'politics is just one item on the larger agenda of personal concerns. For most persons it is found high on the personal agenda only for a short time during election year. A key political role of the press – indeed, a key agenda-setting role – is the movement of politics onto the agenda and to a prominent position during election year' (McCombs, 1981, 135).

Again, this should be remembered when discussing media research in non-democratic societies. It is anecdotally the case that the distance that people seem to feel from everyday political matters is echoed in states where there is little chance of effecting change because the system is locked against participation. More research is needed to see at what point, freedom to act, or – conversely – a lack of freedom to act, provokes more or less political consciousness, and at what level?

Framing and priming

If the media wish to increase the salience of an issue, so as to persuade their audience towards adopting their position on the matter (the media agenda), then they also have to draw attention to and emphasize certain issues and specific flows of arguments – a process known as framing.

> Framing essentially involves selection and salience. To frame is to select some aspects of a perceived reality and make them more salient in a communicating text ... through repetition or by associating them with culturally familiar symbols. (Entman, 1993, 52–3)

Media priming provokes an opinion or a behavioural change by altering the relative weight people give to various considerations that make up the ultimate evaluation

(Mendelsohn, 1996, 113). Entman (2001) describes a news incident in which a (former) Soviet Union aircraft shot down a civilian aircraft as an 'attack', while labelling as a 'tragedy' a similar incident in which a United States aircraft shot down a civilian Iran Air airplane. Certain words activate mental constructs and prime a news audience. Framing and priming are related. Framing makes certain information in a news story salient and depresses the importance of other information. Priming and the spread of activation are the mechanisms through which news frames stimulate thought processes and emotional reactions. Cappella and Jamieson (1997) discuss the cognitive basis of framing effects.

Agenda setting is often labelled as an example of a moderate effects model of media influence. This is because the model argues that the media can be influential precisely because they can affect the amount of attention given to a story or the language used. Noelle-Neumann (1977) goes further with agenda setting and says that the media create a climate of public opinion that can engender fear of isolation among people who judge that their views are outside that 'climate', leading to a spiral of silence. According to Noelle-Neumann, people who think they represent a minority view tend to keep quiet in public debates, whereas those who think they represent a majority point of view tend to make their views known. As most public debates are mass mediated and rarely conducted interpersonally in modern societies, most people have no way of finding out what the majority's thoughts are and rely on public opinion polls or other estimates of what others are thinking. People make judgements about whether they are in the majority or a minority of an issue and if they think they are in the minority will keep silent, for fear of social isolation. Public opinion polls, interestingly, cannot pick up the spiral of silence because people are responding to their perceptions of what the majority thinks. We can see in Noelle-Neumann a return to powerful effects, but in a more sophisticated way that does not deny the existence of active audiences.

> **to recap...**
>
> Agenda setting assumes that when an audience member is exposed to a given medium agenda she or he will adjust her or his perception of the importance of issues in the direction corresponding to the amount of attention devoted to those issues in the medium used. Agenda setting is an example of a moderate effects view of media influence.

Uses and gratifications

> **Uses and gratifications model.** Proposes that people get out of the media what they want of it.

Agenda-setting research shows that there is a range of audience needs. Uses and gratifications research complements the study of the agenda-setting function of mass media. It is concerned with the uses audiences make of the mass media and the gratifications they get from that use. The first studies were published in the 1940s and were concerned with the entertainment, rather than the political, content of the mass media. They studied the ways audiences used radio quiz programmes, classical music and soap operas and the gratification they got from them.

The most famous uses and gratifications work in political communication is that in Blumler and McQuail, *Television in Politics* (1969), a study of the 1964 British General Election. They found that British voters used the mass media for vote guidance, to reinforce decisions about voting that they had already made, for general surveillance of the political environment, for excitement, or because they might be able to use the information in interpersonal communication. Those who avoided politics in the mass media did so because when they saw political material they felt alienation, or did so because of partisanship, or because they didn't find it relaxing. They found that newspapers served British voters best for reinforcing their political attitudes and television served them best for voting guidance.

A fundamental assumption of uses and gratifications research is that mass media audiences are not composed of passive individuals who are operated on by media stimuli, as in the basic stimulus–response model. Rather, they exercise freedom in their use of the media. One theory is that they use the media most useful to them. Another is that they use the media because they have a motivation to do so. A third is that they use the media as part of an effort to remain impervious to influence. But it is fundamental to the theory that media use is goal directed. It is assumed we use the media to satisfy specific needs and that we select particular media and particular content to satisfy those needs. These needs are determined by our social environment, which includes our age, sex, marital status, group affiliations and personality.

Katz, Blumler and Gurevitch have said that uses and gratifications researchers deal with:

> (1) the social and psychological origins of (2) needs, which generate (3) expectations of (4) the mass media or other sources, which lead to (5) differential patterns of media exposure (or engagement in other activities), resulting in (6) need gratifications and (7) other consequences, perhaps mostly unintended ones. (1974, 11–35)

They assume that communication is a transactional process in which parties give and take from the communication approximately equal values. They have even suggested a typology of media-related needs classified into cognitive needs (information) and affective (emotional, aesthetic), personal integrative, social integrative and escapist needs. Some may be satisfied by news, some by soap operas, some by crime drama, or books or newspapers.

Most uses and gratifications studies have not gone beyond describing audience needs and media functions, but Katz, Gurevitch and Haas (1987) went further in a survey of 1,500 people in Israel. They found, among other things, that respondents considered non-media sources to be more important than the mass media in satisfying all needs investigated by the researchers; that mass media were more important for those cut off from family, friends, the state and society; that respondents who say that matters of state and society are important to them consistently rank newspapers as the most important mass medium; and that television serves the greatest variety of needs.

This suggests that although the media offer individuals a variety of material, the degree to which an individual absorbs any of it depends on her reasons for assessing it. If there is close correspondence between the individual's purpose for reading, listening or viewing and the message being disseminated by the chosen medium, the message has the greatest chance of effect. But if there is not much correspondence between motive and message, there will be little chance of effect. For example, if a person watches television primarily for entertainment and relaxation, she will see little or no consequence in televised political discussions and documentaries. Research has shown that those who use television for recreation have less information than those who use it for information – or, indeed, than those who don't use television at all.

The uses and gratifications approach proposes that people get out of the media what they want of it. Thus it avoids the deterministic theory of the hypodermic-effect, or stimulus–response, theory which holds that information transmitted by the mass media has a direct impact on how people view the world, that media coverage of political events is our basis for understanding those events. It also avoids the theory that people screen out undesirable political messages simply by selective exposure, selective perception and selective retention. As Pierce, Beatty and Hagner put it:

> Simply put, the uses-and-gratifications model states that people get out of the media what they want of it. If people approach the presidential debates with the goal of

to recap...

Uses and gratifications
research is concerned
with the uses audiences
make of the mass
media and the gratifica-
tions they get from that
use. The approach
focuses primarily on
the individual but does
argue that there are
social functions of
media.

learning more about the two candidates, the probability is that the debates will have an effect upon their evaluations. If they view the debates to confirm their opinions of the two candidates, then the possibility of debate-induced attitude change is greatly reduced. If the approach to the debates is as a source of entertainment found in the clash of the personalities of two political celebrities, the substance of the debates will be overlooked ... People who rely on television for political information have lower levels of political involvement and information. This may result from individuals who are dependent on television not having information access to their primary goals; their primary goal may be entertainment and relaxation. Then, according to the uses-and-gratifications model, television dependency should be associated with lower levels of political information and awareness. (Pierce, Beatty and Hagner, 1982, 113–14)

The structure and function of mass media in society

Uses and gratifications theory proposes that audience needs are served by several media functions. These functions were outlined by Harold Lasswell in a famous paper published in 1948 'The Structure and Function of Communications in Society' and reviewed by McQuail, Blumler and Brown in 'The Television Audience: A Revised Perspective' (1972). Lasswell's three social functions were:

- the surveillance of the environment;
- correlation of the parts of society in responding to the environment;
- the transmission of the social heritage from one generation to the next.

To these Charles R. Wright (1975) added a fourth function, entertainment. Lasswell said his three functions are performed by three kinds of specialists:

- those who survey the political environment of the whole state, for example, diplomats, attachés, foreign correspondents;
- those who correlate the response of the whole state to the environment, for example editors, journalists, speakers;
- those who transmit responses from the old to the young, for example educators in family and school.

Lasswell's focus on the manifest and latent functions of the mass media reflects the dominant sociology of the time – structural functionalism – which emphasized the role of structures and equilibrium in societies (compared with emphasis on conflict and change in Marxist thought). Lasswell posed the following questions as his formula for studying the social functions of the mass media in society: *Who? Says what? In which channel? To whom? With what effect?* He said that there are five matching areas of communication studies – control analysis (who), content analysis (the study of what is said), media analysis (the study of TV, radio, newspapers, and so on), audience analysis (the study of audiences), and effects analysis (the study of the impact of media messages).

Wright (1975) outlined in depth some of the possible manifest and latent functions of mass communication. Manifest functions of a media campaign, for example, might be to mobilize public opinion in support of a country (such as Kuwait) invaded by an aggressor (such as Iraq). The latent function of the campaign might be push your country to war with Kuwait. Unintended latent functions may have either positive or negative effects. Wright takes Lasswell's functions and gives them greater complexity by asking the question: What are the (1) manifest and (2) latent (3) functions and (4) dysfunctions of mass communication (5) surveillance (news) (6) correlation (editorial activity) (7) cultural transmission (8) entertainment for the (9) society (10) individual (11) subgroups and (12) cultural systems?

The social functions of the newspaper

Some of the hypothesized social functions of mass communications have been supported by empirical evidence. Berelson (2004) for example offered support for the surveillance function of the mass media in a famous study reported in his 'What Missing the Newspaper Means'. When the deliverymen of eight major New York city newspapers went on strike for 17 days in 1945, the Bureau of Applied Social Research at Columbia University conducted intensive interviews with 60 newspaper readers to determine what 'missing the newspaper' meant to them.

The Bureau found that although almost everyone paid tribute to the value of the newspaper as a source of 'serious' information about the world of public affairs, not everyone used it as such a source. Asked why they missed their paper, only a few mentioned missing news of a 'serious' event. Many simply said something like 'to keep informed'. When asked what particular stories they missed in the preceding week almost half were unable to mention any story and others mentioned a 'non-serious' story such as a murder case. Presented with a list of six front-page stories of the week before, only about one-third said they had missed reading any of them. Nevertheless, fully two-thirds confessed they felt that they did not know what was going on in the world during the newspaper strike, although only about half had any notion of what in the world they wanted more information about. Berelson comments: 'To miss the newspaper for its "serious" news value seems to be the accepted if not the automatic thing to say. But this does not mean that the newspapers were not genuinely missed by their readers' (Berelson, 2004, 256).

Some, as we have seen, missed the paper because they missed serious news. Some missed columnists' interpretations of the serious news. Others missed the paper because it had been for them a direct aid in daily living. In fact, half said they had been handicapped in some way – some had been unable to follow the radio programmes without the newspaper's radio guide; some didn't go to the movies because they did not know which movies were showing; some missed business, financial and stock market information; several women missed details of embarkation; and a couple of regular readers of obituary notices were afraid that their acquaintances might die without their knowing about it.

The newspaper also had a respite value – an 'escapist' function. Some people missed the development of a story in the comics and some of the human interest stories. 'When you read it takes your mind off other things', one respondent said. Twice as many people missed the paper more as the week went on than missed it less. Some even missed their daily dose of antipathy as they disagreed with their most disliked columnists.

Clearly these people are hardly alienated from mass society. Rather they seem to be people who used the newspaper to integrate themselves into it. The person from the small town where he had known everyone was using the paper as a substitute – as the 'closest thing' to knowing everyone in New York. Others were identifying with columnists and the public figures reported in the papers. Others identified with the people in the human interest stories. Many used the papers as a guide to the prevailing social morality or as a boost to their social prestige. It would not be difficult to make a case from this small study to support Lasswell's contention that the social functions of the mass media are surveillance of the environment and transmission of social heritage.

During the 1978 newspaper strike in New York City, Leo Bogart (1989) interviewed 90 readers to learn what they missed most, and re-interviewed 71 of them after the strike ended. Eleven per cent most missed the front-page news, and an additional 21 per cent mentioned the other general news pages, 23 per cent mentioned sports, 12 per cent the editorials and 8 per cent the financial news. Another 13 per cent mentioned the retail ads and 7 per cent the classifieds. It appeared that what the readers missed most was in the traditional areas of news coverage rather than the realm of fun and games. 'I don't know what's going on', 'I don't know what's happening locally', were among the reactions.

reflection What would you miss from a media 'absence'? Which medium would you miss most? What would you miss? When would you miss it? Television? Newspaper? Internet news site? Radio?

Think about the time, the place and the content as three aspects that would determine the kind of 'absence' and the way in which you would miss the medium.

The integrative function of mass media

It must be clear by now that the newspaper, and related media, is very much part of social life. The idea of mass media as having 'integrative functions' was taken up by the Chicago School sociologists (such as Park and Wirth) and by Morris Janowitz in his 1952 work *The Community Press in an Urban Setting*. Janowitz saw a two-way relationship between cities and their mass media. The media provide channels of information and symbolism required for integration and social solidarity of the vast aggregates of people concentrated in the cities and the vast aggregates provide audiences large enough and concentrated enough to support mass media.

Janowitz rejected the idea that cities generate impersonality and disorder. He also rejected the view that the moral order is conditioned by the individual's functional and economic interests rather than by a local community social order. He saw the modern city-dweller dividing his or her life between local neighbourhood and remote places of work in the city. Thus a city is a collection of little worlds and local communities and the question he set out to answer in his study of 75 local communities in Chicago was whether the community press helped to maintain local community activities and identifications and whether it helped to interrelate them to non-local activities and identifications. His answer is that it does. Although community newspapers were set up to make money out of the central business district decentralization characteristic of large modern cities, they have come to serve a wider range of unanticipated social, political and affectual needs. Thus, in Wright's (1975) terminology, they have added latent functions to their manifest functions. The large-scale daily newspapers could not maintain individual neighbourhood identities within the broad metropolis so the suburban giveaways have taken over that function.

At every point in its operation the local community press was inextricably interrelated with the personal communications that linked the paper's staff, community leaders and the paper's readers. Thus it operated in an area midway between the mass media (daily press) and informal communication (word of mouth).

Gerbner and the disintegrative functions

Against Janowitz's rather optimistic view of mass media must be placed the more pessimistic views of those who see the mass media as potentially contributing to the decay of primary relationships and the weakening of adherence to social norms and

Disintegrative function of the mass media. Argues that media may contribute to the decay of personal relationships and social bonds.

Integrative function of mass media. Argues that the media provide channels of information and symbolism required for integration and social solidarity in modern society..

to recap...

The idea that media have social functions – **integrative** and **disintegrative** – is an extension of early sociological interest in strict causes and effect in society. While strict causal notions have been modified over time, the concept of social functions of media remains an important one.

values. Because of widespread concern during the 1960s about political assassination, riots and serious crime, the United States National Commission on the Causes and Prevention of Violence conducted a series of studies on violence. George Gerbner (1970) and a team of investigators studied all prime-time television programmes as well as Saturday morning cartoons shown in a typical week in 1967 and compared them with a comparable week in 1968, thus producing the first of a series of annual Violence Profiles. Gerbner reported that the portrayal of violence on television was very pervasive and that the public believed it to be excessive. Heavy television viewers revealed a significantly higher sense of personal risk, of law enforcement and of mistrust and suspicion than did light viewers in the same demographic groups exposed to the same real risks of life. The results also showed that television's independent contributions to the cultivation of these conceptions of a 'mean world' and other aspects of social reality are not significantly altered by sex, age, education, income, newspaper reading, and church attendance (see also Signorelli and Gerbner, 1988).

The tendency of US research findings on mass media effects, however, has been to suggest that even viewing of violence and aggression was not necessarily a cause of violent and aggressive behaviour and, indeed, that portrayal of aggression was sometimes warranted (United States Government, 1982). There are also of course cultural and sub-cultural variations on what counts as media violence and which moral issues predominate. Readers outside the United States would note, for instance, that the capacity to mimic violent behaviour with guns is a problem mainly for the US where there is inadequate gun control, and thus widespread access to and acceptance of small arms in the private and public domains. By contrast, in a study undertaken by Donald (2005) in China, in 2001, parents and teachers reported that they were not concerned about media violence, but were worried about the standards of sexual morality in cartoons from Japan!

The active audience

When uses and gratifications researchers are concerned with the effects of the mass media they assume that the audience is active, not passive, that it might, for example, be concerned with the credibility of the media, its type of content, and the attention it pays to a particular type of content, for example a person might choose to read *The New York Times* because it is reliable, it covers a wide range of topics, and contains the best sports writing in any US American newspaper. Another person may choose al Jazeera television because they want an Arabic language and political perspective on the wars that have followed 11 September 2001. Yet others may choose the BBC because as British expatriates they feel comfortable listening to accents 'from home' whatever the focus of the news itself. Many contemporary media users might access all three kinds of information to achieve a balanced view on world events.

Although most uses and gratifications studies are concerned with the entertainment content of the mass media, some are concerned with their political uses. Studies have found, for example, that large audiences are attracted to US presidential debates and that in countries such as Britain many people are attracted to political commercials and to political appeals of parties. Some studies try to elicit the audiences' motives for this attraction, some try to find out what is behind these motives, some measure the media's ability to meet their political needs, and some study links between the needs and political material. It has been found, for example, that there are three main clusters of audience needs: the needs for information and diversion, and personal needs. O'Keefe and Mendelsohn (1974) found that newspapers were rated highest in supplying information needs in a political campaign. McLeod, Becker and Byrnes (1974) found that television was rated highest in judging candidates' personal qualities and newspapers were rated high for classifying issues. They found that the 1976 presidential debates on television were rated highly for providing excitement and insight into candidates' personal character and into their stands on issues.

An obvious question emerges from research into uses and gratifications. When producing media messages to persuade people is it more effective to present only the evidence supporting the point of view being made, and to satisfy only the need gratifications of the chosen audience, or is it better to introduce also the arguments of those opposed? Carl Hovland's research provided the answer. Hovland, a psychologist, provided wartime research for the Information and Education division of the US army. Early in 1945 the Army reported that morale was being negatively affected by over-optimism about an early end to the war. The Army issued a directive to the troops informing them of the difficult tasks still ahead. The Army wanted to emphasize that the war could take longer than presumed.

The directive provided an ideal topic for research – it was possible to present a one-sided or two-sided message on the progress of the war. Hovland, Lumsdaine and Sheffield (1971) used the directive in an experiment on the effect of presenting 'one side' versus 'both sides' in changing opinions on a controversial subject, namely the time it would take to end the war. The Armed Forces Radio Services, using official releases, constructed two programmes in the form of a commentator's analysis of the Pacific war. The commentator's conclusion was that it would take at least two years to finish the war in the Pacific after Victory in Europe.

'One Side'. The major topics included in the program which presented only the arguments indicating that the way would be long (hereafter labeled Program A) were: distance problems and other logistical difficulties in the Pacific; the resources and stock piles in the Japanese empire; the size and quality of the main bulk of the Japanese army that we had not yet met in battle; and the determination of the Japanese people. This program ran for about fifteen minutes.

'Both Sides'. The other program (Program B) ran for about nineteen minutes and presented all of these same difficulties in exactly the same way. The additional four minutes in this later program were devoted to considering arguments for the other side of the picture – US advantages and Japanese weaknesses such as: our naval victories and superiority; our previous progress despite a two-front war; our ability to concentrate all our forces on Japan after V-E Day; Japan's shipping losses; Japan's manufacturing inferiority; and the future damage to be expected from our expanding air war. These additional points were woven into the context of the rest of the program, each point being discussed where it was relevant. (Hovland, Lumsdaine and Sheffield, 1971, 469)

Hovland conducted an initial survey of the troops in the experiment to get an idea of their opinions about the Pacific before hearing the broadcast in order to compare their opinions after the broadcast. The following tables, adapted from Hovland's data, show that the effects were different for the two ways of presenting the messages depending on the initial stand of the listener. Table 4.2 shows that two-sided messages were effective for those who already estimated a short war and one-sided messages were more effective for those who estimated a long war. Table 4.3 shows that two-sided messages were more effective with high school graduates than with non-graduates.

Table 4.2 **Effectiveness of Programme A and Programme B for men with initially unfavourable and men with initially favourable attitudes**

Among men whose initial estimate was 'Unfavourable' (estimated a short war)	%
Programme A (one side only)	36
Programme B (both sides)	48
Among men whose initial estimate was 'Favourable' (estimated a long war)	
Programme A (one side only)	52
Programme B (both sides)	23

Source: Adapted from Hovland, Lumsdaine and Sheffield (1971).

Table 4.3 **Effectiveness of Programme A and Programme B for men of different educational backgrounds**

Among men who did not graduate from high school (changing to a longer estimate)	%
Programme A (one side only)	46
Programme B (both sides)	31
Among men who graduated from high school (changing to a longer estimate)	
Programme A (one side only)	35
Programme B (both sides)	49

Source: Adapted from Hovland, Lumsdaine and Sheffield (1971).

Hovland's research showed that mass media messages can be used to reinforce and to change attitudes. One-sided messages are most appropriate where people already support a point of view. Two-sided, or balanced, messages are most appropriate when people are better educated and/or opposed to a point of view. Hovland's research differs from a uses and gratifications approach because it does not assume that there is always a status quo of need gratification – that is to say, you should always send a message that meets people's existing needs.

Hovland's research belongs to a limited effects tradition of mass media influence. However, his research contradicts important elements of previous findings on personal influence. The mass media increases its influence in environments where people cannot check what is happening at a personal and interpersonal level. Soldiers in the Second World War had an idea of when the war would end and wanted an idea about when the war would end. Mass media help to construct a model of complex events just as the individual does. As Walter Lippmann said:

> the real environment is altogether too big, too complex, and too fleeting for direct acquaintance. We are not equipped to deal with so much subtlety, so much variety, so many permutations and combinations. And although we have to act in that environment, we have to reconstruct it on a simpler model before we can manage with it. To traverse the world men must have maps of the world. Their persistent difficulty is to secure maps on which their own need, or someone else's need, has not sketched in the coast of Bohemia. (Lippmann, 1922, 11)

Lippmann goes on to argue that what each person does is based not on direct and certain knowledge of the reality of the world but on pictures he or she makes of the world, or on pictures made for him by others. If people believe the world is flat, then they won't sail too near to the edge of the planet. 'Man', he says, 'is no Aristotelian god contemplating all existence at one glance. He is the creature of an evolution who can just about span a sufficient proportion of reality to manage his survival' (1922, 18).

Given this view of the world, reality is not something that can be discovered – the world is too big, too complex, and too fleeting for that. Rather, it is something that is created as limited pictures in our heads. In politics, it is not only something that is created, but also something that is continually being re-created. In the 1970s in Britain, the dominant picture of the political world was one in which big government tried to care for everyone, tried to provide public national healthcare and a wide range of social services. In the 1980s, conservative politicians and business think tanks altered that picture of the world. They promoted 'privatization' – a system in which government would play a lesser role and social services and government services would become the province of private enterprise. In contemporary China there has been a similar shift. In the 1970s the people were conceived of as the masses, with a first allegiance to the state, which would provide totalizing and centralized management of the economic fate of the workforce. In the 1980s, while state allegiance and control remained (and still remain) central to the power of the government, people were encouraged to *xia hai* (jump into the sea) and take personal risks in business enterprises, private ventures, and money-making activities. Now, it is seen as much more important to be a good capitalist than a good socialist, and it appears that neo-liberalism, capital and communism can coexist. Thus political and socio-political reality may be conceptualized not as a given, unchanging, objective thing but as a process: a constantly changing succession of mental pictures of what reality is, or ought to be. It is also a battlefield in which parties and groups are striving to impose their particular pictures of the world on the electorate at large.

Constructivism

The idea that reality is socially constructed and that mass media play an important role in constructing that reality was taken up by constructivism. Swanson (1981) sees constructivism partly as a challenge to the effects tradition based on the largely attitude-oriented national surveys conducted by the Survey Research Center of the University of Michigan in the 1950s. These suggested that people's voting choices were determined mainly by their demographic sociological background, their long-term non-partisan leanings, partisan attitudes, such as their sense of citizen duty and of political efficacy, and partisan attitudes, such as their identification with a political party. In their 1960 study, Campbell et al. proposed their 'funnel of causality' theory, which said that 'party labels enable people to organize their perceptions and preferences' in particular elections. The result of their work led to the belief that people's political behaviour was shaped by their long-term political attitudes rather than by current political communication: they voted 'Labor' because Dad was a worker, a 'Labor' supporter and a slum-dweller rather than because of what was said in an election campaign. In fact, what was said in an election campaign, or in other forms of political communication, tended to reinforce their existing beliefs rather than change them. This led to the 'law of minimal consequences' as a formulation of the impact of political communication. People tended to selectively expose themselves

Constructivism. Argues that people actively construct personal and social schemata and those schemata in turn affect how they perceive and act in the world.

to political communication that was congenial to their long-term political attitudes or selectively perceive those parts with which they agreed.

The constructivists question this. They assume that people interpret political communications and channel their activities and organize their actions as a consequence. They study people's interpretations by trying to map the 'constructs' that make up a person's 'political construct subsystem' – their constructs about, say, a politician's personal qualities, her or his personal background, her or his political background, her or his political ideology, her or his stands on specific issues, and her or his campaign style. Through these interpretive processes campaign communication is seen as influencing people's beliefs and thereby their behaviour.

The constructs people use to make decisions about the world form into schemata, much like Lippmann assumed people created 'maps' of the world in order to simplify the complex of events around them. Doris Graber cites the joke about a Russian who visited Sweden. On his return to the Soviet Union he told everybody that while there was an ample supply of consumer goods in Swedish shops, the Swedes were too poor to buy them. 'When asked how he knew that the merchandise was available only to the wealthy few, he replied: "That's easy, there were no long lines of people queuing up in front of the shops"' (Graber, 1989, 110). Graber's point is that when interpersonal experience diverges from media images, the impact of countervailing information is likely to be complex. People work with 'schemata' in their everyday lives and it is these schemata, personal and social, that form the basis of a theory of media effects.

Schemata are templates that a person creates and then attempts to fit over the realities of which the world is composed. Schemata are acquired from childhood and then developed independently through observation, experience and reasoning. Schemata are both personal and social. 'Thus the young may learn that poverty comes from ignorance and lack of education, or that employment is the consequence of laziness, social malfunctions, or fate. They may learn which dimensions of a given situation are worth noting, and which can be safely ignored' (Graber, 1989, 105–6).

A schemata approach to media effects suggests that the extent to which news provided by the mass media and the schemata created by the individual correspond will depend on news content and the existing schemata of the audience. 'If news stories that survive screening contain messages that are compatible with people's existing schemata, they are readily absorbed. Schemata and media images then tend to be blurred carbon copies of each other' (Graber, 1989, 107).

The influence of media, therefore, increases where:
- schemata of the audience are consistent with the purpose of the messages sent (because it is reinforcing existing attitudes); or
- where there are no set schemata associated with an issue (because there is no point of view on the issues).

Ien Ang (1985) in her study of Dutch viewers of *Dallas* shows how schemata presented in the media intersect in complex way, even though Ang might not call herself 'constructivist'. Women were the main audience of *Dallas*. *Dallas*'s female characters were, for the most part, powerless. Ang argues that fantasy allows people to play with societal representations for their own purposes. Women got pleasure from watching the powerless women on *Dallas* because they could try out the characters in their own minds, at no risk to themselves.

Here it is not primarily a matter of the content of the fantasy, but mainly of the fact of fantasizing itself; producing and consuming fantasies allows for a play with reality, which can be felt as 'liberating' because it is fictional, not real. In the play of fantasy we can adopt positions and 'try out' those positions, without having to worry about their 'reality value'. (Ang, 1985, 134)

case study

Chinese film director Zhang Yimou (*Raise the Red Lantern* and *To Live*) created the movie *Hero* to tell the story of the first emperor of China, Qin Shihuang. Two thousand years ago Qin Shihuang 'unified' China by subduing the six 'warring states' (*zhan guo*), and by unifying the language and the currency system. He also built China's major northern fortification, the Great Wall. He was ruthless and executed anyone suspected of disloyalty or who opposed his ideas, including Confucian scholars. Mao Zedong, unsurprisingly perhaps, was a fan of Qin Shihuang. 'Please don't slander Emperor Qin Shihuang, sir', Mao wrote in a 1973 poem (Kahn, 2003). The story of the Qin emperor is so well known in China that even the Chinese Pod online language service (which is created in Shanghai and downloaded onto MP3 players all over the world) used it to create an 'advanced' conversation between 'history students in a classroom setting'. This is, if you like, diffusion 2000 years after the event!

Hero is the story of an attempt to assassinate Emperor Qin. The story involves a series of flashbacks of different versions of the journey of the assassin, played by Jet Li, from recruitment to finding the Emperor to kill him. When the assassin arrives the Emperor argues with the assassin that what looks like his cruelty and oppression of his people is indeed for their own good, bringing peace and unity to a united China. The assassin is moved and changes his mind. The Emperor sheds a tear with the converted assassin and then orders his execution.

Again unsurprisingly, the 'Chinese authorities love it' (Kahn, 2003). Chinese leaders submitted the movie as nominee for best foreign film at the Academy awards after a premiere screening in Tiananmen Square. The movie was also a box office success with both domestic and international audiences. We need to consider that the motivations for enjoying the film were very different for the Chinese and the overseas audiences however. The first may have appreciated the nationalism that the film espouses, in so far as it deals with a profoundly Chinese narrative of two heroes: the Emperor and the assassin. The second may just have enjoyed the aesthetic richness of the art direction and the feisty glamour of the martial arts.

In interviews after the national release of the film, Zhang argued that the movie was not ideological. 'The only test of a film's success, especially a martial arts film, is whether it can keep the audience's attention for 90 minutes, not its metaphysics' (Kahn, 2003). Zhang has directed movies promoting China's bid to host the 2008 Olympics in Beijing and its entry to stage the 2010 World Exposition in Shanghai. Cynics would suggest that his film *Hero*, pandering as it does to the officially acceptable tale of national unity for China, would have made him a likely choice for these plum jobs.

HERO
by Zhang Yimou

Hero is an example of a movie that is, in fact, ideological, providing support for the concept of a unified China and the role of authorities in subordinating people to the greater good. For Chinese audiences the ideological messages would be clear and fairly unambiguous. For foreign audiences the movie is a fantastic martial arts action film and the underlying ideological messages do not have the same resonance.

Hero underlines the importance of the idea of active audiences. Audiences, as Ang (1985) argues, can play with messages and images. The social schemata of Chinese audiences and international audiences may be very different and each audience will draw different interpretations to the text and bring different interests to it.

Empirical research in media effects has concluded that audiences are active not passive. At the extreme this leads to the idea of limited effects, the notion that media have minimal influence. Other models, like constructivism, hold that audiences are active but that schemata are influential in affecting perception.

The medium

The final kind of effects research discussed in this chapter relates to the work of Marshall McLuhan, and related theorists. McLuhan was concerned primarily with the nature of the medium rather than the message:

> On September 6, 1949, a psychotic veteran, Howard B. Unruh, in a mad rampage on the streets of Camden, New Jersey, killed thirteen people, and then returned home. Emergency crews, bringing up machine guns, shotguns, and tear gas bombs, opened fire. At this point an editor on the *Camden Evening Courier* looked up Unruh's name in the telephone directory and called him. Unruh stopped firing and answered, 'Hello.'
> 'This Howard?'
> 'Yes ...'
> 'Why are you killing people?'
> 'I don't know. I can't answer that yet. I'll have to talk to you later. I'm too busy now.'
> *(The New York Times*, cited in *Understanding Media*, 1964, 220)

McLuhan's example raises issues about the effects of a medium. He belongs to the class of theorists who hold that the medium itself has the greatest effects, not the producers of media content, the content or the audience. He wrote before the rise of networked computers and the Internet and had no interest in the politics of feminism, capitalism or any other contemporary issue. McLuhan's main concern was with the technological colonization of the human body by media and how each medium can change perception and human practices.

McLuhan's main argument was that media were either hot or cold, depending upon the degree of participation and effect on the senses. Print is a hot medium because it engages people's imaginations. Television is a cold medium because it involves people in the visual sensations but leaves little to people's imaginations.

Jerry Mander (1978), in his *Four Arguments for the Elimination of Television*, took the idea of the effects of the medium on the senses to the extreme by arguing that television as a 'virtual' medium has an intrinsic necrophilic bias. Television, for Mander, is better at representing dead things than living things. Mander recounted his story of working for the Sierra Club in the 1960s when it was planning to establish a Redwood National Park in the US to save giant redwoods. He took a camera into the forest to film the trees to show the public the majesty of the forest. 'It didn't work at all. There was absolutely no communication we could have with those trees through technology.' However, when Mander went back and shot images of redwood stumps, the images of the stumps were more powerful than the living trees. 'Death', Mander realized, 'is better for television communication than life is. When you translate images through technology the aura is dropped out and just the image itself remains' (1978).

Mander's ideas go too far but they do show the focus of theorists' concerns with the inherent biases of a medium. Harold Innis, McLuhan's precursor, would not support

Mander's conclusions about the death wish nature of electronic media, but he did hold that concentration on a medium of communication automatically implies a bias in the cultural development of a civilization either towards an emphasis on space and political organization or towards an emphasis on time and religious organization (Innis, 1951, 216). For example, according to Innis, the dominance of parchment in the West gave a bias towards religious organization that led to the introduction of paper with its bias towards political organization. 'With printing, paper facilitated an effective development of the vernaculars and gave expression to their vitality in the growth of nationalism.' The adaptation of the alphabet to large-scale machine industry in turn became the basis of literacy, advertising, and trade. 'The book as a specialized product of printing, and in turn, the newspaper strengthened the position of language as a basis of nationalism.' In the United States the dominance of the newspaper led to large-scale development of monopolies of communication in terms of space and implied a neglect of problems of time. 'The bias of paper towards an emphasis on space and its monopolies of knowledge has been checked by the development of a new medium, the radio.' (Innis, 1951, 216–17).

Innis, as discussed in Chapter 3, made the distinction between time-biased and space-biased media because techniques of production and distribution of knowledge appear for him to produce very different kinds of societies – those with rock as a means of transmitting knowledge are limited in the speed at which knowledge can be transmitted and returned; those with satellites are freed from geographic and time constraints. The former will end up with a religious bias in their societies, the latter with a secular and political bias. Of course, emerging tales of the use of the Internet, television and mobile media by religious groups and extremists who call upon religion for inspiration, require us to either revisit this theory, or to make new judgements about the political nature of religious communications.

McLuhan and Innis work with theories – explanations about the effects of media on society. What cannot be doubted is that different modes of communication in a society have very different requirements for the production and distribution of knowledge and, for the journalist, the production of news. Moreover, those modes of communication affect use of time and space and the everyday practices of cultures. This part of Innis's thesis would appear to be beyond dispute. Once specific techniques are adopted, a certain logic develops around them. Writing parchment, for example, required strength and effort. 'Working six hours a day the scribe produced from two to four pages and required from ten months to a year and a quarter to copy a Bible' (Innis, 1951, 169). Libraries were slowly built up and uniform rules in the care of books became adopted. Demand for space for the standing of books upright led to increased construction of libraries in the 15th century.

to recap...

Some media theorists argue that it is the medium itself that has the greatest effects, not the producers of media content, the content or the audience. Marshall McLuhan, Harold Innis and Jerry Mander are classic examples of this position on media effects.

Summary

Public perceptions about the power of media and public concern about media effects are a constant theme in the history of media effects and are unlikely to disappear. Empirical research suggests that the media are an important, but sometimes limited, source of influence on the attitudes and behaviour of members of the audience. Evidence taken from actual life in experiments and fieldwork by researchers supports the view that:

- the audience, consumers, are as Bauer says, obstinate (1971). It is easier to reinforce people's attitudes than it is to change them;
- media messages are mediated by group processes. Opinion leaders play a major role in shaping attitudes towards issues;

- the persuasive influence of media increases because of processes of mediation such as:
- agenda setting
- personal and social schemata.

Modern media effects research revolves around:
- processes of selection of content for the media, such as agenda setting;
- interpersonal processes of influence, such as opinion leadership;
- psychological processes of defence, such as needs gratification;
- social construction of reality, based on constructs and schemata formation.

The question 'Do the media shape audience experiences or mirror them?' has no simple answer. Much of early media effects research was designed to provide evidence to government or business on how to influence people to behave in a particular way, or watch or listen to particular programmes, or buy advertised goods. While we know that there is no simple stimulus–response in media effects, there continues to this day continuous collection of information about audiences – their values, beliefs, concerns, viewing or listening or reading patterns, consumption patterns, and so on. Media organizations try to stay close to what they think are the interests of their audiences, however defined – by monitoring broadcast ratings or other research.

The authors argue that the evolution of our understanding of media influence has, in fact, returned us to a model of powerful effects. There is no longer a simple model of powerful effects. There is a range of complex theories that provide insights into the relationship between the organization of media and the social and psychological use of media, from the gatekeepers through to groups and individuals. Agenda setting shifted thinking towards a moderate effects model because it became clear that the very process of selection of content by media professionals and organizations meant that some things would be made salient and others not. Individuals in this model, though, might not necessarily blindly follow the media agenda; thus the term 'moderate'. The idea of a spiral of silence also shifted thinking away from a limited effects model and towards powerful effects. The spiral of silence raises the possibility that public opinion formation can involve people suppressing their own views because of a desire to conform to majority views.

A complex model of powerful effects does not by definition mean that audiences are passive. As we will see in later chapters, active audiences can be manipulated, deceived or persuaded, even on a global scale. Modern empirical research on media effects has yielded evidence on how, whom and when to persuade. Indeed, persuasion and manipulation bring us to the topic of the next chapter, ideology. The 'administrative school' represents only one side of the media effects coin.

At the conclusion of this chapter you should be able to:
- distinguish between different models of media effects;
- critically discuss the idea of an active audience;
- recognize the limits of media influence.

Key themes

Active audiences/active interpreters. Audiences are not passive receivers of media messages. They actively interpret what they receive through media or opinion leaders. Paul Lazarsfeld's research on a presidential campaign reported in *The People's Choice* found that whenever respondents were asked to report on their recent exposures to campaign media, 'political discussions with peers' was mentioned more frequently than radio or print. Lazarsfeld found that those most likely to change their vote in the presidential campaign read and listened least. The mass media of radio and newspaper did not change behaviour because the people who did the reading and listening listened or read their own views and were most resistant to conversion. The people in their own social group were, like them, also resistant to calls for them to change their vote. The idea of 'active audiences', therefore, does not mean that mass media have no influence but that any model of media influence must be complex and must account for people being active interpreters.

Media influence. Early theorizing about media influence concluded that there was a 'hypodermic needle' effect from mass media – the media injected the message into society and society reacted as a result. Its origin was in the rise of propaganda and new broadcast media at the time such as radio. This was a simple one-step model of media influence. Paul Lazarsfeld and Carl Hovland and others, employed by either business or government, found that the interactions between mass media and the individual were far more complex than assumed. A model of personal influence, or a two-step, limited effects model, ensued that introduced the opinion leader as a possible mediator of mass media messages. The limited effects model, however, missed in its analyses much of the behind-the-scenes social system that delivers media messages and how that system might affect which messages were chosen and with what emphasis. Agenda setting and diffusion of innovations emerged as moderate-effects models that dealt with the psychological reception of media messages and the structures and organizations of society that delivered those messages. For example, the selection of news by journalists, the emphasis placed by news organizations on one kind of news rather than another, precedes individual psychological choices of the individual who receives the news. This 'agenda setting' has influence over people's view of the world and what is happening. Constructivism, like agenda setting and diffusion of innovations, deals with both individual and society through cognitive schemata. Noelle-Neumann's model of the spiral of silence takes individual psychology and the structures and organization of media and argues that the climate of opinion created by the media can constrain how people think and act in modern society. This is a step back towards powerful effects, but with a far more sophisticated notion of the intersection between audiences and the media.

*Discussion
questions*

1   Why are people so concerned about media? Which groups and individuals in our society express most concern about media effects? And how do those groups and individuals express those concerns?

2   Why does the statement 'the media have powerful effects' need caution?

3   Which issues do you think need to be debated in the study of mass media effects? Why?

4   Summarize the main features of the media effects approach. Why do you think this approach is so vigorously criticized in Marxist and neo-Marxist studies on the media?

5   Select a news story from a magazine, newspaper, television (video record it) or the Internet that deals with the effects of media on people. Bring the story or stories to tutorial and discuss the assumptions the writer(s) had about the power of the media.

6   Do you think heavy viewing of violence leads to violent behaviour? How did you establish your conclusions? What are some social and cultural conditions that might affect your conclusions?

7   Personal and social schemata are the templates through which we see the world – this is the constructivist view. Are the media professionals, the image tribes, who produce content for the media affected primarily by the schemata of the 'middle class' – if so, then what do such schemata contain?

8   Consult a journal relevant to your specialization (for example *Media, Culture and Society*,

European Journal of Communication, Journalism Quarterly, Public Opinion Quarterly) and summarize an article that deals with the effects of media. What approach did it take? What hypotheses or research questions did it pose? What were the results? Discuss your summaries with the tutorial.

9   McLuhan said 'the medium is the message'. Do different media have different effects on the way society is organized? On this view, what are some of the possible effects of the new media, cyberspace, on social organization?

10   The trajectory of American research is clearly attached to US models of society and communication. What kinds of issues need to be re-addressed in the light of alternative and perhaps contrasting models of international social and cultural organization?

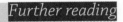*Further reading*

McCombs, M.E., and Zhu, J. (1995). Capacity, diversity and volatility of the public agenda: Trends from 1954 to 1994. *Public Opinion Quarterly*, **59**, 495–525.

McQuail, D. and Windahl, S. (1981). *Communication models for the study of mass communication*. London: Longman.

Rogers, E.M. (1982). The Empirical and the Critical schools of communication research. In M. Burgoon (ed.) *Communication Yearbook 5* (124–44). New Brunswick: Transaction Books.

Rogers, E.M. (1994). *A history of communication study*. New York: Free Press.

Classics in media and ideology

chapter

5

This chapter will introduce you to:

- the concepts of ideology and hegemony in media studies;
- the emergence of postmodernism as a way of thinking about discourse and language

and the role of power;
- theorization about the public sphere.

Chapter 4 introduced some of the major models in media effects research, many originating in the 'administrative research' tradition. In this chapter we will explore the 'critical research' tradition and its variations. This chapter will introduce you to:

- the concepts of ideology and hegemony in media studies;
- the emergence of postmodernism as a way of thinking about discourse and language and the role of power;
- theorization about the public sphere.

> 'Newspapers should blacklist poorly performing industries and denounce the inefficient. They should uncover the bad types in all parts of society and punish them!'

This proposed aim of newspapers did not come from a sour economist or a moral rights crusader. The proposal is Lenin's, the communist revolutionary, who argued for 'an effective, ruthless and truly revolutionary *war* against the *specific* wrongdoers'. The primary role of the press, he says, is to condemn the bad and to make appeals to 'learn from the good' (Lenin, 1918, in Mattelart and Siegelaub, 1983). Lenin is talking about

Ideology. The means by which dominant economic classes, ruling classes, extend their control over others so that their rule is accepted as natural and inevitable.

the exercise of power and the role of media in serving communist goals. In the previous chapter we talked about research into how people use media. This research is often termed 'administrative' because of its links to problems of modern industry in reaching audiences and selling products. In this chapter we examine the 'critical' tradition that has as its focus problems of ideology. We need to know the key classics in media and ideology because they tell us about how power is theorized, and how the social and political consequences of media are debated.

Ideology and hegemony

Lenin wrote at a time when there were virtually no modern media in Russia. For the Soviet leadership in 1926 it was technology, and media technology in particular, that was going to be the index of communist success. Leon Trotsky made this quite clear: 'Victory over poverty and superstition is ensured to us, provided we go forward technically. We must not lag behind other countries. The first slogan, which every friend of radio must fix in his mind is: Don't lag behind!' (Trotsky, 1926, in Mattelart and Siegelaub, 1983, 257).

In 1926, according to Leon Trotsky, who in many senses was the logistical genius of the Russian Revolution and the subsequent Civil War, the United States' railway network amounted to 405,000 kilometres, Britain's 40,000, Germany's 54,000 and the Soviet Union's 69,000. The US carried 600 million ton-kilometres by rail, Britain 30 million, Germany 69 million, and the Soviet Union 48.5 million. The US spent a billion and a quarter rubles, 9 rubles 40 kopeks per head, on postal services. The Soviet Union spent 75 million, 33 kopeks per head. The US had 60 million kilometres of telephone wires, Britain 6 million and the Soviet Union only 311,000.

Trotsky took the media to be a powerful tool for development and policy but he was more circumspect about the nature of its effects:

What is the relation between radio technology and the social system? Is it socialist or capitalist? I raise the question because a few days ago the famous Italian, Marconi, said in Berlin that the transmission of pictures at a distance by means of Hertzian waves is a tremendous gift to pacifism, foretelling the speedy end of the militarist epoch. Why should this be? These ends of epochs have been proclaimed so often that the pacifists have got all ends and beginnings mixed up. The fact that we shall be able to see a great distance is supposed to put an end to wars! Certainly, the invention of a means of transmitting a living image over a great distance is a very attractive problem, for it is insulting to the optic nerve that the auditory one is at present, thanks to radio, in a privileged position in this respect. But to suppose that from this there must result the end of wars is merely absurd. (Trotsky, 1926, in Mattelart and Siegelaub, 1983, 255)

The communist revolution had social change as its objective, with media subordinated to the creation of the good socialist worker. Trotsky thought that if the media were in capitalist hands, then there would be capitalist propaganda, and if in socialist hands, then there would be socialist propaganda. Lenin and Trotsky were interested in indoctrination, what media *should* do to transform the worker into the socialist worker. The media at the service of revolutionary scientific Marxism in Russia were taken to be a means of getting rid of non-scientific, 'superstitious thought', such as church sermons broadcast by radio. 'What, indeed, does a "voice from heaven" amount to when there is being broadcast all over the country a voice from the Poly-technical museum?' (Trotsky, 1926, in Mattelart and Siegelaub, 1983, 257).

class discussion Trotsky was sure that media would be used as a tool of propaganda whatever system of political organization was in place. Think about the radio, 'audio' media that you consume through radio and the Internet. Is there an equivalent 'voice from heaven' in the content to which you are exposed? Are there single or competing voices? Do they reinforce your ways of thinking about world issues, or do they challenge them? How do you identify a 'voice from heaven' (we are of course referring to this ironically and metaphorically), and what is your response?

Stalin sent an assassin, to Mexico City, with an icepick to kill Trotsky before Trotsky could undertake any media studies of his own. However, when Bauer conducted a study of Soviet refugees in the 1950s, he found that Soviet methods of indoctrination were singularly unsuccessful. Bauer knew that virtually every Soviet citizen was regularly exposed to meetings at which were conveyed some news, the party line on various issues, general political agitation and indoctrination. The Soviet refugees were asked 'From what sources did you draw most of your information about what was happening?' Only 19 per cent specified the meetings, compared with 87 per cent citing newspapers, 50 per cent radio, and 50 per cent word of mouth. 'Gradually the obvious dawned on us', said Bauer, 'our respondents were telling us where they learned what *they* wanted to know, not where they learned what the regime wanted them to know' (1971, 338–9). The higher Bauer went up the social ladder of the Soviet refugees, the more likely those groups were to rely on word of mouth to better understand the official media. 'Viewed from the vantage point of the regime's intention, the widespread dependence upon word of mouth was a failure in communication. From the point of view of the citizen and what he wanted, his own behaviour made eminent sense' (Bauer, 1971, 339).

It is not surprising that there is continual change both in the way people use media and also in the ways media analysts understand that use. Research technology, such as survey and sampling design, was still in its infancy at the time when Trotsky addressed the Friends of Radio in 1926 over 80 years ago. Social and psychological theories and many of the theories of media effects, and the media technologies associated with them, developed side by side in the equivalent of a single person's lifetime.

Marxist perspectives on the media have dominated the development of mass media research in communication in the UK and Europe, in contrast to the empirically based tradition of the United States covered in the previous chapter. The influence of Marxism on US media studies came much later leading to a 'ferment in the field' debate in a special 1983 edition of the *Journal of Communication*. Marxist and related perspectives on the media, which emerged in a European context, have led to questions about conflict, control, ideology and class struggle in modern media. Commercial perspectives, which emerged in public opinion research in the United States, led to questions about audiences, persuasion, attitude change and the nature of public opinion.

Political economists in particular look at the intersection between economic forces and political forces and in media studies often draw on Marxist or neo-Marxist perspectives. Political economists Edward Herman and Noam Chomsky (2002) in their book *Manufacturing Consent* outlined a propaganda model that focuses on the effects of US capitalist ideology on agenda setting in the media, including the role of news. They said that there were five main filters, or ways, that media content is controlled in western societies:

- by size, concentrated ownership, owner wealth, and profit orientation of the dominant mass media firms;
- by advertising as the primary income source of the mass media;
- by the reliance of the media on information provided by government, business, and 'experts'
- by 'flak' as a means of disciplining the media;
- by 'anticommunism' as a control mechanism.

'Flak' for Herman and Chomsky refers to negative responses to media news or programmes, whether letters, phone calls, petitions, law suits, speeches and so on. The ability to produce flak, in their account, is greatest for the powerful institutions most committed to the capitalist cause. Media professionals, in Herman and Chomsky's model, are puppets of capitalism. 'In the media, as in other major institutions, those who do not display the requisite values and perspectives will be regarded as "irresponsible", "ideological" or otherwise aberrant, and will tend to fall by the wayside' (Herman and Chomsky, 2002, 304) For Herman and Chomsky everything media professionals do can be explained in terms of ideology and its effects.

The idea that ideology explains media effects takes many theoretical forms. The power of the media for political economists, however, is clearly different from that of a McLuhan or an Innis. Herman and Chomsky say that there is a ruling class and that this ruling class controls the media and their effects. McLuhan says that the medium has its own intrinsic effects, independently of its content or its owners. The United States is put forward in the Marxist perspective as the arch-villain of capitalism, the principal global disseminator of the information revolution. It is 'American' (he refers specifically to the US, not to Canada or to the Latin and South American states) society, says Brzeninksi, that is having the greatest impact on all other societies, prompting a far-reaching cumulative transformation in their outlook. 'This is all the more likely because American society more than any other, "communicates" with the entire globe. Roughly sixty-five per cent of all world communications originate in this country ... For the first time in history the cumulative knowledge of mankind will be made accessible on a global scale and it will be almost instantaneously available in response to demand' (Brzeninksi, 1970, cited in Mattelart, 2003, 93).

According to the Council for the Development of Community Media in Canada (Mattelart and Siegelaub, 1983, 397), mass media, through processes of control, filtering and censorship, renew capitalist ideology and relegate us, the audience/consumers/subjects/individuals, to the status of mere message consumers, 'turning this non-communication into an instrument of social control and maintenance of bourgeois power. On top of this hold over information, the mass media are also characterised by a maximisation of profits, from advertising to cable distribution'.

Ideas about global social-class conflict, ownership and control are key Marxist themes and often stand in stark contrast to traditional media effects studies. The Marxist perspective has been especially influential in teaching British and European students about the influence of mass media. In what follows we will explore the nature of Marxist thinking, especially as it relates to the effects of mass media. Marxism has been in decline as a political movement since the collapse of the USSR in 1991, but its intellectual effects can still be felt, including within the postmodern concerns with language and discourse.

Marx

Karl Marx grew up in the oppressive state of Prussia as its economy was making the transition from agrarianism to industrialism and as its society was shifting from folk society to mass society. As farms were consolidated into larger units and as manufacturing moved from small-scale to mass production, small farmers and small producers were ruined and forced to live in poor conditions around factories. Hours of work were high, wages low, and women and children joined the men as factory fodder with children as young as eight being made to work up to fourteen hours a day in mines and mills in most European countries.

Marx, along with many other observers, was appalled by what he saw but unlike the others Marx sought to analyse and find solutions to the problems to which he objected. Industrial society, indeed all societies, Marx thought, were motivated by materialistic determinism. The way people organize their lives is determined primarily, but not exclusively, by the prevailing modes of production, distribution and exchange of commodities in the community. Materialism dominated society because humans must eat, drink, dress, and find shelter before they could concern themselves with anything else. Thus productive forces caused a division of labour and a division of the physical means of production. They forced people into productive relations. Manufacturing labour was separated from commercial labour and both were separated from agricultural labour. But within each category individuals cooperated in distinct kinds of work.

class discussion The previous explanation is in the past tense as a description of Marx's analysis, but of course there is much that is true of the present, and indeed of all human experience. Consider the society in which you live. What are the key determinants of how people have organized that society? How much is dependent on local, national or global solutions or influences? Is it true in the contemporary world that the bare necessities of 'eat, drink, dress and find shelter' are achievable without other 'rights': education, equality, and communications for instance?

What are the contemporary divisions of labour in your society? How important are the service, communications and finance sectors for instance (as opposed to industrial sectors)? What differences does the division of labour make to how people communicate?

The division of labour also generated corresponding property relations and the result was to divide society into classes. The trend was towards two classes – those who owned the means of production and those who owned only their labour power. Under the capitalist mode of production, capitalists, landowners and wage labourers formed the great classes of society. But gradually the distinction between landowner and capitalist was disappearing and soon there would be only two important classes, the bourgeoisie and the proletariat. The bourgeoisie would own all the means of production but needed the labour power of the proletariat because the means of production were useless unless labour was applied to them. The historic task of the bourgeoisie, or capitalist, class was to accumulate capital.

If materialistic determinism was the main motive force in Marx's conception of industrial society, it was not the only one. Other important forces included the state, education, and propaganda. The modes of production comprised the substructure, base or economic foundation of society. But it was protected by a great superstructure of political, legal, educational, spiritual and artistic institutions and by patterns of relationships between such institutions and chains of authority. These reconciled members of society to the existing system by moulding their opinions, customs, moral and ethical values, expectations and behaviour patterns. Thus whenever new forces of production gained importance they caused new productive and property relations and transformed the superstructure of institutions so as to assist, rather than hinder, material production. In a famous formulation of this idea, Marx and Engels wrote in *The German Ideology*:

> The ideas of the ruling class are in every epoch the ruling ideas, i.e. the class which is the ruling material force of society, is at the same time its ruling intellectual force. The class which has the means of material production at its disposal, has control at the same time over the means of mental production, so that thereby generally speaking, the ideas of those who lack the means of mental production are subject to it. (1972, 64)

Hegemony. The consensus of society given to the mode of life impressed on society in general by the ruling class.

Many of the theorists after Marx have developed this aspect of 'ruling ideas'. The influential Italian Marxist Antonio Gramsci (1891–1937), for example, developed the concept of hegemony. He said there were two levels of the superstructure, the 'civil' or 'private' society and the 'political society or state'. The ruling class exercised its intellectual dominion through the civil or private level and its direct dominion through government and law.

Gramsci (1968) said that hegemony was the 'spontaneous consensus' the mass of society accorded to the mode of life impressed on society in general by the ruling class. This consensus was achieved because of the prestige and trust the ruling class (or dominant group) enjoyed due to its position. Gramsci said that hegemony exists when a ruling class is able not only to coerce a subordinate class to conform to its interests but also to exert a 'total social authority' over the subordinate class and the whole society. Thus hegemony depends on both force and consent. In liberal-capitalist states it depends more on consent, but the same players are involved in manufacturing that consent where possible to do so. It is achieved not only in the productive substructure but also in the superstructure of state, religion, education and propaganda. It is achieved by the containment of the subordinate classes and by ideology.

False consciousness. When people are dominated by others and accept that domination as natural and legitimate.

The subjugation of the subordinate classes is achieved by making the ruling class's definitions of reality the lived reality of everyone else. In Marxist discourse this is false consciousness. False consciousness is when people dominated by others take their domination by ruling classes to be legitimate. For example, if a woman believes arguments in a patriarchal society that she should be controlled by men, and subordinate to men in all things, emotionally and physically and intellectually, then that woman has a false consciousness. She cannot see that she should be free. In this way ideology binds together the ideological unity of the entire society. The ruling class is successful in this when it manages to frame all competing definitions of reality within the range of its own conceptions of what is real. Thus it sets the limits in which everyone perceives reality.

Hegemony is achieved through such agencies of the superstructure as the family, the church, the education system, cultural institutions and the media, as well as through the coercive instruments of the state. It is not a given or permanent state of affairs but has to be constantly fought for and secured. Nor can it be total, for the subordinate classes have their own systems of values, but when it is successful these can be contained.

In his two major works *Reading Capital* (1970) and *For Marx* (1970) the French philosopher Louis Althusser elaborated on the ideas of Marx and Gramsci. He argued that capitalism as a system reproduces the conditions of production, including the conditions of social reproduction – the reproduction of labour power and of the relations of production. This includes wages, without which labour power cannot reproduce itself as a developing productive force. The reproduction of labour power through wages (salaries) requires the family; the reproduction of advanced skills and techniques requires the education system; the reproduction of the submission to the ruling ideology requires cultural institutions, religion and the media, the political institutions and the overall management of the state. Althusser calls these the ideological state apparatuses and argues that they operate primarily through ideology. They provide the 'system of ideas and representations' by means of which people understand and live an imaginary relation to their real conditions of existence.

What is represented in ideology is therefore not the system of the real relations, which governs the existence of people, but the imaginary relation of those individuals to the real relations in which they live. These apparatuses for Althusser establish a hegemony as an order in which a way of living and thinking is dominant and where one concept of reality is diffused through society – including tastes, morality, customs, religious and political principles.

Mass media and the process of legitimation

How capitalist-conservative hegemony tends to hold sway even in the theoretically open societies of contemporary democracies is a question that continued to preoccupy Marxists. The outstanding fact about the competition for popular support in such societies, admits Ralph Miliband in *The State in Capitalist Society* (1973), is that parties of the Left have won little support. He suggests several reasons for the success of capitalist-conservative ideologies. They are supported by activist members of the middle class and by well-funded agencies in the field of macro-politics, in which members of the dominant classes are able, by virtue of their opposition, for instance as employers, to dissuade members of the subordinate classes, if not from holding, at least from voicing unorthodox views. Nor of course does this only affect members of the working classes or of the lower middle classes: many middle-class employees are similarly vulnerable to pressures from 'above'. 'This process of dissuasion need not be explicit in order to be effective. In civil life as well as in the state service, there are criteria of "soundness", particularly in regard to politics, whose disregard may be highly disadvantageous in a number of important respects' (1973, 163).

The process of legitimation, or the reinforcement of the existing social order, it is claimed, is assisted by the media. Although the media appear to reflect liberal society's pluralist diversity and competitive equilibrium, they are a crucial element in the legitimation of capitalist society. They are both the expression of a system of domination and a means of reinforcing it. The absence of state dictation to the media and the presence of debate and controversy in their content serve only to mask their true function:

Pluralism. Conceives of power as distributed across different groups in society, shifting over time and issues.

consistently, the press for the most part has always been a deeply commit
trade union force. Not, it should be said, that newspapers in general oppos
unions as such. Not at all. They only oppose trade unions, in the all too fa
jargon, which, in disregard of the country's welfare and of their members' own i.
ests, greedily and irresponsibly seek to achieve short-term gains which are blir
self-defeating. In other words, newspapers love trade unions so long as they do bac
the job for which they exist. (Miliband, 1973, 198–9)

The media, Miliband argued in 1973, control much of the means of mental production,
as their ownership is overwhelmingly in the private domain and is part of large-scale
capitalist enterprise, they are controlled by 'men [sic] whose ideological dispositions run
from soundly conservative to utterly reactionary' (1973, 204). These views are either
imposed directly on editorial staff or 'seep downward'. Thus journalists learn to spare the
conservative susceptibilities of the men or women who employ them and to take a proper
attitude to free enterprise, to conflicts between capital and labour, to trade unions, left-
wing parties and movements, to the Cold War, revolutionary movements and the role of
the United States in world affairs. Moreover, they feel directly or indirectly the influence
of advertisers. The media learn to show exceptional care in dealing with such powerful
and valuable customers and treat them with sympathetic understanding.

Mass media also feel the influence of government because all governments:

now make it their business, ever more elaborately and systematically, to supply
newspapers, radio and television with explanations of official policy which naturally
have an apologetic and tendentious character. The state, in other words, now goes in
more and more for 'news management', particularly in times of stress and crisis,
which means, for most leading capitalist countries, almost permanently; and the
greater the crisis, the more purposeful the management, the evasions, the half-
truths and the plain lies. (Miliband, 1973, 208)

Those who work for the media may be divided into members of the Left, conserva-
tives and people with blurred political commitments who wish to avoid trouble. This
last group, 'like their committed conservative colleagues mostly "say what they like";
but this is mainly because their employers mostly like what they say, or at least find
little in what they say which is objectionable' (Miliband, 1973, 211).

Many other Marxist and neo-Marxist analysts hold or have held similar views.
Stuart Hall (1977a and b) says that quantitatively and qualitatively the media have
established a decisive leadership in the cultural sphere and progressively colonized the
cultural and ideological sphere. The media construct images of the meanings, practices
and values of groups and classes. They integrate images, representations and ideas into
coherently grasped 'wholes'. They provide an inventory of the lifestyles and ideologies
of modern capitalism. The media as a consequence give some voices and opinions
greater weight to the powerful over the weak. For media professionals this process of
reproduction of ideology is not fully conscious because it is masked partly by what
makes news news – routinization of practice. Audiences will not necessarily decode
the messages in the way intended by the message or the media but they often do so at
least within the dominant codes (Hall, 1977a and b; 1989).

Theorist snapshot: Stuart Hall

Stuart Hall became Director of the Birmingham Centre for Contemporary Cultural Studies in the UK in 1968, following its 1964 founder Richard Hoggart. The Centre became a focus for the development of the new field of cultural studies:

> Unlike traditional academic disciplines, cultural studies did not have (or seek) a well-defined intellectual or disciplinary domain. It flourished at the margins of and by successive encounters with different institutionalized discourses, especially those of literary studies, sociology and history; and to a lesser extent of linguistics semiotics, anthropology and psychoanalysis. (O'Sullivan, 1983, 61)

The media group at the Birmingham Centre for Contemporary Cultural Studies contested the traditional models of direct media influence that, as we found in Chapter 4, had characterized many of the models of media research. The Centre drew attention to the ideological and linguistic structures of media texts. Hall had an interest in the role of codes in 'the circulation and securing of dominant ideological definitions and representations' (Hall 1980, 118).

Hall argued that there were three interpretative codes or positions that a reader might bring to a text:

1. A dominant (or hegemonic) reading – the reader fully shares the text's code and accepts and reproduces the preferred reading (the reading which may not have been the result of any conscious intention on the part of the creator of the text);

2. A negotiated reading – the reader partly shares the media text's code, but may resist and modify the reception of the code in a way that reflects their own life and personal or group contexts;

3. An oppositional (counter-hegemonic) reading – the reader understands the preferred reading but does not share it and may bring alternative ways of dealing with it.

Hall's work, which was to be influential in the US in the 1990s, and that of David Morley (1980) in his study *Nationwide*, shifts media theory away from the idea of passive audiences and further enchances the idea that audiences are active even if they are subject to powerful forces that seek to control them.

Empirical evidence for Marxist views

All this is Marxist or neo-Marxist theory. Is there any empirical proof of it? Well, there is certainly some hard evidence to support some aspects of the theory. In *Bad News, More Bad News*, and *Really Bad News*, the Glasgow University Media Group presented the results of six years' research into the coverage of news about trade unions, industry and the economy (1976; 1980; 1982). They concluded that television has the power to tell people the order in which to think about events and issues – to set the agenda. It also largely controls what people will think with.

The Group found that television routinely presents trade union wage gains as the cause of inflation, without giving alternative explanations, such as lack of investment. Moreover, its industrial coverage concentrates on only a few industries. In the first half of 1975, one out of two industrial stories on British television was about transport, communication or public administration and the 2 per cent of British workers who worked in motor manufacturing featured in nearly one quarter of television's general industrial coverage. The coverage of strikes was very distorted. Although the engineering industry had a high incidence of strikes, it had negligible coverage. Of the 90 main disputes in Britain nine were never mentioned on television. Moreover, strikes were presented as if labour was consistently the cause and on television news 'trouble' was more likely to come from low status or marginal groups – from the bottom of society rather than the top. On British television in the 1970s and 1980s strikes are always bad, unless they happen in Poland. The Polish strikes at the end of the 1980s, which were crucial in the rise of the Solidarity movement, were portrayed in terms of people fighting for democracy and freedom. Other, more local struggles, were portrayed as politically inept and economically naive. Whatever your view of the particular issues, this disparity was indeed telling.

The news, moreover, had a male bias. The 1975 study showed that only 8 per cent of all named interviewees were women and most of these were sportswomen, women involved in disasters, Margaret Thatcher, or the Queen. The Group found that the boards of the BBC and the Independent Broadcasting Authority were drawn mainly from the ranks of the power elite and they directly or indirectly set limits on what the employees were allowed to do or say.

Moreover, the journalists themselves were much better paid than most members of society and certainly better paid than many of the people whose activities they reported. Most journalists had few experiences outside their own class and culture and were not well placed to speak about what it was like to be unemployed or to be scrutinized for cohabitation by social security investigators. Generally they shared a common culture with the most powerful groups and interests in society:

> The backgrounds of most journalists in broadcasting and the world in which they live mean that they share a common culture with the most powerful groups and interests in our society. Furthermore, official sources such as the Treasury and the Ministry of Defence gain routine access for their views on television, since they have the power to make sure their views are heard. In a sense they control the livelihood of journalists, since given the type of news journalists have to produce, these sources have a monopoly over certain kinds of information. For example, they might leak the content of cabinet discussions. Press briefings are given to favoured journalists and the more powerful the interests that are at stake, the more tightly the vision will be controlled. The Ministry of Defence for example has more press and information personnel than any other government department (including the Central Office of Information). Senior news journalists in this area tend to have a close affinity with these interests and sometimes have a military background themselves. (Glasgow University Media Group, 1976, 13)

After it has presented a book full of specific studies, the Group concluded that the media have accepted the ideology of consensus. Instead of presenting the economic system as a battleground for a conflict between capital and labour, they begin from the assumption that there should be no such conflict. They present any evidence of 'trouble' as the work of 'unacceptable' elements. They are reluctant to scrutinize the actions of middle or upper classes as the source of trouble and even more reluctant to examine the economic system on which this class structure rests.

> The search for the source of trouble focuses instead on the actions of the workforce. Stories then abound of pigheadedness, wreckers, reds under the bed, exorbitant wage claims, strikes, people who are work-shy, or think the country owes them a living. There is no comparable list relating to the activities of management or the owners of capital – there are no routine references to management intransigence, incompetence, expense account lunches, perks, fraud, manipulation of wage deals, lock-outs or tax avoidance. (Glasgow University Media Group, 1976, 129)

More evidence for some of the Marxist views may be found in an American book, Todd Gitlin's *The Whole World Is Watching: Mass Media in the Making and Unmaking of the New Left* (1980). Although never himself a Marxist, Gitlin's theoretical position blends the neo-Marxist thought of Antonio Gramsci on ideological hegemony with the Frankfurt School theory of co-option. Gitlin studies the relationship between the media and the New Left, particularly the Students for a Democratic Society, in the 1960s. His book begins with the familiar assertion that people can know directly only tiny regions of social life. For much of the remainder they must rely on the manufactured public world that the media bring into their private space. They soon find themselves relying on the media for concepts, images of heroes, guiding information, emotional charges, recognition of public values, and for symbols in general. The media, he says, name the world's parts. They certify reality as reality. 'To put it simply: the mass media have become core systems for the distribution of ideology' (Gitin, 1980, 2).

Although so-called free societies theoretically allow the expression of a wide range of viewpoints, they are structured so as to make it extremely difficult, perhaps unimaginable, for an opposition movement to define itself and its worldview outside the dominant culture. Picking up some Marxist notions, Gitlin says:

> Truly the process of making meanings in the world of centralized commercial culture has become comparable to the process of making value in the world through labor. Just as people **as** workers have no voice in what they make, how they make it, or how the product is distributed and used, so do people *as producers of meaning* have no voice in what the media make of what they say or do, or in the context within which the media frame their activity. [emphasis in original] (1980, 3)

Essentially this argument follows Marx's line that modern production has effectively alienated the worker from his work. Gitlin goes on to argue that the mass mediated meanings produced by the media stand outside the people who were involved in expressing them (for example speakers or demonstrators) and confront them as an alien force because they have been distorted by the professional and ideological practices of the media in reporting them. Moreover, marginal groups seeking media coverage must distort their messages to make them newsworthy. They have to couch their messages in forms that conform with journalists' notions of what is a 'story', an 'event', or a 'protest'. If they are successful, the messages-as-pseudo-event is reported and it becomes 'the movement' for the audiences of the mass media. It is that *mediated image* that is accepted or opposed in the political arena. Moreover, the mass media certify some people as leaders or noteworthy 'personalities' in movements that are reported in the media. Thus the mass media convert leaders into celebrities. Often, flamboyance is, in the media's mind, a key characteristic of an acceptable celebrity and the presence of such a flamboyant celebrity can assure the coverage of an event such as a protest or demonstration.

Gitlin concedes that while media distort movements they also amplify the issues that give them life. But in exposing the scandals, which might be the basis of protests, they like to reserve to duly constituted authority the right to remedy them. He attributes this to the operation of Gramsci's notion of hegemony. Journalists view events through frames that they have picked up through family, church, school, state, the corporate economy increasingly based on oligopoly rather than competition, the bureaucratic national security state and the values and attitudes they have absorbed in their own professional training as journalists. These hegemonic frames are persistent patterns of cognition, interpretation, and presentation, of selection, emphasis, and exclusion, by which media workers routinely organize their messages. These frames are useful in allowing journalists to process large amounts of information quickly and routinely. But because they have been constructed from the dominant culture, they reflect, rather than challenge, its values.

Thus the media routinely divide political and social movements into legitimate and illegitimate and in doing so they apply values that they see as 'natural' or 'common sense', thus supporting Gramsci's notion that those who rule the dominant institutions secure their power largely by impressing, directly or indirectly, their definitions of situations upon those they rule or by limiting the range of what is thought throughout society. Consequently the media are likely to present, say, radical students, feminists, or environmentalists as stirrers, troublemakers, or, in the Australian idiom, ratbags, or they may accept the core of their protest but present duly constituted authority as the appropriate power to deal with it.

Media images are biased towards order. They rarely challenge the pre-eminence of the corporate economy, the militarized state, and authoritarian social relations as a whole, nor do they normally violate core hegemonic values or contribute too heavily to radical critique or social unrest:

> most of the time the taken-for-granted code of 'objectivity' and 'balance' presses reporters to seek out scruffy-looking, chanting, 'Viet Cong' flag-waving demonstrators and to counterpose them to reasonable-sounding, fact-brandishing authorities. Calm and cautionary tones of voice affirm that all 'disturbance' is or should be under control by rational authority; code words like disturbance commend the established normality ... Hotheads carry on, the message connotes, while wiser heads, officials and reporters both, with superb self-control, watch the unenlightened ones make trouble. (Gitlin, 1980, 4)

Gitlin's study of the relationship between the New Left and the mass media in the 1960s may be usefully compared with such British studies as Halloran, Elliott and Murdoch (1970) and several of the studies in Cohen and Young (1973) and also with Blumler and Ewbank (1970). For an elaboration of Gitlin's thought see Gitlin (1982) and (1983).

to recap...

Empirical evidence appears to support the Marxist view that the media have accepted the ideology of consensus. Instead of presenting the economic system as a battleground for a conflict between capital and labour, they begin from the assumption that there should be no such conflict.

activity   Select five news websites, five newspapers circulated in your area, and five celebrity magazines. Taking the front page on each, do a brief visual content analysis of the images used. How many are of men, women and children respectively? What sort of news story attaches to what image? How many of the images refer to the main 'doers' or active agents in the stories? How many refer to victims or passive players in the story? What class or social stratum of people would you say they represent? Is there a discernible 'best point of view' presented in these news and opinion sources? How does the class or gender of a person support that? Then write a short piece analysing the degree to which class and gender politics in your society match with or differ from those described in the UK in the 1970s and 1980s. Remember, there is no right or wrong answer, but we do want you first, to count carefully and second, to be highly critical in your approach to the use of images and people in the creation and distribution of meaning through news.

Critical theory

For a significant critique and departure from traditional Marxism, exhibited in some of these studies, see Steve Chibnall's sociological study, *Law and Order News: an analysis of crime reporting in the British press* (1977). Steve Chibnall interviewed fourteen specialist crime reporters representing eight of the ten Fleet Street daily and Sunday papers, which employ such specialists. He also interviewed about twenty other journalists whose experience seemed relevant to understanding law and order news. In addition, Chibnall monitored law and order news in Britain's national press from January 1971 to December 1975 (1977, 8). He used his study of this special kind of news as a way of understanding news in general and concluded that news was a form of 'commercial knowledge' – 'a saleable product designed with consumers in mind, yes, but still produced by men who retain a certain kind of integrity, who generally "believe" in their product and whose allegiances extend beyond their immediate paymasters' (1977, 223–4).

Professional communicators, for Chibnall, are not simply puppets on strings pulled by capitalists. They do not necessarily feel oppressed and they exercise choice and construct their own realities within the constraining parameters. This acceptance allows the professional communicator 'to get on with the job' of reporting the news (1977, 224). In reaching this conclusion, Chibnall rejects the simplistic approach of the traditional Marxists and finds more refined Marxist explanations inadequate. He also rejects the explanations of news offered by empirical social science:

> We might say that the difference is that social science research often fails to see the wood for the trees while Marxist approaches rarely give one the impression that the wood is composed of trees at all. The Marxist perspectives provide a valuable counter to the type of *laissez-faire* model of mass communications ... in that they unsuccessfully identify the overall political role of the media in the continuing hegemony of a capitalist class and assert the overriding importance of the media's structure of ownership and control in that process; but they generally fail to go beyond this insight. They fail to relate a political economy of mass communications to a *sociology* of mass communicators. For the most part, writers in the Marxist tradition ... seem to settle for a crude determinism relating ownership and control to the maintenance of class relations thus:

Control of mass media by capitalist interests	=	Production of dominant ideology	=	Mystification, false consciousness and the reproduction of class relations.

> (Chibnall, 1977, 207–8)

Chibnall says that the assertion by Marx and Engels in *The German Ideology* that the class that is the dominant material force in society is at the same time its dominant intellectual force, because those who control material production control mental production, fails to tell us about the orientations and motivations of professional ideologists themselves. Down to our own days, he says, Marxists have failed to analyse closely the production of knowledge at the mundane level of everyday life. Gramsci distinguished between 'traditional' professional intellectuals, administrators, scholars, scientists and theorists and 'organic' intellectuals who accompany an emergent class formation, becoming functionaries in the bureaucracies of its superstructure and contributing to its hegemony. Journalists may be considered to be members of the Ideological State Apparatus, which crams every citizen with daily doses of nationalism, chauvinism, liberalism and moralism. Miliband acknowledges that the mass media do not form an unqualified ideological monolith. They do publish a diversity of opinions and perspectives but they are, nevertheless, a 'crucial element in the legitimation of capitalist society because they have a 'passionate hostility' to anything outside the liberal-democratic consensus.

Chibnall also argues that the ideological dispositions of media owners reflect their economic interests and that these dispositions 'seep downwards' in the media hierarchy. But Chibnall says none of these Marxist interpretations explain in detail how the process of hegemony operates sociologically – at the mundane level of daily life in media organizations.

Chibnall himself develops the idea that a newspaper is a business oriented to serving advertising and that it makes news a commodity to be slickly handled and brightly packaged. The mass-circulation newspaper itself is a commodity, which creates the conditions for its reproduction by selling other commodities including news itself, which becomes a standardized commodity to be judged by the standards of the market. It presents us with a stereotyped, top-down view of reality. Nevertheless, news is not necessarily perceived as a commodity by everyone involved in its production – for some of these people it is a creative expression.

Chibnall insists that 'we cannot legitimately reduce the explanation of newspaper representations to a single causal factor' (1977, 225). When the production of news is viewed at the level of daily life it is not so simple. Similarly, the journalists who produce it are ambivalent about what they produce and how they do it:

> When combined with the routine, work-a-day nature of professional journalism, the endlessly-repeated procedures of 'newsgathering', concerns of profitability and financial shortages create a *tendency* among communicators to see news as a commodity. It remains essentially a tendency, however, rather than a permanent definition. Like most definitions of the situation, the definition of news as a commodity is probably evoked when it suits the particular purposes or mood of the definer, in this case the professional communicator. (Chibnall, 1977, 220–1)

Critical theory approaches tend to be neo-Marxist in their inflection. Generally, they focus on how radical inequalities in the distribution of rewards are presented and accepted (even by those who get least) as if this were natural and inevitable. The basic theory stems from Marx, even though he never developed a systematic theory of communication. The 'first force' school was German in origin – the Frankfurt School – and was an attack on scientific positivism and an assertion of the importance of ideology in analysing political communication. The 'second force' school began in various countries and was often non-Marxist (for example in a concern for political language).

Culture industry. Frankfurt School argument that capitalism standardizes culture under the guise of individualization.

Theorist snapshot: The Frankfurt School

The Frankfurt School represented the first Marxist attempt to analyse media. Theodore Adorno, Max Horkheimer, Herbert Marcuse, Walter Benjamin, Leo Lowenthal, Erich Fromm and Jürgen Habermas were associated with the School. The Institute for Social Research (Frankfurt School) was set up in Germany in the 1920s but some of its members fled to the US with the rise of Nazi Germany.

Adorno and Horkheimer coined the term culture industry in one of their best-known works *Dialectic of Enlightenment* to describe what they saw as the dominant means of oppression in modern society. The culture industry, they argued, standardized culture and while the culture industry promoted individualization the whole process was, in fact, designed to commodify consumers and audiences and to control them:

> Marked differentiations such as those of A and B films, or of stories in magazines in different price ranges, depend not so much on subject matter as on classifying, organizing, and labelling

consumers ... Consumers appear as statistics on research organization charts, and are divided by income groups into red, green, and blue areas; the technique is that used for any type of propaganda. (Adorno and Horkheimer, 1979, 123)

The Frankfurt School was opposed to the industrialization of culture. The culture industry they argued reflected the use of science to standardize audiences and consumers. Scientific positivism for the School was at the heart of this 'scientization' – the idea that all knowledge was quantifiable and only the application of scientific method and finding out natural laws mattered in any empirical investigation. Paul Lazarsfeld and Theodore Adorno argued exactly on this point. Lazarsfeld was one of the key founders of modern multivariate statistics and survey. Adorno doubted that these 'positivistic methods' were beneficial.

Unlike the Marxists, the neo-Marxists seek reform by democratic transformation of the prevailing conditions in the entire scope of mass communications. They want to democratize the media by changing the emphasis on materialism in media content, by dismantling the capitalist system and thus the media system, by encouraging worker participation in all areas of media production, by transferring media control from private owners to producers, by forming advertising and publicity cooperatives, and by activating the masses for 'communicative emancipation'.

Critical and neo-Marxist media theoreticians focus on the media as instruments of liberation – as means by which authentic interests of the masses can be articulated. They concentrate not on the distribution of mass communications through the mass media but on absolute societal communication about the needs and interests of the masses. But both Marxists and neo-Marxists are agreed that the ruling class, partly through the mass media, exercise hegemony over our view of the world. Although the mass media pose as neutral and impartial, they really are not. They take for granted the conventional views of society. As Richard Hoggart has said:

The fourth and most important filter – since it partly contains the others – is the cultural air we breathe, the whole ideological atmosphere of our society, which tells us that some things can be said and that others had best not be said. It is that whole and almost unconscious pressure towards implicitly affirming the status quo, towards confirming 'the ordinary man' in his existing attitudes, towards discouraging refusals to conform, that atmosphere which comes from the morning radio news-and-chat programmes as much as from the whole pattern of reader-visual background-and-words which is the context of television news. (cited in Bennett, 1982, 303)

Having noted the general areas of agreement in Marxist and neo-Marxist theory, we should also note that not all critical theory is Marxist, but almost all of it is opposed to quantitative empiricism, functionalism and positivism that dominated media analysis in the 1940s, 1950s and 1960s. In his excellent review, 'The Empirical and the Critical Schools of Communication Research' (*Communication Yearbook 5*, 1982, 124–44), Everett M. Rogers says that the empirical school of communication research has emphasized the effects of communication and paid little attention to the broad context in which communication occurs whereas the critical school emphasizes philosophy, dialectics and the broad social structural context of communication. It believes that a theory of communication is impossible without a theory of society.

Many other criticisms can be found in the 368-page special issue of the *Journal of Communication* entitled *Ferment in the Field*, **33**(3), Summer 1983) which brings together 35 essays on critical theory by 41 authors from 10 countries. Here a handful of US empiricists confront a big team of critical theorists. Generally the North Americans claim that critical research is narrow and negative. It is too concerned with media ownership and the control of communication empires. Further, it was claimed that critical theory delegitimizes western journalism, opposes empirical research and is ethically unclear and politically unrealistic. The empiricists claim the critical researchers are biased. They are politically and morally committed, play to an international crowd, make themselves sole judges of the news and rely on either Marxism or rehashed Marxism for their theoretical propositions. According to the empiricists, critical research is unscientific methodologically and logically unsound; it is seduced by big words; avoids measurement; illustrates rather than tests concepts; fails to meet empirical criteria for causality, inference and explanation; overgeneralizes from cases to classes and from individual behaviour to collectivities and vice versa.

For their part, the critical theorists rebutted these views arguing that critical research is diverse and innovative and seeks alternative models and new paradigms. Most importantly, it emphasizes issues not stressed in administrative behaviour research. These issues include the sources and exercise of power in society and the centralization of communication power. It looks at control and dominance through the media and the resulting dependency of underrepresented or oppressed groups. It is concerned with economic and political forces at all levels – structurally in production industries, ideologically in the text, motivationally among consumers. It stresses that communication cannot be isolated from its social context or from its history. *Ferment in the Field* was subjected to a systematic review by Michael Real in the *Journal of Communication* of Autumn 1984.

Generally the critical school is stronger in Europe and the empirical school stronger in the United States. The Frankfurt School was set up in Germany in 1923 with Marxism as its ruling principle but when its Jewish scholars moved to New York in 1934 they began to refer to themselves as the critical (rather than Marxist) school and in the 1950s even dropped the idea that class conflict was 'the motor of history'. And by the time some of them returned to Frankfurt in 1949 they were even integrating empirical investigations into their dialectics. Nevertheless their emphasis remains essentially philosophical and their focus remains on the broader social structural context of communication. Rogers summarizes the differences between empirical and critical traditions:

> Here we see an illustration of the contrasting orientation of empirical and critical communication scholars: (1) empirical researchers emphasize understanding communication effects on an audience, and they conduct content analysis in order to infer such effects, while (2) critical scholars emphasize understanding the control of a communication system, so they conduct content analysis in order to make inferences about mass media institutions ... [its] central concern [is] with the issue of who controls mass communication systems. (1982, 127)

Rogers also notes that empiricists tend to be optimistic: they feel that the mass media can sometimes contribute to social change at least by providing information about social problems as a first step towards solving them whereas in Europe, Marxists tend to see mass media chiefly as agents of social control that block opportunities for radical social change and prop up the status quo. For more about the critical and empirical schools in Europe, see Richard Fitchen (1981).

to recap...

Critical theory went beyond traditional social class analysis and took an interest in 'the cultural air we breathe, the whole ideological atmosphere of our society' (Hoggart cited in Bennett, 1982, 303). Critical theorists, compared with traditional Marxists, identified with democratic, rather than physical, force as the means for change.

case study

The image of Nazi Germany in many people's minds is of marching stormtroopers under the swastika – a martial and frighteningly memorable image. Leni Riefenstahl's film *The Triumph of the Will* is a classic in this genre. But this type of propaganda was far from the norm in Nazi Germany. Of the approximately 1,100 feature films produced between 1933 and 1945, 80 per cent of them were not officially coded as political by the regime. Half of all films were comedies or musicals (Reimer, 2000).

Adolf Hitler, tyrant of Nazi German's Third Reich, and Joseph Goebbels, his Minister for Propaganda, had diametrical views on propaganda and media influence. For Hitler, propaganda served purely ideological purposes first and foremost. For Goebbels, the main purpose of propaganda was entertainment. Entertainment, for the propaganda minister, could reinforce ideological propositions better than any compact ideological message.

There were reasons for Goebbels' conclusion that entertainment was the best propaganda. Anti-Jewish films like *The Eternal Jew* showed shocking scenes of rat infestations and compared the Jews with rats. The effect in the German cinemas was immediate. People threw up in or walked out of cinemas (Reimer, 2000). Goebbels had robustly opposed the film, but Hitler was adamant in showing it.

Goebbels had also gained his lessons about entertainment from the success of Leni Riefenstahl's film *Olympia*, a documentary of the 1936 Berlin Olympic Games. Riefenstahl's two-part documentary won international prizes before the outbreak of the Second World War and was a success domestically and internationally. It showed little of Nazi German ideology and even little of Adolf Hitler but was thoroughly infused with Nazi ideology with its constant iterations of mass adulation and the symbols of Nazism such as the swastika, a sun wheel symbol with a completely different meaning in Hindu culture.

View and discuss: Do you remember the musical

ADOLF HITLER AND JOSEPH GOEBBELS

'marching hyenas' sequence in Disney's *The Lion King*? The sequence quoted (visually) from the Riefenstahl films, thus employing the cinematic look and feel of Nazi power to emphasize Scar's brutality and potential for evil. Have another look at the sequence What do you make of the crescent moon 'shot' at the end of the sequence? Have the animators deliberately spliced a known image of evil with the symbol of Islam to make a more contemporary point? Is that a fair or useful approach to children's entertainment? Or, does it continue the regime of malicious propaganda, which the Frankfurt School so vehemently opposed?

The success of entertainment in conveying propaganda became especially apparent in the increasing anti-Semitism of the German people. Goebbels' entertaining films built anti-Semitism into their discourse in subtle and sometimes comic ways. Storybooks for children that drew on German folklore and contrasted the past with the present eras reinforcing existing anti-Semitic attitudes were widely distributed. For example, in *Trau keinem Fuchs auf grüner Heid und keinem Jud bei seinem Eid!* (Don't Trust a Fox in a Green Meadow or the Word of a Jew!) a fox plans to trap its prey while a Jew makes a deceitful oath under his Star of David. The film links the common and deeply held German folkoric view that neither foxes nor Jews can be trusted. In one part of the book it says quite explicitly: 'Like a fox, he slips about. So you must look out.'

Joseph Goebbels' principles of propaganda reflected the empirical research findings among the allies during the Second World War. In order to change behaviour it is best to reinforce existing attitudes rather than to make a direct appeal to change behaviour. Citizens of the Third Reich were on the whole, and as Goebbels knew, only mildly anti-Semitic when the Nazis came to power. At war's end Germans were radically exterminationist (Rees, 1992).

Anti-Semitism was – and perhaps still is – a global phenomenon. Nazi ideology is a case of false consciousness. People who deny Jewish people – or any ethnic or religious group – their humanity are deluded.

Discourse

Marxist and critical theories seek to identify the rationalities that underpin social development and social inequality and how power is exercised in social relationships. *Postmodernism* is a reaction against the idea that any rationalities can be identified and that anything can be true. Friedrich Nietzsche (1844–1900), Roland Barthes and Michel Foucault, among others, have heavily influenced the postmodern movement.

Postmodernists argue that we can only come to know reality through language or discourse or signs. 'Reality does not exist ... language is all there is and what we are talking about is language, we speak within language' (Foucault, quoted in Macey, 1994, 150). Jean Baudrillard, elaborating on principles found in Barthes's work, argues that contemporary society is one of proliferation of signs without significance. In fact, modern society has become sign-saturated, with signs about news, signs about self, signs about environment, signs about advertising, and so on. Everything has become **hyper-real**, simulations and not representations. Everything has become artifice where signs refer to nothing but themselves. 'Disneyland is presented as imaginary in order to make us believe that the rest is real, when in fact all of Los Angeles and the America surrounding it are no longer real, but of the order of the hyperreal and of simulation' (Baudrillard, 1993, 25). Nothing, for Baudrillard, is any longer authentic. Postmodernism has a strong social constructionist bent, suggesting that much of what we know is socially constructed.

The science of signs is called **semiology** or **semiotics**. There is the *signified* – that to which a word or other signifier refers and the *signifier* – that which signifies. Semiology draws on theories in linguistics as well as other traditions. Semiotics is used in media studies to analyse popular culture. Semiology acts as a direct counterpoint to content analysis in the media effects tradition. Content analysis counts units (such as word, paragraphs, and so on) and makes conclusions on the content of stories based on frequency. However, as Burgelin points out, solely focusing on frequency of occurrence of a message has its own problems:

Hyper-real. The idea that everything has become artificial and where signs refer to nothing but themselves.

Semiotics/semiology. The study or science of signs and meaning.

> But above all there is no reason to assume that the item which recurs most frequently is the most important or the most significant, for a text is, clearly, a *structured* whole, and the place occupied by the different elements is more important than the number of times they recur. Let us imagine a film in which the gangster hero is seen performing a long succession of actions, which show his character in an extremely vicious light, but he is also seen performing one single action, which reveals to a striking degree that he has finer feelings. So the gangster's actions are to be evaluated in terms of two sets of opposites: bad/good and frequent/exceptional. The polarity frequent/exceptional is perceptible at first sight and needs no quantification. Moreover we clearly cannot draw any valid inferences from a simple enumeration of his vicious acts (it makes no difference if there are ten or twenty of them) for the crux of the matter obviously is: what meaning is conferred on the vicious acts by the fact of their juxtaposition with the single good action? Only by taking into account the structural relationship of this one good action with the totality of the gangster's vicious behaviour in the film can we make any inference concerning the film as a whole. In more general terms one could say that the meaning of what is frequent is only revealed by opposition to what is rare. In other words, the meaning of a frequently-recurring item is not essentially linked to the fact that it occurs ten times rather than twenty times, but it is essentially linked to the fact that it is placed in opposition to another item which occurs rarely (or which

is sometimes even absent). The whole problem is therefore to identify this rare or absent item. (Burgelin, 1972)

Burgelin's reading of the text as a whole can, of course, be extended to the reading of the text within an ideological context. Barthes (1972) for example made the central semiological distinction between the signifier, the signified and the sign, but went further and suggested that mythology operates at another level. He gave the example of a young negro in French uniform saluting the flag on the front page of *Paris Match*. Barthes argued that beyond the immediate meaning of the picture it signifies a metalanguage, that France is a great empire, that all her people, without colour discrimination, faithfully serve her. It is in this second order semiological system that myth, and the role of ideology, is found.

Postmodernists are concerned with how power is exercised or how inequalities come about. Postmodernism, as Anthony King says in his introduction, is the 'discourse of emerging voices':

> These are the voices that literary critics call subaltern voices, that feminists have named the muted voice, that folklorists denominate the voice of the trickster or coyote, and that linguists call the code-switcher's voice. It is the voice of the periphery, not of the centre. It is the voice of the silent ones who are struggling to speak. It may be the ultimate postmodern voice – the anonymous voices of crowds, the muffled roar of rumor and of threats, or even insults and obscenities gouged on public walls. (King, 1992, 2)

Postmodern discourse, in this sense, concentrates on speakers and groups that have historically lacked access to large audiences, political apparatus, and public media. The media for King (1992) have become pivotal in using language and images to develop stereotypes and perpetuate myths. Webster thinks though that the idea of postmodernism and postmodernism as a way of life often seem to come together and, indeed, might fracture society:

> Postmodernism's emphasis on differences – in interpretation, in ways of life, in values – is in close accord with the abandonment of belief in the authentic. For instance, the postmodern outlook encourages rejection of elitisms, which proclaim a need to teach children a unifying and enriching 'common culture' or the 'great tradition' of literature. All this and similar such protestations are dismissed as ideology, instances of power being exercised by particular groups over others. However, postmodern culture goes further than this: it contends that those who fear what they regard as that fragmentation of culture if people are not taught to appreciate, say, the literature and history which tells us 'what we are' and thereby what brings us as citizens together, should be ignored. (Webster, 1995, 173)

Postmodernism is a general term which describes approaches that are opposed to ideas of laws of behaviour, behaviourist, empiricist, traditional Marxist, or otherwise. Baudrillard and Foucault are two important influences on postmodernist thought, but there are various theoretical approaches in cultural studies. The phenomenological and existential approaches are exemplified by Alfred Schutz (1962) and Karl Jaspers (1951), who coined the phrase 'truth begins with two'. Phenomenology is one of the philosophical bases for constructivism discussed in Chapter 4. Berger and Luckmann's (1976) seminal work *The Social Construction of Reality* was directly influenced by the work of Alfred Schutz. Berger and Luckman argue that humans are active interpreters of their environments and that much of what we interpret is created by social actions and meanings. A cultural studies approach, such as that made possible through phenomenology, does not seek to explain human behaviour, but to understand it. 'It does not seek to reduce human action to underlying causes or structures but to interpret its significance. It does not attempt to predict human behaviour, but to diagnose human meanings' (Carey, 1977, 418).

Theorist snapshot: Toby Miller

The work of Toby Miller exemplifies some of the new directions in which media studies has moved in recent years. There are many scholars who might be cited as innovators, but Miller is a good example of the breadth and diversity of topic and approach that are possible in the discipline. Two of his key interventions have been on sex and sport, and on cultural citizenship, particularly in respect to the idea of an 'international division of cultural labour'. These subjects can be explored in detail in his books and articles, but we will give a very brief explanation of why this kind of work is valuable to students and emerging new scholars (as we hope some of you will decide to be at the end of your first degree!).

Sex and sport may seem to be topics that, although both much deployed in media content, are not necessarily related. Toby Miller demonstrated in his book *Sportsex* (1971) that cultures surrounding sporting activity are complex, and that a key feature of this complexity is how these two themes constantly interact. Sports are central to the content of many media, providing entertainment that is visceral and visual. Male and female sports stars and team members are required to be excellent sports performers but they are also scrutinized for their physical strength and beauty. The impact of advertising and sponsorship is part of this development, but so too is the core human desire to look at other people and to consume their image. Such a desire may not be directly about sexual fulfilment, but it is very much associated with the scopophilic desires that are associated with sexuality and the pleasures of 'looking'.

In a rather different part of his work Miller has focused on migration and its role and impacts within globalization. Migration patterns, he argues, are an important part of understanding culture, and by extension, media. There are those who obtain great benefits from partial migrations, and these tend to be the wealthy cosmopolitans of the corporate world, but also those highly skilled artists and crafts-people who work in successful sectors of the arts and media. On the other hand, there are many millions of migrants who support globalization through their labour, but who derive minimal benefits – other than basic survival – and who do not draw down the rights of citizenship and belonging through the moves they make across borders and across the world. Crucially they do not earn enough money to be sufficiently valued by governments and corporations as the leading edge consumers whose choices drive policy in contemporary states and societies.

Miller's major contribution has been therefore to draw our attention to the complicity of culture and media industries in these uneven experiences of global development.

We have chosen Miller as an example because he works on the political, social and cultural aspects of media. He is as interested in how footballers hug one another in public displays of joy when they score a goal, as he is vigilant in documenting the fates of those who cannot easily access the benefits of consumption-led wealth but whose labour is nonetheless central to the infrastructure underpinning such wealth.

The public sphere

Public sphere. An institutionally guaranteed space where people can communicate without threats or force.

Second force Frankfurt School theorist Jürgen Habermas (1962) went further than his counterparts and sought a theory of communicative action. Habermas's idea of the public sphere or *Öffentlichkeit* emerged out of his historical analysis of the emergence of communicative spaces over time. The concept of the public sphere has become influential in debates about how structures can be created and maintained to ensure that people can communicate freely.

The ideal public sphere is an institutionally guaranteed space where people can communicate without their communication being distorted by threats or by force. Centres of sociability in the 19th century like coffee houses in London and taverns all over Britain were public-sphere-like for Habermas because they were places where serious and not so serious business could be discussed without traditional political constraints. Note, though, women were not normally allowed in these particular communicative spaces, or if they were, tended to be working as servers rather than joining the conversation. This is relevant to the question of who gets included in a public sphere, an issue that is still of genuine interest to media studies scholars. Women were, though, a part of the circulating libraries of the poor and Habermas would count these as part of a public sphere.

Traditional public service broadcasting, like the BBC (British Broadcasting Service), ABC (Australian Broadcasting Service) and PBS (Public Broadcasting Services) in the USA, also has public sphere characteristics because it has a constitutionally and legislatively guaranteed space where governments cannot, or are expected not to, interfere in the freedom of the broadcaster in its day to day work. Habermas's theory is discussed further in the next chapter.

Habermas shares many of the Frankfurt School concerns with capitalist control over communicative practices. However, he is more optimistic about the possibilities of genuine communication than the idea of the culture industry allows in Adorno and Horkheimer's work.

activity Use online resources to investigate the models of funding for the BBC, the ABC and PBS. If you live somewhere else with a publicly owned broadcasting service, look at that situation as well. The questions you should be asking are:

Who funds the broadcaster?

What evidence of (a) freedom of expression and (b) constraints on freedom are available for research: through a case study, or through its constituted codes of practice, or perhaps in vision statements?

What value does such a constituted broadcast system bring to society, and how important would you say that it is to a functioning public sphere?

The Marxist and postmodernist traditions are often labelled by their opponents as 'non-empirical' or 'grand theoretical' because they do not rely heavily on fieldwork data. The effects tradition, addressed in the Chapter 4, is often labelled pluralist by Marxists, because it conceives of power as distributed across different groups in society, shifting over time and issues:

> The pluralists see society as a complex of competing groups and interests, none of them predominant all the time, in which alignments shift from issue to issue and from time to time. Media organizations are seen as bounded organizational systems, enjoying an important degree of autonomy from the state, political parties and institutionalized pressure groups. Control of the media is said to be in the hands of an autonomous managerial elite who allow a considerable degree of flexibility to media professionals. (Open University, 1977, Unit 7/8, 4–5)

Different perceptions of the power of the media often stem from different definitions of what constitutes 'effects', rather than from disagreement about the consequences of media in society. For example, both Marxist and pluralist perspectives on media effects can agree on issues of enforcement of social norms. However, the Marxist perspective is that of mass media as part of a powerful ideological apparatus within the class relationship of capitalist society. This focus on ideology represents a fundamental rift between Marxist and pluralist approaches to media research.

There are also rifts in Marxist thought. Traditional Marxism is concerned with the structural effects of capitalist society. It argues that these structures and the laws that govern them can be studied scientifically. 'Natural science will eventually subsume the science of man [*sic*] just as the science of man will subsume natural science: there will be a single science' (Marx, cited in Habermas, 1981, 46). Orthodox Marxism holds that there are absolute truths about capitalist society and class conflict. *Poststructural* Marxism, on the other hand, is concerned more with hegemony and discourse and how people come to believe that capitalism is a natural way of life rather than laws or truths of history that govern capitalist development.

All Marxist approaches to media analysis adopt a 'grand-theoretical' position in which both the issues and the methodologies for exploring media are explicitly taken from an over-arching theory of society. This is the opposite of the media effects tradition which sees itself as holding an empirically based conception of the media in which theorizing is subject to modifications and revisions based on empirical research findings (Open University, 1977, 65).

At the conclusion of this chapter you should be able to:
- distinguish between the traditional Marxist and the neo-Marxist positions on media influence;
- critically apply the ideas of ideology and hegemony to the operations of modern media;
- critically discuss the rise of postmodern ideas on media influence, especially the role of signs and meaning.

Social class. Marxist approaches to media analysis look at the role of social class in influencing media structures and organizations and individuals. Traditional Marxist analysis holds that there are scientific laws governing how social class works. Base and superstructure interact, but it is the material needs of society that drive development, the future and how we think. In its raw form this approach is deterministic. Neo-Marxist approaches, like the Frankfurt School, focus more on the superstructure – culture and media in particular – and their relationship to capitalism and domination. Both Maxist and neo-Marxist traditions brought ideology, power and legitimation to the fore in media analysis. Issues of social class and inequality have not disappeared.

Postmodernism and poststructuralism. Postmodernism is a general term which describes approaches that are opposed to ideas of laws of behaviour and reality, whether behaviourist, empiricist, or traditional Marxist. Poststructuralism, similarly, holds that there are no law-like structures in human society. Postmodernists and poststructuralists hold that power certainly exists in society but it is maintained through the discursive or semiotic practices that occur in everyday life. Cultural studies, as a discipline, draws on a range of perspectives in its analysis of media.

Discussion questions

1 Marx employed a base/superstructure model. Describe this model and discuss some of the advantages/problems when applying it to the study of the influence of media on society.

2 Pick a specific kind of 'deviance' identified by the media as deviant behaviour. What patterns do the media follow? How is the issue:
   • identified;
   • contrasted with normal behaviour;
   • linked to other problems;
   • part of calls for something to be done.
   Does the treatment of deviance align with elite or ruling class interests?

3 Select a media news programme – through traditional or new media. Try to identify the unexamined assumptions that limit the terms of the discussion (ask yourself what issues are NOT raised). Try to identify the key concepts, especially those with political content, whose meaning is taken for granted.

4 Select a given media news story that is running in traditional and new media (with the Internet this can include blogs as well as commercial outlets). Monitor the story for two to three nights in succession and try to identify those working habits and conventions that seem to you to be bound to ideological assumptions or that seem to give rise to ideological outcomes. Be sure that you pay attention to as many aspects of the news message as possible – the news script itself, visual material, the relationship between the two, interviewing techniques, narrative style, the semiotics of the newsdesk, and so on. Do blogs provide more objective accounts?

5 Who are the elites in your society? Do they influence the nature of content in media? Give examples.

6 Choose a series of items from popular literature or television or the Internet (for example detective/police stories, love stories, and so on). In what ways would you say that the narrative patterns in that literature embody 'ideology' or 'mythology', in Barthes's sense?

7 In the 1996 Massey Lectures, John Ralston Saul (*The Unconscious Civilization*, Penguin 1977) argued that the world in the 20th century had been gripped by a series of holistic ideologies and all had failed. Is the current popular ideology of corporatism (let free markets determine everything) a better analytical tool?

activity   Choose one of the following theorists and thinkers (or find another in conversation with your lecturer) in media and communications studies (we have included media anthropology as well). Research and read as much of their work as you can: books, media interviews, journal articles, research reports, and opinion pieces. Write a short account of their work to date and why it is influential in the field in general, and what impact it has on the way you think about media. Report back to tutorial at the end of semester.

Sonia Livingstone	Jing Wang	John Hartley	Mick Taussig
Roger Silverstone	Laura Mulvey	Faye Ginsburg	Simon During
Manuel Castells	David Buckingham	Toby Miller	Howard Tumber
James Katz	Graeme Turner	Geert Lovink	James Curran

Further reading

Carey, J. (1977). Mass communication research and cultural studies: an American view. In J. Curran, M. Gurevitch and J. Woollacott (eds) *Mass communication and society* (409–26). Edward Arnold in association with Open University Press.

Couldry, N. and Curran, J. (eds) (2003). *Contesting media power: Alternative media in a networked world*. Feldham: Rowman and Littlefield.

Miller, T. (2001). *Sportsex*. Philadelphia: Temple University Press.

Miller, T. (1998). *Technologies of truth: Cultural citizenship and the popular media*. Minneapolis: University of Minnesota Press.

Miller, T., Govil, N., McMurria, J. and Maxwell, R. (2001). *Global Hollywood*. London: British Film Institute.

O'Sullivan, T., Hartley, J., Saunders, D. and Fiske, J. (1998). *Key concepts in communication and cultural studies*. London: Routledge.

Williams, R. (1985). *Keywords: a vocabulary of culture and society*. Oxford: Oxford University Press.

Classics in reasoning about information and its ownership

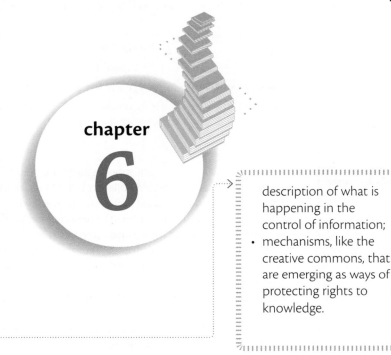

chapter

6

This chapter will introduce you to the:
- major styles of reasoning about information;
- concepts of copyright and the public domain;
- idea of a second enclosure as a

description of what is happening in the control of information;
- mechanisms, like the creative commons, that are emerging as ways of protecting rights to knowledge.

Chapters 4 and 5 introduced the concept of active audiences or active interpreters. They also introduced the ideas of ideology and hegemony that relate directly to issues in media and in the power that media create. Information, its ownership and its control are an important part of theorizing in media studies and in understanding important issues in media globalization. However, the first step in understanding ownership of information is to grasp the *conceptions* or *discourses* on information. This chapter will introduce you to the:

- major styles of reasoning about information;
- concepts of copyright and the public domain;
- idea of a second enclosure as a description of what is happening in the control of information;
- mechanisms, like the creative commons, that are emerging as ways of protecting rights to knowledge.

The principle that ideas are free has a long history in the philosophy and law of democracy. This principle has led to legal paradigms that aim to strike a balance between public and private ownership of creativity. Copyright and patent laws hold that the community owns knowledge, while authors are granted temporary rights to make money from their creations. Protecting this principle has become problematic because 'information' is now treated as a highly prized commodity. Many people state that we live in an information age, a statement that explicitly values knowledge above other forms of wealth. 'Information', though, is a complex phenomenon and talking about 'ownership' is equally problematic. In this chapter we look at the key debates about ownership of information and definition of information.

The reality of information

Who owns information is the underlying problem in any debate about global inequalities in access to and use of information. This raises an obvious problem. What is information? Balnaves and Caputi (2000) proposed a way of investigating different styles of reasoning about social phenomena. Their theory provides a framework for understanding how people construe things as 'natural'. They give an illustration of how Christians in Nazi Germany reasoned about Jewishness. For example, in *The Information Bulletin of the Reich Association of Aryan Christians* there were question/answer segments to problems of what constituted 'Aryan'. Think about it as a vicious caricature of the 'problems page' in a women's magazine.

> Question: A man has two Jewish grandparents, one Aryan grandmother and a half-Aryan grandfather; the latter was born Jewish and became Christian only later. Is this 62 percent Jewish person a Mischling or a Jew?

> Answer: The man is a Jew according to the Nuremburg Laws because of the one grandparent who was of the Jewish religion; this grandparent is assumed to have been a full Jew and this assumption cannot be contested. So this 62 percent Jew has three full Jewish grandparents. On the other hand, if the half-Aryan grandfather had been Christian by birth, he would not then have been a full Jew and would not have counted at all for this calculation; his grandson would have been a Mischling of the First Degree. (Friedlander, 1997, 158)

Being a Mischling meant survival, of course. Mischling were treated better than full Jews. There is no natural law to which we can refer to determine the quantity 'Jewishness'. The quantities are determined by what Balnaves and Caputi (2000) call 'corporate constructs', systems of styles of reasoning about Jewishness.

'Information' as a phenomenon may be real in the same way that 'Jewishness' is real in Nazi Germany. It is tempting to think of 'information' as real in the same way as natural phenomena are thought to be real. Such assumptions need scrutiny. This chapter will provide an overview of how some disciplines construe 'information'. It will show how disciplines define 'information', the reasons for those definitions, and their effects on the way we think about 'information'. The authors are interested in the 'scheme of reference', much in the way Hacking (1983) was interested in styles of reasoning, established by disciplines when dealing with information as a construct and how each discipline anticipates the phenomenon 'information'. The authors argue that any measurement of the value of information, whether individual or organizational, national or international, is dependent upon styles of reasoning about the reality of information. These styles of reasoning affect directly the choice of empirical indicators for measuring information. They also affect how we understand the nature of society and mind and the effects of global information flows on culture.

Reflection Have you experienced a 'house' system at school or college? What are the effects of being put in a 'house' or named fraternity or sorority? Do assumptions of value and correct behaviour arise from this membership? How would you evaluate this knowledge from your current perspective?

Styles of reasoning about information

Styles of reasoning about information can be found at definitional level. *Lord of the Rings* has a good everyday conception of 'information':

> 'But I should like to know –' Pippin began.
>
> 'Mercy!' cried Gandalf. 'If the giving of information is to be the cure of your inquisitiveness, I shall spend all the rest of my days in answering you.' (Tolkien, 1965, 260)

Tolkien's definition of 'information' as 'answers to questions' is a common and perhaps the simplest conception of 'information' we are likely to encounter in the literature. When we enter disciplines associated with the construct 'information', however, we encounter specific theoretic frameworks. Usage of the term 'information' varies widely. For example:

- *Data:* 'Information ... is essentially raw data. Knowledge is interpreted data' (Kochen, 1983, 49).
- *Decision-making:* 'The information contained in a decision-state is related to the mean square variance of the expected values of the courses of action' (Yovits and Abilock, 1974, 166).
- *Information transfer:* 'Inherent in at least one set of definitions of the words "knowledge" and "information" is the concept that an item of knowledge becomes an item of information, when it is set in motion' (Murdock and Liston, 1967, 197).
- *Perception:* Information is 'the experience arising from the direction of attention through the gestures of others to objects and their characteristics and cannot be called "knowledge" ... Perception is not itself to be distinguished from information' (Mead, 1938, 54–5).
- *Propositions:* 'Ontologically information is propositions' (Fox, 1983, 12).
- *Resource:* (where no formal definition has been supplied) 'This information decade will be the effort to bridge the widening information gap between supply and demand and to curb the technically speaking high under consumption of information' (Coltoff, 1984).
- *State-change:* 'The information of *s* is the amount of uncertainty we are relieved of when we come to know that *s* is true' (Hintikka, 1968, 312). Information is 'the alteration of the Image which occurs when it receives a message. Information is thus an event which occurs at some unique point in time and space to some particular individual ... [It is] that-which-occurs-within-the-mind-upon-absorption-of-a-message' (Pratt, 1977, 215).

According to Levitan (1980, 244) 'information' is infinitely variable in that it characterizes every different subject one is able to recognize and 'it is ubiquitous in that it pertains to everything.' Conventionally, information carries with it a variety of meanings ranging from news to acts of informing or conveying. The Latin word *forma* is derived from the Sanskrit word *dhar*. *Forma* means shape, figure or contour. The verb *formo* means to give form to something, to form an idea of a thing, to sketch or represent (Lewis and Short, 1900, 768). Modern meanings of information tend to be more discipline dependent. The definitions above suggest that there are significant differences in conceptions about the reality of information – what information is and what information does. The authors will now turn to the reasoning behind different conceptions of the reality of information.

Information as the medium

'Information theory' has become associated not only with the coding and transmission of signals, but also with the construct of 'uncertainty' or 'curtailment of variance' of a human's mind or cognitive state, that is, the human receiver of a message. Campbell (1982, 61) said, for example, that a message conveys no information unless some prior uncertainty exists in the mind of the receiver about what the message will contain. Similarly, according to Sampson, 'it seems intuitively plausible that receipt of a less likely message conveys more information' (1976, 9).

Claude Shannon, an electronic engineer, is often held up by European scholars as an example of how *not* to think about media studies and by early United States' scholars as an example of how human communication works. Many models of communication in mass communication textbooks talk about send-message-receiver as a basic model of communication and cite Shannon's mathematical work in communication theory for electronic transmission as the source. The authors will use some of the logic involved in Shannon's information theory because an understanding of the scheme of reference in information theory requires an understanding of the techniques used.

Shannon's schematic diagram of the communication system is well known. The system consists of information source, transmitter, channel, receiver and destination (Shannon and Weaver, 1964, 33–4). 'Noise' we are normally told constitutes a distortion of the message. It is worthwhile outlining basic details of signal transmission. Imagine there is a head office in London and a branch office in Paris connected by a simple telegraph line. (If you do not know what a telegraph line means, think of a simple wireless transmission method, crude now but revolutionary in the 1890s!) Once every second along this line, from London to Paris, travels a signal. The signals repeat exactly the same pattern and we are unable to stop and start the stream of signals. From the engineering point of view no information has been sent on this channel because it is impossible to vary the pattern of the signal. Where there is a variation of the pattern there is information. In Shannon's mathematics, information is measured, for the source, by the number of alternative messages at the source's disposal. For the receiver, information is measured by the degree of initial uncertainty as to which of several alternative messages will be sent. The greater the number of messages available to the transmitter, the greater the initial uncertainty at the receiver.

Lathi provided the following example. In a morning paper there are three headlines: (1) Tomorrow the sun will rise in the east; (2) United States invades Cuba; and (3) Cuba invades the United States. 'If we look at the probabilities of occurrence of these three events we find that the probability of occurrence of the first event is unity (a certain event), that of the second is very low (an event of small but finite probability), and that of the third is practically zero (an almost impossible event)' (1983, 608). Information is, in this context, connected with the element of surprise, which is the result of uncertainty or unexpectedness (Lathi, 1983, 608).

Campbell (1982, 61) argued that probability measures both knowledge and ignorance, just as Shannon's entropy does. If entropy is a maximum, that is to say, if all the possible messages are equally probable, then an individual's ignorance is also a maximum (Campbell, 1982, 63). The engineering and commonsense viewpoints converge, says Lathi, on the notion of *source choice*. In the ideal system, where source and destination begin from the same set of presumptions, the receiver's uncertainty about the transmitted message is equal to the source's freedom of choice in constructing the message.

However, *amount of meaning* and *amount of information* are not equivalent in this context. For example, the statement 'Mark is a mammal' is less probable in normal conversational English than the statement 'Mark is a man'. Yet it is not reasonable to assume that because the statement 'Mark is a mammal' is less probable in conversation it is, therefore, more informative. Nonsense sequences or structures require as much information as do those that carry functional meaning (Wicken, 1987). Preoccupation with entropy does not allow us to deal with the semantic content of particular messages in Shannon's theory. According to Shannon, the fundamental problem of communication from an engineer's point of view is the reproduction at one point, either exactly or approximately, of a message selected at another point. The semantic aspects of this communication are 'irrelevant to the engineering problem' (Shannon and Weaver, 1964, 31). Information theory is not associated with the meaning of the message, or the message itself, but rather with the probabilities associated with the message.

For Shannon, in electronic engineering accuracy of signals is important. The signal received should be the signal sent. Shannon used specialized techniques in mathematics and engineering in order to measure signals. Shannon identifies information with the media that carry it. In Shannon's discourse 'information' is the signals and the probabilities associated with signals. For Shannon, information is not separate from the media that carry it. The authors will call this perspective *Information as the Medium*.

The idea that information and the media that carry it are identical can be found in other disciplines. For example, the information retrieval expert Lancaster holds that an information retrieval system 'does not inform (i.e., change the knowledge of) the user on the subject of his [*sic*] inquiry. It merely informs him of the existence (or nonexistence) and whereabouts of documents relating to his request' (1968, 1). Metcalfe (1959) also argued it would be a mistake to suggest that information retrieval systems, through manipulation, create new knowledge. It had been suggested that there would have been much earlier discovery of DDT as an insecticide if there had been coordinate indexing of documents on DDT and on insecticides. But 'this is utter nonsense. Until there was an experiment about 1939 in which DDT was rediscovered and found for the first time to be insecticidal, and until there was a document stating this, information on it could not be retrieved because it had not been put into a document and didn't even exist as knowledge' (Metcalfe, 1959, 203).

Van Rijsbergen (1975, 1), on the computer side of information retrieval, accorded with the view that one can adequately describe information in information retrieval by simply substituting 'document' for 'information'. He also took the view that information retrieval systems do not inform, but rather locate documents that are relevant to a request. This perspective accords with the non-realist perspective of Shannon. Information is not real in the same way that informed people are real. Information retrieval creates systems that provide an adequate indication to documents – the document retrieved is the document sought. Electronic engineering creates systems that provide adequate transfer of signals – the signals sent are the signals received.

Information as order

Norbert Wiener is an example of realist styles of reasoning about information. Wiener was one of the founders of information theory and variants of his cybernetic approach can be found in various contemporary works. Wiener classed communication and control together:

> Why did I do this? When I communicate with another person, I impart a message to him [*sic*], and when he communicates back with me he returns a related message which contains information primarily accessible to him and not to me. When I control the actions of another person, I communicate a message to him. (1950, 24)

This process is regarded by Wiener as the essence of the rational being's life (1950, 27). The structure of the human mind, following the principle of feedback, is an index of the performance expected from it. Wiener argued that society can be understood only through a study of the messages and the communicative means that belong to it. The fundamental idea of communication is that of transmission of messages (1950, 141). (For the cybernetician, the human body is information that could, in theory, be transmitted over the telephone line.)

A message, in cybernetics, is form or organization, but the form is not incorruptible. Sets of messages have entropy like sets of states in the external world. Just as entropy is a measure of disorganization, the information carried by a set of messages is a measure of organization. It is possible, therefore, to interpret the information carried by a message as, essentially, the negative of its entropy, and the negative logarithm of its probability (Wiener, 1950, 131). One might still ask of Wiener: what is information? 'It emerges through effector organs, generally [our] muscles. These in turn act on the external world, and also react on the central nervous system through receptor organs such as the end organs of kinaesthesia; and the information received by the kinaesthetic organs is combined with [our] already accumulated store of information to influence future action' (1950, 26). A kinaesthetic sense is a record of the positions and tensions of muscles (1950, 35). The term kinaesthesia refers to movement, so we can say from this that knowledge is dependent on movement. From this we can metaphorically infer that knowledge is *dynamic*, and that it is *changeable* both in time and space.

In the afterword of Wiener's *The Human Use of Human Beings* it says that there is little point in 'deriving here the mathematical formula in the manner of information theorists' (1950, 277). The 'commodity' that circulates in a communication system for Wiener no matter what its physical form, is *information* (1950, 277). Information is, in this view, the content of that which is exchanged with the outer world as we adjust to that world and make our adjustments felt upon it. 'The process of using information is the process of our adjusting to the contingencies of the outer environment, and of living with that environment ... To live adequately is to have adequate information' (1950, 26–7). Again, while Wiener sees information as a physical thing that leads to social order, we also see that *adjustment*, *movement*, *dynamism* and *process* must be factored into any discussion of knowledge and knowledge transmission between rational beings.

The amount of information held by an individual is not to be equated with the amount of information held by the community. 'Whatever means of communication the race [humans] may have, it is possible to define and to measure the amount of information available to the race, and to distinguish it from the amount of information available to the individual ... Certainly, no information available to the individual is also available to the race, unless it modifies the behaviour of one individual to another' (Wiener, 1951, 183). Indeed, a community tends to have less information than any one individual. 'In connection with the effective amount of communal information, one of the most surprising facts about the body politic is its extreme lack of efficient homeo-static processes' (1951, 185). Wiener's idea is counterintuitive here – the community collection of knowledge is greater than the individual.

A signal or code is not to be equated with information under Wiener's analysis. The odours perceived by an ant may appear to lead to standardized conduct, 'but the value of a simple stimulus ... for conveying information depends, not only on the information conveyed by the stimulus itself, but in the whole nervous constitution of the sender and the receiver of the stimulus' (Wiener, 1951, 183). Without a code of sign language all I need to do is to be alert to those moments when another shows signs of interest or emotion; that is to say, a signal does not require intrinsic content (1951, 183).

Wiener expressed a concern for order and disorder, organization and disorganization. His concern is with negative entropy. Beniger, in a more recent study, supported Wiener's thesis. He said that the subject matter of the social and behavioural sciences, if they are to complement studies of the flows of matter (input–output) economics and energy (ecology) 'ought to be information: its generation, storage, processing, and communication to effect control' (Beniger, 1986, 38). The authors will call this style of reasoning about information *Information as Order*. It is characteristic of theorists within this style to conceive of all human communication and society as a move toward order, organization and equilibrium. Information is a real entity, merely instantiated in individual acts of informing or being informed. It moves all human society toward order.

activity Why might information conceived as order – or even social order – be a dangerous assumption to make? Why would a move towards 'order' in Nature be the same as a move towards 'order' in a society? Is, indeed, Nature organized? Or is it dynamic? How do you discover new information and is it necessarily orderly? Look up and list some famous examples where new ideas have emerged. What benefits of order, or just change, did those new ideas make possible?

Information as cognitions

Styles of reasoning about information in computer science differ from cybernetic conceptions of information in electronic engineering and the more speculative ideas of those like Wiener. The interest taken by artificial intelligence scholars in cognitive psychology during the 1950s signalled a fundamental change in computer science. 'The key to the chance was the concept of *information*' (Cohen and Feigenbaum, 1982, 5). Research into short-term memory indicated that measurements of memory are best made in terms of 'semantic *chunks* – meaningful units of information – not abstract *bits*' (Cohen and Feigenbaum, 1982, 5). The result of this shift in emphasis was that Shannon's mathematical formulation 'has been largely abandoned' (1982, 5).

Minsky (1979, 400), one of the founders of artificial intelligence research, said that computer science attempts to understand ways in which information processes act and interact. Information processes means the processes involved in knowledge representation. Levesque characterized the knowledge representation hypothesis as follows: 'Just as there is a calculus of arithmetic, where numerical expressions are formally manipulated in a value-preserving way, so might there be a calculus of thought, where propositional expressions could be formally manipulated in a truth preserving way' (1986, 257).

In Marvin Minsky's theory our thoughts are largely shaped by things that seem most similar. Standard situations are 'frames'. Each type of knowledge needs some form of 'representation' and a body of skills adapted to using that style of representation (Minsky, 1987, 72). Mind is made up of 'agents' who turn other agents on and off in a 'society of mind'. Agents form into agencies. 'When you drive a car, you regard the steering wheel as an agency that you can use to change the car's direction. You don't care how it works. But when something goes wrong with the steering, and you want to understand what's happening, it's better to regard the steering wheel as just one agent in a larger agency' (1987, 23). A frame is a skeleton, like an application form, with many blanks or slots to be filled. 'We'll call these blanks its *terminals*; we use them as connection points to which we can attach other kinds of information' (1987, 245). For example, a frame that represents a table might have terminals to represent the top, legs, and so on.

Mind is described by Minsky in terms of goal-directedness, effort of processing stimuli and problem solving. Information is realized in the act of comparing, examining, relating, distinguishing, abstracting, deducing, demonstrating – all of which are forms of intellectual effort. The end result, cognitions, guarantees the agent a better representation of the world. It is the effort of processing that is, in some sense, a guarantee of the material truth of the information acquired.

Bobrow and Hayes assessed the state of the art of artificial intelligence research in 1985 and cited an interesting comment by Newell as the best expression of the intention of the discipline:

> One of the world's deepest mysteries – the nature of mind – is at the centre of AI. It is our holy grail. Its discovery ... will be a major chapter in the scientific advance of mankind ... There will be a coherent account of the nature of intelligence, knowledge, intention, desire, etc., and how it is possible for the phenomena that cluster under these names to occur in our physical universe. (Bobrow and Hayes, 1985, 388).

What we call consciousness for those like Minksy consists of little more than 'menu lists that flash, from time to time, on mental screen displays that other systems use' (Minsky, 1987, 57). The authors will call this style of reasoning *Information as Cognitions*. It is characteristic of this style of reasoning to assess the value of information solely in terms of decision-making or problem solving.

Information as uncertainty

According to Wilbur Schramm, communication research in the United States is concerned with *all the ways* in which ideas are exchanged and shared: 'Thus we are talking about both mass and interpersonal communication. We are talking about the spoken word, signal, gesture, picture, visual display, print, broadcast, film – all the signs and symbols by which humans try to convey meaning and value to one another' (1963, 6). Schramm's description of the process of human communication is interesting. In its simplest form, he said, the communication process consists of a sender, a message, and a receiver. The sender and the receiver may even be the *same person*, 'as happens when an individual thinks, or talks to himself. But the message is at some stage in the process separate from either sender or receiver. There comes a time when whatever we communicate is merely a sign that stands for some meaning to the sender and that stands to the receiver for whatever meaning he reads into it' (1963, 7).

Some internal activity precedes the offering of signals or signs or messages. 'One must feel a reason for communicating in the first place' (Schramm, 1973, 48). That internal activity involves 'information processing' and results in message encoding and 'giving orders to the musculators of the body that produce the signs' (1973, 48). According to Schramm, this is a Type A communication act. When someone makes use of the signs or signals, this is called a Type B communication act: 'That is, someone must direct his [sic] attention to them, extract certain information from them through his sensory channels and (in his black box) process that information' (1973, 48). Signals have the capacity to represent. These signals, at some point in the process, fall out of our control. 'For a moment it may seem strange to think of the signs as being separate. Yet if we recall one of our own common experiences with communication – mailing a letter or a manuscript and then wishing one had it back to make some changes or perhaps to reconsider whether to send it at all – we can understand this situation' (Schramm, 1973, 49).

Schramm (1973, 38) wrote that information is the 'stuff' of human communication. By information, he did not mean facts or truth nor did he mean instruction or the kind of knowledge we find in an encyclopaedia. 'We are using the term in a way not unlike that in which Shannon and Wiener used it when they wrote about information theory and cybernetics, anything that reduces the uncertainty of a situation … This idea has influenced the thinking of scholars who know little of physics and engineering and who have never "looked an information-theory formula in the face"' (1973, 38). But Schramm's interpretation of Shannon is suspect. For example, for Shannon, a bit is a useful device for calculation; for Schramm a bit is that which *resolves uncertainty*. We should also be suspect of Schramm's original claim that information that resolves uncertainty includes cultural interventions and acts of communication, like film. Many have argued that a film contains bits of information that resolve uncertainty, that the viewers do indeed apply cognitive means to comprehend those bits, but that notwithstanding all this, a film may also be about uncertainty on the plane of the human psyche, where formations of fantasy are more cogent than verifiable information or narrative.

The influence of the 'uncertainty', or 'negative entropy', approach should not be underestimated. In pChina, social scientists have adopted the conception with vigour (Li Ming, 1985). Schramm is not alone in his interpretation of information theory. Krippendorf, for example, wrote:

> The second concept in the title of this paper is information. By this I do not mean a statement of fact (as opposed to entertainment or pleasure), knowledge about the world, or the content a message conveys. Although facts, knowledge, and message content involve information in some way, I find it useful to regard information as a change in *an observer's state of uncertainty* caused by some event in this world. This conception of information is not new, although its process nature is rarely realized. By way of explanation, let me compare information with the more acceptable concept of energy: I would suggest that information is related to uncertainty as energy is related to matter. (1984, 49)

The authors will call the style of reasoning of those like Schramm *Information as Uncertainty* because we are dealing with individual decision-making but information is still conceived as an external force. In this style of reasoning information is a real entity leading to decision-making and resolution of uncertainty in individuals.

Information as code

Schramm also argues that a *message* is *encoded* into a *natural language sign*. We are to think of signs as encoding the messages they convey. We have to interpret the sign in order to decode the message. The assumption is that we cannot directly say what we wish. The authors will call this style of reasoning *Information as Code*. It is common. It is characteristic of this style of reasoning to treat language as a channel. Thoughts must be sent off across a gap (in introspection or human interaction). At the other side of a 'gap' we must interpret the sign within which thoughts are encoded in order to decipher the message. This reasoning about information thoroughly separates subject and object. It gives the impression that meaning is *fixed* in the object (message) by a code and not through the justifying practices that operate among us. It is worthwhile reasserting evidence from the literature in this regard:

> Words emerge in acts of encoding and decoding, and as tools of message transmission in a shared non-linguistic world ... What is being conveyed, however, are *not* word meanings. (Rommetveit, 1968, 304–5)

In the work of Schramm it is 'signs' or 'codes' or 'messages' that bridge a 'gap' between two individuals, or between one thought and another, in the process of communication. We are asked to believe that *messages* are *encoded* in language signs by a sender and transmitted by *sounds* to a receiver. The message is *deciphered* by a receiver capable of *interpreting* the sign. Schramm would argue that we come to understand what someone is saying by the *way* it is said.

Information as being informed

Styles of reasoning about information in the cultural studies tradition entail an explicit rejection of cybernetic ideas about information. According to Jonas, for example, whether individual or social, intentional action in the case of humanity may well be 'in a sense very different from cybernetics, *in-formation*' (1953, 192).

> It is I who let certain 'messages' count as 'information', and as such make them influence my action. The mere feedback from sense-organs does not motivate behaviour, in other words, sentience and motility alone are not enough for purposive action – not even for the original conditioning of reflexes which once set up, may then substitute for purposive action. (Jonas, 1953, 185)

Information exists in a community of interpretation in use. In this sense, information is not located in the individual or outside the individual in some physical form. The authors will call this style of reasoning *Information as Being Informed* because it is characteristic of this scheme of reference to consider information as both individual and public. Information does not exist by transmission or by communication but *in* transmission and *in* communication.

Speech according to the German political philosopher Jürgen Habermas reflects a twofold structure of work and interaction. He attempted to outline the universal conditions that apply to all speech acts. Instrumental action (work) entails *perlocutionary* aims, and communicative action (interaction) entails *illocutionary* aims. Perlocutionary effects exist under descriptions of states of affairs brought about through intervention in the world. Illocutionary effects are achieved through interpersonal relations in which participants 'come to an understanding with one another about something in the world' (Habermas, 1984, 290). Speech acts serve to establish and renew interpersonal relationships; represent states and events; and make experiences manifest (1984, 75–101). All speech acts oriented to reaching understanding are subject to validity claims, that the statement made is true; that the speech act is right with respect to the existing normative context; and that the manifest intention of the speaker is meant as it is expressed (1984, 99).

activity If you are familiar with theatre scripts you might think about examining some classic dialogues, just a few lines, and work out what kinds of aims and motivations lie inside the text. Think about the decisions you would need to make about the lines if you were an actor. Harold Pinter, William Shakespeare and David Hare are all good starting points. Then, move on to films by the Coen Brothers, and Hal Hartley, and try the same exercise there.

While Habermas used the term 'communication' to refer to 'interaction', he also made the concept of 'intention' primary. The communicative intent of the speaker is basic to critical theory. Intentions are the basis of interaction. Illocutionary aims of speech acts are achieved when *all* participants 'harmonize their individual plans of action with one another and thus pursue their illocutionary aims *without reservation*' (Habermas, 1984, 294). Habermas's work is essentially about moral conduct. Human communication that does not allow freedom and participation is systematically distorted. Emancipatory interest is that realm of reason that seeks to ensure autonomy and responsibility and a balance of interests. 'A speaker can pursue perlocutionary aims only when he deceives his [*sic*] partner concerning the fact that he is acting strategically – when, for example, he gives the command to attack in order to get his troops to rush into a trap' (Habermas, 1984, 294).

Information as commodity

Styles of reasoning about information as a commodity are the opposite of Habermas's ideas about the ideal speech situation. Commodity notions about information are not necessarily discipline-specific. According to Black and Marchand (1982, 2), the problem of assessing the value of information is fundamentally due to the scope and imprecision of the terms used to describe information. Lytle has written that 'as every library science student knows, no sound theoretical or practical means have been found to establish the value of information for an individual or an organization' (1986, 319). In information policy (and information economics) literature it is generally agreed that information is a vague concept, difficult to operationalize. For the United States National Commission on Libraries and Information Science (NCLIS) task force report on public sector/private sector interaction in providing information services, for example, the concept 'information' 'appeared and was generally understood to refer to the content or symbolic substance of a communication, as separate from the physical form in which the communication occurred. But despite the appearance of a general understanding of the term, it simply eluded definition' (NCLIS, 1982, 16). One resolution of this dilemma, adopted by task force members, was to treat information 'as a commodity, as a tool for better management of tangible resources, as an economic resource in and of itself' (NCLIS, 1982, 26).

There have been two major developments in the information policy literature. The first involved a resurgence of the entrepreneurial ethic. The second involved the perception of information as a saleable commodity. 'In 1985 one can state that "information is a valuable resource" without attracting much attention. In 1980 that statement would have been regarded as odd' (Lytle, 1986, 310). However, the resource conception of information was considered as early as 1973 in Australia. Tell (1974, 31), for example, asked, 'Is it in fact desirable to have certain prices and fees connected with information and information about information to guide the economic development and to safeguard the public respect for information as a resource just like other forms of energy such as natural gas, water, electric power, etc?' Lamberton also anticipated the resource issue, 'Even if nobody "owns" the unexpected in a legal sense, it seems likely that information resources, like land, minerals, buildings and machines, will become the basis of economic and political power' (1975, 13–14).

In ordinary discourse we use the notion of 'resource' in many ways. For instance, we might call our family a 'resource' because we get advice from family members. Equally, we might say that our friends have great 'resources' of will. But the resource conception of information is not of this kind. According to Paulsen (1980, vi), for example, the adage 'information is power' properly refers to the role of information in social power. Perspectives on information power can be examined as 'control of information and communications technology, information as a resource to control other resources, information as cybernetic control, and information as a power/work transformation variable' (Paulsen, 1980, v).

Proponents of the resource doctrine of information do not support the idea of information as documents, signals or data structures. The NCLIS report is a paradigm example. It specifically avoided identifying information with the media that convey it: 'That definition (in identifying "information" with the media that convey it, and with a limited set of such media at that) is irreconcilable with the usage in the Task Force' (NCLIS, 1982, 16).

When supporters of the conception of information as a resource call information a resource it is not always clear to what they refer. Definitions tend to be highly ambiguous. However, if we examine the literature carefully, among those who call themselves information managers, we find that 'information' refers to 'knowledge' in some way. According to Cronin (1986, 128), for example, information activity 'is cerebral activity (be it at a low or high level). Inputs and outputs are "soft"'. And it is information that 'has all the hallmarks of the new capital' (Cronin, 1986, 129).

The authors will call this style of reasoning *Information as Commodity*. It includes those in the literature of information policy or information economics who hold information to be a resource, in the sense we have examined above. For the commodity theorist, information is a real entity that may be manipulated as a commodity or resource (for example Cronin, NCLIS, Paulsen and Tell).

to recap...

Conceptions of information as a commodity are at the opposite ends of conceptions of information as informed people. There is a range of styles of reasoning about information and these have an impact on how we treat knowledge and its distribution.

case study

Google's motto is 'Don't Be Evil'. However, it became embroiled in controversy over its attempt to create a universal library. It collaborated in 2005 with university libraries in the US in its Google Print project. This project involved digitizing all the libraries' books at no cost to the libraries. Google argued that it was not breaching copyright because it was only going to put up snippets of the books online, for searching purposes, meeting 'fair use' rules that say a small proportion of copyrighted material can be put in the public domain.

About twenty per cent of all books are fully in the public domain. This includes books that were never copyrighted (such as government publications) or expired copyrights (such as Shakespeare). Google copies non copyright books and puts them online for the public. About ten per cent of books are copyrighted and in print. Google tries to create arrangements with publishing company partners that allow the company to scan and display parts of the work (Toobin, 2007). 'The vast majority of books belong to a third category: still protected by copyright, or of uncertain status, and out of print. These books are at the center of the conflict between Google and the publishers' (Toobin, 2007).

Publishers and the Authors Guild took Google to court. They argued that the act of copying the full text is a breach of copyright, even when only snippets provided online after someone has done a search.

'What they are doing, of course, is scanning literally millions of copyrighted books without permission,' Paul Aiken, the executive director of the Authors Guild, said. 'Google is doing something that is likely to be very profitable for them, and they should pay for it. It's not enough to say that it will help the sales of some books. If you make a movie of a book, that may spur sales, but that doesn't mean you don't license the books. Google should pay. We should be finding ways to increase the value of the stuff on the Internet, but Google is saying the value of the right to put books up there is zero.' (Toobin, 2007)

Libraries in democracies have traditionally been owned by the public through its government. Google's intention is to provide easy access to the world's published works and of course to make money from it. The publisher and author court action is not necessarily designed to benefit the public. Their interest is in getting a monetary benefit from Google's action, not preservation of the public domain. One way to do this, of course, is for Google to argue that the way it has presented or transformed the original non copyright texts is different from the original and therefore copyrightable. Google could then claim ownership to those works.

GOOGLE 'DON'T BE EVIL' AND THE UNIVERSAL LIBRARY

There are also other forces at work in restricting access to knowledge. Yahoo! and Microsoft have conformed to censorship rules in countries that have strict censorship. Indeed, Yahoo! was accused of supplying search engine records to China that in turn were used as evidence to jail a Chinese journalist for 10 years (Ghitis, 2006). The BBC news site is not accessible through Google, Yahoo! or other international search engines in China (and it is not possible to find the word 'censorship').

The flip side to censorship issues is privacy issues. Google saves every search and every email that you send through its service. Does Google have a right to monitor your behaviour?

Reflection

What is your point of view? Is Google part of the process of commodification of information?

Or, is it a part of expanding the public domain and making knowledge more accessible to rich and poor alike?

What is the difference between a novel and a blog, and why might one need stricter copyright than the other?

What, would you argue, constitutes *fair use* of copyright materials?

The second enclosure

Information commons and the public domain. The information commons is the public domain where the community's knowledge is accessible to all.

First enclosure. Involved privatizing the commons – public land ('the tragedy of the commons') – in order to enhance property rights over lands.

Copyright. Holds that the community owns knowledge while authors are granted temporary rights to make money from their creations.

Different disciplines define 'information' in different ways, but it is not only the use of the words and the use of the definitions that are relevant here. The ways of thinking in disciplines about 'information' are clearly different and have consequences for: (1) how mind, human action and communication and media are conceived and analysed, and (2) how the information is valued and owned.

The idea of the information commons becomes important in the debate about the value and ownership of information. In the feudal era the lords of the manor would invest in drainage, sheep purchases and crop rotation in the commons (land for the whole community) because they knew that there were social and economic benefits. The first enclosure movement involved privatizing the commons ('the tragedy of the commons') in order to enhance property rights over land. There is economic debate about the benefits of the first enclosure (Boyle, 2003). However, the idea of enclosure is relevant to debate about ownership of information. The second enclosure movement involves taking knowledge – which is owned by the community – privatizing it and closing it off.

The idea that the community owns published knowledge is enshrined in law. Intellectual property law tries to protect the individual and the community interest in knowledge. There is no freedom of access to what a person knows, for example, unless that person publishes what he or she knows. Under common law you own your own ideas completely until they are published. 'Ideas are free; but while the author confines them to his study they are like birds in a cage, which none but he can have a right to let fly; for, till he thinks properly to emancipate them, they are under his own dominion' (Briggs, 1906, 19). People who decide to 'let fly' their ideas gain a reward because of their contribution to the public domain. 'Copyright, which defines the right of an author with regard to his production, is undoubtedly given him to recompense for his creative work' (Briggs, 1906, 22). While the right to tangible expression of knowledge is called a property right, it is more precisely a right to reward for those who surrender their exclusive control of their own thoughts. Freedom of access to the public domain, to the totality of published works, refers to access to the tangible expressions of knowledge, such as documents, signals and data structures.

Copyright – the traditional legal assertion that ideas are free – and the public domain emerged together. Libraries are themselves an extension of the ethos of the public domain and the benefits of making knowledge available to all, rich and poor. Larry Lessig provides a more specific conception of the commons in the era of the Internet:

It is commonplace to think about the Internet as a kind of commons. It is less commonplace to actually have an idea what a commons is. By a commons I mean a resource that is free. *Not necessarily zero cost, but if there is a cost it is a neutrally imposed, or equally imposed cost.* Central Park is a commons: an extraordinary resource of peacefulness in the center of a city that is anything but: an escape and refuge, that anyone can take and use without the permission of anyone else. The public streets are a commons: on no one's schedule but your own, you enter the public streets, and go any direction you wish. You can turn off of Broadway into Fifty-second Street at any time, without a certificate of authorization from the government. Fermat's last theorem is a commons: a challenge that anyone could pick up: and complete, as Andrew Wiles, after a lifetime of struggle, did. Open source, or free software, is a commons: the source code of Linus, for example, lies available for anyone to take, to use, to improve, to advance. No permission is necessary; no authorization may be required. These are commons because they are within the reach of members of the relevant community without the permission of anyone else. They are resources that are protected by a liability rule rather than a property rule. Professor Reichman, for example, has suggested that some innovation be protected by a liability rule rather than a property rule. The point is not that no control is present: but rather that the kind of control is different from the control we grant to property. (Lessig, 2002, 1783)

The modern push to treat information as a commodity and to restrict access to information goes counter to the origins of copyright and the public domain. As we have seen from disciplinary conceptions of information it is odd in most cases to talk about 'ownership'. What does it mean to 'own' decisions? or uncertainty? The second enclosure movement is about ownership of ideas and the tangible expressions of those ideas.

The creative commons

New media allow people to appropriate the work of authors without paying for it. File-sharing software like Limewire and others enable individuals to download movies, songs and other creative works without paying for them. Creating a balance between everything being free and rewarding the author is at the heart of the debates on the second enclosure movement. The creative commons movement is a response to the pressures of access and reward. From Australia (http://creativecommons.org.au/) to China (http://cn.creativecommons.org/) there are attempts to provide a licensing environment that strikes a balance between author rights and public access. It is worthwhile citing at length the Australian introduction to its creative commons site:

Creative commons. Provides a licensing environment that strikes a balance between author rights and public access.

From a legal perspective, one of the most significant responses to these changes has been the development of new licensing systems designed to open up access to and use of protected material. These 'open content licensing' models preserve the creator's intellectual property rights whilst giving permission in advance for the content to be used more broadly than would be permitted under default copyright law. These licences differ from those commonly used before the advent of digital technologies in that they are typically generic (ie standard terms apply to all users), non-discriminatory (ie anyone can access the content) and at a minimum provide the user with the right to reproduce, copy and communicate the content, subject to prescribed terms or conditions. In addition, they are generally relatively short, simple and easy to read, conceptually interoperable with other open content licences, and machine enabled. The most popular and widespread of these licensing models in relation to creative material is Creative Commons.

to recap...

Creating a balance between everything being free and rewarding the author is at the heart of the debates on the second enclosure movement. The creative commons movement is an attempt to create this balance.

It might appear odd for a book on media studies to be looking at the discursive practices of electronic engineering and other sciences, like computing, and how they construe the concept 'information'. However, it is important for you to know that disciplinary conceptions of information have (1) influenced media scholars' conceptions of how human communication works and (2) influenced more broadly conceptions of society and human action. For example, the transmission model of human communication (send-message-noise-receiver-feedback) found in communication and media textbooks has its source in scientific ideas about the transmission of physical signals. The idea of information as uncertainty reduction and order, found in theories of entropy, has tripped over into the realm of theorizing about human action and what media do. There were several major styles of reasons identified by the authors:

- *Information as the medium:* Information and the media that carry it are the same thing;
- *Information as order:* All human communication is a move towards order, organization and equilibrium;
- *Information as cognitions:* The value of information is conceived solely in terms of decision-making or problem solving;
- *Information as uncertainty:* Information is a real entity leading to decision-making and resolution of uncertainty in individuals;
- *Information as code:* Information is 'signs' or 'codes' or 'messages' that bridge a 'gap' between two individuals, or between one thought and another, in the process of communication. *Messages* are *encoded* in language signs by a sender and transmitted by *sounds* to a receiver. The message is *deciphered* by a receiver capable of *interpreting* the sign;
- *Information as being informed:* Information is both individual and public. Information does not exist by transmission or by communication but *in* transmission and *in* communication. There is no 'gap' to be bridged by codes;
- *Information as a commodity:* For the commodity theorist, information is a real entity that may be manipulated as a commodity or resource.

Understanding our styles of reasoning about information is also important to our ideas about whether or not information can be owned. Traditional copyright law treats ideas as free with a temporary reward to authors for the tangible expression of those ideas. Tangible expressions, like patents and copyright, have a set timeline. When that timeline finishes, the knowledge and ideas return to the community. The contemporary ideas of information as a commodity, however, make all knowledge and ideas subject to property rights and in perpetuity. The public domain potentially disappears in the second enclosure movement.

When people download songs from the Internet without paying for them they are in one sense stealing. In another sense they are exercising a feeling that there is a public domain within which things are free, in Lessig's sense. Working out this balance between community ownership of knowledge and individual reward to authors is part of the complexity of contemporary times.

Google's aim to become one big electronic library holding all the world's knowledge and books looks, on the surface, to be in the public interest. But Google is a profit company not a public service. The authors would argue that Google is in fact a part of the second enclosure movement and not an advocate for an information commons.

As we have seen, information can be construed in a variety of ways, from information as the media that carry it through to people being informed. How we construe information as a phenomenon has consequences beyond theory. Conceptions of information bear directly on how we think about the public domain and modern media.

At the conclusion of this chapter you should be able to:

- critically analyse concepts of information and recognize the complexity of the different discourses that attempt to define information;
- apply concepts of information to key debates in the ownership and distribution of knowledge;
- apply the issue of ownership and control of knowledge to human rights issues locally and globally.

Reasoning about information and its ownership. Media studies is interested in the social distribution of knowledge. The mediation process has implications for that distribution, especially issues of equity in a globalized world. If the disadvantaged cannot afford knowledge then they will not be able to access the world's knowledge. In Chapter 2, the circulating libraries of the poor in London were cited as way that disadvantaged people tried to access literacy and knowledge when they could not afford personal libraries or books. Public libraries and intellectual property laws have, in the past, been designed not to serve the rich but to ensure that the community's knowledge is accessible to everyone. How 'information' is construed, therefore, has implications for its legal status and how people might access that information. Information, construed as a commodity, draws on the idea that information is a real thing – a resource – that can be traded like any other physical thing. Information as a commodity also turns upside down the idea that information is, first and foremost, owned by the community. Habermas's and Jonas's conceptions of information are at the other end of information as a commodity. They shift information back to the informed citizen as the real thing.

The second enclosure. The second enclosure has been used to describe the shift to the commoditization of information. Treating information as a commodity is often shorthand for commoditization of knowledge. Land was the subject of the first enclosure. Land as a commons is public and theoretically usable by all. Enclosure meant privatizing the commons. Knowledge is the subject of the second enclosure. Knowledge, though, is not a commodity like land and has special public-good characteristics. The amount of knowledge that you have does not decline when you talk to your mother, father, boyfriend or girlfriend. Your relatives or friends gain knowledge from you and you all have knowledge. This is a different arrangement, from, say, a box of chocolates. Once you give the box of chocolates away then you have none left. Traditional intellectual property laws do not 'enclose' knowledge. If you charge your mother for your advice, then you have entered the 'second enclosure'.

1   Do you download music or films or other materials from file-sharing software, without paying for it or acknowledging the owners or authors? Discuss in class how you think 'ownership' works in an online world.
2   What do you think 'information' is? Can it be owned?
3   Who owns the text in a chat room? No one?
4   What are some of the threats that are emerging to public access to knowledge?
5   Is Google a threat or an opportunity in the global distribution of knowledge?

Bollier, D. and Watts, T. (2002). *Saving the information commons: A public interest agenda in digital media*. Washington, DC: Public Knowledge.

http://www.publicknowledge.org/pdf/saving_the_information_commons.pdf

The UN General Assembly called a World Summit on the Information Society (WSIS) to develop a clear statement on the foundations for an Information Society.
http://www.itu.int/wsis/basic/about.html

Content, audiences and effects

part

3

Part 2 provided an overview of some of the key classics in media studies and changes in theoretical and empirical perspectives that have emerged as a result. In Part 3 the authors start to look in more detail at three of the components of the mediation process – audiences, content and effects. Clearly, structures and organizations are also embedded in what is happening globally. Governments are organizations and are involved in propaganda. Corporate monopolization of international news affects the structures of news distributions. The primary focus of the chapters in this section, though, is on the implications of propaganda, cultural imperialism, and global flows on audiences and cultures nationally and internationally, including the rise of national brands.

Chapter 7, Information Warfare and Modern Propaganda, investigates the rise of perception management and issues management as well as techniques of propaganda. The chapter looks at:

- key components of public opinion;
- the rise of information warfare and perception management and their application in a global context;
- the devices of propaganda, including rhetoric;
- the application of principles of image restoration and issues management in professions like public relations, including the issues cycle.

Chapter 8, Transforming Cultures, discusses the concept of culture, the study of intercultural communication and issues in cultural imperialism. The chapter investigates:

- the concept of culture and intercultural communication and their relevance to media studies and globalization;
- attempts to define the dimensions of culture;
- the arguments of cultural imperialism;
- the continued monopolization of news agencies at global level;
- types of resistance to dominant cultures that are emerging within nations and internationally, including culture and political jamming, and radical and rebellious media.

Chapter 9, Brand China and Bollywood India, provides case studies of the impact of social class in both countries and the impact of their international cinema. The chapter examines the:

- idea of *brand* as it applies to nation states and globalization;
- importance of social class to understanding media and social change;
- globalization of cinema and the importance of India and China to modern international cinema.

Information warfare and modern propaganda

chapter

7

This chapter will introduce you to:
- key components of public opinion;
- the rise of information warfare and perception management and their application in a global context;
- the devices of propaganda, including rhetoric;
- the application of principles of image restoration and issues management in professions like public relations, including the issues cycle.

Chapter 6 in Part II argued that our reasoning about information has consequences for how we think about ownership of information. The very idea of 'information warfare' shows that the importance of the idea of information has expanded into all domains, including the military. How governments and corporations manipulate public opinion is important to our understanding of audiences and content in the media process. This chapter will introduce you to:

- key components of public opinion;
- the rise of information warfare and perception management and their application in a global context;
- the devices of propaganda, including rhetoric;
- the application of principles of image restoration and issues management in professions like public relations, including the issues cycle.

Perception management. Conveying or denying selected information to foreign governments, intelligence systems, leaders or audiences in order to influence their emotions, motives, and objective reasoning.

After the terrorist attack on New York's twin towers on 11 September 2001 national governments increased the size and scope of their activities in perception management and psychological operations (PSYOPS). This response indicated another area in which we are part of an information era – warfare too is about the management of information. That has always been true (which is why there have always been spies) but arguably the conduits and means of creating and sharing knowledge have increased exponentially with the growth of new media communications. Information warfare is then the modern term that covers propaganda and persuasion campaigns, including deception. These campaigns have become an accepted part of military and government thinking, but they can also pose a threat to the public sphere and the public domain.

Elements of public opinion

When the planes hit the twin towers in New York on 11 September 2001, public opinion in the United States changed. It changed from a predominant feeling of safety within the physical borders of the US to unfamiliar feelings of anxiety and threat. Sympathetic countries overseas also felt threatened. The US government legitimately needed to manage that public opinion locally through the media or overseas through cultural diplomacy and public diplomacy. But managing and manipulating public opinion are

Propaganda. Lies and manipulation (black); the nature of the source unclear (grey); truth but biased (white).

very different things. Manipulation of public opinion represents the dark side of perception management where propaganda – black, white or grey – is used to influence people. Propaganda is defined by its source. Black propaganda involves lies and the manipulation is covert (hidden). White propaganda can involve the truth and is not hidden (overt). The information looks legitimate and independent but the aim of the propagandist is to put only one side of the story. For example, fast food hamburger chains might cite only those independent studies that say that their food is not harmful, but exclude all those that say that it is. Grey propaganda, on the other hand, is where the source of the information is unclear and might or might not be legitimate.

Information warfare. Refers to enemy attacks against information infrastructures in modern societies.

PSYOPS. Psychological operations – involves overt and covert psychological techniques to influence audiences.

Perception management is a part of modern information warfare. Modern perception management involves actions by a government or the military to convey and/or deny selected information to foreign governments, intelligence systems, leaders or audiences in order to influence their emotions, motives, and objective reasoning. Modern perception management combines truth projection, operations security, cover and deception, and psychological operations (PSYOPS).

Public and cultural diplomacy can be tools of perception management. In the US, *Voice of America*, through to less formal channels like trade associations, professional associations, and joint national associations, can be used in perception management campaigns. Indeed, the Central Intelligence Agency Fact Book can be listed as a part of 'public diplomacy' as it projects through its public website an image about a country (its profile, and so on) (http://www.cia.gov/cia/publications/factbook/). In the People's Republic of China (PRC), the Chinese state television apparatus, whose channels range from CCTV channels 1–9 to the education network CTV, is all connected to the promulgation of state sanctioned news, culture and information. This is quite explicit in the deployment of the English language Channel 9, to 'discuss' Chinese issues in a fashion acceptable to the state and decipherable by foreign viewers.

Public diplomacy has, of course, a legitimate role in national relationships. It can involve white, grey and black propaganda. China began in 2005 an image campaign to bolster its global economic and political ambitions. Beijing opened 27 branches of the Confucius Institute around the world in less than a year with a budget of US$200 million annually to teach Chinese in overseas countries. These could be described as analogous to the British Council, the Goethe Institut and the Alliance Française (and especially the impressive Maison Française in east Beijing, where a cinemathèque, a bookshop, Internet facilities, a library and a cafe work to create a good environment for immersion in French culture for young urban Chinese). These organizations use soft culture strategies to reach out to the world's populations to 'sell' or brand the idea of their national leadership and cultural cache. The thin line between cultural diplomacy and propaganda is an interesting one to tread when making judgements on the character of a communication policy – peaceful connections or information warfare?

Information warfare however is of course a much more direct, and usually pernicious, mode of attack. The origins of the term 'information warfare', according to Hutchinson (2006), can be traced back to the late 1980s when the term was used by the military. Information warfare's origins are in electronic warfare, military deception, psychological operations (PSYOPS) and information/operational security.

> However, the most significant element in its evolution was the development of electronic computing and communications technology. By the mid-1990s information warfare, driven by considerable developments in computer and communications technology, was developing into an integrated doctrine. It was still technology focused with command and control dominating, and with media management still as a separate entity. However, technological innovations were beginning to see them merge. It was becoming clear that modern wars were also media wars. (Hutchinson, 2006, 212)

In the movie *Die Hard 4.0* an ex-government programmer seeks to control all the computing systems in the United States. This is 'hacking' if you are the enemy and 'information warfare' if you are the attacker. Information warfare at the computing end can include attacks on data stores, for example computer and human memories; communication channels, for example humans, telecommunication systems; sensors/input devices, for example scanners, cameras, microphones, human senses; output devices, for example disk writers, printers, human processes; as well as manipulators of data, for example microprocessors, humans, and software (Hutchinson and Warren, 2001). Every day people receive emails pretending to be from banks in order to obtain their passwords to their accounts. This is called a social engineering attack because it is the human and not the computer that is the weakest link. This type of attack is persuasion in a minimal sense. It is a hoax, a trick, to get you to reveal to criminals your bank details. Persuading individuals, groups or nations to change their attitudes and behaviour can occur, however, on a government supported level, overt and covert. These 'attacks' are not just on networks but on minds. The 'media wars' component of information warfare tries to manipulate public opinion.

What, then, is public opinion, this force that Pascal called Queen of the World and Montaigne called a 'powerful, bold and unmeasurable party'? In 1965, Harwood Childs argued that in democracies public opinion was a matter of widespread interest. It was venerated, feared, praised, cursed and solicited. Politicians courted it; statesmen appealed to it; philosophers extolled or condemned it; merchants catered to it and pollsters analysed it. But few people agreed on what it was. He surveyed and classified a wide range of definitions (Childs, 1965, 195). Many of the classic definitions are collected in the papers in Part 1 of *Reader in Public Opinion and Communication*, edited by Bernard Berelson and Morris Janowitz (1966), and in Part 1 of *Voice of the People*, edited by Reo M. Christenson and Robert O. McWilliams (1967). For our purposes the most useful definition is that in Bernard C. Hennessy's *Public Opinion*: *Public opinion is the complex of beliefs expressed by a significant number of persons on an issue of general importance* (Hennessy, 1965, 13).

Hennessy goes on to argue that there are five factors in public opinion. First is the presence of an issue, with an issue being defined as a contemporary situation in which there is a likelihood of disagreement. Second is a recognizable group of persons concerned with the issue – the public of public opinion. Third is a complex of beliefs – the totality of opinions members of the public hold on the issues. Fourth the opinions must be publicly expressed whether in words or in actions such as demonstrations. Fifth the interested public must represent a significant number.

As Ian McAllister (1992) points out in *Political Behaviour,* a widely supported opinion may have little political consequence because it does not stir up conflict and therefore become an issue whereas an intensely held opinion supported by a small group of effective activists can become politically consequential. He offers the examples of the pro-gun lobby in the United States that for decades has effectively prevented any US government from restricting access to firearms and the anti-abortion lobbies that have made government wary about completely free access to abortion. Other intensely held opinions include opposition to smoking in public eating places and the view that high taxes make people less willing to work (McAllister, 1992, 81).

Perceptions are the very essence of our cognitive map of politics because that map is mainly a mediated picture of political reality. As Nimmo and Combs point out, people's pictures of political reality are 'not the products of direct involvement but are perceptions, focused, filtered and fantasized by a host of mediators, the press, entertainment programming on television, movies, popular magazines, songs, and group efforts in election campaigns, political movements, religious movements, and government policy making ... mediated, second-hand reality is one's politics' (1983, 9, 18).

Public opinion is dependent upon the existence of a public sphere, referred to in Chapter 5. Without a communicative space where public opinion can be expressed there is no real public domain, mediated or not. There is, of course, 'public opinion' in authoritarian and dictatorial regimes but it does not express itself as a democratic force and it cannot find expression through media.

Issues

The existence of a public sphere is a crucial aspect of social access to public opinion as a meaningful force. At an even more fundamental level, however, it is humans and groups of humans that attach significance to an issue or a problem. The way in which an issue emerges as such is about the way in which humans think and make sense of the world and its events, and the impact of those events on their lives and values. There is therefore an art to capturing, understanding and dealing with issues before they become crises. Public opinion is of interest to all media disciplines but so are issues. Public relations professionals deal with issues from a strategic issues management perspective. Identifying and dealing with issues before they become crises is the bread and butter of the public relations strategist. Issues and crises have life cycles. Issues and their publics can be *latent* (in the process of being formed), *emerging* (begins to appear in the public domain), *hot* (in current debate) and *fallout* (possibility of rekindling). Other descriptions of the issues life cycle include stages of potential, imminent, current, critical and dormant (Crable and Vibbert, 1985).

Grunig (1979) proposed a situational theory of publics to explain the different stages of public response to emerging issues:

When a group is in an indeterminate situation but does not recognize the situation as problematic, the group can be called a latent public. When a group recognizes a problem – what is missing in the situation – the latent public becomes an aware public. When a public organizes to discuss and to do something about the situation, it can be called an active public. (Grunig, 1979, 242)

The situational theory explains why some groups are active on a particular issue and others might be apathetic. In order to understand how to persuade people, therefore, it is essential to understand where different groups might be in their understanding of an issue and where the issue is in the public or organizational discourse (remember, this theory can be used within organizations as well as between organizations and their publics).

An application of the issue life cycle and issues management can be found in Benoit's (1997) image restoration strategies. Benoit (1997) found that there is a range of strategies that famous people use or could use to restore their reputation when those reputations have been damaged:

- **Denial** or simple denial involves shifting the blame. A person accused of wrongdoing may simply deny committing the offensive action – 'victimage'.
- **Evasion of Responsibility** can involve *Provocation* (I was provoked by someone else); *Defeasibility* (I lacked control or information over the event); *Accident* (It happened by accident) or *Good Intentions* (I had good intentions).
- **Reducing Offensiveness of the Event** includes *Bolstering* (creating positive feelings towards the accused); *Minimization* (offsetting negative feelings towards the offensive act); *Differentiation* (the act was not as bad as other acts); *Transcendence* (placing the bad act in a favourable context); *Attack the accuser*; *Compensation* (promise to repair the problem, which includes restoring the state of affairs existing before the offensive action).
- **Corrective Action and Mortification**. Confess and beg forgiveness. If the audience believes the apology is sincere, they may pardon the wrongful act.

activity Most of us can point to incidences of all the above at some time in our lives. Working with a fellow student, try and find a concrete but unexceptional example of each 'error', or 'strategy'. Then give the examples a rating of 1 to 5 according to how dishonest (1) or strategically sensible (5) you consider the behaviour in the example you have chosen.

Is it difficult to make this rating in some cases? Are there conditions where moral considerations are incommensurate with strategic decisions in the management of information? Now do the exercise again, but this time use examples where something serious has been at stake (the conduct of a war, the state of the environment, a child's well-being). What happens to the severity of your moral decisions in these contexts?

Benoit (1997) used the famous actor Hugh Grant as a case study. Grant had his mugshot printed in the Living Arts section of *The New York Times* after being charged with engaging in lewd conduct in public in his white BMW with a 23-year-old prostitute named Divine Brown. Benoit examined videotapes of Grant's appearances and found four strategies: mortification, bolstering, denial and attacking one's accusers. Grant did not attempt to minimize the offensiveness or significance of his act and did not try to make any excuses for his behaviour. This is classic mortification. He told the show host of *The Tonight Show*, Jay Leno, that he had 'done an abominable thing' and to *Larry King Live* that 'it was an atrocious thing to do and disloyal' (to his partner Liz Hurley).

On *The Tonight Show* Grant said:

> People give me tons of, ah, ideas, ah, on this one, ah. I keep reading psychological theories and stuff like this, ah, you know, that I was under pressure, I was over-tired, or I was lonely, or I fell down the stairs when I was a child or whatever. But I, you know, I think that would be bollocks to hide behind, ah, something like that, you know. I think you know in life pretty much what's a good thing to do and what's a bad thing, and I did a bad thing, and there you have it. (Benoit, 1997, 257)

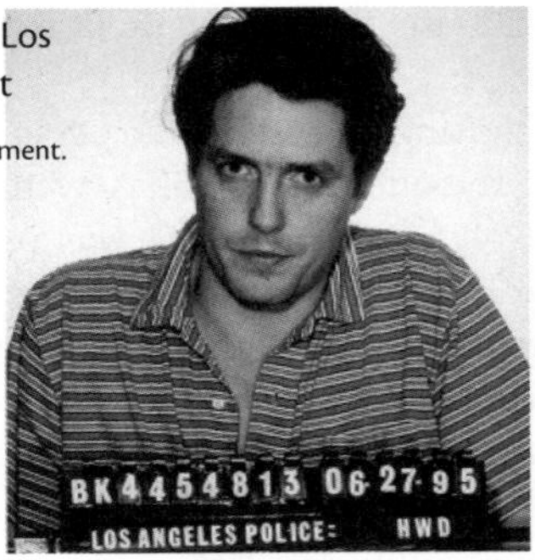

Figure 7.1 **Hugh Grant at Los Angeles police department**

Source: Los Angeles police department.

Hugh Grant's approach to his situation was very successful and diffused much of the damaging negative publicity that first emerged. Grant is also a highly educated, ethical, and articulate human being – who may not have needed advice on how to deal with the situation. Perhaps his responses were based on common sense, actual remorse and a habit of truth telling? Grant's problems are also a cultural marker showing the rise of a whole field of strategic issues management. The flip side of dealing with the impact of news on reputation is the role of the journalist in setting the news in the first place.

Journalists have an impact on issues as agenda setters. (Agenda setting was discussed in Chapter 4.) Journalists can focus on news stories that attract people's attention. 'Framing' and 'priming' are an important part of 'agenda setting'. *Frames* call attention to some aspects of reality rather than others. They make interpretation possible through a journalist's use of syntax, themes, script and rhetoric. *Priming* in conjunction with framing is a psychological process where news emphasis on specific issues or events activates other memories associated with those issues or events. For instance, media reference to 'David Hicks', depending on how the story is framed, might elicit in Australians' minds images of Guantanamo Bay and unjust incarceration or of the Taliban and treacherous Australians who were trained by them. Cognitive priming linked with agenda-setting research enables us to look at how the media influence a person's perception of the importance of issues or events. 'News stories, even those strategically framed, often carry substantive information about issues, albeit set in the context of self-interested manipulation. Attentive exposure can alter political knowledge by increasing the accessibility of information, changing the associations among the constructs and cuing and strengthening existing localized networks of concepts' (David and Pavlik, 2003).

The word 'activist' for example does not by definition mean 'terrorist', but framing and priming in future may correlate the two. In a *Sunday Times* (18 September 2005, 36) article, 'Ousted activist "baffled"' it was reported that 'American peace activist Scott Parkin is back in the US, saying he is still baffled about his expulsion from Australia as a national security risk'. The linking of the word 'peace activist' with 'national security risk' may, over time, have an effect. At present, the rhetoric used by journalists to describe Parkin does not highlight people like him as a national security risk even though the news reports did say that the Australian intelligence agency identified Parkin as a risk. If journalists automatically call all 'activists' 'national security risks', promoting the assumption that the one is the other, then we start to see framing and priming that may change perceptions. For example, a phrase by a journalist 'peace activists, like Al-Qaeda known nationally and internationally as serious risks to security and an Australian way of life, yesterday ran a protest rally in Victoria Street' is framing and priming an audience. Al-Qaeda as a word 'primes' because it would automatically trigger memories, visual and otherwise, of terrorist acts, and secret fanatical groups with influence worldwide. The journalist's language would have set the 'frame'. The Australian intelligence agency does not release its reasons for identifying someone as a security risk. From what can be discerned, Parkin is opposed to the arms trade and was in Australia to protest, among other things, the operations of a major company in trading arms.

It is not that there is an overarching conspiracy in the process of framing and priming, although of course in areas like perception management and psychological operations, the modern versions of grey and black propaganda, there may well be. There will in any democratic society be a series of 'labellings' and discourses that become well known and are common. What makes a democracy a democracy and the Fourth Estate a fourth estate is the capacity to recognize and to correct serious wrongs that emerge or have emerged over time.

Anchors

Journalists and public relations experts are involved in shaping the agendas that end up in the public domain and the issues that may or may not be perceived as important. Some of those agendas may involve persuasion, consciously or not. Jowett and O'Donnell (2006) distinguish between propaganda and persuasion. Propaganda involves control of the information flow by the source of the propaganda, management of public opinion and manipulation of behaviour patterns. The propagandist seeks to change a person's attitudes, beliefs, values or behaviour to meet their objectives. Persuasion, like propaganda, tries to create changes in attitudes and behaviour but it is not necessarily propaganda. For Jowett and O'Donnell (2006), the persuader sees the process as voluntary.

Persuasion involves response shaping, response reinforcing and response changing. Response shaping is where the persuader is a teacher and the audience is a student. 'A persuader may attempt to shape the response of an audience by teaching it how to behave and offer positive reinforcement for learning' (Jowett and O'Donnell, 2006, 32). Response reinforcing is where the audience already have positive attitudes and the persuader reminds them about the positive attitudes and stimulates them to feel even more strongly by demonstrating their attitudes through specified forms of behaviour (for example blood drives). Response changing, the most difficult type of persuasion, involves asking people to switch from one attitude or behaviour to another. 'People are reluctant to change; thus, to convince them to do so, the persuader has to relate the change to something in which the persuadee already believes. This is called an anchor because it is already accepted by the persuadee and will be used to tie down new attitudes or behaviours' (Jowett and O'Donnell, 2006, 33).

Anchor. Deeply held values/ beliefs/attitudes that are targeted by propagandists.

Anchors in public opinion, for Jowett and O'Donnell (2006), can be attitudes, beliefs, behaviours, values or group norms. Attitudes are predispositions towards things. The statement 'I hate smoking' expresses an attitude towards smoking. This might be one among many attitudes towards smoking. Beliefs are more factually oriented. 'Smoking will kill you' is a belief. Behaviours are what people actually do and are guides to what people will do in the future. Attitudes and behaviour can contradict each other. It is, indeed, possible to be anti-smoking and smoke cigarettes. Values are special kinds of belief that pull in ideas of right and wrong. 'It is wrong to smoke' is making a value statement. Values are more difficult to change than attitudes or beliefs. Group norms include all these possible anchors. The groups we belong to can often share similar attitudes, beliefs, behaviours and values.

Lee and Lee's (1939) early research into propaganda came up with simple descriptions of possible propaganda techniques, based on what they had witnessed. It is possible to see anchors in their descriptions of the devices:

- *Name Calling* – giving an idea a bad label. Name calling is used to make an audience reject and condemn the idea without examining the evidence (Lee and Lee, 1939, 26);
- *Glittering Generality* – associating something with a 'virtue word'. Glittering generality is used to make an audience accept and approve the thing without examining the evidence (Lee and Lee, 1939, 26);
- *Transfer* – carries the authority, sanction, and prestige of something respected and revered over to something else in order to make the latter acceptable. Transfer uses authority, sanction, and disapproval to cause an audience to reject and disapprove something the propagandist would have the audience reject and disapprove (Lee and Lee, 1939, 69);
- *Testimonial* – involves having a respected or hated person say that a given idea or programme or product or person is good or bad (Lee and Lee, 1939, 42);
- *Plain Folks* – is when the propagandist attempts to convince the audience that their ideas are good because they are 'of the people' (Lee and Lee, 1939, 92);
- *Card Stacking* – using selective facts or falsehoods or logical or illogical statements in order to give the best or the worst possible case for an idea, programme, person, or product (Lee and Lee, 1939, 95);
- *Band Wagon* – 'Everybody – at least all of us – is doing it'. A band wagon appeal attempts to convince the audience that all members of a group will follow our crowd and 'jump on the band wagon' (Lee and Lee, 1939, 39).

Of course, many of these devices are commonplace in modern advertising. Theories of persuasion and related findings have emerged for each component in the communication process 'who, said what, to whom, with what effect?'; the Yale communication research framework. Hovland's work on one- and two-sided messages, part of the Yale communication research programme, was mentioned in Chapter 4. The Yale and related research discovered that source credibility, for example, is part of the 'who'. Both physical attractiveness and attractiveness based upon similarity of a source can influence us if we are not motivated to think deeply or if the issue is one of subjective preference (celebrity endorsement is based on this idea). A sleeper effect, part of the 'what', can happen with media messages. There can be a delayed impact as we remember the message but forget why we might have discounted it. Arousing both positive and negative feelings – fear appeals or humour appeals – can lead to attitude change. Making people happy makes them easier to persuade (happy people rely heavily on peripheral cues, discussed below). Fear arousing messages can change attitudes and behaviour, if specific directions are included for avoiding the negative outcome. Shock advertisements designed to stop people speeding have this role. Research suggests the people who are easiest to brainwash are those whose beliefs have never been challenged. It is possible to *inoculate* people against arguments, over time. Distracted people do not tend to counter argue.

Petty and Cacioppo (1986) produced a well-known contemporary model of persuasion, combining many of the elements found from the Yale research and other psychological studies. They divided the routes of persuasion into 'central' and 'peripheral' (Figure 7.2). People who are educated on the topic and highly motivated on an issue are more likely to process the argument and, if the argument is successful, to change their attitudes and behaviour. If people are not motivated by an argument, then a peripheral route might be more effective. Creating a very attractive source, for instance, might attract people to the message.

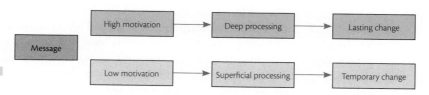

Figure 7.2 **Central and peripheral routes of persuasion**

Source: Adapted from Petty and Cacioppo (1986).

Modern persuasion and propaganda campaigns draw on a range of techniques to influence publics and audiences. These have become highly sophisticated in perception management campaigns. Language is also an important part of the process of persuasion and it is rhetorical devices that sophisticated propagandists draw on to influence audiences.

Rhetoric

Euphemisms. Replaces one expression with another that carries with it positive associations.

Dysphemisms. Replaces one expression with another that carries with it negative associations.

Rhetoric can draw on rhetorical devices, slanters, in order to persuade an audience. Slanters are words or phrases or indeed grammatical structures that present a positive or negative slant. Euphemisms and dysphemisms, for example, replace one expression with another that carries with it positive or negative associations. 'Special action' was a euphemism for 'killing' in Nazi Germany. *Youde ren* (some people)', in certain circles in the PRC in the 1960s and 1970s, meant those who might be blamed for inappropriate politics, but not named explicitly by the speaker. Neutral language can function as euphemism or dysphemism. 'Negative income', neutral as it sounds, is a euphemism for 'debt'. Rhetorical comparisons link our feelings about something to something we are comparing it to: 'He had a smile like a bent street sign'. Rhetorical definitions use loaded language: 'Abortion is the killing of innocent human life'. Rhetorical explanations use loaded language while telling the reason for an event: 'He lost his job as a journalist because he lost his nerve'.

Rhetorical language often uses stereotypes as slanters. Stereotypes are popularly held, but often not evidence based, images of a group: 'All women, as we know, are poor drivers'. This statement also includes, though, innuendo by implying what it does not say – that women are not smart. Rhetoric when used inappropriately can be very closely linked to tactics of bullying and discrimination. Loaded questions follow the logic of innuendo by suggesting something through the very existence of the question. 'Do you still hit your husband?' condemns the person who replies if they say 'yes' or 'no'. Weaslers are rhetorical devices, often legitimate, that allow the speaker to qualify what she or he says, shielding a claim from criticism. 'Possibly', 'as far as we know', are weasler words. 'As far as I know, she is the best journalist in the city'. This last sentence is like proof surrogates, which refer to evidence without providing the details. 'She is obviously the best journalist in the city' or 'Most people agree that she is the best journalist in the city'.

Stereotypes, persuasive comparisons, persuasive explanations, and innuendo can all be a part of downplaying. A downplayer is a rhetorical device to make something seem less important than it really is. For example, adding 'quotation marks' to a word can downplay a person's achievement: 'His "theory" of the media is well known'. Adding the words 'so-called' might achieve the same effect: 'His so-called theory of the media is well known'.

Ridicule, sarcasm and hyperbole, or exaggeration, are a part of the world of slanters. As you might guess, rhetorical devices can backfire, but for the most part we use them in everyday language without knowing the art of rhetoric. War, in particular, brings rhetorical language to the fore. Table 7.1 shows words used by journalists in different British papers, tabloid and broadsheet, during the first Gulf war. A *Guardian* journalist analysed the news reporting to see if there were differences in the way the allied forces and the enemy forces were reported. In the left-hand side are the words used in reporting allied forces and in the right-hand column words used to describe the enemy, Iraq.

Table 7.1 Rhetorical language in news reporting during the Gulf War

We	They
Have Army, Navy and Air Force, press briefings reporting guidelines	Have a war machine, censorship, and propaganda
Take out, suppress, neutralize	Destroy, kill, cower in their foxholes
Launch strikes pre-emptively	Sneak missile attacks without provocation
Have boys, lads	Have troops, hordes
Are professional lion-hearts, cautious	Brainwashed, paper tigers, cowardly, bastards of Baghdad
Motivated by an old-fashioned sense of duty	Fear of Saddam
Fly into the jaws of hell	Cower in concrete bunkers
Have missiles like Luke Skywalker zapping Darth Vader	Ageing duds (rhymes with Scuds)
Cause collateral damage	Cause civilian casualties
Have precision bombs	Fire at anything in the skies
Our POWs are gallant boys	Their POWs are overgrown schoolchildren
George Bush is at peace with himself	Saddam is demented, defiant, a crackpot monster
Our planes suffer a high rate of attrition	Fail to return from missions

Source: Mad Dogs and Englishmen. *Guardian* 23 January 1991.

to recap...

Rhetoric is the art of using language in persuasion. There is a range of rhetorical devices that can be deployed to influence audiences to persuade them towards the propagandist's objectives. Rhetoric is not in itself unethical but, clearly, its application can be either ethical or unethical.

Of course, rhetoric fails if it neglects to take into account its audience or, indeed, simply does not know how to write in the language of the audience. Nazi Germany, for example, was famous for both sophisticated domestic propaganda and crude and unsophisticated foreign propaganda. In an airdrop in Britain a leaflet was titled *Naziministerium des 3ten Deutsches Reiches*. It then said in English: 'To the men of Britain and Eire. You have proved yourselves a race of abject COWARDS unwilling to leave your Mamas' & Wifey's apron strings and FIGHT ME. YOU LICE, VERMIN, SPAWN of PROSTITUTES' (Reynolds, 2005). Covert weapons going with leaflets like exploding boxes of chocolates and canned peas also failed.

Modern companies also apply the principles of propaganda and rhetoric in their branding. The word 'green' has taken on a particular significance in the modern world of global climate change.

case study

BP is one of the largest oil companies in the world. In 2000 it launched a public relations and advertising campaign blitz to introduce its new slogan *Beyond Petroleum* with a green and yellow sun logo. Ogilvy & Mather won the *PRWeek* 2001 Campaign of the Year award for its work on the campaign.

An advertisement in the *International Herald Tribune* in November 2000 stated 'Beyond – means being a global leader in producing the cleanest burning fossil fuel. Natural Gas – means being the first company to introduce cleaner burning fuels to many of the world's most polluted cities; means being the largest producer of solar energy in the world; means starting a journey that will take a world's expectations of energy beyond what anyone can see today' (SourceWatch July 2008 http://www.sourcewatch.org/index.php?title=BP). 'Clean fossil fuel', 'cleaner burning fuels' – do these phrases represent rhetorical devices?

GREENWASHING

In the blink of an eye every global company was becoming 'green'. Sir Richard Branson's Virgin Blue ran advertisements saying that the airline wanted to 'contribute to a greener world' by allowing passengers to pay extra to plant a tree to offset emissions from the flights. The advertisements showed a picture of a giant hand planting a tree while a Virgin plane flies past in a blue sky, with the conclusion of course that Virgin was now a green airline.

The United Nation's *Intergovernmental Panel on Climate Change* notes that aircraft emissions are almost three times as damaging to the atmosphere as carbon dioxide from ground traffic. 'When an airline starts calling itself green you have to wonder how much of the marketing around the environment is based on fact and how much of it is simply hot air' (Lee, 2007). In response to questions about Virgin Blue's green advertising, spokeswoman Heather Jeffery wrote back: '"Congratulations, you took the bait. The green ad is part of our campaign to provoke public awareness and public discussion on offsetting, abatement and the role of aviation in planning to mitigate climate change."' (Lee, 2007).

'Glittering generality' involves the use of virtue words. Green is a virtue word. Words like natural, carbon-neutral and environmentally friendly are also virtue-oriented and represent a particular ethos. But bogus claims do not help if they are not followed up with reality. 'Greenwash' has emerged as a term to describe companies or organizations that attempt to preserve and expand their markets or power by posing as friends of the environment, even if they are in fact socially and environmental destructive. Lead brands like Lexus, Volkswagen and supermarket chain Tesco have been accused by the British Advertising Standards Authority of making false green claims. According to a study by TerraChoice Environmental Marketing, of 1,018 consumer products making 1,753 environmental claims only one came out squeaky clean.

In Australia, supermarket retailer Woolworths and Saab have been picked up by the Australian Competition and Consumer Commission. Woolworths sold its Select brand of toilet paper and tissues as 'sustainable' after it ordered the paper from an Indonesian company that, apparently, illegally cleared rainforests. Woolworths blacked out the claims and left the products on the supermarket shelf. Saab in its advertisements claimed that 'every Saab is green'. Saab told consumers that for every car sold the company will plant 17 trees to offset the emissions in the first year. Given that car-use is one of the problems, rather than the solution to global climate change, this was difficult to sustain as more than greenwash.

The ancient art of rhetoric, therefore, has not disappeared. Nor is propaganda a purely political tool. Modern businesses are engaged in propaganda at national and international levels.

Perception management

> 'I volunteered at the al-Addan hospital,' Nayirah said. 'While I was there, I saw the Iraqi soldiers come into the hospital with guns, and go into the room where … babies were in incubators. They took the babies out of the incubators, took the incubators, and left the babies on the cold floor to die.' (Stauber and Rampton, 1995)

This is an example of black propaganda. It was a lie. 'Nayirah' had never visited the hospital. The story was made up as part of a campaign by the public relations firm Hill and Knowlton to convince US public opinion to support a war against Iraq's dictator Saddam Hussein after he invaded Kuwait. US public opinion, to that point, had been decidedly against military action.

Three months passed between Nayirah's testimony and the start of the war. During those months, the story of babies torn from their incubators was repeated over and over again. President Bush told the story. It was recited as fact in Congressional testimony, on TV and radio talk shows, and at the UN Security Council. 'Of all the accusations made against the dictator,' MacArthur observed, 'none had more impact on American public opinion than the one about Iraqi soldiers removing 312 babies from their incubators and leaving them to die on the cold hospital floors of Kuwait City' (1992).

Nayirah was not a nurse. She was a member of the Kuwaiti Royal Family. Her father Saud Nasir al-Sabah was Kuwait's ambassador to the US. The Caucus did not tell the US public that Hill and Knowlton had coached Nayirah. Hill and Knowlton, however, had found the key anchor that would sway US public opinion – human rights abuses. The Kuwaiti government, through a front group Citizens for a Free Kuwait, paid Hill and Knowlton $12 million to develop an integrated campaign to influence US public opinion. Hill and Knowlton employed the Wirthlin group to conduct extensive research into which issues would sway opinion in favour of Kuwait and military action against Iraq.

> After the war ended, the Canadian Broadcasting Corporation produced an Emmy award-winning TV documentary on the PR campaign titled 'To Sell a War.' The show featured an interview with Wirthlin executive Dee Alsop in which Alsop bragged of his work and demonstrated how audience surveys were even used to physically adapt the clothing and hairstyle of the Kuwait ambassador so he would seem more likeable to TV audiences. Wirthlin's job, Alsop explained, was 'to identify the messages that really resonate emotionally with the American people.' The theme that struck the deepest emotional chord, they discovered, was 'the fact that Saddam Hussein was a madman who had committed atrocities even against his own people, and had tremendous power to do further damage, and he needed to be stopped.' (Stauber and Rampton, 1995)

Hill and Knowlton used a range of pre-packaged media versions of events in Kuwait, from human rights abuses through to positive images of the Kuwaitis. The media campaign included very successful Video News Releases (VNRs) that provided visuals with and without voice-overs. TV directors ran these VNRs without reference to their source, Hill and Knowlton, giving the impression of editorial independence.

Hill and Knowlton were not employed for the second Gulf War and the invasion of Iraq. However, techniques of perception management were employed.

Operation Iraqi Freedom

Public diplomacy, a tool of perception management, was used to provide the context for the invasion of Iraq, or Operation Iraqi Freedom. US Secretary of State Colin Powell appeared at the UN Security Council, broadcast live around the world, to argue that Saddam Hussein, dictator of Iraq, supported Al-Qaeda and had at his disposal Weapons of Mass Destruction. This, Powell, said, was ground for the UN Security Council support to invade Iraq. The UN Security Council did not ratify the US call for an invasion. The US, Britain, Australia and others – the Coalition – went ahead and invaded Iraq. No Weapons of Mass Destruction were found.

Over 40 million propaganda leaflets were dropped on Iraq before the first attack and over 40 million during the campaign. Radio was the main propaganda medium, although SMS and email were also used in direct messages to Iraqi leaders. Radio Tikrit was the 'black PSYOPS' radio station that pretended to be managed by local loyal Iraqis in the Tikrit area with editorial that sounded like it was supportive of Saddam Hussein. After a while, however, Radio Tikrit became critical of the Iraqi regime, hoping to sway loyal Iraqis away from Saddam Hussein. 'The hope of Black PSYOPS is that the target audience does not see through the ruse and believes the information is coming from the wrongly attributed source, which it sees as more credible. The risk, of course, is that if the ruse is discovered, the trustworthiness of the entire PSYOPS effort, both White and Black, is damaged' (Collins, 2007).

The Coalition forces 'embedded' journalists into the military forces to enable them to report directly on what was happening. This was also a means, of course, of controlling what journalists reported. Annie Lawson et al. (2008) in a *Guardian* article, provided an overview of the claims and counterclaims made during the media war in Iraq: 'The worst example of false claims relates to the battle to take control of Umm Qasr, the southern Iraqi deep-sea port and one of the key targets in the early war. On Sunday afternoon, it had been "taken" nine times. By Sunday night there were still ugly skirmishes between coalition forces and irregulars loyal to Saddam operating out of the old town. Umm Qasr was not, in fact, taken until Tuesday.'

Umm Qasr

Claim
Thursday, March 20, 7.33pm

US-led troops have taken Iraqi border town of Umm Qasr, Iraq's only deep-water port in the south, wires and TV report.

Counterclaim
TV reporters, including Mark Austin on ITV's News Channel, challenge the claims. They have it on Iraqi authority that Umm Qasr has certainly not been taken. 'Iraqi troops deny anyone has surrendered.'

Confirmation
Friday, March 21, 11.35pm

Admiral Michael Boyce, chief of the British defence staff, confirms the off-the-record briefings received by media in Kuwait and southern Iraq. 'Umm Qasr has been overwhelmed by the US Marines and now is in coalition hands,' he says.

Further confirmation
Friday, March 21, just after midnight

US defence secretary Donald Rumsfeld says US forces have taken Umm Qasr. The fog of war thickens.

Challenge
Saturday, March 22, breakfast time

TV reporters on Sky and BBC say Umm Qasr has witnessed fighting and dispute claims that the port has been 'taken'. They explain the new town is under coalition control but the old town is putting up resistance and therefore Umm Qasr cannot qualify as 'taken'.

Challenged again
Sunday, March 23, 05.53am

A heavy firefight breaks out between US Marines and Iraqi forces, witnesses say.

Confirmation again
Tuesday, March 25, 9.53am

Reuters: 'The southern Iraqi port town of Umm Qasr, where US and British forces have faced Iraqi resistance for days, is now "safe and open", a British commander said on Tuesday. Brigadier Jim Dutton, commander of the British Royal Marines' 3rd Commando Brigade, told reporters he hoped the first ship bringing aid to Iraq would arrive within 48 hours.'

51st Division

Claim
Friday night, March 21

Wires, TV and radio report official claims that coalition commanders have accepted the surrender of the 8,000-strong 51st Iraqi infantry division near the southern city of Basra on Friday.

Counterclaim
Sunday March 23, 10.33pm

Reuters: 'Iraqi officials denied US statements that the commander of the Iraqi division had surrendered, which US officials said on Friday.'

Counterclaim number 2
Monday, March 24, 3.22am

New York Times wire service: 'US officials were quick to announce the surrender of the commander of the 51st Division. On Sunday they discovered that the "commander" of the surrendered troops was actually a junior officer masquerading as a higher-up in an attempt to win better treatment.'

SCUDS

Claim
Thursday, March 20, 10.15am

An Iraqi Scud missile fired at US troops on the Kuwaiti border was intercepted by Patriot missiles, the US military says. Reports of scud attacks widespread.

Admission

Sunday, March 23, 4.30am

US general Stanley McChrystal says: 'So far there have been no Scuds launched. We have found no caches of weapons of mass destruction to date.'

Attempts to influence world public opinion by deception or false news stories can be undermined by the simple proliferation of news sources. One can watch al Jazeera, the Arabic satellite news channel, and see a perspective of the world perhaps more consistent with his own.

Source: Lawson, A., O'Carroll, L., Tryhorn, C. and Deans, J. (2008). War Watch: Claims and counter claims made during the media war over Iraq. *Guardian*, 11 April. Reproduced with permission. Copyright Guardian News & Media Ltd 2008.

With the proliferation of news sources and individual sources, like blogs, it is much more difficult for governments to uniformly influence world audiences. An Arab and a western audience, for example, can switch to al Jazeera, the Qatar based television news channel (now with London headquarters also), for a different version of events. The first time most western audiences heard about al Jazeera was on 7 October 2001 when US, British and Australian forces, as part of the so-called 'coalition of the willing' initiated the 'war on terror' with an assault on Afghanistan. The timing of al Jazeera's broadcast of a videotaped statement by the alleged mastermind of September 11, Osama bin Laden, praising the attacks on the World Trade Center and the Pentagon, brought condemnation from the White House. The US Secretary of State, Colin Powell, attacked al Jazeera for broadcasting 'vitriolic, irresponsible kinds of statements'. Al Jazeera quickly became likened to former communist mouthpiece *Pravda* and Hitler's National *Zeitung*.

The CIA expressed concern that bin Laden might be using the videotaped statements to transmit coded messages. This culminated in the revelation that the Bush administration had in fact planned to bomb al Jazeera. In 2001 the US bombed the al Jazeera Kabul office and in 2003 the Baghdad office was attacked by a US missile. Both attacks were claimed to be accidental. Then on 22 November 2005, British tabloid the *Daily Mirror* claimed access to a 'top secret' memo that revealed a plot by President Bush to bomb al Jazeera headquarters in Doha and which shed doubt on the US claim that the attack on the Kabul office was a military error. Prime Minister Tony Blair quickly dismissed the claim as a 'conspiracy theory'.

The history of al Jazeera can be traced to the demise of the BBC's Arabic service in 1996. The BBC partnership with a Saudi Arabian company was shut down amid attempts by Saudi Arabia to censor a documentary on executions. The void created by the BBC was quickly filled by al Jazeera, a satellite channel funded by the Emir of Qatar and other Arab moderates who believed in the need for uncensored news for the Middle East. For many, al Jazeera would fulfil the promise of uncensored news devoid of and unencumbered by conspiracy theories and anti-Israeli sentiment that characterizes much of the state-controlled networks in the Middle East. Despite this, there are those who take a more critical view of al Jazeera's mission to air stories about the corruption of governments in Egypt, Saudi Arabia, Syria and many other parts of the Middle East embodied succinctly in its motto 'We get both sides of the story.' Critics of al Jazeera claim a salient absence of stories that expose corruption in

Qatar and that, despite its purported status as an independent news network, al Jazeera is subject to the same kinds of state controls and censorships as many other Middle Eastern networks.

Al Jazeera has met with resistance from both the US and Arab regimes. Kuwaiti officials protested against its pro-Iraqi stance, Saudi Arabian officials protested against anti-Islamic programming and the former Palestinian President Yasser Arafat frequently protested against its interviews with militant Islamist Palestinian groups.

In 2004, the Iraqi interim government announced a one-month closure of al Jazeera's Baghdad office amid claims by Iraqi officials that the station was advocating violence 'inciting hatred and problems and racial tensions.' The ban followed accusations from US Defence Secretary, Donald Rumsfeld that al Jazeera was inciting hatred of the US in the Middle East. American condemnation of al Jazeera as a terrorist network suddenly shifted in 2005 when Washington granted interviews to al Jazeera with Powell and Rice, interviews that they had long denied, and with rumours that the US would even consider buying time on al Jazeera to broadcast political messages. In another twist, rumours had emerged that al Jazeera had an agreement to supply CNN with all video messages from known terrorist cells prior to broadcasting them on its network. The irony of the newfound friendship between the US and al Jazeera, a London office and an English language channel has not been lost on viewers of al Jazeera.

Islam goes online

It is not only the western nations that use perception management techniques. Islamic countries are equally likely to resort to propaganda practices. However, Islamic countries also encounter the fact that their own media have become extremely diverse, with the Internet providing voice for both traditional and non-traditional views. Islam came online through what Anderson (1999) calls 'technological adepts' who have the skills to bring interests they have as Muslims to the new medium. This includes students who go abroad to study, émigré professionals, political exiles and labour migrants. These adepts put up texts of the Qur'an and electronic discussion forums on Islam and related subjects that engaged Muslims. What emerged was an arena of contest, challenges to authority and responses – or as Anderson (1999) says – 'the real diversity of the Muslim world and Muslim opinion.'

An example of a middle-ground Islamic portal is the islamonline.net site produced in Qatar with content created in Cairo. Islamonline.net includes religious lessons and sermons but also instructional material for children and services that provide interaction directly with sheikhs or with databases of fatwa, other advice, religious lessons, sermons, hajj guides, health information, entertainment, personal testimonials and interviews with public figures. The site draws an audience interested in lifestyles that they cannot find at home. It is very much a transnational audience.

Islamic portals, therefore, tend not to be tied to existing institutions, even though traditional Islamic websites still exist. On the Internet people can find alternative sheikhs who speak to their situation and provide an Islamic expression not available at their neighborhood mosque or from local sheikhs. 'Their religion does not become private, but [is] transferred to another public and style of interaction' (Anderson, 1999).

9/11

Insecurity ... is the new normal. (Massumi, 2005, 31)

The trauma that Americans experienced in response to the 9/11 terrorist attack was similar in some ways (but different in others) to the cultural trauma that many indigenous peoples experienced in response to colonization by European and American countries over the last few centuries. (Pyszczynski in Prewitt et al., 2004)

The perception management, or propaganda, campaigns from the Gulf wars and in subsequent continuation on the 'war on terror' have had effects outside the well-defined military events. Since 11 September 2001 and the ensuing war on terror, a new discourse of terrorism has emerged as a way of expressing how the world has changed and defining a state of constant alert (Altheide, 2004). Theorizing about this constant alert has also become a part of the discourse. 'The war on terror' refers as much to a perpetual state of alertness as it does to a range of strategic operations, border control policies, internal security measures and public awareness campaigns.

In his speech delivered at the United Nations Security Council Ministerial Session on Terrorism on 20 January 2003, Colin Powell invoked the rhetoric of a clash of civilizations and urged 'We must rid the civilized world of this cancer ... We must rise to the challenge with actions that will rid the globe of terrorism and create a world in which all God's children can live without fear'. It is this construction of the war on terror as a global battle between 'the West and the rest' that appears to enable and facilitate the affective response to political fear – a reaffirmation of identity and membership of a collective. As Robin states 'Understanding the objects of our fear as less than political allows us to treat them as intractable foes. Nothing can be done to accommodate them: they can only be killed or contained. Understanding the objects of our fear as not political also renews us as a collective. Afraid, we are like the audience in a crowded theatre confronting a man falsely shouting fire: united, not because we share similar beliefs of aspiration but because we are equally threatened' (2004, 6).

Affective modulation. The idea that fear is becoming ingrained and routinized in all of us.

Brian Massumi (2005) uses the phrase affective modulation to describe the human response to the fear of terror. The actual level of alerts in the United States, for example, is for Massumi one of reinforcement and renewal of collective identity, modulated and transformed from an affective response to an affective state of anxiety. If you think that this sounds complex, then you are right. Massumi is basically saying that we are getting so used to alerts about fear that fear is becoming ingrained in us. Frank Furedi (2002) argues that fear has progressively dominated our society to the point where we live in terror of disease, abuse, stranger danger, environmental devastation and terrorist onslaught.

Summary

In this chapter the authors have explored propaganda and persuasion, and some of its applications, together with the rise of specific disciplinary areas such as strategic issues management. Propaganda and persuasion are related to ideas of power. One way to look at persuasion is through concepts of power. Hannah Arendt (1958) argued that, from Voltaire to Dahl, the traditional conception of power has been force and violence. However, for Arendt force and violence are instruments, or implements, of power and not power itself. If one person wants to dominate a group, then violence is the most efficient way to achieve command-obedience, but not power. Power always stands in need of numbers, says Arendt; violence always relies on implements.

Power corresponds to the human ability not just to act but to act in concert. Power is never the property of an individual; it belongs to a group and remains in existence only so long as the group keeps together. When we say of somebody that he is 'in power' we actually refer to his being empowered by a certain number of people to act in their name. (Arendt, 1958, 64)

For example, putting a gun to a person's head and asking them to hand over their money is force. For Arendt this is the perfect command-obedience relationship. Propaganda, on the other hand, requires voluntary support from its audience and this gives it power and legitimacy, until, of course, people find out that they are being manipulated – as in the case of the first Gulf War.

Management of public opinion in modern democratic societies has a legitimate side to it. However, modern publics need balanced information in order to participate meaningfully in the political choices they make, the political processes they are involved in, and in the debates that emerge on important issues. Many of the issues that emerge can be national and global, from climate change to the future of oil. The public sphere and the public domain are fragile spaces. The active participation of citizens and media in these spaces acts as a counterbalance to those forces that might seek to distort an informed public.

Key themes

Image restoration and issues management. Not all techniques for influencing public opinion are unethical or undesirable. Image restoration has emerged as a strategic approach because of the complexities of dealing with millions of people on a controversial issue that has affected a well-known person. Issues management has emerged as a way of identifying and dealing with issues before they become crises and is the bread and butter of the public relations strategist. Issues and crises have life cycles. Issues and their publics can be latent (in the process of being formed), emerging (begins to appear in the public domain), hot (in current debate) and fallout (possibility of rekindling). Public opinion in issues management is a complex phenomenon. First, public opinion generally involves the presence of an issue, with an issue being defined as a contemporary situation in which there is a likelihood of disagreement. Second, it involves a recognizable group of persons concerned with the issue – the public of public opinion. Third, it involves a complex of beliefs – the totality of opinions members of the public hold on the issues. Fourth, the opinions must be publicly expressed whether in words or in actions such as demonstrations. Fifth, the interested public must represent a significant number.

Persuasion. Persuasion involves response shaping, response reinforcing and response changing. Response shaping is where the persuader is a teacher and the audience is a student. 'A persuader may attempt to shape the response of an audience by teaching it how to behave and offer positive reinforcement for learning' (Jowett and O'Donnell, 2006, 32). Response reinforcing is where the audience already have positive attitudes and the persuader reminds them about the positive attitudes and stimulates them to feel even more strongly by demonstrating their attitudes through specified forms of behaviour (for example blood drives). Response changing, the most difficult type of persuasion, involves asking people to switch from one attitude or behaviour to another.

Discussion questions

1   Construct a multimedia presentation for class drawing material from one or more of the following archives:
    US government and educational archives
    http://www.archives.gov/exhibits/powers_of_persuasion/powers_of_persuasion_home.html

http://digital.lib.umn.edu/warposters/warpost.html

Information Warfare

http://www.iwar.org.uk/

National Library of Scotland

http://www.nls.uk/propaganda/index.html

2   Bring to class news stories that you think exemplify different stages of the issues life cycle.

3   Bring to class any websites that try to expose propaganda or deception. Are those sites reliable?

4   Can you find website examples of white, grey and black propaganda?

5   Can you identify the key 'anchors' used by the propagandist in those examples?

6   Bring to class examples of advertising that use each of Lee and Lee's propaganda techniques.

7   Do you think that 'information warfare' has extended beyond military campaigns?

8   Is public opinion only important in liberal democracies? Research at least one non-western political system to see how public opinion is formed and informed to create collective debate.

Further reading

Jowett, G.S. and O'Donnell, V. (2006). *Propaganda and persuasion*. Sage: London.

This site outlines the basic elements of propaganda, its use during wartime, with examples on how propaganda works psychologically.
http://www.globalissues.org/HumanRights/Media/Military.asp

Transforming cultures

This chapter will introduce you to:
- the concept of culture and intercultural communication and their relevance to media studies and globalization;
- attempts to define the dimensions of culture;

- the arguments of cultural imperialism;
- the continued monopolization of news agencies at global level;
- types of resistance to dominant cultures that are emerging within nations and internationally, including culture and political jamming, and radical and rebellious media.

As we witnessed in Chapter 7 attempts to transform global public opinion through propaganda are alive and well. Early approaches to communication and development assumed that modern media transformed cultures and led them to economic prosperity. Daniel Lerner (1958) proposed a theory of 'rising expectations' because he thought that media fast-tracked industrial development. When he realized this was not so, he proposed a theory of 'rising frustrations'. There is little doubt, however, that there is communication across borders and between cultures on a scale never before experienced. In this chapter we look at theories of intercultural communication, flows of communication like advertising and news and patterns of ownership of media.

Intercultural communication

As a child I remember going with my grandmother in early spring to her allotment on the edge of the small town. There was great activity; everyone was pulling out old vegetables, hoeing, raking, measuring, drilling holes for seeds. Some weeks later the scene and the activities had changed. Neat rows of seedlings, symmetrically spaced, had appeared, and the people were now transplanting, weeding, watering … To me, then, all that activity and all the changes seemed entirely natural, ordinary and quite unremarkable. As I reflect on it now it seems to me a most fitting metaphor for the description of culture. Nature provided the ground (literally) on which culture could work: the soil, the seeds, the weather, the water. The decision, however, to place the allotments on the southern edge of the town was an entirely cultural matter, as was the size of each allotment (or even the concept of an allotment!). Culture, too, had its effect on what kinds of tools would be used: forks and spades, hoes and rakes of certain kinds, dibble-sticks, balls of string and sticks to mark the rows, and so on. (Kress, 1998, 5)

Kress sees culture as natural and ordinary but at the same time defining what we do in practice. We attach meanings to people and to practices as well as to our physical environment. Culture is so deep in us that it is, for all intents and purposes, reality. Each cultural artefact carries with it a whole system of significations. The very fact that we call something a 'mobile phone' signifies a human technology, especially in Germany where the mobile phone is called 'a handy'.

Worldview. Each culture has its own worldview or expectations about its cultural artefacts, human conduct and identity.

Communication and culture are intimately linked. Signs and symbols are communicated through language and through cultural artefacts. Each culture also has its own worldview or expectations about its cultural artefacts, human conduct and identity.

The *United Colors of Benetton* advertising campaigns are a good example of cultural artefacts and global campaigns where worldviews are explicitly challenged. The campaigns for the Italian clothes manufacturer began in 1984 as a means for communication and as expression of what the company took to be universal equity themes such as human rights and racial equality. The advertisements were designed to challenge stereotypes and to be controversial. Figure 8.1 shows one of the advertisements from the AIDS campaign. The advertisements generated news interest and provided Benetton with huge exposure, including scepticism from social activists at the deployment of suffering for advertising outcomes. Benetton's argument was that the advertisements served a profit motive but were also genuinely designed to tackle morally important issues.

Benetton used the same approach of tackling controversial issues when it wanted to increase its market share in the United States. The worldview it wished to challenge was the US support for the death penalty. The creative mind behind the advertising campaigns, Oliviero Toscani, spent two years visiting death row inmates. The campaign was launched worldwide in 2000 and highlighted the plight of 26 convicted murderers on death row in the anti-death penalty theme (Figure 8.2).

The campaign, however, quickly came under attack by the families of the victims and the legislatures that had allowed Benetton into the prisons to interview the inmates. They were not only upset about the advertisements. A 100-page supplement provided by Benetton did not mention any of the crimes committed. Various advocacy groups called for a boycott on all Benetton products. There was public outrage at Benetton's approach and vocal and successful opposition from the advocacy groups. Sears Roebuck was one of the targets of the boycott. It had signed a contract with Benetton to sell its products in its stores throughout the US. Sears Roebuck withdrew its contract both in opposition to Benetton's campaign and in response to the public outrage expressed by the victims of those condemned to be executed.

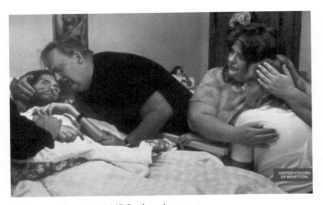

Figure 8.1 Benetton AIDS advertisement

Source: AIDS. David Kirby Copyright 1992 Group S.p.A. Photo: Therese Frare. Concept: Oliviero Toscani. Reproduced with permission.

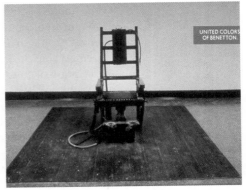

Figure 8.2 Benetton death penalty campaign

Source: Electric Chair. Copyright 1992 Benetton Group S.p.A. Photo: Lucinda Devlin. Concept: Oliviero Toscani. Reproduced with permission.

Dimensions of culture

Benetton's challenge to the idea and practice of the death penalty was within cultures that shared similar cultural characteristics, even if they did not share the same language. Italians and Americans are *low context cultures* and *individualistic*. The controversy expected by Benetton in the United States was unlikely to happen in *high context cultures*, where deference to the group and to authority is much greater. For Edward Hall (1976), cultures have different styles of communication and different contexts that reflect their individualism or collectivism. High context cultures tend to have greater conformity to group expectations than individualistic, or low context, cultures. In Table 8.1 Japan would be at the top of high context cultures with the highest degree of conformity to group expectations and German-speaking countries the lowest.

Geert Hofstede (1982) measured different dimensions of culture in his study of employees in IBM, expanding the ideas of context. For Hoftstede, individualistic countries (for example US, Australia, UK) personal goals take priority over their allegiance to groups like the family or the employer. Competition rather than cooperation is encouraged and personal goals take precedence over group goals. These cultures emphasize individual initiative and achievement. In collective societies (for example Pakistan, Taiwan, Peru) people are born into extended families or clans that support and protect them in exchange for their loyalty. The individual is emotionally dependent on organizations and institutions. The culture emphasizes belonging to organizations. Individuals trust group decisions. Hofstede ranked countries on an individualism and collectivism scale. A high ranking in Table 8.2 means the country has an individualistic orientation.

Hofstede also identified other major dimensions of culture, including masculine and feminine orientations; power distance and uncertainty avoidance. Masculinity is the extent to which values within a society are male-oriented and those values correspond with behaviours such as assertiveness, ambition, achievement, the acquisi-

Table 8.1 Spectrum of high and low context cultures

High Context Cultures
Japan
Middle East countries
Greece
Spain
Italy
England
France
North America
Scandinavian countries
German-speaking countries
Low Context Cultures

tion of money, signs of manliness, material possessions, and not caring for others. Femininity on the other hand stresses caring and nurturing behaviours. The connection between these values and the masculine or feminine is cyclical as the one defines the other. Actual behaviours and manifestations of gender we will explore later on. The higher ranked countries in Table 8.3 represent a stronger masculine orientation.

Power and authority are a part of Hofstede's idea of power distance. In some cultures people are not perceived to be equal and they have a rightful place – they are, literally, distant from real power and are expected to show deference to those with authority. Children in high power distance cultures, for example, will seldom interrupt a teacher and show great reverence and respect for authority. Low power distance countries, such as Austria, Finland, Denmark, on the other hand, hold that inequality in society should be minimized. People in these cultures hold that they are close to power and should have access to that power. Table 8.4 shows Philippines with the highest ranking on power distance.

High uncertainty avoidance cultures try to avoid uncertainty and ambiguity by providing stability for their members. This is done by not tolerating deviant ideas and behaviours and believing in absolute truths and the attainment of expertise. Uncertainty avoidance cultures tend to be characterized by a higher level of anxiety and stress than other cultures because people think of the uncertainty as inherent in life and as a continuous hazard that must be avoided. As a consequence there is a strong need for written rules (for example Portugal, Greece, Germany). Countries like Sweden and Denmark, on the other hand, prize initiative, are more willing to take risks, are more flexible, and think that there should be as few rules as possible. Table 8.5 has Greece at the top of the rank of those countries that seek to avoid uncertainty.

The different dimensions of culture on Hofstede's analysis can lead to social problems if they become too dominant. For example:

Table 8.2 Countries ranked by individualism

USA	1	Columbia	9	Hong Kong	32
Australia	2	Sweden	10	Chile	33
Great Britain	3	France	11	Singapore	34
Canada	4	Ireland	12	Thailand	35
Netherlands	5	Norway	13	Taiwan	36
New Zealand	6	Switzerland	14	Peru	37
Italy	7	Germany	15	Pakistan	38
Belgium	8	...		Venezuela	40

Source: Adapted from Hofstede (1982).

Table 8.3 Countries ranked by masculinity

Japan	1	Germany	9	Finland	35
Austria	2	Philippines	10	Yugoslavia	36
Venezuela	3	Columbia	11	Denmark	37
Italy	4	South Africa	12	Netherlands	38
Switzerland	5	USA	13	Norway	39
Mexico	6	Australia	14	Sweden	40
Ireland	7	...			
Great Britain	8	Chile	34		

Source: Adapted from Hofstede (1982).

Table 8.4 Countries ranked by power distance

Philippines	1	France	9	Sweden	35
Mexico	2	Columbia	10	Ireland	36
Venezuela	3	Turkey	11	New Zealand	37
India	4	Belgium	12	Denmark	38
Yugoslavia	5	...		Israel	39
Singapore	6	Switzerland	32	Austria	40
Brazil	7	Finland	33		
Hong Kong	8	Norway	34		

Source: Adapted from Hofstede (1982).

- masculinity: violence;
- uncertainty avoidance: xenophobia;
- collectivism + high power distance: blind followers;
- individualism + masculinity: anonymity, depersonalization;
- collectivism + uncertainty avoidance: ethnic violence.

Table 8.5 **Countries ranked by uncertainty avoidance***

Greece	1	Turkey	11	Canada	31
Portugal	2	Mexico	12	USA	32
Chile	3	Israel	13	Philippines	33
Belgium	4	Columbia	14	India	34
Japan	5	...		Great Britain	35
Yugoslavia	6	Switzerland	25	Ireland	36
Peru	7	Netherlands	26	Hong Kong	37
France	8	Australia	27	Sweden	38
Spain	9	Norway	28	Denmark	39
Argentina	10	South Africa	29	Singapore	40
		New Zealand	30		

* The authors have artificially provided a rank where some of the countries are equal in rank (for example Chile and Belgium). See Hofstede's (1982) original work for full rankings.

Source: Adapted from Hofstede (1982).

Time and *high* and *low context communication* are other important dimensions that affect how people communicate. Western cultures for instance tend to be *monochronic*. Time is divided into intervals and the clock helps to regulate behaviour and actions. If a person makes an appointment to see their bank manager in the United States, then the bank manager is expected to turn up on time or near to time. Not all cultures, however, follow this seemingly simple rule. *Polychronic* cultures hold the *relationship* to be more important than times set for meetings.

Our everyday communication – how we speak, write and read – is also affected by our culture. Japanese culture uses communicative cues other than speech, including use of the situation, body language and even silence. Bowing to an elder can signify many things, depending on the nature of the bow. No words are needed to explain it. This is called high context communication. High context communication is ambiguous, indirect, maintains harmony, understates and is reserved. Low context communication is precise, direct, open and based on explicit statements in text or in speech. On this view, the closer a relationship becomes and that a situation is understood the less need there is for explicit statements (high context). The more difficult it is to understand the meaning of a situation the more there is a need for explicit statements (low context). Parts of western culture may involve high or low context communication. For example, the modern court system requires everything be explained, quite literally. Clothes, as codes in western culture, may or may not tell you who a person is or what their status is. You have to ask people where they are from and what they do (low context communication). A Roman Catholic priest in traditional clerical dress in contrast is easily identifiable.

The authors have not yet directly covered language and its importance to cultural identity. However, as will become apparent, it is their belief that these powerfully influ-

Table 8.6 Languages on the Internet

Per cent of all Internet users	
English	29.9
Chinese	14.0
Spanish	8.0
Japanese	7.9
German	5.4
French	5.0
Portugese	3.1
Korean	3.1
Italian	2.8
Arabic	2.6
Rest	18.2

Source: US National Virtual Translation Center (http://www.nvtc.gov/).

ence global communication patterns. Most of the resistance encountered with the introduction of satellite transborder communication arose from the fear that national or regional or ethnic cultures would be overwhelmed by the messages carried in the new technology, giving rise to a global culture that closely resembled something like contemporary American popular culture, which may be deemed highly offensive, for example, in Islamic cultures. The cultural dimensions, of course, interweave with language and are not separate from verbal or nonverbal communication. Table 8.6 gives an overview of the current languages on the Internet.

There is empirical evidence that the different cultural dimensions, such as collectivism and individualism, and high and low context communication, exist and are important in our understanding about how different communication patterns occur in different societies. However, it would be a mistake to think that these cultural dimensions or patterns of communication determine behaviour. Cultural or linguistic determinism can be as problematic as technological determinism because a deterministic approach often misses other influences on human behaviour. For example, the different cultural dimensions do not tell us about social inequality – social stratification – phenomena associated with, say, gender. A society could have individualism as a value, have a feminine cultural dimension and still be stratified by gender. Adoption of the Internet by women in high context cultures provides some insight into the complexities of global media trends and culture.

Women and the Internet: the Stainless Steel Mouse and the Burma uprising

China and Japan are traditionally high context cultures with the individual deferring to the group and women deferring to men. However, one of the most interesting trends of the 21st century has been the extraordinary growth and activism of women Internet users in both these countries and elsewhere. By the beginning of 2002 between 40 per cent and 50 per cent of Chinese and Japanese women were using the Internet (McLaren, 2003).

McLaren (2003) gives an overview of Guo Liang and Bu Wei's major 2001 survey of Internet use in five Chinese cities. A total of 3,000 men and women aged 17 to 60 were surveyed in Beijing, Shanghai, Guangzhou, Chengdu and Changsha. Chinese-language websites were the most popular with 76 per cent of people using them. Only 14.6 per cent admitted to viewing overseas Chinese language sites and 9.2 per cent to visiting foreign language sites. Seventy-two per cent used email, the most popular Internet tool, 57 per cent used the Internet for news, 52 per cent to pursue personal interests, 50.6 per cent to enter chat rooms, and 45 per cent for musical or other artistic appreciation. The survey confirmed a desire for openness and access to alternative points of view.

Guo and Bu also note the relative 'openness' (*kaifang*) nature of the web with regard to sources of information and channels of expression, especially the interactivity of bulletin boards and chat rooms, where users can put forward their own ideas. One of the goals of their survey was to investigate whether Internet usage had an impact on what they call 'the extent of openness' of the individual (*kaifang chengdu*). An 'open' individual is defined as one who is willing to understand and accept completely unfamiliar phenomena and who is willing to experiment and trial new ideas or goods. (McLaren, 2003)

New media technology does not naturally lead to a rise in status for women. Women can also easily be marginalized. By the late 1990s the Chinese-language Internet in China looked radically different from the western versions. McLaren (2003) summarizes the main differences as:

1. Internet access is controlled through state controlled backbone networks, the opposite of western designs. Chinese web users log on through controlled web portals such as Sina.com, Sohu.com, Net Ease and Chinese Yahoo! and others;

2. China also has a national intranet with firewalls to control the flow of information and communication. There is strict censorship and monitoring of email traffic and violators are arrested and detained. There is a Surveillance Centre for National Information Security. Western Internet providers, including Google, have signed self-discipline protocols and indeed may even provide information back to Chinese officials about users. 'According to Xiao Qiang, Director of a Chinese diasporic organization based in the US called Human Rights in China, "More than 30,000 state security employees are currently conducting surveillance of web pages, chat rooms, and private email messages"' (Xiao cited in McLaren, 2003).

McLaren (2003) concludes that in spite of the extraordinarily intensive efforts of the Chinese state to control the flow of information the government is fighting a losing battle. 'It appears that for every tactic employed by the state, Internet users and web site providers come up with a counter policy (in line with the well-known Chinese strategy of "those on top issue a policy and those underneath come up with a counter policy"). For example, when the government tried to ban Google, online protests forced the state to accept a modified version of this popular Western search engine' (McLaren, 2003).

· McLaren (2003) provides an interesting insight into one Chinese woman who attempted take advantage of the expressive possibilities of the web and in the process became a high profile cause célèbre. Liu Di, nicknamed *Bu xiugang laoshu* or stainless steel mouse, was on 7 November 2002 a 22-year-old psychology student at Beijing Normal University. On that day she was taken into detention for offences while using the Internet, with no notice to friends or relatives. She was released one year later without being charged. McLaren (2003) analysed her online written work for the Western Temple Alleyway Bulletin Board (*Xici hutong*) a discussion group named after the lanes and alleys (*hutong*) encircling the traditional walled-in compounds of old Beijing.

Liu Di's compositions, McLaren says, are whimsical and sardonic essays influenced by the novels of East European dissident writers. In one work she directly challenges the authorities by dedicating a mock play to the Beijing and Jiangsu province Security Bureau, featuring as a patient in an asylum for the insane, 'the mad one – stainless steel mouse'. 'Who is this "stainless steel mouse"? A timid child, a ridiculous mouse, a cunning conspirator, or a traitorous "dangerous element"?' The mouse is diagnosed as deluded, paranoid and a dangerous conspirator and in the conclusion of the play dies of laughter. In another composition, *Yinmou lun*, On Conspiracy, the mouse says she is a conspirator. The stainless steel mouse defends a webmaster, Huang Qi, who she says was wrongly charged for putting up web content from an overseas contributor. 'Finally, let me introduce a wonderful conspiracy. Let us one day speak the truth. In our daily lives it is unavoidable that we speak falsehoods. But if one day we could speak the truth then on that day we would become free people. Then we can write about that day and put it up on the web to allow everyone to exchange their experience.'

McLaren concludes that one could perhaps find fault with Liu Di for her rashness and naivety, 'but she is hardly a dangerous subversive conspirator.' The draconian reaction of the Chinese state to her youthful ramblings demonstrates the limitations of freedom of expression for women activists.

In Burma's September 2007 uprising against the military junta it was women who actively organized with monks and civilians protests against Burma's military regime. Burma's women activists were also adept at using the Internet internally for organizing protests and in highlighting the country's problems to the international community. Although less than one per cent of Burma's population has access to the Internet, and only 25,000 people have email addresses, skilled female bloggers bypassed official firewalls and developed links with local embassies or overseas visitors who do not have restricted access.

Figure 8.3 Liu Di – the Stainless Steel Mouse

Burmese activists have considerable support from exiles, including websites The Democratic Voice of Burma operating out of Norway and Mizzima News operating in Delhi India. These activist sites herald the advent of 'citizen reporters' taking video and text from Burma and writing up stories for the international news communities. The military junta thought it had cut all access to the Internet when it continued its crackdown on activists, but many women activists still managed to get news out to exiles and the international audience. This is an extract from one of the citizen reporter and activist blog entries in Burma at the time:

> The authorities refused to open the eastern gate of Shwedagon pagoda, the monks stood in front of the gate and recited Metta Sutta [Buddhist teaching for loving kindness]. Then the soldiers charged the monks with batons and started beating and kicking the monks. We heard that an elderly monk died because of the beating. I saw one monk beaten severely. I guess that he is the same monk who is reported to have died. The monk must be over 80 years old. The monks were peacefully demanding opening of the gate and the soldiers just charged into them and arrested five people. I heard that two of the monks who were arrested were forced to take off their robes. Their robes were burnt. And the police also stamped on the Sasanah flag [religious flag]. In all, about 12 monks and civilians were injured. The police fired teargas from four directions. (Pallister, 2007)

The Burma example, like that of the stainless steel mouse, shows how governments attempt to adopt new media that are perceived to contribute to their economies but end up having to deal with their democratizing potential. The individualism of the Internet is not necessarily identical with consumerism but it is most certainly linked to low context expressive communication. The high context–low context ideas, therefore, are not simple dichotomies in the current global media environment. OpenNetInitiative, set up by Oxford, Cambridge, Harvard and Toronto universities, with its own website, tracks these tensions and Internet restrictions around the world. Low context media can also contribute to communality and media richness, a characteristic of high context cultures.

Communal use of the Internet: Berbers and the Korean Minihompy

There are 6,000 languages spoken in the world. Of these 50 per cent are regarded as endangered. A language disappears from the world every two weeks. Of all the world's languages and cultures, perhaps that of the Berber (Amazigh) people of northern

Africa, is the oldest. Imazighen, the traditional Berber name, means free people (Almasude, 1999). The Berber territory reaches from Egypt to Mauritania and from the Mediterranean to the boundaries of historic sub-Saharan Black Africa. There are an estimated 20 million Berber within the following countries:

- Morocco 8.3 million
- Algeria 7.7 million
- Libya 2.3 million
- Tunisia 1.2 million
- Egypt 500,000

The Berber language was not primarily at risk from western popular culture broadcast through Hollywood or global television. Standard Arabic has been held in higher esteem than other languages within the region. It is the language of the Qur'an and used as a first language in schools, television broadcasts, newscasts, newspapers, magazines, and literature. Until a few years ago, being Berber was to be second class. Even in the most modernized society in North Africa, Tunisia, being Berber was synonymous with being an illiterate peasant dressed in traditional garments. The Berber, however, rallied by recording Berber songs, poems and the language generally for distribution locally and then internationally. These recordings started when the first reel-to-reel recordings emerged and progressed through to broadcasting and the Internet. As a result of pressure brought to bear by the growing awareness of Berber music through recording technology and a worldwide audience, the King of Morocco, Hassan II, felt compelled to recognize the importance of the Amazigh culture and language in Moroccan identity and integrated it into the school curriculum.

The Berber case study showcases the use of media technology by marginalized individuals and communities to sustain cultural identity and language. The *minihompy* – mini home page – of Korea's Cyworld showcases the use of the Internet to retain the communal feel of Korean society. The online service through Cyworld combines homepage building and social networking, including role playing. According to Cyworld's owners a quarter of Korea's 48.2 million population have signed up, with the majority from the 24- to 29-year-old age group. Cyworld subscribers get their own page, a virtual living room called a *minihompy* where they can create diaries, publish images, network, host legal background music and more.

While Cyworld looks like other services such as Friendster it brings with it social obligations more appropriate to high context cultures. The word Cy means 'realtionship' in Korean and the social customs associated with relationship dominate the communicative practices. In Korea, not responding in a timely fashion to a message is seen as rude and upsetting. People literally spend all day on their minihompy sites writing replies or sending messages to maintain relationships. There are as a consequence billions of web page impressions each year. High context cultures, therefore, are not necessarily undermined by low context communicative means. The issue of cultural identity and the possibility of cultural erosion, however, take centre stage when we turn to debates about national development and global flows of media and communication.

to recap...

Many of the world's languages are under threat because of dominant cultural influence over minority languages. This is not just a 'western' issue but can occur wherever one culture has supremacy in setting the cultural agenda. The Internet and other media of global communication can have a democratizing role for those resisting authoritarian governments and an agenda-setting role for those who can access the global audience.

Global flows

Our identity is intimately linked to the culture that we live in. As nations and societies become more closely linked, through media participation, tourism and trade, fears of cultural erosion have become a part of the debate about globalization. However, early

Ethnocentric. The tendency
for us to see everything
through our own cultural lens.

theorists of modernization thought in terms of development rather than in terms of cultural erosion. They also tended to be ethnocentric, assuming that what happened in western cultures was, indeed, the model for all other countries.

Daniel Lerner (1958) in his work *The Passing of Traditional Society* is a good example of western expectations about 'underdeveloped' societies. Lerner argued that rising media participation in any society tends to raise participation in all sectors of the social system.

> Two observations appear to hold for all countries, regardless of continent, culture, or creed. First the direction of change is always from oral to media system (no known case exhibiting change in the reverse direction). Secondly, the degree of change toward media system appears to correlate significantly with changes in other key sectors of the social system. If these observations are correct, then we are dealing with a 'secular trend' of social change that is global in scope. (Lerner, 1958, 56)

Non-secular organizations and individuals, of course, use the same trajectory to build anti-modern power bases. Secularity does not any longer have a hold on global media.

Non-western societies had something to say about the idea that western 'global media' are good for everyone. Debates about the nature of a new world communication or information order took centre stage in UNESCO debates in the 1970s. The global impact of mass media and the issue of cultural erosion became top priority in the UNESCO General Conference in 1976, where non-aligned non-western countries wanted a declaration on mass media that acted as a demonstration against western dominance of media and information flows. Instead of a declaration UNESCO set up The International Commission for the Study of Communication Problems, known famously as the MacBride Commission. 'One of its chief tasks was to analyse communication problems, in their different aspects, within the perspective of the establishment of a new international economic order and of the measures to be taken to foster the institution of a "new world information order"' (UNESCO Work Plan for 1977–1978, 19C/5 Approved §4155).

The MacBride Commission recommended that there be a 'new more just and efficient world information and communication order'. Such a world order might be possible with:

1. The development of third-world countries so that they become truly independent and self-reliant and develop their cultural identities. This would include tailoring national communications policies to suit the conditions in the country, building infrastructure, equitable distribution of common global communication resources, limits on the activities of transnational corporations, preferential treatment of non-commercial media, and balanced flows of technical information.

2. Better international newsgathering and better conditions for journalists.

3. Democratization of communication (access and participation, the right to communicate). This included guarantees of human rights, acceptance of 'the right to communicate', abolition of censorship, editorial independence, limits on media concentration and monopolization, limits on the influence of advertisers on editorial policy/media content, attention to the communication needs of women, children and minorities, and facilitation of horizontal communication.

4. Furtherance of international cooperation.

Table 8.7 **Modernization**

1. Western societies as a model – emphasis on economic growth
2. Causes of underdevelopment inherent in the countries themselves
3. Focus on the nation state
4. Emphasis on individual freedoms
5. Mass media accorded a central role in the development process
6. Vertical pattern of communication – from the elite to the people

Table 8.8 **Dependence**

1. World systems perspective – development defined in terms of centre and periphery
2. Underdevelopment ascribed to the industrialized capitalist powers of the West
3. Information gaps – underdevelopment in the periphery is prerequisite to development in the centre
4. The mass media reinforce the dominance of the metropole over its satellites
5. A country in the periphery must strive for self-reliance and liberation from the world system
6. Emphasis on social equality

The MacBride recommendations went against the free flow doctrine of the United States that held that there should be no restrictions on the flow of information or communication around the world. The poorer nations, however, argued that this 'flow' was primarily to the benefit of the wealthy (north) nations at the expense of the poorer (south) nations, leading to dependency. Tables 8.7 and 8.8 summarize the modernization and dependency perspectives.

The idea that there is a global centre and periphery that affects communication, culture and economy was part of Immanuel Wallerstein's argument in *The Modern World System: Capitalist Agriculture and the Origins of the European World Economy in the Sixteenth Century* (1974). Wallerstein, a Marxist, proposed that core countries, like the United States and Britain, had other countries dependent upon them, but in different stages of exploitation. In the days of colonial expansion, for instance, core nations would take the resources of peripheral countries that had been conquered or occupied. They might also change (or destroy) the indigenous cultures as a result. Those peripheral countries would, over time, develop their own middle classes and industrialize. The emerging semi-peripheral countries would then themselves exploit other countries.

As you can see, Wallerstein's theory is the Marxist flip side of Lerner's theory of development. Wallerstein sees the capitalist enterprise as pure exploitation. Lerner sees 'development' as a natural and good thing. Both theoretical approaches have a deterministic flavour. Wallerstein and Lerner, however, provide an entrée to the idea of global flows and whether there are dominant cultures with dominant flows that erode cultures or lead to dependency.

It is worthwhile turning to some of the contemporary mapping of global flows to see what is happening. The Princeton International Networks Archive has and is mapping different kinds of flows from telephone calls to student exchanges www.princeton.edu/~ina. What its work has found is that rich regions tend to enjoy ties with many other parts of the world while poorer regions have at most one dominant partner. Figure 8.4, exam-

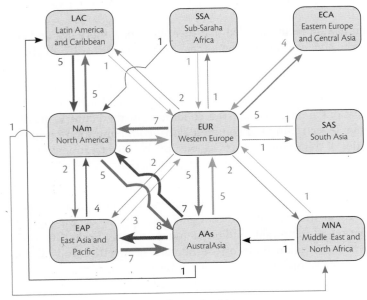

Figure 8.4 Trade links between major trading blocs

Source: Used with permission, Centeno (2005).

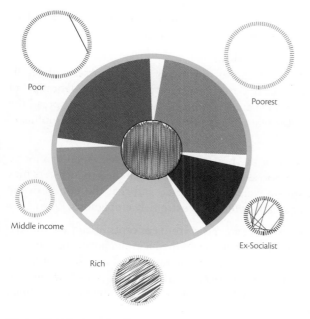

Figure 8.5 Telephone traffic in the 1990s

Source: Used with permission, Centeno (2005).

ining trade flows, shows that South Asia, for example, has one dominant tie to western Europe. Figure 8.5 shows how much the rich nations communicate among themselves, by telephone. The large circle in Figure 8.5 represents the entire globe and the large doughnut hole in the middle shows significant ties between individual countries. The smaller circles on the periphery represent connections within the various colour categories. These categories represent World Bank national wealth categories. The wealthy countries not only call each other quite often, but the poor ones have little communication with one another and only seek to call the rich.

These maps tell us that there is US and western domination of trade and telephone flows. That domination extends to online and offline media and information flows, as Bagdikian (2004), Boyd-Barrett (2007), Thussu (2006; 2007) and others have shown. Thussu (2007) in the context of media uses the expression 'dominant media flows' and subaltern flows to conceptually describe the current situation.

> **Subaltern flows.** A second layer of international media players and include private and state sponsored flows.

Subaltern flows are a second layer of international media players and include private and state sponsored flows: the Indian film industry, Bollywood, and Latin American televnovelas, South Africa based, pan African network M-Net, Euronews, the 24/7 multilingual news consortium of Europe's public service broadcasters, TV5 and Radio France Internationale, aiming at the francophone market, al Jazeera, the pan Latin American TV channel Televisor del Sur (Television of the South) in Venezuela, Russia Today (RTTV) the English language CCTV 9 (China Central Television) – 'These orginators of transnational media flows have a strong regional presence but are also aimed at audiences outside their primary constituency' (Thussu, 2007, 12).

> **Glocalization.** A glocal media product involves media content and services being tailored to specific cultural consumers.

Thussu (2007) sees glocalization as central to the acceleration of western media flows: 'What seems to be emerging is a glocal media product, conforming to what Sony once characterised as "global localisation": media content and services being tailored to specific cultural consumers, not so much because of any particular regard for national cultures but as a commercial imperative.'

The global flows do not give us a picture of cultural erosion even though they may imply dependency and if not dependency, dominance of the flows themselves. Debates about the content of the media flows, however, have raised problems of cultural erosion or cultural imperialism. Political economist Herbert Schiller (2000, 101) argues that 'corporate influence pervades nearly every aspect of society. From simple things, like our daily diet and the clothes we wear, to matters of larger scale, like the way we communicate with each other.' For Schiller, this corporate influence is international. His definition of cultural imperialism is:

> **Cultural imperialism.** Involves the transfer of a dominant ideology to other cultures, potentially destroying the indigenous culture or making it dependent on the dominant culture.

the sum of the process by which a society is brought into the modern world system and how its dominating stratum is attracted, pressured, forced, and sometimes bribed into shaping social institutions to correspond to, or even promote, the values and structures of the dominating center of the system. (1976, 9)

That dominating centre, for Schiller, is capitalism.

John Tomlinson (2001) provides an insightful analysis of the discourses and definitions of cultural and media imperialism. After looking at a dictionary definition of cultural imperialism, 'The use of political and economic power to exalt and spread the values and habits of a foreign culture at the expense of a native culture', Tomlinson thought that:

a moment's reflection will show that the practice of watching television cannot be deemed to be straightforwardly imposed, that the intention of the broadcasters may not be directly to 'exalt and spread' values and habits, and that the notion of the process being at the 'expense of a native culture' is extremely ambiguous. (2001, 3)

The aim of this discussion is not to scare you away from concepts of cultural imperialism but to emphasize that debates about cultural and media imperialism are complex. It is worthwhile looking at how some theorists have attempted to show how cultural or media imperialism may work. Donald Duck became a famous focus of debates on ideology when Ariel Dorfman and Arman Matterlart published *How to read Donald Duck: imperialist ideology in the Disney comic*.

Chile under its military dictatorship banned *Para Leer al Pato Donald*, later published in English under the title *How to Read Donald Duck*. Disney tried to ban the book, but it went on to sell hundreds of thousands of copies in myriad languages. The authors, Ariel Dorfman and Armand Mattelart, deconstructed the Donald Duck characters in order to show the capitalist ideology that underpinned them. For example, Donald Duck is talking to a witch doctor in Africa. He says:

'I see you're an up-to-date nation! Have you got telephones?'
'All colors, all shapes', the African assures him. 'Only trouble is only one has wires! It's a hot line to the world loan bank.'

For Dorfman and Mattelart we can here see both attitudes towards developing nations and of course ideas of what counts as a developed nation. In a tale about Donald Duck's nephews in kindergarten we can see role playing for the capitalist world:

'Today, we will play that we are all big business men', says the teacher.
'I'll pretend I'm a big landlord with lots of land for sale!' exclaims Dewey.
'That's the spirit', responds the teacher. 'Who wants to buy some land from Dewey?'
'I will!' says another of Donald's nephews, donning a top hat, monocle and cane to emulate billionaire Scrooge McDuck. 'I want to buy an island!'
'How big an island, and in what ocean, stranger?' replies Dewey.

Dorfman and Mattelart's play on Disney has been called polemical (Tomlinson, 1992). It is not necessary to be a Marxist, however, to appreciate the point that Dorfman and Mattelart are making about ideological messages and how the values of one country might affect another. A person's culture can be eroded if alternative values and symbols are adopted. But the impact of these cultural values and symbols is not necessarily uniform or unidirectional. Using a geology metaphor Duane Varan (1998) identifies different kinds of erosion and reactions that might occur as a result.

Cultural abrasion. Where media systems produce in local cultures a fear of cultural domination.
Cultural deflation. Where a local culture is carried off by an erosive cultural agent.

Cultural abrasion is where media systems can act as cultural abrasive agents, producing in local cultures a fear of cultural domination. Cultural deflation, from the Latin 'to blow away', is where a local culture is carried off by an erosive cultural agent. This is especially

Cultural deposition. Where people will adopt a foreign value, but it comes at the expense of another value.

Cultural saltation. Where foreign media systems help stimulate local cultural expression.

the case where parts of a local culture might be weak and are most likely to be uprooted by contact with a foreign media agent. Cultural deposition is where people will adopt a foreign value, but it comes at the expense of another value. Cultural saltation is similar to deposition, but foreign media systems help stimulate local cultural expression (Varan, 1998).

A simple example would be denim jeans. In one culture, adopting jeans might affect the dress code so drastically that it changes perceptions of fashion and even perceptions of gender (cultural abrasion). In another culture, adopting jeans might only represent a minor change to symbols and values (cultural saltation). Romania's Communist dictator Nicolae Ceauşescu experienced cultural deflation at first hand when he decided as policy to increase the amount of entertainment on Romanian television. He thought that entertainment would cause no harm to the regime and indeed that it might ease domestic unrest at the state of the economy. Shows like *Dallas* from the United States and *Onedin Line* from the United Kingdom were purchased by the Romanian dictator and became overwhelming hits with the Romanian population. So much so that Ceauşescu became concerned that Romanians were not watching the communist propaganda, including poems read on television praising the communist dictator. He decided to cancel the foreign shows and limit television to three hours a day, all of which was spent broadcasting communist propaganda, including extreme imported North Korean propaganda that talked about how the Americans boiled children in oil. The result of Ceauşescu's acts involved subversion from his citizens and government agencies. Illegal television aerials were made in government factories and set up on people's households in order to get access to Hungary's more liberal television programmes. The BBC documentary *The Power of Soap*, an episode in *We Have Ways of Making You Think* (1992), argues that the collapse of the Communist regime in Romania was very much linked to its encounter with television and its dictator's actions in restricting access to entertainment.

There can be varying and sometimes confusing reactions to the introduction of a new medium to a culture. Granzberg's (1985) longitudinal eight-year study of the Canadian indigenous Algonkian communities in Northern Canada compared residents in a village that received satellite television services with another village that did not, until later. Those children exposed to television became more aggressive and saw themselves as Canadians. Popular music also displaced record sales in traditional music. This was a case of cultural abrasion. 'In a surprising twist, however, a similar trend did not repeat itself following the control population's eventual encounter with television. In other words, while direct and immediate effects associated with television seemed apparent in the initial treatment population, it did not occur when the treatment was administered to the control population. How could such contrasting encounters be explained?' (Granzberg, 1985).

to recap...
Cultural imperialism is, at base, the domination of one culture over another. Media imperialism is an extension of this idea. Media are the vehicles for this domination. However, empirically, what is happening can be complex and involves different levels of domination or erosion of cultures.

Granzberg (1985) had found that the village first exposed to television saw the medium as an extension of its belief system. The village not yet exposed to television saw the medium as a threat. 'Elders in the treatment village, for example, had experienced dreams fore-telling of the arrival of television. Parents integrated television with their own traditions by explaining to their children how television was like the "conjuring tents" of traditional shaman. Yet villagers in the control group used similar traditions as proof of the evils of television – as harmful White Man conjuring which captured people's souls and made them crazy' (Varan, 1998).

Varan (1998) concludes that for indigenous societies the struggle for cultural preservation will continue. Indigenous cultures will resist attempts to erode their way of life and their values.

case study

The problem of cultural erosion, however, is not only and necessarily an international one. The Center for Communication and Civic Engagement at University of Washington, http://depts.washington.edu/ccce/Home.htm, for example has highlighted the need for active involvement by citizens against human rights abuses or curtailment of civil rights, even when individuals are mismatched against executive governments and corporate power. Culture jamming has emerged as one of these means of becoming active. It is 'an attempt to reverse and transgress the meaning of cultural codes whose primary aim is to persuade us to buy something or be someone' (Jordan, 2002, 102). It is an interception or counter message that hacks 'into a corporation's own method of communication to send a message starkly at odds with the one that was intended' (Klein, 2000, 281). Bart Cammaerts (2007) gives examples of *political jamming* that use culture jamming practices. Greenpeace, the environmental movement, in its 'Stop E$$O'-campaign substituted the S with a US-dollar-sign. 'Esso/Exxon/Mobile then decided to sue Greenpeace for infringing the copyright of its logo and for reputational damage. In reaction to the court case Greenpeace launched a call to the general public to use the Esso logo in graphical jams … The results were often cunning and witty fake logos' (Cammaerts, 2007, 72).

The *meme* is the basic unit of communication in culture jamming. Memes are symbols that stimulate visual, verbal, musical, or behavioural associations. Culture jammers use these memes in ways that make people think about their behaviour and their beliefs. Jonah Peretti's email exchange with Nike over his online order for personalized Nikes is a classic culture jam. Nike's website allows people to order personalized labels on shoes. Peretti asked Nike to put the word 'sweatshop' on his pair of Nikes. Nike is, not surprisingly, sensitive over anything to do with sweatshops as it had been accused of using cheap sweatshop labour in developing countries in order to reduce costs and increase profits. The resulting email exchange between Peretti and Nike was broadcast around the world. The actual exchange is provided below.

CULTURE JAMMING

Culture jamming. An attempt to reverse and transgress the meaning of cultural codes whose primary aim is to persuade us to buy something or be someone.

Jonah Peretti's email exchange with Nike

From: 'Personalize, NIKE iD' <nikeid_personalize@nike.com>

To: "Jonah H. Peretti" <peretti@media.mit.edu>

Subject: RE: Your NIKE iD order 016468000

Your NIKE iD order was cancelled for one or more of the following reasons.

1) Your Personal iD contains another party's trademark or other intellectual property.
2) Your Personal iD contains the name of an athlete or team we do not have the legal right to use.
3) Your Personal iD was left blank. Did you not want any personalization?
4) Your Personal iD contains profanity or inappropriate slang, and besides, your mother would slap us.

If you wish to reorder your NIKE iD product with a new personalization please visit us again at www.nike.com

Thank you,
NIKE iD

From: 'Jonah H. Peretti' <peretti@media.mit.edu>

To: 'Personalize, NIKE iD' <nikeid_personalize@nike.com>

Subject: RE: Your NIKE iD order 016468000

Greetings,

My order was canceled but my personal NIKE iD does not violate any of the criteria outlined in your message. The Personal iD on my custom ZOOM XC USA running shoes was the word 'sweatshop.' Sweatshop is not:

1) another's party's trademark,
2) the name of an athlete,
3) blank, or
4) profanity.

I choose the iD because I wanted to remember the toil and labor of the children that made my shoes. Could you please ship them to me immediately.

Thanks and Happy New Year,
Jonah Peretti

From: 'Personalize, NIKE iD' <nikeid_personalize@nike.com>

To: "Jonah H. Peretti" <peretti@media.mit.edu>

Subject: RE: Your NIKE iD order 016468000

Dear NIKE iD Customer,

Your NIKE iD order was cancelled because the iD you have chosen contains, as stated in the previous e-mail correspondence, 'inappropriate slang'.

If you wish to reorder your NIKE iD product with a new personalization please visit us again at www.nike.com

Thank you, NIKE iD

From: 'Jonah H. Peretti' <peretti@media.mit.edu>

To: 'Personalize, NIKE iD' <nikeid_personalize@nike.com>

Subject: RE: Your NIKE iD order 016468000

Dear NIKE iD,

Thank you for your quick response to my inquiry about my custom ZOOM XC USA running shoes. Although I commend you for your prompt customer service, I disagree with the claim that my personal iD was inappropriate slang. After consulting Webster's Dictionary, I discovered that 'sweatshop' is in fact part of standard English, and not slang. The word means: 'a shop or factory in which workers are employed for long hours at low wages and under unhealthy conditions' and its origin dates from 1892. So my personal iD does meet the criteria detailed in your first email.

Your web site advertises that the NIKE iD program is 'about freedom to choose and freedom to express who you are.' I share Nike's love of freedom and personal expression. The site also says that 'If you want it done right … build it yourself.' I was thrilled to be able to build my own shoes, and my personal iD was offered as a small token of appreciation for the sweatshop workers poised to help me realize my vision. I hope that you will value my freedom of expression and reconsider your decision to reject my order.

Thank you,
Jonah Peretti

From: 'Personalize, NIKE iD' <nikeid_personalize@nike.com>

To: "Jonah H. Peretti" <peretti@media.mit.edu>

Subject: RE: Your NIKE iD order 016468000

Dear NIKE iD Customer,

Regarding the rules for personalization it also states on the NIKE iD web site that 'Nike reserves the right to cancel any Personal iD up to 24 hours after it has been submitted'.

In addition it further explains:

'While we honor most personal iDs, we cannot honor every one. Some may be (or contain) others' trademarks, or the names of certain professional sports teams, athletes or celebrities that Nike does not have the right to use. Others may contain material that we consider inappropriate or simply do not want to place on our products.

Unfortunately, at times this obliges us to decline personal iDs that may otherwise seem unobjectionable. In any event, we will let you know if we decline your personal iD, and we will offer you the chance to submit another.'

With these rules in mind we cannot accept your order as submitted.

If you wish to reorder your NIKE iD product with a new personalization please visit us again at www.nike.com

Thank you, NIKE iD

From: 'Jonah H. Peretti' <peretti@media.mit.edu>

To: 'Personalize, NIKE iD' <nikeid_personalize@nike.com>

Subject: RE: Your NIKE iD order 016468000

Dear NIKE iD,

Thank you for the time and energy you have spent on my request. I have decided to order the shoes with a different iD, but I would like to make one small request. Could you please send me a color snapshot of the ten-year-old Vietnamese girl who makes my shoes?

Thanks,
Jonah Peretti

{no response}

Adbusters (www.adbusters.org) is another example of culture jamming. It is a global network of artists, activists, writers, pranksters, students, educators and entrepreneurs who, according to their website, work to challenge the way information flows, institutions wield power, and multinational companies set their agendas. They engage 'in fearless anti-corporate criticism, Adbusters treads contentious political terrain in a way that publications dependent on ad revenue or foundation money can't' (www. adbusters.org).

Who owns the media and who makes a profit from them, of course, plays a major role in what happens with information and communication flows, nationally and globally. The trend worldwide has been towards concentration of ownership and vertical integration of media industries.

Media ownership

Ulla Carlsson's Nordic Information Centre for Media and Communication Research (NORDICOM) at Göteborg University published in 2003 *The Rise and Fall of NWICO – and Then? From a Vision of International Regulation to a Reality of Multilevel Governance*. The report concludes that there is 'a new international order' of the sort envisaged in the 1970s. 'Now we see the era of multilevel governance of the media system – the interplay between many different actors, public and private, on multiple levels, from the local to the global' (Carlsson, 2003, 34).

The reality of the modern media landscape, as we have seen, is very complex and reduction of that landscape to simple causal factors does not help in analysing that landscape. However, this does not mean that problems in media ownership and regulation are no longer important. The concentration of ownership is mapped on a continual basis by independent groups like *Mother Jones*'s 'smart, fearless journalism' (http://www.mother-jones.com) and by *Columbia Journalism Review* (http://www.cjr.org/resources/). The NORDICOM report showed in 2003 how conglomerates have dominated media sales, as outlined in Table 8.9. This ownership group has now been reduced to eight. Each of these organizations owns subsidiaries in a range of media from radio to television to the Internet and book publishers, and includes the production and distribution organizations behind those media (vertical integration).

At the same time, media densities and accessibility to media have changed. Table 8.10 shows the trend towards greater diffusion of media in those least developed countries in the world.

Table 8.9 The largest media corporations in the world, by media sales volume 2001 (US$ billions)

1.	AOL Time Warner USA	38
2.	Viacom (Inc.) USA	23
3.	Vivendi Universal France/USA	19
4.	The Walt Disney Company USA	16
5.	Bertelsmann AG Germany	15
6.	News Corporation Australia	13
7.	Sony Corporation Japan	9
8.	Reed Elsevier The Netherlands	7
9.	Gannett Co., Inc. USA	6
10.	Pearson PLC Great Britain	6

Source: Carlsson (2003).

Table 8.10 Media densities in the world 1970 and 1997. Units per thousand inhabitants

	Daily newspapers		Radio receivers		TV sets	
	1970	1996	1970	1997	1970	1997
The world, total	107	96	245	418	81	240
Africa	12	16	93	216	4.6	60
America	170	141	698	1017	209	429
Asia	49	66	81	255	20	190
Europe	281	261	465	29	205	446
Oceania	269	227	779	1071	188	427
Least developed	4.5	8	56	142	0.5	23
Developed	292	226	643	1061	263	548

Source: UNESCO (2003).

Culture has a role in diffusion of media and its control. Different national cultures have different perceptions on the freedom of their media and on regulation of content and ownership. Some countries, for example, have strict censorship laws affecting how advertising, news and programmes are made. Showing a woman's bare leg in an advertisement is banned in Arab countries but allowed in western countries. Reporting a news story criticizing your leaders might get your killed in one country and rewarded in another.

Models of regulation and media freedom

Siebert, Peterson and Schramm (1963) provided one of the early attempts to conceptualize the different ways nations were regulating their media. They distinguished between Authoritarian, Libertarian, Communist and Social Responsibility approaches to regulation. *Authoritarian* models allow no public criticism of the state or leadership through the media, with media owned by a monarch or ruler, a party or private individuals. The purpose of the media is to support the state and leadership. *Libertarian* models separate the state and media. Nothing is forbidden from publication prior to publication. There is private ownership. The purpose of the media is to inform, interpret and entertain. The *Communist* model involves control of the media by the Communist Party and is there to serve Party objectives. Under this model the media are theoretically owned by the people. The *Social Responsibility* model limits publication of information that might be socially harmful or invade private rights. There is private ownership but greater government interference than in the Libertarian model. Social responsibility of the media is more important than their freedom. The purpose of the media is to inform and educate to help social progress. There have been updates of this model, including Altschull's (1984) typology that distinguishes between Market (First World), Marxist (Second World) and Advancing (Third World). The Communist-Soviet bloc no longer exists but the overall philosophical ideas behind the models remain.

Non-profit organizations such as Freedom House, http://www.freedomhouse.org, have attempted to put flesh on different aspects of regulation of the media by different countries. In their freedom of the press ranking Freedom House rates various questions against legal, political and economic dimensions. The *legal environment* category includes questions that rate the positive impact of legal and constitutional guarantees for freedom of expression; the potentially negative aspects of security legislation, the penal code, and other criminal statutes; penalties for libel and defamation; the existence of and ability to use freedom of information legislation; the independence of the judiciary and of official media regulatory bodies; registration requirements for both media outlets and journalists; and the ability of journalists' groups to operate freely. The *political environment* category includes questions that evaluate the degree of political control over the content of news media; the editorial independence of both state-owned and privately owned media; access to information and sources; official censorship and self-censorship; the vibrancy of the media; the ability of both foreign and local reporters to cover the news freely and without harassment; and the imprisonment, violent assaults, and other threats. The *economic environment* includes questions about the structure of media ownership; transparency and concentration of ownership; the costs of establishing media as well as of production and distribution; the selective withholding of advertising or subsidies by the state or other actors; the impact of corruption and bribery on content; and the extent to which the economic situation in a country impacts the development of the media. Table 8.11 presents the 2007 press freedom rankings.

Table 8.11 Global press freedom rankings, 1–74 free, 75–132 Part Free, 133–195 Not Free

1 Finland	Austria	India	Kuwait	Singapore
Iceland	Belize	Mongolia	Sierra Leone	Iraq
Belgium	France	Bolivia	Colombia	Bahrain
Denmark	Hungary	Croatia	Georgia	Oman
Norway	Japan	Montenegro	Cambodia	Chad
Sweden	Slovenia	Antigua & Barbuda	Central African Republic	Togo
Luxembourg	Cyprus	Burkina Faso		Venezuela
Switzerland	Poland	Fiji	Nepal	Azerbaijan
Andorra	Spain	Serbia	Niger	Russia
Netherlands	Suriname	Dominican Republic	Guatemala	Brunei
New Zealand	Grenada	Mozambique	Haiti	Kazakhstan
Liechtenstein	Mali	Ecuador	Kenya	Swaziland
Palau	Trinidad & Tobago	Brazil	Lebanon	Tajikistan
Portugal	Vanuatu	East Timor	Thailand	Burundi
Jamaica	Greece	El Salvador	Paraguay	Ethiopia
Estonia	Ghana	Lesotho	**132** Seychelles	Gambia
Germany	Mauritius	Nicaragua	Jordan	Vietnam
Ireland	Kiribati	Peru	Algeria	Congo-Kinshasa
Monaco	Tuvalu	Romania	Angola	Yemen
Saint Lucia	Nauru	Panama	Bhutan	Laos
United States	South Africa	Bosnia	Egypt	Sudan
Bahamas	Cape Verde	Macedonia	Morocco	Saudi Arabia
Barbados	Guyana	Philippines	Pakistan	Syria
Canada	Israel	Senegal	Qatar	Tunisia
Marshall Islands	Italy	Comoros	Sri Lanka	China
Malta	Sao Tome & Principe	Guinea-Bissau	Armenia	Iran
Saint Vincent & the Grenadines	Benin	Mexico	Zambia	Israeli-Occupied Territories / Palestinian Authority
	Chile	Argentina	Liberia	
San Marino	Hong Kong	Turkey	Moldova	Rwanda
Czech Republic	Namibia	Albania	Bangladesh	Somalia
Lithuania	Papua New Guinea	Madagascar	Cameroon	Belarus
Latvia	Samoa	Congo-Brazzaville	Guinea	Equatorial Guinea
United Kingdom	Solomon Islands	Honduras	Kyrgyzstan	Zimbabwe
Costa Rica	South Korea	Tanzania	Côte d'Ivoire	Uzbekistan
Dominica	Uruguay	Malawi	Malaysia	Eritrea
Micronesia		Ukraine	Maldives	Burma
Saint Kitts & Nevis		Indonesia	United Arab Emirates	Cuba
Slovakia	**75** Tonga	Uganda	Afghanistan	Libya
Taiwan	Bulgaria	Mauritania	Djibouti	Turkmenistan
Australia	Botswana	Nigeria	Gabon	**195** North Korea

Free 74 (38 per cent) Partly Free 58 (30 per cent) Not Free 63 (32 per cent) **TOTAL 195**

Source: Global Press Freedom (2007).

Table 8.12 **A region's interest in news stories about itself, as a percentage of all news received**

Australia and New Zealand	56
Eastern Europe	80
Japan	78
China	64
Middle East	85
North America	80
Southern Africa	80
Latin America	92
Western Europe	63

Source: Adapted from Stevenson (1994).

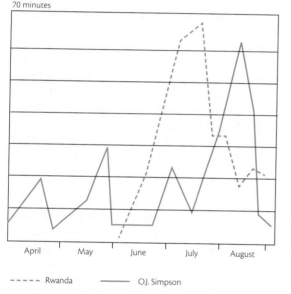

70 minutes

April   May   June   July   August

- - - - - Rwanda   ———— O.J. Simpson

Figure 8.6 ABC, CBS and NBC nightly newscasts, by minutes, 1994

Source: Adapted from Linda Melvern (2007).

International news has a major role in conveying ideas about other countries and their cultures. Table 8.12 gives an idea of which regions are more receptive to news stories from outside their own countries. Interestingly, China, and Australia and New Zealand are least ethnocentric in this regard. While Stevenson's (1994) data are relatively old and this type of data is difficult to keep current, these figures provide interesting insights into the effects of culture on news selection.

International agenda setting of news affects what individual cultures might see, from the little that they do choose, and count as important. Humanitarian crises, in particular, fall into this category. When the massacre of 800,000 Tutsi by Hutu was underway, international news broadcasters focused on the O.J. Simpson murder case. From Figure 8.6 we can see that reporting on Rwanda only gained news broadcasting interest when the Hutu refugee crisis had also peaked.

Ownership of the major international news agencies that distribute news about what is happening in each country remains monopolized. However as the Internet grows in importance in the distribution of news, the nature of this monopolization is itself being transformed.

News agencies and news aggregators

News agencies collect news stories from around the globe and set the agenda for the possible choice of stories available to local news outlets. These stories include moving images for television, stills for newspapers and magazines and both for web broadcasters. Associated Press (AP), United Press International (UPI), Reuters and Agence France-Presse (AFP) have dominated this global news flow.

Chris Paterson (2006) says that the rise of news aggregators in an online environment is a signal of the continuation of global news dominance by a few. There is no doubt that people in western societies are accessing news online. Twenty-three per cent of Americans reported online news as their main news source in 2000 and 42 per cent by 2004 (Paterson, 2006).

Dominant online news providers by 2001 took two main types. The first type was a website of major conglomerates that passed on news agency content to audiences. Yahoo! was the first company in the mid-1990s to develop a relationship with the British Reuters news agency. The second type combined original content written by the organization's own journalists with news agency content. The BBC and the *New York Times* are paradigm examples.

The term news aggregator emerged to described websites or search engines that select, retrieve and link news from anywhere on the Internet. *Google News* and Yahoo! ended up aggregators of news from thousands of news sources. But reproducing news agency content led to a lawsuit against Google in 2005. Google did not pay for news directly produced by news agencies. Agence France-Presse (AFP) sued Google for 17.5 million dollars for breach of copyright. Google removed the content from its websites and has agreed to give AFP samples of its news content (Cozens, 2005). Google's position is that news headlines are not protected by copyright even though this is not statute in the US. 'Google also argues that their linking to AFP content at the websites of AFP clients brings profit, not loss, to AFP, which increases the possibility of the American courts seeing aggregation as "fair use" of copyrighted material' (Paterson, 2006).

Most audiences go to the news aggregators or the news services. Forty-six per cent of US Internet users go to the national television news website, for example CNN or MSNBC, Thirty-nine per cent go to news aggregators like Yahoo! or Google (Horrigan, cited in Paterson, 2006). Table 8.13 gives the top online news services in the US.

Paterson concludes that this will leave the online news world (in the English language) with only four organizations doing extensive international reporting (Reuters, AP, AFP, BBC): 'a few others do some international reporting (CNN, MSN, *New York Times*, *Guardian* and a few other large newspaper and broadcasters), and most do no original international reporting' (2006).

to recap...

International agenda setting of news affects what individual cultures might see, in particular humanitarian crises. Monopolization of the news agencies affects what goes on to the agenda. Internet news is following this trend. The term news aggregator emerged to described websites or search engines that select, retrieve and link news from anywhere on the Internet. This is a new form of agency dominance of the news.

Table 8.13 Top online news services in the United States

Corporation	Audience
Microsoft	52,873,000
Google	45,069,000
Yahoo!	44,111,000
Time Warner	40,895,000
New York Times Company	21,118,000
News Corp. Online	20,867,000

Radical and rebellious media

The outcome of monopolized international news services is homogenized news that tends to be bland precisely because it seeks to keep a range of local country audiences happy. Despite the popularity of the news aggregators among modern news audiences there are also radical and rebellious media that attract large news audiences.

Indymedia has emerged as 'almost mythic' in proportions as a radical media news site (Jankowski and Jansen, 2003). Indymedia (or independent media centre) was created as a result of protests at the World Trade Organization (WTO) in Seattle in 1999. The website was created as a hub for distributing independent news about what was happening, including video documentaries. Indymedia from then took off as an international phenomenon with groups set up in countries around the world.

Jankowski and Jansen (2003) adapted from Atton a typology to describe alternative media, represented in Table 8.14. Two key features of alternative media are their democratic and collective production process and the commitment to experimentation. Jankowski and Jansen (2003) compare this typology with the Indymedia organizational structure and ethos, presented in Table 8.15.

One of the Indymedia promotions is featured in Figure 8.7. Regardless of the success or not of Indymedia in the future, modern media appear to provide the potential for expression of radical thought (see Boler, 2008, for a contemporary discussion on use of Web-based media in shaping political and social movements).

Table 8.14 **Typology of alternative media**

Product
• Radical formulation of political, social and cultural positions
• Redefinition of traditional news values
• Innovative presentation through language and illustrations
• Adaptation of conventional production technologies process
• New modes of media distribution
• Redefinition of copyright and use regulations
• Transformation of conventional journalistic roles
• Horizontal organizational structures and working networks

Table 8.15 **Typology of Indymedia features**

Policies and Principles
• Collective ownership and management
• Open access
• Transformation of copyright and use regulations
• News construction and production
• Redefinition of news
• Transformation of conventional codes of news production
• Limited editorial restriction
• Involvement of non-professionals
• Fusion of standard one-way publication with interactive communication
• Multimedia presentation of news
• Contextual components
• Distribution via electronic networks
• Intertwining of local and global issues
• Emphasis on movement-based news, demonstrations and protests

to recap...

The Internet has corporate voices dominating much of the global distribution of news. However, the global mediascape has also been transformed by the possibilities for an alternative voice. Some of these voices are subaltern, like al Jazeera and others are more independent, like the Indy networks.

Radical and rebellious media may be linked to cultural or political jamming, but for the most part they are a *contra-flow* (Boyd-Barrett and Thussu, 1992) with a more specific and enduring purpose. It is of course much more difficult to run an independent media centre in authoritarian and dictatorial regimes than in democratic societies. However, the media landscape has transformed the possibilities for an alternative voice and many groups in 'not free' regimes have developed independent media sites, at risk.

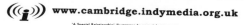

Figure 8.7 Indymedia promotion

Summary

New phrases are still emerging and will continue to emerge to describe or to try to analyse the relationship between culture and globalization, not least new phrases like 'cultural economy'. Anheier and Isar in their edited collection present what they call 'indicator suites' on aspects of the relationship between culture and globalization' (2008, 2). The modernization and dependency models, however, dominated much of the early international media governance and academic discourses. Modernization theorists held that there were law-like processes associated with media and development. Introducing western media into 'underdeveloped' countries was seen to be a good thing and would help those countries to 'develop'. Dependency theorists held that western perspectives on modernization were ethnocentric and an abbreviation for cultural imperialism and cultural domination. Those like Dorfman and Mattelart, for example, argued that media systems act as vehicles for cultural imperialism.

The concept of culture becomes fundamental in these discourses because national and ethnic identities are at stake. Do dominant media flows – whether trade, telephone or news – erode national and local cultures? As the authors have attempted to show, the idea of dominant flows has not disappeared in the discourse on cultural domination, but there has been a shift away from focusing solely on the foreign violation of national boundaries. The potential empowerment of local audiences through radical media, cultural jamming or other means is now a part of the discourse and practice.

The demand for a new international information or communication order was a result of resentment of the imbalances in international news flows and a lack of respect for peoples' cultural identity. Many of these issues remain current, not only for nations and cultures that cannot match the West but for groups within western cultures who seek an independent voice.

At the conclusion of this chapter you should be able to:
- critically discuss the concept of culture in intercultural communication;
- evaluate arguments about cultural imperialism and identify contexts where there may or may not be dominant culture influence through the media;
- recognize alternative voices in the global and local mediascapes.

Key themes

Culture. Culture is so deep in us that it is, for all intents and purposes, reality. Culture seems natural and ordinary but at the same time it defines what we do in practice. We attach meanings to people and to practices as well as to our physical environment. Intercultural communication has, at its core, the attempt to find better ways to understand different cultures other than our own and better ways to communicate as an international community. Geert Hofstede's work was one of the early attempts to try to define different dimensions of culture and how they affected communication and behaviour. His dimensions – individualism/collectivism, masculine/feminine power distance, uncertainty avoidance – may not be perfect representations of how different cultures act or react but they are guides to real differences in how we communicate. Some cultures are high context and deference to the group has priority over the individual. Some cultures do value individualism more highly than the collective. Different cultures also have different styles of communication. It is important in media studies to understand the importance of culture on the mediation process and the impact of communicative differences on interpretation.

Global flows. Globalization at the minimum involves networks – of media, goods, people – that cross national boundaries and can vary in their extent, intensity, tempo and influence. It is possible to map some of the flows between countries. In this chapter, for example, we have looked briefly at trade flows and international telephone traffic. In terms of extent, intensity and tempo we can see that the wealthier nations tend to trade with each other and communicate with each other on a scale that dwarfs more disadvantaged cultures. Media ownership, similarly, seems to be in a narrow set of hands at global level, with news agencies and news aggregation concentrated in a few companies. The dominant flows and the concentrated ownership of media do appear to support a cultural imperialism argument that the wealthier nations are dominating the whole global media agenda. However, the picture starts to change when we look at the contra and subaltern flows. Second tier news groups like al Jazeera are not US or western Europe owned and have established international influence. Independent media exist that do not replicate the global news agenda of the wealthier nations. Culture and political jamming are ways of expressing dissent within wealthier nations. Even when international advertising campaigns are designed to influence other cultures there can be resistance, for example in the case of Italian company Benetton's anti-death penalty campaign in the United States.

Discussion questions

1 Investigate the corporate websites of high and low context cultures. Bring to class your examples. Discuss in what ways, if any, websites are affected by high and low context culture or high or low context communication, in their design or in any other way.

2 See if you can find examples of culture or political jamming. Bring them to class and discuss their efficacy or usefulness as a protest tool.

3   Which model of globalization do you think best represents what is happening? Can you find examples to discuss in class that support your point of view?

4   The Berbers were given as one example of a culture attempting to preserve its past and to maintain its language. Can you find any other examples where cultural groups have adopted modern media technology to assist their cause?

5   Does media ownership really bias what we see and hear in our national and international news? Is the 'citizen reporter' a more honest approach to news and a guide to the future of global journalism?

6   Bring to class what you think are examples of cultural abrasion, cultural deposition and cultural saltation.

*Further reading*

Boler, M. (ed.) (2008). *Digital media and democracy: tactics in hard times*. Cambridge, MA: MIT.

Miller, T., Nitin, G., McMurria, R. and Wang, T. (2005). *Global Hollywood* 2. London: British Film Institute.

Williams, R. (1981). *Culture*. Fontana.

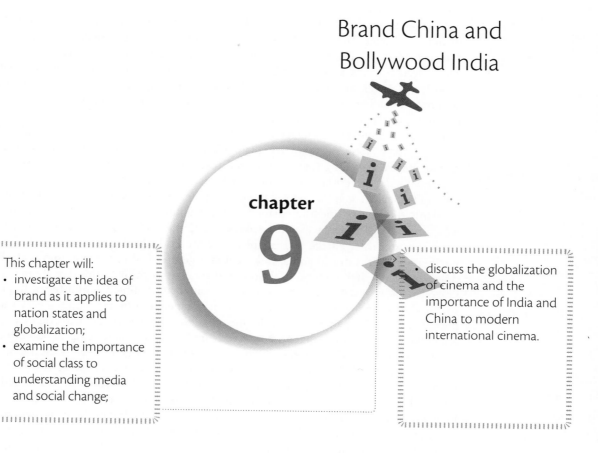

Brand China and Bollywood India

chapter

9

This chapter will:
- investigate the idea of brand as it applies to nation states and globalization;
- examine the importance of social class to understanding media and social change;

- discuss the globalization of cinema and the importance of India and China to modern international cinema.

In Chapter 8, we found that there is significant debate about the nature of cultural change in a globalized world. In this chapter we examine India and China as two major, non-western, cultures that are involved in or have been affected by global media. This chapter will:

- investigate the idea of *brand* as it applies to nation states and globalization;

- examine the importance of *social class* to understanding media and social change;

- discuss the globalization of cinema and the importance of India and China to modern international cinema.

Soon we will find that in order to make a hugely successful film you have to match Tom Cruise with an Indian or a Chinese actor.

(Indian film director Shekhar Kapur, 2002)

Kapur, a director who has worked in both the Bollywood and Hollywood systems, is reflecting on the changing nature of the global film audience and the types of films that will be produced for that audience. He is also making a point about the size of audiences from two of the world's largest nations, India and China. Kapur's prediction has also become reality.

German audiences, and not just the Indian audience in Germany, have become fans of Indian cinema. The Hindi-language movies of film director Shah Rukh Khan are shown on local German TV channels and German fans mob the director when he visits Germany. 'It's a very humbling experience for me', Khan told the *Hollywood Reporter*. 'I never imagined that, not knowing the language or the culture of our country, the audience would react to a movie that is a take-off on the Indian movie industry and like it so much' (Advani, 2008).

But India's and China's engagement with the West and its culture, media and technology has a long history. In 1896 Maurice Sestier, the Lumière Brothers' representative travelling the world to sell their cinematograph, stopped in Bombay and screened a selection of brief films at Watson's Hotel. The advertisement for the screening clearly suggests that the intended audience for this novelty were the British residents of the city and the cosmopolitan, Anglophile Indian middle class. There was no hint that cinema would become a national Indian obsession within a few years. By 1913 D.G. Phalke had established a studio in Nasik, a pilgrimage town in northern Maharashtra in India and created a genre of film, the mythological, that draws on India's rich cultural traditions and remains popular to this day. By 1927 the Government of India established the Indian Cinematographic Committee of Inquiry that undertook a detailed study of the extent of cinema in India. Within a very short period of time film had become a significant addition to the Indian cultural mix. The Shanghai cinemas in the 1920s were already multiplexes screening up to 90 per cent American imports. The film scene was also mixed up between the two cultural influences. The film scholar Fu Poshek has written of two great Chinese actresses Ruan Lingyu and Chen Yunshang, that while the first was very 'Chinese' and restrained in her clothing style, Chen went for an athletic American 'sporty look' to emphasize how modern she could be (Fu, 2003, 14). Meanwhile, the Chinese-language cinemas, in Singapore, Hong Kong, Taiwan and on the mainland of China, have continued to develop strong stylistic and social characteristics. As the industry has opened up to more and more co-productions, there has also been some synergy between the worlds of film so that the two-way street between early Indian, Chinese and western film worlds still continues.

activity Name three Chinese and three Indian stars that you know. Have you seen them in English, or Hindi or Chinese language films? Have any acted in more than one language? Do you have any comments on their style of self-presentation as a star? Do their films reflect a local culture or a global one?

What does non-English language film mean to you? Name your favourite from recent years. Why did it entertain or move you?

Whatever the depth and achievements of Chinese and Indian film cultures, indeed of any film cultures outside the very powerful Hollywood mainstream, these have often been unacknowledged on a global scale. The power of Hollywood's vertically integrated distribution systems has made it possible to ignore other people's film. This is tied to the broader question of colonial vision. In media and film studies one must take this factor into account when describing the relative influence and wealth of particular media industries. In a sense it is immaterial when western colonialism began, what is important is that imperialism and colonialism provided the lens through which western scholars have interpreted Asia. Edward Said (2003) called this Orientalism. Said was describing the aesthetic as well as the political appropriation of cultures in his analysis. In terms of media this may be understood as a kind of willed cultural ignorance on the part of western media producers and consumers, often echoed in the scholarship of film and media communications. The other side of Orientalism is an affected representation of eastern cultures, that tries to make them seem outdated, obscure, dramatic or over-feminine. For those of us who are feminists, we may not worry about the latter, as what is wrong with the feminine after all! However, in an Orientalist aesthetic it is certainly not intended to denote respect.

Such ignorance or rudeness is no longer supportable or wise. India and China have become major manufacturing powers with an expanding middle class to support their claim to be emerging world leaders in many areas. China is the world's major manufacturer and exporter of consumer products. India has become a major provider of services, largely associated with computers and outsourcing of financial services. Their media now support the communicative channels for almost half the world's population, and significant segments of that population are getting richer and more powerful as those economies grow. In such a context Orientalism looks plain silly, to the populations of the world who know very well that their choices, tastes and media cultures matter a great deal on their own terms and in languages other than English.

This shift in economic power is beginning to manifest itself politically, militarily and culturally to the extent that prestigious western journals such as *The Economist* describe the 21st century as the Asian century. In this chapter the authors will discuss some aspects of the Asian century so far and draw your attention to the ways in which key categories – media structures, media audiences and media content – help us to understand the social issues of class and change that Asian populations are confronting as their role on the global stage increases.

An overview of China and India

India and China, as Tables 9.1 and 9.2 show, have among the largest populations in the world, roughly the same in size. Their economies differ in several important ways, with China still emerging into a free market structure while India aspires to be a fully free market although residual elements of *autarky*, the desire to be economically self-sufficient, remain. There is also a strong anti-western capitalism strand of political activity in India that manifests itself in attacks on iconic western (US) companies like KFC and McDonald's. India is, however, a democracy. China is not. India, as we shall see, has had significant state intervention in the development of media and in the creation of rules to limit the foreign influence of media. China has a highly controlled media, but the market forces now in play are forcing some changes in content as people choose new forms and genres for entertainment and information. In China there was also, at an institutional level, a great deal of conglomeration activity in the late 1990s and early 21st century in preparation for membership of the World Trade Organization (WTO) and then for the 2008 Olympics. In both countries the rise of the Internet is a key factor in the creation of the new mediascapes and the ways in which the respective states seek to maintain control or, as they would argue, communication sovereignty.

The Internet patterns of each country are significantly different. In Table 9.1 by 2000, India's rate of adoption of the Internet by users was much lower than in China.

By 2006, 10.35 per 100 of the Chinese population were Internet users compared with 5.44 per hundred in India. There were also 20.8 million bloggers in China in 2006, and that number increases every year. The pattern of Internet users in China is related to region of course, with the greatest number of users residing in the great cities of China, including Shanghai, Beijing, Guangzhou and major but not leading cities such as Wuhan. While over 20 per cent of people in Beijing and Shanghai, and about 10–19 per cent in other eastern provinces, were online; less than 5 per cent had access in Tibet (in the west), Henan (in the centre), Jiangxi (in the southeast) and Guizhou (in the south). This is important, as all national stories have some regional variations and you should be prepared to look for them when thinking about comparisons across the world.

Table 9.1 Brief country comparison of China and India

	China	India
Population	1.3 billion	1.1 billion
Economy	Command, although entrepreneurship encouraged and overseen by state	Mixed, although free market economy now dominant
GDP	US$1,835 average (2006)	US$720 (2005)
Political System	One Party State (smaller parties allowed in theory but only under the leadership of the CCP)	Democratic, follows modified Westminster system with separation of powers and multi-party elections.
Political Organization	Centralized and hierarchical cascading down from national, through regional, municipal and county levels	National, regional and local governments
Language	One official language, Mandarin (*putonghua*) but multiplicity of regional 'dialects'. Some languages are from different language families (Turkic for example) and cannot be described as dialects	Polyglot: two official national languages, Hindi and English, and 18 approved regional languages
Mediascape	Closed but increasingly marketized (except in the news sector)	Open
Bureaucracy	Arm of the state at four levels of government	Officially separated from politics, competitive, hierarchical and regionalized

activity   In order to extend your understanding of what Table 9.1 means in your context, add and research a third column for the United States and a fourth for a European, Oceanic or South American example.

It is perhaps ironic that the democratic state, India, has slower diffusion of media like the Internet, compared with China, a more censorship driven society. However, each country has a dialogue with the media it wishes to adopt and to use and these dialogues are often related to a sense of identity and purpose. There are a number of points that need to be made, therefore, about what has led to the current situation:

1. The media in India are a significant part of what can be called the colonial or imperial legacy. That is, media were introduced, developed and designed, often by Europeans in the first instance, to serve the interests of the colonial masters. Local

cultures took up the various media and used them to promote different causes, for the most part independence from the imperialists. Sometimes this has included banning certain media. China does not have a colonial past in the same way that India has experienced. There was partial European and American occupation of key port cities beginning in the late 19th century. There was also Japanese occupation of northern China, and attempts to colonize the south during the Sino-Japanese War in the 1930s and into the 1940s world war. Local media did of course become voices of resistance, although sometimes local and foreign interests (businessmen) worked together to bring certain media to their province. This was the case in Ningbo where the Dutch and the Chinese collaborated to bring in the telegraph system, even though the Manchu government miles to the north in the capital Beijing, refused to authorize it.

Table 9.2 **Brief country comparison of Internet use, China and India**

		China	India
Internet users	1993	2,000	2,000
	1994	14,000	4,000
	2000	23,000,000	10,000,000
Education of Internet users	High school and below	29	15
	College	30	9
	Bachelor	39	37
	Postgraduate	2	39
Average weekly Internet use		14	2
Gender of Internet users	Male	70	77
	Female	30	23
Age of Internet users	Under 24	56	61
	25–39	35	28
	Over 40	9	11

Sources: NUA Internet surveys; CNNIC (2001); Euromonitor estimates (www.euromonitor.com/); World Bank (www.worldbank.org).

2. The press, radio, television and the new media are based on technologies ultimately derived from the technological revolution begun in the West in the 19th century and exported to the rest of the world. Traditionally this is discussed in terms of technological transfer or technological dialogue. One of the key turnarounds in contemporary media is that new media tend to be most popular in Asia, with innovations in style and application coming out of Japan and Korea, but quickly adopted elsewhere in the region.

3. It is important to recognize that the construction of the various Asian mediascapes has never been uniform or homogeneous. Rather the creation has been asynchronous (varying over time) depending on the material conditions current at particular moments of national development and whether there have been indigenous elites prepared to assume the burden of producing a local press, for example.

4. While the Asian media bear a resemblance to the western media it is important to remember that they do not necessarily serve the same purpose.

5. The creation of a national mediascape is resource intensive. It requires expensive technology and an educated elite to produce and consume the product and a degree of prosperity where the consumer has discretionary money to spend on a radio or a television, for example. In China, even large numbers of the rural population has access to a shared television. Most urban families have their own set at home.

6. When we are working with national identities in international and global contexts then we are talking about imagined communities. One of the most influential modern theories of nationalism was proposed by Benedict Anderson (1991) in his book *Imagined Communities*. Anderson, an Indonesianist with a deep knowledge of Javanese politics, traced the development of the role of newspapers in the Indonesian independence struggle against the Dutch, which led him to argue that a sense of national identity was a necessary feat of the imagination required to achieve independence. Anderson argued that it was impossible for all Indonesians (or Americans or Australians or Indians or British or Chinese for that matter) to physically know one another at any given time and yet they can all claim a relationship – we are Americans, Australians or Indians. In short we inhabit an imagined community that is horizontal (we are all equal), bounded (this is the US or United Kingdom or India or China) and sovereign (we are in control of the territory we claim to be American or British or Chinese or Indian). In addition, as we claim a nationality we also claim an identity, often several identities all at once.

> **Imagined communities.** Members of even the smallest nation will never know most of their fellow citizens, meet them, or even hear of them, yet in the minds of each lives the image of them as a nation or community.

The idea of imagined communities fits in well with our discussions in Chapter 1, and following chapters, about globalization, at minimum, being concerned with the extent of networks and the intensity of the links. Once a culture knows what another culture is thinking and starts to understand the main forms and characteristics of its identity, and to notice that there are links between their different ways of being, then you will start to see adaptations and changes in both cultures.

China

At the time of writing, Beijing was getting ready for the Olympics – 'New Beijing, Great Olympics' is the motto. The Olympic brand is supported by five mascot dolls called 'Friendlies' or, since their change of name in October 2006, 'Fuwa' (*fu*/good fortune + *wa*/baby = good and fortunate child). The Fuwa were created specifically to build what Donald and Gammack in *Tourism and the Branded City* (2007) call Brand China. Beibei, the fish, Jingjing, the panda, Huanhuan, the Olympic flame, Yingying, the (Tibetan) antelope and Nini, the swallow, symbolize aspects of China's land, its animals and culture. These names, and the animals themselves, were chosen carefully. Qinghai, a large province in the far west was given the antelope, which is an endangered animal from the region. In international political circles this was a problem, because of the connection between China's brand and disputed territories. Xinjiang, a largely Islamic region, has a separatist movement. Tibet, a predominantly Buddhist area and also in the far west of China, is a contested autonomous region, which some Tibetans feel should not be part of the mainland at all. Meanwhile in Qinghai, while there are both Han people and about 900,000 Tibetans, the main minority group is Hui, a Muslim minority nationality in China. The complications of allocating a Chinese identity through a brand symbol to this part of the country should be becoming clear! Of course, we need then to understand that sometimes a national imagination works on its multicultural, geo-political identity, in this case, 'China', rather than basing its brand on individualized ethnic or religious claims to identity.

The idea of a mark or a *brand* signifying a reputation or a signifier of identity is not new. However, what is new is the attempt to brand nations, something often associated with tourism campaigns originally and seen by many as representative of a shift away from the nation state towards the concept of the market state. Here we look more closely at this idea.

At one end of the spectrum we can think of tattoos, or even heraldry, as branding while at the other end of society the branding of criminals or prisoners and farm cattle with hot irons has been common practice around the world for many centuries. Contemporary branding is much more usually associated with the emotive and reputational power of a product or firm. A brand is not accidental as the business of brand creation and maintenance is a major industry, arguably a media industry given its close links to advertising and marketing communications. Places and nations are also subject to branding, and that is often linked to mega-events and major incidents. The Olympics, the World Expo, a football World Cup, or a major political meeting (OPEC or APEC) may all be used as springboards from which to build or enhance a brand identity – usually for a city or country, or both.

The Beijing Olympics is a case of *co-branding*. Co-branding is when two or more products form an alliance that enables the transfer of certain aspects of an image from one brand to another (Rao and Ruekert, 1994). John Gammack (Donald and Gammack, 2007) has pointed out that product–place co-branding, in which products associated with a place help establish terms that have a public meaning (for example Cornish pasties, Peking duck) is a sort of place branding, even if the association is no longer unique to that place, as in the case of Parma ham (Kavaratzis and Ashworth, 2005). Brand equity is ideally increased for both – so Beijing and the Olympics would benefit from a successful Games in 2008. Likewise, if anything goes wrong, the image of both the place and the event, or Olympic movement, will suffer. Olympic cities are not chosen lightly, nor would either brand wish to risk its reputation publicly by a poor decision or subsequent delivery. Each successful Olympic Games strengthens the Olympic brand, and for a brief period of time the showcased city is provided with a global platform upon which to stand and establish or promote its image. Nonetheless there are problems that might arise. Both Beijing and the next Olympic city, London, have used their Olympic bids to stress urban regeneration. In both cases the media, often the new media in Beijing's case, have been used to show that this regeneration might be delivered at the direct expense of the poor. In London, there are protests, for instance, from Romany people, market gardeners and council apartment residents, claiming that their land and homes are being sacrificed to London's Olympic image. In Beijing, construction workers have died during the preparations for the big event, and pictures and discussions on this have been circulated on blogs and through photographs taken by fellow workers' mobile phones. It is not the job of this chapter to make judgements on these incidents, but we would like you to think about how the unexpected use of media affects the carefully orchestrated work of something as important as a branding strategy in a nation with the ambition and power of China.

Brand image is shaped by marketing and media activities, including film, television and other visual communications. It seeks to create strong, positive and memorable associations, by word of mouth, by direct experience and by identification with particular events, people or places. If you try to imagine, pace Anderson's 'imagined' communities of the nation, what a certain city looks and feels like, and what *you* think and feel about that place, how much is dependent on tourism websites, blogs, films, television coverage and even postcards? How much comes from word of mouth (in which we could include blogs and wikis) or your actual experience?

class discussion For Brand China, what criteria would be most
important for maintaining or improving its
image? Probably it needs a mixture of things to make the brand strong. Discuss and prioritize
the aspects of a city brand that would improve both local and, by association, national reputation. Use Beijing, London or other global cities to illustrate your argument.

First, certain cities have to be 'headlined' as representative both of their own special characteristics, and of China as a whole. Shanghai is the most successful in this, possessing as it does a place in the index of world cities (the GaWC index was created in the UK), albeit on the third tier in that hierarchy. Shanghai has placed a great deal of emphasis on its image and brand in recent years, emphasizing its role as the city of exhibitions, of green spaces, and of modern urban cosmopolitanism. This is the image that film-makers are encouraged to project if they shoot a film in Shanghai, but it is also the story that comes out of the advertising industry and from international media accounts of living as an expatriate or an executive in the city. China's other cities are also under pressure to define themselves as part of a new Creative China brand, what we might think of as a sub-theme of the overall Brand China. In most cases, the aim is to connect history, culture, infrastructure and the environment, and to link all those endeavours with creative media activities and industries. Thus each part of the branding activity is linked to the programmes of change that can make it happen. So, cities and city planning are both important to the national brand. The national brand is a further iteration of 'the imagined community', supported by media industries, government, and commerce.

Second, *Brand China has to use media to support its communication strategies both inside and outside the country*. Those communication strategies are very important when (a) the mediascape is essentially a closed system, but (b) China wants to present a strong but friendly (aka Friendlies) face to the outside world. Sometimes this means that two different stories are available to different audiences; sometimes this means that all stories about an issue are suppressed or highly manipulated. Perhaps the worst outcome is when stories are banal or without any interesting substance. For instance, a government approved magazine like *Jinri Zhongguo* (China Today) is sent to Chinese readers all over the world, and is also available in China. It emphasizes positive stories and upbeat analyses of China's modernization. (The English language version is similarly optimistic.) In an article on where to stay during the Beijing Olympics (2008.2), the page was bordered in red (the preferred colour of Brand China) and carried pictures of the Friendlies, and the Beijing 2008 logo in the title and borders. The main picture was of air hostesses practising how to offer water and reading matter to prospective visitors. The text itself was a low-interest piece on whether to stay in a small hotel or a boarding house in Beijing. The article was therefore all part of the Brand China drive, and had very little to do with real news or even lifestyle information.

Third, Brand China has to deliver in all kinds of areas and products if it is to retain international credibility. So, Chinese products need to be safe, reliable, and well made as well as cheap and plentiful. If this does not occur, China will remain as a factory for cheap goods, rather than an equal partner in the economic system of innovation and creative diversity. The role of media in managing this face of the Brand is crucial. Official media can be firmly persuaded within China not to report some of the problems with, say, food safety. Indeed there are laws that forbid undermining national security or cohesion, which can be adapted to punish over-diligent reporters. Reportage of national disasters, another blemish on the Brand if they are too frequent, has to be approved before publication in print or broadcast media. Nonetheless there are often individuals who are willing to take a risk online to get a story out, or even a whole group of people who 'take a walk' together to protest some kind of environmental or development issue. These stories, and mini-events, are picked up by international media from the endless stream of data flowing on from the global news agencies, mainly because the big events such as the Olympics help these same media attract global interest to anything Chinese. *Thus, one brand strategy (visibility on the world stage) can undermine another (positive stories only about Chinese goods and products).*

Industrial Community Television (ICTs)

Branding is relevant to this chapter because engagement in the process and execution of branding on the international stage is part of a media process. It is one of projecting China's identity to outside national and ethnic borders while at the same time reinforcing cultural identities inside the geo-political territories of the nation.

This is a far cry from the world of Industrial Community Television (ICTs) in China that dominated the Chinese mediascape in the 1990s but have largely been replaced by commercial cable operations as the Chinese economy moves more and more to the market model of production. Cable television took two forms in China; the ICT, which is community-based, and commercial cable operations, which began in the urban centres in the 1990s. The ICTs, introduced in the 1970s, were a response to changing political and cultural conditions at a time when the centre seemed to be devolving ideological power. Television relay stations in the work units appeared to fulfil two functions: first, to provide an effective means of saturating the country with CCTV in a cheap and effective manner, and second, at the same time to meet the growing demand for television programmes. By contrast the commercial cable stations are a product of the 1990s and represent the move towards the increasing commodification of culture in China. The ideological enterprise at the heart of China's political system is maintained through a strong line (*tifa*) on all news and current affairs issues. Cultural programming tends not to challenge the main policies of the government, which currently focus on harmonizing social attitudes and aspirations, with the desire to get rich and the need to stabilize class relations.

The ICT operations were attached to factories, manufacturing plants and other institutions in the 1970s. They were important for local communities, which these workplaces represented, as they carried information and gossip that appealed to very particular interests and tastes. These communities have now broken down and ICTs are quickly replaced in the audience's affection by programming provided by large entertainment oriented conglomerates, such as the Shanghai Media Group and major provincial TV stations. The provincial TV stations are often more popular nationally than the Chinese Central television station. Their programming is lively and relevant to people in smaller cities as well as in the major capitals. Provincial broadcasters focus mainly on entertainment, necessary to bring in advertising revenue of course. This means that the working population can sit down and share in an 'imagined community' of social satire, formulaic game shows and the occasional formatted 'winner' (US readers will know of Big Brother and Survivor, examples of format television in the States and Europe). They can also share passions and excitement around media personalities, gossip and fashion.

In rather the same way that brand strategies create internal problems for the overall aim of Brand China, so the loosening and commercialization of television policy in China create schisms in the system. Unwittingly, the Chinese authorities, with their policy to encourage the widespread cabling of China in the 1980s, set in place a communication infrastructure that both encourages regionalism and provides the space for the articulation of difference. In the early period, before the provincial and metropolitan stations began to get their programming flow working well, it also led to the influx of foreign content. This was unacceptable to many old-fashioned patriots for reasons of cultural contamination and undesirable political influences perceived to come in with such content. Perhaps they worried needlessly for Chinese audiences embrace local, Chinese shows and content with great enthusiasm, as long as they are entertaining. There are always segments of the population who look for more serious and challenging information, but arguably this is sought mainly in Internet discussion and through interpreting the politics of everyday in comedy formats and in conversation.

The entrepreneurial rich become the revolutionary class

In Chapter 8 we saw how the Stainless Steel Mouse, a quasi-dissident Chinese writer, was arrested by officials for her writings and later released. The social and economic pressures from outside China have affected the way it deals with its communication and media. This includes China's relationship to the World Trade Organization (WTO). China for example now permits overseas owners to control up to 50 per cent of the Internet companies that operate domestically. The Chinese government, therefore, is committed to the development of the Internet while at the same time controlling it. With no sense of irony, the Chinese government created a Ministry of Information that on the one hand promotes the development of the Internet and on the other hand censors and controls its spread and use.

An important part of the reason for the compromises that the China government makes in communications policy, and in the actual practice of censorship, is *economic*, and thus *social*. China has an emergent aspirational middle class. Their best interests are China's best interests – economic growth, a stable society and a working communications infrastructure.

Social class[1]

Class is not a new word in Chinese politics, but it is a newly articulated notion (Bian et al., 2005), which allows the concept of 'harmonious society' to hinge on the elaboration of the success of the middle-income (actually high income but the harmonious term '*zhong* = middle' is preferred) consumer and the wealthy to a wider population. The likelihood of that extension is doubtful in the immediate future, especially given the environmental problems of modernity, which hit the poorest, hardest and first. The emergence of a class discourse in China is associated with two moments of Party history.

The first, in 1949, was the victory of the CCP and the establishment of the People's Republic of China. At that point, what Apter and Saich (1998) have called the 'exegetical bonding' of identity to Maoist-Marxist-Leninist orderings of peasant, worker, landlord and intellectual classes (to name a few in a more complex system), became an important political fact. Words and stories became deeds. This prefigures media as the carrier of political truth in China today. The second iteration is much more recent, and has grown from the post 1978 Reform era (reforms it should be noted that were planned at least fifteen years earlier by Deng Xiaoping), and the appearance of new social stratifications and regional differences, haves and have-nots, and – most recently – new

---

1 The following section is taken from Donald's work on class and film in Malpas (Donald, 2008).

structures of taste and feeling in people's approach to their priorities and lifestyle choices. Class is again an important category, but it must be approached as a complex phenomenon stemming from reform economics, personal wealth creation, and a society newly oriented to money as the most important marker of success, and aspira- tion as a core value in everyday life.

The scope of the category of the Chinese middle class is somewhat more porous than that, especially given that it is not merely the possibilities for conspicuous consumption (Wang, 2005; Wang and Zhang, 2005) but also the taste for 'quality' of life that characterizes the new urban so-called 'elites'. They are indeed determinedly pursuing the tasteful consumption of cultural goods, but they are also articulating a desire to achieve the best possible lifestyle for themselves and their children according to quite varied levels of income, means and social relations. So, class is something more than origin and production, and is very much associated with how people imagine their place in the national community.

case study

Jia Zhangke's *Sanxia Haoren* (*Still Life*, literally *Good People of the Three Gorges*) (2006) can be viewed as landscapes of class, book-ending the Reform era from the early nineteen-eighties to the present. In *Still Life*, the setting is contemporary. Jia is a film-maker from Shanxi who has done a great deal to correct the need for films which essay the provincial urban landscape of small towns (*Unknown Pleasures*, *Platform* and *Xiao Wu*), and the relatively modest but potentially divisive aspira- tions of their people. In another recent film, *The World* (2004) Jia follows a family of Shanxi migrants into a Beijing theme park, and narrates the painful contingencies of the underclass of migrants in the capital. The argument of that film is that although migrants are utterly necessary to the everyday workings of Beijing's interna- tional, reform economy model, they have little or no access to either the real 'world', or to the reality of a middle income success story, and are more likely to die in an under- compensated industrial accident than to achieve the modern life for which they made the trek to the metropolis. In *Still Life*, Jia visits the classic land- scapes of China's hinterland and makes them central to his narrative of China's modernization. Here, his key characters are again from Shanxi, one

is a coal miner (Sanming – who also appears in minor roles as a character in *The World* and *Platform*), a quiet man whose reasonableness is apparent but whose quiet stoicism makes him a subject rather than an agent of the change around him. The other major character is a nurse (Shen Hong), also visiting the area from Shanxi to find her husband. Indeed both are coming south to find their spouses. Sanming is seeking his estranged wife, simply because he wants to see her and, especially, his daughter, after a sixteen year absence. Hong wants to tell her husband, who has all but deserted her whilst making a fortune in construction and destruction in the Three Gorges Dam project, that she is leaving him for someone else and moving to Shanghai. Thus the narrative of the film is centred on movement between and across the key sites of Chinese history, development and outlook. Between Shanxi, Sichuan and the idea of Shanghai, *Still Life* traverses the scope of China. The film requires an under- standing of the present as premised on the past, as much as the face of reform (Shanghai) is dependent on the ravages of development in China's West and on the movement of peoples from the northwest to populate (and indeed de- populate) that development.

STILL LIFE

Source: Excerpt from Donald (2008).

The films of film-makers like Jia Zhangke highlight the issues of social stratification in Chinese society and also point out that these class issues should be discussed in the media, so that the whole nation can appreciate how the impact of modernization is affecting not just those who are getting richer, but those whose work make that wealth possible.

Class is important to media studies first, through the issue of representation of different experiences to help create or repair the imagined community of the nation; second in that different classes have unequal access to media production and consumption; third, that governments favour one class over another in making and enforcing media policy.

Another major issue in media studies is the question of language. This is highly important in both China and India, given the scope and scale of their populations. It is also a class issue, as those of higher incomes and better access to education are more likely to speak and understand the national language fluently and with pleasure. In China there are 17 minority peoples with a population over a million. There are 35 other groups with smaller numbers. Most of these groups speak a language other than standard Chinese as their mother tongue. In all provinces in China there are dialects that are incomprehensible or opaque to one another. Meanwhile almost all programming is in the national or 'common' language, *putonghua* (Mandarin). You can see then that watching television for those who speak putonghua as a second language is dependent on having had some education and on being able to understand at least two ways of speaking 'Chinese'.

Language policy in China favours a national language paradigm. This discriminates against minorities who speak Turkic, Manchu, or southern dialects. It also undermines the cultural strength of rural people with a stronger tie to local versions of Chinese.

Table 9.3 provides a brief summary of the Chinese mediascape. The post 2000 Chinese mediascape is a long way from the days of the ICTs and CCTV domination of television.

Table 9.3 **Chinese mediascape**

	Pre-reform	1980–1999	2000–
Economic system	Command economy	Market reform	State capitalism
Media regulation	Engineer/state model	Deregulation	Bureaucratic model
Social stratification	Egalitarian/rice bowl	New middle class	Emerging digital divide
Function of media	Propaganda	Reform of attitudes	Part information provision for market demand; part governmental voice
Types of media	Print, posters, radio, loud-speaker, film, terrestrial TV (for example ICTs)	Online, satellite and pay TV, video, mobile phone	Broadband
Media characteristics	Mass; cultural despotism	Shift to entertainment function and entrepreneurialism	Convergence
Crisis	Establishing control	Changing roles of media workers and problems with maintaining traditional roles	WTO; high cost of upgrading media infrastructure; control of the Internet

Source: Adapted from Donald and Keane (2002).

India

By the late 1980s and early 1990s questions were being asked as to why India had not fulfilled its potential compared with the Asian tigers (Japan, South Korea, Taiwan, Singapore and Malaysia). China had yet to embark upon its bold embrace of capitalism that has transformed the country. The conclusion was that the planned economy approach, or autarky, that had shaped India since 1947 was inadequate and that if India was to progress economically and assume a more positive role on the international stage it was necessary to reform economic policy.

In 1992 the minority Congress government of Namasinha Rao introduced cautious reforms of the financial markets that have subsequently multiplied the effects of changing government economic policy to transform the Indian economy and create a consumerist middle class of some 300 million people. India has a thriving computer software industry based on Bangalore, Hyderabad and Delhi. Mumbai (Bombay) is a major international financial hub and cosmopolitan city and other regional cities including the Marxist-governed Kolkata (Calcutta) have created economic zones that encourage economic investment and development. Moreover, education has been mobilized to support national development in a significant way in India and China. For example, India is now training 25 per cent of the world's engineers and Tamilnadu, a southern state, is training 25 per cent of the Indian total, through an extensive and complex collegiate system of tertiary education. In these sorts of circumstances it is difficult to talk in terms of technology transfer through donation. The economic transformation of India coincides with the deregulation of the Indian airwaves. The Indian press has a long tradition of independence from government policy but the airwaves were strictly a state monopoly.

India unlike China has an independent press. The press in India comprises a healthy daily sector with the *Times of India* (Mumbai), *The Hindu* (Chennai) and *The Statesman* (Kolkata). This includes a strong weekly journal section (*India Today*) and other respected journals like *The Economic and Political Weekly*. The Indian government inherited All India Radio (AIR) from the British and continued the British policy of state control of broadcasting. AIR and later Doordashan, the state TV broadcaster, operated under the control of the Ministry of Information and Broadcasting (MIB), where they became little more than mouthpieces for the government of the day. As broadcasters they were highly bureaucratized, unadventurous and dull, high minded and restricted to major cities, although by the 1980s AIR had begun to expand (it is now the world's largest radio broadcaster). The advent of transborder satellite television broadcasting transformed the Indian mediascape. Originally, the Indian state sought to ban satellite broadcasting but in a landmark decision the Indian High Court determined in the 1990s that the ether or airwaves were a commons and that while they could be regulated by the state they were not owned by the state.

The emerging satellite television blossomed for a number of reasons. First, like China, there was a rapidly emerging urban middle class with money to spend on what had hitherto been regarded as luxuries like TVs. Second, there were local entrepreneurs, called 'cable wallahs', willing to invest in the changing economy. 'Cable wallahs' illegally downloaded satellite signals from international broadcasters and then redistributed them via cable links to individual buildings and even localities for a fee. Indeed the cable wallahs were the people who recognized the transformative power of the new communication technologies such as the VTR, VHS tapes, cable and satellites and appropriated them for commercial gain outside of the established international networks. Third, the sheer size and potential of the Indian market proved an irresistible attraction to global broadcasters like Rupert Murdoch.

In 1997 Murdoch visited India to negotiate the broadcast rights for StarTV on the subcontinent. Two things of note occurred during the visit. First, Murdoch was treated like a visiting head of state, signifying two things; the perceived power of Murdoch as the head of one of the world's major transborder media companies News Corp, and the eagerness of the Indian government to attract foreign investment in India thereby ending autarky as the dominant Indian economic model. Second, at the time of his discussions with the authorities Murdoch declined to meet with the cable wallah associations that had emerged in India. They immediately announced that they would boycott StarTV broadcasts. Murdoch immediately grasped the significance of this gesture and met with the cable wallahs.

StarTV was conceived as a conduit for pre-packaged US American programmes and global advertising for famous brands. The opposition to this concept from the governments of Asian nations as diverse as Malaysia, Singapore, China, Indonesia and Vietnam (all of whom sat snugly in the AsiaSat broadcast footprint that powered StarTV) and the subsequent lack of audiences caused StarTV to refine its programming policies and develop a concept of 'cultural sensitivity'. In reality this meant that StarTV met with the various national authorities, forging a compromise where Star avoided broadcasting material that would upset the conservative cultural sensitivities of various states it was incorporating into its pan-Asian market. The actions of the Indian cable wallahs were interpreted by StarTV within this framework and Murdoch's rapid shift of position to meet with the association's representatives, set the ground for a transformed Indian broadcasting regime comprising the state, global commercial broadcasters and localized distribution networks. India now has eight permanent geostationary broadcast satellites servicing 250 television channels, broadcasting into seventy-two million homes.

While there is no doubt that satellite TV has brought great changes to Indian society and culture – the representation of women on the screen is an obvious example – it is necessary to strike a cautionary note. The beneficiaries of these changes are the urbanized middle classes who comprise between 25 per cent and 30 per cent of the Indian population. In other words, between 70 per cent and 75 per cent of the Indian population still live in dire poverty, living in the horrendous urban slums (*bustees*) and villages in the rural areas (*mofussil*). Moreover, there remains strong political and cultural opposition to the changes associated with the process of modernization India is currently undergoing.

activity   Create a map of India and use colours or symbols to indicate the following information – which you will need to research in groups or as an individual project through the online atlas or through other sources:

1. Language distribution
2. Political divisions (formal)
3. GDP
4. Media saturation
5. Media capitals (major media producing cities).

If this is done and you want to know India even better – create a grid demonstrating which media are created in which part of India and for what audience. Bollywood is a starting point, but also consider the more mundane service industries; outsourced telephone work, IT and software design and support.

The independent Indian state inherited from the British an extensive and finely tuned censorship apparatus. The British had always been conscious of their disparity in numbers; the fact that so few ruled so many. To ensure their rule progressed smoothly the British developed a model of governance based on an ideology, supported by an elaborate censorship network and guaranteed by a large, powerful volunteer army officered by the British. The ideological underpinnings of the Raj were based on a belief in European cultural and technological superiority, which manifested itself in a doctrine of European prestige under threat. Whenever British prestige was perceived to be at threat the British swung into action. Between 1857 and 1947 the British created an elaborate and vast network of control that included the Indian Civil Service (ICS) where every District Officer was a magistrate and expected to enforce the rules, the Criminal Investigation Department (CID) who kept an eye on dissidents and created a vast archive of reports, the Dramatic Performances Act of 1876, which was designed to control stage performances that were perceived to be critical of the British, and the Indian Cinematographic Act (1918, 1920, and 1922) which was introduced to control the manufacture, exhibition and distribution of cinema in India.

The culture of control permeated British India and was inherited by the Indian state, which embraced it and applied it even more rigorously than the British up to the 1990s when the advent of satellite broadcasting challenged the model of state control then in place. This culture of control and the tensions it created will be discussed below in relation to the Indian film industry.

In 1947, when Britain relinquished rule, two nations were created on religious lines out of the Raj – India and Pakistan. In 1971 the sundering of Pakistan created Bangladesh. The three successor nations to the British Raj have fought wars over territory and in the name of national identity. In Table 9.4 the authors try to show two things. First, the features and contours of nationalism change over time in response to political and economic conditions. Second, that at each stage of nationalism there is a dominant medium of communication that gives expression to the type of nationalism and is crucial in formulating a sense of national consciousness. In order to give shape to these contentions we will look at the way in which two media, radio and film, have been used in India to advance particular nationalist agendas.

Table 9.4 **Nationalist agendas and India**

Type	Motivation	Communication	Typology
Bengali nationalism	Anti-British sentiment	Print nationalism	Linguistic and Cultural
Communalism	Religious identification	Combination of texts, including religious writings plus orality	Ethnic and Religious identity
Gandhian	Compassionate and inclusive	Print and secondary orality in that Gandhi exploited the new media successfully	Inclusive based on Nostalgia
Nehruvian	Socialist, secular and inclusive	Print based but augmented by film	Rational, Humanistic and Secular
Bangladeshi	Linguistic	Print and radio	Ethnic, Linguistic and Cultural
Communalist	Hindutva	Print, film and TV	Religious
Secular	Modernity	Mass media, satellites computers and consumerism	Mass consumption

Radio

In 1971 the creation of an independent Bangladesh was announced over the radio, thereby signalling the importance of the medium in largely illiterate cultures. The independent, and at this point illegal, radio station was a successor to All India Radio (AIR) established by the British. In 1947 AIR, in line with the political division, was divided along communal grounds with stations in Lahore, Karachi and Dhaka going to Pakistan. Subsequently all three nations, India, Pakistan and Bangladesh, expanded their respective radio networks under state sponsorship. AIR is now the world's largest radio broadcaster with 146 stations, broadcasting in the two national languages, Hindi and English, as well as eighteen regional languages. In most studies of global media, radio is neglected but it is worth remembering that radio is as much a beneficiary of technological progress as television. The transistor made radios small, cheap and highly portable, indeed the ideal medium for communications in a developing nation.

AIR sought to assume a key role in shaping modern India. It continued to expand its reach, covering all the geographical regions of India including the remote northeast (Assam, Nagaland and Manipur) and its range of programmes. On the surface AIR was engaged in the process of modernization but at another level AIR was also engaged in the process of forging a modern state in which national consciousness in a linguistically and ethnically diverse polity was paramount. In extending its scope and range AIR became an important tool of nationalism. Its remit to modernize India was also a brief to 'Indianize' the population through the Hindi language.

Television

Television came rather late to India for economic and ideological reasons and in 1975 it could be watched in only five cities. Since then it has undergone amazing growth as a result of the introduction of satellite broadcasting and decisions to improve the service of the national broadcaster Doordarshan (literally 'television'). Doordarshan retained a monopoly on television until the early 1990s but became fully commercial in 1985. As a monopoly broadcaster it was noted for its boring and predictable scheduling and bureaucratized approach to broadcasting, which was challenged by the introduction of satellite broadcasting in the 1990s. However, the MIB had begun to change before that by expanding the service; Doordarshan now has 1,400 terrestrial transmitters, 11 regional language satellite channels, 48 studios scattered throughout India and delivers 19 channels. The catalyst for this growth was a decision to introduce national programming to coincide with the Asian Games in New Delhi in 1982. A colour service was also inaugurated. By the mid-1980s television had become a mass medium in India largely because of the change in programming practices on the part of Doordarshan management. Television was no longer just a medium of development but also one of entertainment and the organization made several very popular soap operas in the 1980s, the best know being *Hum Log* (We the people), and dramatized the *Ramayan* (1987) and *Mahabharat* (1988–1989). The Ramayana and Mahabharat are the two foundational texts of Hindu culture and the decision to dramatize and broadcast them had significant consequences.

Satellite television

The hunger for television in India did not abate. StarTV and Zee TV, launched in 1992, made their programming free and available on satellites and via local cable markets. There were by 1992 over 400,000 Indian homes with cable television. By 1999 there were 22 million (Thomas, 2006). The spectacular manner in which StarTV expanded

Table 9.5 Household penetration of StarTV, 1992–2001

Country	1992 June	1994 January	1996 August	1999 April	2001 October
India	1,282,500	7,278,000	14,000,000	18,000,000	27,000,000
Pakistan	30,195	77,038	150,000		1,300,000
Bangladesh			205,000	305,000	317,565

Source: Adapted from Thomas (2006).

in South Asia is best represented in tabular form.

There are now a number of published books that examine in detail the phenomenon of satellite television in South Asia (Page and Crawley, 2001; Butcher, 2003: Thomas, 2006). They all agree on one point; that the introduction of satellite broadcasting transformed the Indian mediascape, contributing to what Singhal and Rogers call 'India's communication revolution' (2001).

The major private all-India satellite broadcasters in India are:

- StarTV
- Zee TV
- Sony Entertainment Television
- MTV India
- Discovery India.

Most broadcasters work in close cooperation with the various local cable networks. However, Direct TV and Tata Sky have begun direct to home (DHS) broadcasts. The cable wallahs have gained a pivotal role in the Indian mediascape as they are no longer confined to the densely populated urban areas but can also be found in the rural areas as well. In the south, Sun Network, comprising Sun TV, Gemini TV, Udaya TV and Surya TV, dominates the mediascape for cultural reasons. StarTV, Zee and Sony tend to broadcast mainly in Hindi or English whereas the stations associated with Sun Network broadcast in regional languages – Tamil, Telegu, Kannada and Malayalam, all of them substantial audiences. Local soap operas are popular throughout the south.

Zee TV was created by Subbash Chandra, now one of India's richest men, in 1992, after CNN's coverage of the first Gulf War demonstrated the efficacy of satellite broadcasting. He has worked closely with Rupert Murdoch over the years. Zee now operates independently in India and has movies, sports and general entertainment channels. Zee is also popular in Mauritius, which has a large Indian population and over 65 per cent of Indian homes in England subscribed to Zee services in 2001 (Singhal and Rogers, 2001, 113).

In addition to a full array of Indian programmes Indian audiences can access, depending on their cable provider, CNN, BBC World Vision, NHK, CCTV (Chinese overseas service), HBO, Die Welt, TV Monde, Islamic TV, al Jazeera (English), al Jazeera (Arabic) and MNet from Africa. In short, South Asia is a visually saturated culture with terrestrial television, satellite and cable services, DVDs and CDVs and a remarkably vibrant film culture. The region has in many respects become a marketplace of ideas, a site where different visions of a world order contest for audience share.

to recap...

All India Radio (AIR) is an example of a medium that was used to modernize a nation with diverse languages and ethnic identities. It is also an example of media used in the service of nationalistic goals.

activity   India and the World: Now, contextualize your map of India with a visualization of the flows of media content coming in from the rest of the world through TV and film, but also remember the content flowing out in other directions. What does this tell you about the problems with Orientalist approaches to media studies? What theoretical concepts might be more useful in explaining the map or visualization that you have created?

The rise of Indian cinema

Indian cinema is now recognized as an important expression of Indian nationalism but this was not always the case. India adopted the British system of classifying industries as nation building based on their capacity to produce goods rather than services. Film was not perceived as contributing to the nation and was viewed merely as entertainment, without substance and ultimately lacking in cultural depth despite the fact that by 1938 the film industry was the eighth largest industry in India. The film-makers themselves claimed an allegiance to the nationalist cause and pointed out that the use of Hindi advanced the independence cause, but they were ignored by politicians. This situation has changed significantly and Indian cinema is now considered to be a major factor in generating a sense of Indian nationalism. In the 1990s a series of films were made about the war with Pakistan over Kashmir. In 2001 *Lagaan* (directed by Ashutosh Gowarikar), a film that combined two Indian passions, film and cricket in the context of the nationalist struggle against the British, won the Best Foreign Film Award at the Oscars. In 2007 *Chak De! India,* a film about the Indian women's hockey team was screened with great success. Previously we have spoken about how the media brand the nation. This is precisely what these films do for India. In fact Mishra argues that Bollywood has become the global brand for India (2002). The trajectory taken by Indian film since 1931 when *Alam Ara*, the first Indian talkie, was made is an extraordinary one. The elements of costume drama, fantasy and songs, dance and music remain (Gokulsing and Dissanayake, 1998). Some would argue that for the Indian audience, music and fantasy are now basic elements of their experience. This is partly true but the full story is more complex, as the timeline provided in Table 9.6 suggests.

Table 9.6 A timeline of Indian film

Date	Development
1896	Cinema brought to India by Maurice Sestier, the Lumière Brothers' travelling representative, who subsequently went on to Australia. Screenings occurred at Watson's Hotel, Bombay, and were aimed at the British expatriates.
1911	A number of short documentaries are made and screened, largely in the major cities.
1912	R.G. Tourney and N.G. Chitra make *Pundalik*, regarded by some as the first Indian fiction film.
1913	D.G. Phalke, widely regarded as the father of the Indian film industry, makes *Raja Harischandra* after viewing an Italian film on the life of Christ. Phalke makes Nasik his base and creates the mythological genre. Aligns himself politically with nationalist struggle led by B.G. Tilak.
1918	After agitation from London the Government of India drafts the Indian Cinematographic Act, which is finally implemented in 1920, making film censorship a provincial responsibility.
1920s	Film-making established principally in Bombay, Calcutta, Madras, and the satellite cities of Kolhapur, Poona and Salem. However, most films screened in India still come from overseas, mainly the USA.
1927–28	The establishment of the Indian Cinematographic Committee of Inquiry (ICC). It became the most comprehensive investigation of cinema in any society at the time, publishing a report and four volumes of evidence that ran to over 2,000 pages. A fifth volume, the in-camera evidence, was circulated only among government departments. The ICC became enmeshed in controversy because it refused to endorse a quota system along British lines for Indian films but otherwise adopted a remarkably benign view of cinema in India that became the blueprint for all subsequent industry demands for government interventions in the industry.
1930s	Growth of the studios in Bombay, Calcutta and Madras. Creation of the industry organizations such as the Indian Motion Picture Society (1932) and the Indian Motion Pictures Producers Association (1933) whose sole purpose was to represent the industry to the government and protect the studios from the activities of the 'freelancers'. Main activity is generic production, with Socials, Historicals and Costume Dramas dominating.

Date	Development
1931	Release of *Alam Ara* (Imperial Studios), the first Indian sound film. The introduction of synchronized sound guarantees the future success of the Indian film industry and effectively ends the reliance on imported Hollywood films, something the British endorse. Within a decade Indian film industry becomes world's third largest industry after Hollywood and Japan.
1939	The Viceroy, Lord Linlithgow, unilaterally declares war on Germany, taking India into the war without consultation with the Indian National Congress or other Indian political parties, thereby antagonizing most political parties and creating a dilemma for the film industry.
1940s	Problematic relationship between the film industry and the British Government of India over propaganda and access to raw materials. The Defence of India Act was imposed, superseding all other acts. It placed restrictions on raw materials for film. Censorship now centralized and emphasis placed on support of war effort. Government of India co-opts industry with the establishment of the Film Advisory Committee (1941) that allocated film stock to compliant producers.
1947	India achieves independence but at a cost as the country is partitioned into India and Pakistan, which witnessed one of the largest mass movements of refugees in human history and which was accompanied by unparalleled bloodshed. Film industry in transition. Domination of studios under threat as 'freelancers' enter industry by offering established stars huge salary increases. New Congress government remains unsympathetic to film industry.
Post-1947	Film industry still dominated by the Bombay studios and looked to the new independent government for support, arguing it had always supported the nationalists' struggle with its use of Hindi as the preferred language of film. The government refused to take the industry seriously seeing it as a source of revenue by placing a new Entertainment Tax on the sale of tickets. At the same time the 'freelancers' increased their challenge to the studios.
1950s	Regarded by many as the 'heyday' of the studios, which continued to produce high quality films exploring social and historical issues. Most of the great stars of the Bombay industry – Raj Kapoor, Dev Anand, Dilip Kumar, Dhamendra, Guru Dutt, Nargis, Waheeda Rahmin – began work in the industry in the 1950s. Export of films to the Indian diaspora (Caribbean, East and South Africa, Mauritius, Malaya) increased as well as to the Soviet bloc.
1951	The Patil Committee report – essentially a re-run of the 1927/28 ICC report. Its report led to the establishment of the All India Film and Television School in the old Prabhat Studios in Poona with Jerzy Teoplitz (who later went on to be the foundation head of the Australian Film and Television School) as its Principal.
1960s	Freelancers, in association with the film distributors, assert control of the industry, especially in Bombay, changing the nature of production. Most film financing is done through film distributors who are more concerned with box office than art. Regional differences become more pronounced, with Satyajit Ray epitomizing the more artistic Bengali approach to film-making while Madras continues to focus on mythologicals. Madras is also different as the industry becomes enmeshed in and subsequently dominates Tamil politics. In Bombay the costume drama becomes the dominant film genre and later morphs into the *masala* film, which then became the Bollywood extravaganza.
1970s	The emergence of Amitabh Bachchan as the dominant male star of the Bollywood film (see separate box). The *masala* film, characterized by a reliance on music, melodrama, action and exotic locations, becomes the major formula for popular film. Directors like Satyajit Ray, Ritik Gathik, Mani Kaul, Kumar Shahani reject the formula to create a parallel cinema that gains international recognition.
1980s	The *masala* film becomes dominant in popular Hindi cinema based in Bombay and in regional variations. UK now a major consumer of Indian films, reflecting importance of the Indian diaspora for film production.
1990s	Awareness of Indian cinema grows at international level through museum retrospectives in USA and film festival screenings of Satyajit Ray films in USA, Britain, Europe and Australia. Diaspora continues to be an important influence on industry as demands for Indian films grows, utilizing VHS and then DVD for distribution.
2000s	Bollywood becomes a global phenomenon through branding and marketing. The Bollywood formula emphasizes exotic locations and well-known stars as its core features. The creation of Bollywood maps on to changing India social and economic conditions, with its growing middle class. Bollywood becomes popular with new middle classes, non-resident Indians and the dispossessed masses in urban slums and rural areas. Bollywood was for several decades regarded as an entirely marginal, localized cinema without international appeal. This has changed dramatically.

Creating a star dynasty

Each of the periods outlined above is marked by difference – in funding, in government relations, in audience expectations – but, at the same time, there is a continuity in film production, irrespective of its regional base. The continuity is largely rhetorical – a reliance on music, song and dance that draws heavily on traditional Indian theories of dramaturgy. Another consistent feature of Indian film, since the 1930s at least, has been the creation of the star as a vehicle for the drama. Satyajit Ray, the great modernist Bengali film-maker, suggested that it did not really matter what was in the film, they were all the same, so the *star* becomes the focus of the drama, the object of both desire and expectation.

In many respects the origins of the star system in the Indian film industry lie in its admiration and desire to emulate Hollywood from the 1920s. It was difficult however to introduce a modernist system into what was essentially a pre-modernist economy. In addition there were social prohibitions against women appearing in drama and there were few men adept at acting in the new medium. Consequently stars came from a diverse number of backgrounds. In the 1920s Anglo-Indian and Jewish women adopted Hindu names to become stars. One particularly famous star was an Australian. Fearless Nadia (Mary Evans) was born in Perth and moved to India as a child as her father was in the British army. She married J.B.H. Wadia, a major figure in the Bombay film establishment, who directed his wife in a series of famous adventure tales where Nadia triumphed over evil on all occasions. The industry looked to the north and made stars of men from the so-called 'martial races', a British concept designed to justify their recruiting practices for the volunteer Indian army, many of whom were Muslims who also adopted Hindu names. The most famous was Dilip Kumar, born Yusuf Khan. The regional cinemas produced their own stars. The most famous of these was MGR or M.G. Ramachandran, who served as Premier of Tamilnadu continuously between 1977 and 1987. The Union government dismissed his government in February 1980 but he was quickly re-elected. The remarkable thing about MGR was the fact that he continued to make films while he was a member of parliament, which of course enhanced his popularity and meant that he continued to be the premier of Tamilnadu while he was incapacitated with a stroke suffered in 1984. He appeared in his last film, *Madurai Meeta Sundarapandian*, in 1978.

Politics in Tamilnadu are complex and totally dominated by people from the Tamil film industry based in Chennai (Madras) since the 1960s. In part local Tamil politics are informed by a strong anti-Hindi language sentiment and rejection of what is viewed as North Indian cultural imperialism based on a reverence for the Sanskrit-based languages as opposed to Dravidian language and local culture. Film became the pre-eminent expression of a cultural movement based on language and local cultural symbols. In 1967 the Dravida Munnetra Kazhagam (DMK) trounced the Congress Party in the state election. MGR broke with the DMK in 1972 and founded the Anna

Dravida Munnetra Kazhagam (ADMK). These two parties have dominated local politics ever since. The present Premier, M. Karanidhi, who has headed the local government five times, currently heads a DMK government. He began his career as a scriptwriter. He succeeded Jayalalitha who led the ADMK. There have been similar political/film links in other states in India but none is as pronounced as Tamilnadu. The strength of this relationship points to an interesting development in a culture that is still largely illiterate in the rural areas. Film can have enormous persuasive power, a fact not lost on the Bharati Janata Party (BJP), the right-wing Hindu party that came to central power in the mid-1990s. L.V. Advani, the chief ideologue of the BJP, organized rath yatras or 'chariot trails' that toured the rural areas with people dressed and performing as if they were in a mythological film (Mecklai and Shoesmith, 2007).

Stardom in Indian film has always been a heady mix of sex and sex appeal, politics, gossip and money, and over the years a large number of stars have graced Indian film. However, there is a consensus that the greatest star of all is Amitabh Bachchan.

Table 9.7 **A star dynasty**

Stages of career	Features	Key Films
Early Bachchan	Bachchan's physique separated him from earlier representations of Indian masculinity; tall, brooding and very handsome, he insisted on doing all his own action sequences. Bachchan is credited with introducing the angry young man to Indian popular film in the 1970s.	*Zanjeer* (Chains) (1973)
Mid-career	In the 1970s and 1980s Bachchan dominates the screen, making 72 films. He becomes the ideal male type – lean, active, socially aware and against injustice. He stars in films with his wife Jaya Bhaduri.	*Sholay* (1975) *Kabhi Kakhu* (1976) *Amir Akbar Anthony* (1977) *Don* (1978)
Apotheosis	In 1982, when making *Coolie* (1983), Bachchan badly injured himself performing a stunt. He was hospitalized and for a time it looked as if his life was in danger. Huge crowds gathered outside the hospital performing *pujas* for his recovery. Rajiv Gandhi (a future Prime Minister and friend) visited his bedside and Indira Gandhi (the Prime Minister) delayed an overseas trip pending Bachchan's recovery. Bachchan subsequently entered the Lok Sabha, the Indian lower house of parliament, as a Congress member, unsuccessfully as it turned out.	*Coolie* (1983)
The Decline	In the 1990s Bachchan's appeal declined and he was replaced as the leading star by younger, more muscular and modern males such as Hrithik Roshan and Shah Ruk Khan. Bachchan's ascendancy seemed over.	*Hum* (1991)
The Resurrection	In 2000 Bachchan made the transition to TV, hosting *Kaun Banega Crorepati* (KBC), the Hindi language version of *Who Wants to be a Millionaire*. At the same time he took on roles as the avuncular, smooth, cosmopolitan father figure in a number of films with great success. In the meantime his son, Abhishek Bachchan had become a star in his own right. In 2005 Abhishek married Aishwarya Rai, the former Miss World, and Bollywood star. Amitabh, Abhishek, Aiswarya and Jaya Bhaduri now star in films together. A dynasty had been created.	*KBC* *Kabhi Khushi Kabhie Gham* (2004)

activity   Star theory has been explored in film and media studies in many contexts. Select two film industries other than India (those of the USA and Germany would give you historical and global perspectives). Select stars within those industries and map their careers. What are the crucial factors of their success? How has stardom shifted between what was expected and involved in the early part of the 20th century compared with current versions of stardom? Compare and contrast the concept of star with celebrity.

Bollywood

Bollywood made the *Oxford English Dictionary* in 2005: 'a name for the Indian popular film industry, based in Bombay. Origin 1970s. Blend of Bombay and Hollywood.' The dictionary definition, as Mishra (2006) notes, displaces earlier descriptors such as Bombay Cinema, Indian Popular Cinema and Hindi Cinema:

> The triumph of the term (over the others) is nothing less than spectacular and indicates, furthermore, the growing global sweep of this cinema. (2006, 1)

Bollywood serves not just a domestic Indian audience but the Indian *diaspora* (Indians living overseas). Indeed, by 2006 the overall monetary intake for Bollywood films outside India was almost the same as that inside India. If we compare the government taxes taken on movies, which are roughly comparable, then India took US$2,427,510 in 2001 while the combined tax intake of the US and UK was US$1,546,734. As Table 9.8 shows, Bollywood is big business.

Table 9.8 **The Indian movie industry, 2006**

Overall size of Indian movie industry	US$2 billion
Total number of multiplexes	480
Revenue from box office	85 per cent
Home video share of overall movie market	8 per cent
Bollywood movie tickets sold	3.8 billion

Source: *India Today* (2007).

Ninety-seven per cent of Indian urban youth prefer to watch movies at multiplexes and 75 per cent of Indian non-urban youth prefer to watch movies at home. Hindi movies account for 20 per cent of movies made in India, and Tamil and Telugu movies account for 40 per cent. Multiplexes account for 10 per cent of screens but 37 per cent of cinema revenue. *Taal* (Rhythm) was the first Indian film to open in the Top 20 in the US and Top 10 in the UK (Prasad, 1999). Bollywood also moved into co-productions. For example, the films *Marigold* and *The Invaders* were financed by UK, German and Indian investors.

A classic case of the crossover into cinema of 'the Bollywood thematic' referred to by Rajadhyaksha (and an instance of a diasporic nationalism based on homeland fantasies made possible through computer technology) is the film *Swades* ('We the People', 2004), in which a highly successful NRI NASA scientist returns to an Indian village to generate hydro-electricity. The kind of techno-nationalism undertaken in this act implies that the hero is addressing the nation's own pre-modernity and its age-old traditions and prejudices by embracing 'instrumentally', western technology. Mohan Bhargava, the rational modern scientist, comes back to India again when he is tempted by the ancient call of home. He opens a box full of Indian seeds and soil that, for him, confirm the eternal verities and wonder of his homeland, Mother India. This film demonstrates how a nationalist ethos can combine the drive to modernization (through the building of the hydro-electric plant) with an appeal to land and ancient culture. It is notable that Bollywood film is pursuing a nationalist ethos. The writer Rajadhyaksha (2003, 37) has commented: 'In the Bollywood sense of the export of the Indian spectator to distant lands, I want to suggest another kind of export: the export of Indian nationalism itself, now commodified and globalized into a "feel good" version of "our culture'".

In the film, *Moulin Rouge* (2002), the director Baz Lurhmann used Bollywood songs in the context of 19th century France. The film was copied in a Bollywood version in 2005 with an ageing but still glamorous Rekha taking on Nicole Kidman's dance in *Parineeta* (2005). This is a case of a foreign film using Bollywood as a model, but then Bollywood using the film for its own remake. However we should not think that Bollywood is all that matters in Indian film history. This common distortion arises from the fact that the scholarly and popular interest in Indian film has focused almost exclusively on the product of one, and very important, site of production in India. If we focused on Bengali or Malayali (from Kerela) films we would find a different cinema at work (although there would of course be similarities). Furthermore, India has a long tradition of art house production, or parallel cinema, with Satyajit Ray its best-known exponent. Nevertheless it is Bollywood that has become the global product and here we examine its evolution in graphic form.

Table 9.9 **The transition to Bollywood**

Period	Style	Features
1920s to 1940s	Generic production	Regionally based studios specialized in specific film genres. For example, New Theatres in Calcutta specialized in atmospheric melodrama while Kohinoor Film Company, Bombay, specialized in Socials, films that explored social issues in a modernizing society.
1950s	The rise of the costume drama	Ever since the screening of *Alam Ara* (1931) the first Indian-produced sound film, music and song played an increasingly important role. The producers sought to maximize their audiences by making the films conform to Indian dramaturgy, where music, song and colour are important signifiers of mood, emotion and meaning. The costume drama was the genre most suited to this transformation.
1960s to 1980s	The dominance of the *masala* film	*Masala* quite simply means spicy. The received Indian wisdom was it was the way the various ingredients of the Indian film were mixed that distinguished them from western films. Thus the formulaic *masala* film would contain a minimum of twelve song and dance routines, action and adventure, romance, comedy routines, melodrama, a spotless hero (Ram), the virginal heroine (Rana), a 'vamp' and villain, who usually drank alcohol. The music director and play back singers tended to receive equal billing with the stars. There was a trend towards shooting song sequences in exotic locations – Holland, Sydney, New York could all appear in the same sequence. A particular way of shooting (extensive use of zooms) and editing (on movement) evolved. The films were principally made for local or diasporic consumption.
1990s and 2000s	Bollywood	The globalized version of the *masala* film. The films retain all the features of the *masala* film but are shot on larger budgets and marketed as global products. Their difference – in style, context, content – is celebrated rather than seen as an impediment to consumption. The Bollywood films mark a particular kind of cultural crossover characteristic of the postmodern era.

As early as 1938 there were 68 magazines devoted to the Indian film industry. There are even more today, and these are augmented by thousands of websites exploring some aspect of the industry. They range from pure gossip to serious scholarly sites. If you are interested in this topic we suggest you surf the Web and find some. It could be fun!

Language and film

Language has always been a highly contentious and political issue in India. The country is organized politically along linguistic lines. Linguistic nationalists have renamed major cities in India abandoning the names of the British era for more authentic Indian names. Thus Calcutta has become Kolkota, Madras has become Chennai and Bombay has become Mumbai. The last is the most contentious and many people still refer to the city as Bombay. Further, many people in the southern states will not use Hindi and insist on the use of English in official correspondence because they see Hindi as a manifestation of north Indian cultural imperialism. Finally, the education system is organized along linguistic lines. A child can attend an English medium school, a Hindi medium school or a Tamil medium school, depending on the wishes of the parents, and their economic status. The outcome of all of this is a richly complex linguistic mix in which films have played an important role.

Table 9.10 provides an overview of the Indian mediascape.

Table 9.10 The Indian mediascape

	Pre-reform	1980–1999	2000 to present
Economic system	Autarky – self sufficiency	Open markets with some state ownership	Internationalization of markets
Media regulation	Electronic media under control of government	Open skies policy	Deregulation
Social stratification	Caste system; urban/rural divide	Growth of middle classes; worsening urban/rural divide	Attempts at positive discrimination
Function of media	Indianization; Press Fourth Estate	Education; lessening of bureaucratic control	International and diasporic
Types of media	Print, radio, TV and film	Rise of cable wallahs	Emergence of caste and regional media
Media characteristics	Bureaucratic nationalism; development	Diversification with emphasis on entertainment and celebrity	Convergence and globalization – StarTV and Sony
Crisis	Controlling press, maintaining development emphasis	Issues with cultural imperialism; urban/*mofussil* (rural) divide continues	Modernization of the state sector; All India Radio world's largest radio broadcaster; competition between private and state sectors

Hinglish films, a combination of Hindi and English, have also become popular in the international market. *Everybody Says I'm Fine* and *Bombay Boys* were successful low budget releases. Bollywood also readapts foreign movies that touch on sensitive topics. *Jism* (Body), released in 2003, is a mirror of *Double Indemnity* and caused a sensation. In 2002, *Kabhi Khushi Kabhie Gham*, which for many is the ultimate diasporic film, made over US$1 million on only 73 screens in its opening weekend in the US (Tsering, 2003). The most successful Hindi language film of 2005 was *Namastey London* (Vipul Amrutlal Shah) and starred Akshay Kumar and Katrina Kaif. The film was an unashamed articulation of the superiority of Indian values over British values. Jazz (Kaif) is a London born and bred 'British brat', smart and sexy and in love with an

Englishman, Charlie Brown. Her parents want her to marry a Punjabi man and trick her into marriage to Arjun (Kumar), who is an unsophisticated, although handsome and dogged 'funjabi boy' (http://www.erosentertainment.com/namasteylondon/). Charlie proves to be a 'rotter' and Arjun finally wins over Jazz through his simplicity, devotion and love, and she quite happily transforms herself from a modern London girl into a contented Punjabi housewife accepting as natural what in reality is a completely alien value system. In modern India such fantasies have tremendous purchase. They not only reproduce the changed economic basis of contemporary India but they also play on the reversal of fortunes between the former colonial masters and the colonial subjects. In theoretical terms the subaltern has learned to speak.

Summary

India and China are paradigm examples of changes in all the elements of the mediation process discussed in this book – structures and organizations, content, audiences and effects. The rise of aspirational social classes has affected both China and India and shaped their economies and their expectations. The formal media structures and organizations in those countries have changed over time, with the once colonized India now exporting media content to other countries or, in China's case as well, creating content that reflects the interests of their own domestic aspirational classes. Inequalities in a country's social matrix may also be exacerbated by the dominance of one language over another or one class over another, with the media of communication having a fundamental role in this process.

Globalization at minimum involves networks – of media, goods, people – that cross national boundaries and can vary in their extent, intensity, tempo and influence. Countries like China are building a national brand identity that is conveyed, in part, through the media. India already has its international sub-brand in Bollywood cinema. At the same time, India and China have adopted social networking media like the Internet, even though their patterns of adoption and diffusion are very different. These media, driven by economic demands, put countries like China in a contradictory position, promoting the development and spread of the Internet on the one hand and trying to curtail its use on the other.

At the conclusion of this chapter you should be able to:
- apply the concept of brand to issues in nationalism and globalization;
- critically discuss the influence of Indian and Chinese cinema in the global contexts;
- critically apply the idea of social class to the mediascapes of different countries.

Key themes

National brands. The idea of a mark or a brand signifying a national reputation or a signifier of a national identity.

Social class. Class is something associated with *origin* and *production*, but is also associated with how people imagine their place in the national community. India, like China, has a significant urban and rural divide. Media in these contexts tend to reflect the aspirations of the wealthier classes.

Discussion questions

1 Bring to class a selection of corporate and non-corporate international brands that you think are controversial. Discuss what those brands mean to international audiences and why you think that they are controversial. What are some of the problems of the concept of 'brand' in terms of a country?

2   Choose a country other than your own. Make a multimedia presentation for your class that you think demonstrates the impact of that country's social class on its media, audiences and content.

3   Find a movie that you enjoy but that is not related to your own culture. Show selections of that movie to your class and discuss why you enjoyed it but also how your interpretations might differ from the audiences of the culture from whence the movie came.

4   Look for subcultural and linguistic differences in media, audiences and content within your own country. Bring examples to class for discussion.

5   Look at the English version of news in China and India. Are the stories that they select as leads similar or different? How are they similar or different?

Further reading

Donald S.H., Keane, M. and Hong, Y. (eds) (2002). *Media in China: Consumption, content, and change*. London: Routledge-Curzon.

Donald S.H. and Gammack, J.G. (2007) *Tourism and the branded city: Film and identity on the Pacific Rim*. Aldershot: Ashgate.

Keane, M. (2007) *Created in China: The great leap forward*. London: Routledge.

Sen, K. and Lee, T. (eds) (2008) *Political regimes and the media in Asia: Continuities, contradictions and change*. London: Routledge.

Thomas, A.O. (2006). *Transnational media and contoured markets: Redefining Asian television and advertising*. New Delhi: Sage.

Zhu, Ying (2008). *Television in post-reform China: Serial dramas, Confucian leadership and global television market*. London: Routledge.

General

Asian Studies WWW Virtual Library: http://coombs.anu.edu.au/WWWVL-AsianStudies.html
One of the largest aggregations of Asia-related web pages.

China Mainland

Sina – China site:	http://www.sina.com.cn
Baidu	http://news.baidu.com
21cn	http://www.21cn.com
Net Ease	http://www.163.com
Sohu	http://www.sohu.com
Xinhua News	http://www.xinhuanet.com
Renmin Daily	http://www.people.com.cn
Phoenix News	http://www.ifeng.com
Beijing Review	http://www.bjreview.com.cn
Youku Video Share	http://www.youku.com

Hong Kong

Yahoo – HK site	http://hk.news.yahoo.com
Ming Pao	http://www.mingpao.com
Sing Tao Daily	http://www.singtao.com
South China Morning Post	http://www.scmp.com/portal/site/SCMP
The Standard	http://www.thestandard.com.hk
Ta Kung Pao	http://www.takungpao.com.hk
Atnext – Apple Daily	http://home.atnext.com
Youtube – HK site	http://hk.youtube.com

India

Doordarshan	http://www.ddindia.net/	*Official Government of India television network*
Planet Bollywood	http://www.planetbollywood.com/index2.html	
SARAI	http://www.sarai.net/	*A media initiative based at the Centre for the Study of Developing Societies in New Delhi*
Yahoo India Entertainment	http://in.dir.yahoo.com/Regional/Countries/India/Entertainment/	

Structures and organization

part

4

Part 3 examined concepts like public opinion and culture and how audiences and content might be affected by perception management, media ownership and dominant media and cultural flows. The rise of China and India as global media nations was also discussed, together with the influence of their aspirational and entrepreneurial social classes. In Part 4 the authors turn to structures and organizations like e-government, the media professions, the games industry and media research. Participational media challenge traditional and organizational centric ways of dealing with news, publics and the creation of content.

Chapter 10, Governance and Digital Identities, looks in detail at media's role in participation in modern democracy. The chapter examines:
- the concepts of e-government and e-governance;
- the hacktivist and electronic disobedience movements;
- the capacity of new media to create active and passive digital personae;
- some of the implications of digital personae for privacy.

Chapter 11, Interactive Media and News, investigates the relationship between participational media, news and public relations. The chapter discusses the:
- characteristics of news and the idea of typifications, journalists' ideas of what news is and how those typifications affect their choices of news;
- impact of push media and active forums on journalism and public relations;
- emerging alternative models to persuasion.

Chapter 12, Media Economics, discusses public service broadcasting as a public good and the possible shift in advertising from exposure as the basis of measuring audience to co-creation. The chapter looks at:
- the public broadcasting service as an economic model and as a public good;
- changes to traditional media economics in commercial media, especially changes in advertising;
- piracy and its implications for commercial media.

Chapter 13, Games, introduces you to both the games culture and the industry as an international phenomenon. The chapter examines the:
- evolution of the digital games phenomenon;
- ideas of world building, media liminality and play as a part of theorizing about audiences;
- marketing concept of age compression;
- role playing games as an international phenomenon;
- rise of pervasive games.

Chapter 14, Media Research, will introduce you to media research, especially the role of qualitative research. The chapter examines the:
- terminology of research and the differences between quantitative and qualitative research;
- interpretative paradigm in media studies research.

Governance and digital identities

chapter

10

The chapter will introduce you to:
- the concepts of e-government and e-governance;
- the hacktivist and electronic disobedience movements;
- the capacity of new

media to create active and passive digital personae;
- some of the implications of digital personae for privacy.

Chapter 9 in Part III provided an overview of some of the transformations in Indian and Chinese mediascapes brought about by rising aspirations of their wealthier social classes and the rapid adoption of new media. Brand China and Bollywood India work on the global stage and affect wider questions of international identity and power. In this chapter the authors look closely at how participational media are affecting the very idea of government, governance and identity. The chapter will introduce you to:

- the concepts of e-government and e-governance;
- the hacktivist and electronic disobedience movements;
- the capacity of new media to create active and passive digital personae;
- some of the implications of digital personae for privacy.

In the previous chapters we found that modern governments have developed and deployed complex perception management techniques in order to influence national and international populations. We also saw a significant concentration in ownership of media, traditional and new, in advanced industrial societies. However, there has at the same time been an explosion in peer-to-peer communication, from downloading songs in Napster to uploading videos in YouTube. A decline in traditional civic participation, documented by Putnam (2000), has its counterpart in the rise of participatory technologies like the Internet, theorized by Coleman, Taylor and van de Donk (1999). Putnam acknowledges the significance of interactive media and their potential to contribute to both civic participation and to democratic processes. In this chapter we explore the emergence of the idea of e-democracy and attempts by groups such as Cult of the Dead Cow and World Trade Organization (WTO) protesters to mobilize public opinion and protest through new media. We also look at the surveillance trends with the rise of digital personae.

Media activism, citizenship and participation

> With great power comes great responsibility
>
> (Spiderman, 2002)

Sian Kevill in February 2003 announced the BBC's plans for digital democracy. 'Internet-based political activism is happening. But so far, it is a world very much dominated by a small number of Internet-smart activists; see, for example, www. stopesso.com. The BBC wants to help a wider audience find their voice by tackling obstacles to greater participation' (http://www.opendemocracy.net, retrieved February 2003). The idea that public broadcasters should be at the forefront of democratic dialogue is interesting, even if it appears to be unique to the BBC.

Early founders of public broadcasters quickly recognized the difference between sending out information, education and entertainment and genuinely engaging in democratic dialogue. Lord Reith, a founding head of the BBC, argued that broaching controversial subjects was central to the BBC's role. Moreover, the BBC should not broach controversial subjects in a 'halting, inconclusive and even platitudinous manner' (Briggs, 1965, 128–9). Reith, though, had additional important insights. Public broadcasters were not 'factories of dreams', they had to be 'active for democracy', generate a sense of 'trust and engagement' and could lose the trust of citizens if they were not seen to be active for democracy (1965). For Reith, if citizens rejected the BBC as an informed, engaging and trusted source then those citizens might seek sources that were far less trustworthy and perhaps not healthy for democracy. Sian Kevill's announcement about the BBC's role in digital democracy, therefore, fits well with Reith's ethos.

Internet and media activism sounds like something you would not want your kids to be involved in – the phrase hints at questioning authority and rocking the boat. But as Mueller and Page (2004) point out, media activism is about becoming an informed citizen and this has always been at the heart of democracy. Abusive control of information is possible in a modern democracy and a modern dictatorship. Community media, radical media and marginalized media are all attempts to provide communicative spaces for democratic dialogue and diversification of sources of opinion. Habermas (1984) made it axiomatic that people act in ways that distort communication but essentially humans want to know the truth.

Access to the media is a vital component in 'the architecture of the democratic process' and an essential element of citizen participation. It seems significant that advances in new media, most recently the Internet, appear to have stimulated much of the debate about citizenship and participation in society.

Citizens may be said to have two broad categories of rights – political rights (suffrage, freedom of speech, right of assembly, eligibility for public office) and social rights (access to health, education and welfare services). Most notions of citizenship entail the rights and obligations of every citizen to political, social and economic participation. Participation means participation in 'the process of sharing decisions which affect one's life and the life of the community in which one lives. It is the means by which a democracy is built and it is a standard against which democracies should be measured' (Hart cited in Balnaves, Shoesmith and Walsh, 2006).

Participation is traditionally seen as a way of gaining access to the sites of decision-making and power, but it can be argued that participation also allows *regimes of truth* to be challenged (Foucault, 1998). That is, participation can give people a voice to either publicly affirm 'true' discourses or alternatively challenge 'false' discourses and attempt to replace them with other discursive formations.

But while people may have the opportunity to participate within their own communities, few do so. 'Every year over the last decade or two, millions more have withdrawn from the affairs of their communities' (Putnam 1995). Robert Putnam argues that norms and networks of civic engagement intimately affect the performance of representative government. Civic engagement – participating in voluntary associations and helping your neighbour – and a healthy democracy are directly related. His 20-year study of local governments in Italy found that while many of them seemed almost identical on paper their effectiveness as local governments varied greatly.

> Systematic inquiry showed that the quality of governance was determined by long-standing traditions of civic engagement (or its absence). Voter turnout, newspaper readership, membership in choral societies and football clubs – these were the hallmarks of a successful region. In fact, historical analysis suggested that these networks of organized reciprocity and civic solidarity, far from being an epiphenomenon of socioeconomic modernization, were a precondition for it. (Putnam, 1995)

activity   Conduct an informal survey in your study group. Questions should include:

- How many activities that demonstrate and enhance citizenship do you undertake as a regular part of life, sometimes, or on special occasions (an election day)?
- What are the activities that you would like to engage in, but which you see as unavailable to you?
- What would you say are the five main communicative activities (or types of activity) necessary to be a participating citizen?

Putnam says that there have certainly been significant increases in membership in activist or lobbying associations such as the Sierra Club, the National Organization for Women and American Association of Retired Persons (AARP). However, at the same time, 'the proportion of Americans saying that most people can be trusted fell by more than a third between 1960, when 58 percent chose that alternative, and 1993, when only 37 percent did. The same trend is apparent in all educational groups; indeed, because social trust is also correlated with education and because educational levels have risen sharply, the overall decrease in social trust is even more apparent if we control for education' (Putnam, 1995).

Participation is neither a single nor a unified act, but rather a process that may have varying levels of involvement. It is possible, however, to dis-empower people. Societies, for example, put definitions on access to resources and to citizenship. Children are in this position and denial of choice applies to them. A well-publicized example of the denial of choice is the case of Jonathon Lebed, the New Jersey teenager who started online stock-market trading from his home computer (Lewis, 2001). He created his own website devoted to companies with small capitalization and at one point was receiving up to 1,500 hits a day. Lebed would choose companies that he thought showed potential, widely publish his enthusiasm for such stock online, thus advising people to buy. Thus too, he made money, not only for himself, but for those who followed his advice. That is, Lebed behaved like any other broker on Wall Street and earned about US$800,000 within six months. The Securities and Exchange Commission (SEC) investigated him after complaints from adult brokers and analysts who no doubt felt threatened by the fact that an untrained fifteen year old could do their job as effectively as they did, and without charging commissions for the advice. Eventually the SEC forced Jonathon to hand over $285,000 and yet he had done nothing illegal. What he had done was to contravene the commonsense idea that children cannot perform the function of highly paid adults and so he paid the price, literally. That is, he was denied his right to participate in the economy because of his age.

Lebed's actions may represent more than those of a smart teenager with a talent for the Internet and the stock market. Perhaps the structures for participation and representation are changing or need to change. Democratic governments are exploring the potential for e-democracy and e-participation. Online activists in electronic civil disobedience movements are also using the new communicative structures made possible by the Internet to influence decision-making.

Electronic civil disobedience. The use of new communicative structures like the Internet for protest to influence decision-making.

to recap...

Civic engagement – participating in voluntary associations and helping your neighbour – and a healthy democracy are directly related. Traditional civic engagement is, though, in decline in modern democracies. Will the Internet and other forms of new media enhance participation in democracy?

class discussion As we note in Chapter 13, games marketers presume that children are cleverer than in previous generations, so they target them for sales. If they are advanced beyond previous expectations, why should their rights as active participants in the economy not be similarly advanced? Of course this raises the worldwide spectre of child slavery and child labour, so it is not an easy question to address. Try and weigh up the interests of an individual like Jonathan Lebed against the rights of children in economies with little or no access to education or media. How would you conceptualize their equivalent but very different needs in relation to social power?

E-democracy

Whether direct Internet democracy is good or bad is, however, quite beside the point. It is inevitable. It is coming and we had better make our peace with it. We have to better educate ourselves so that we can make good decisions. Restricting the power of the people is no longer a viable option. The Internet made it obsolete. (Morris, 2000, 31)

Morris (2000) argues that pressure for increased participation by citizens in the societal decisions made about them will only increase with the advent of the Internet. Coleman (1999) agrees and also sees the new participatory technologies as a way of enhancing civic participation. At present, modern democracies are representational, where a few people are elected to govern millions of people. Modern corporations, where most people work, are not democratic. The only time most people get a choice about who governs them, and with what policies, is at local, state or national elections every few years. In western industrial countries there has emerged a civic deficit with increased citizen disengagement from the traditional processes of communication and politics (Putnam, 2000).

E-democracy. The ultimate form of e-democracy would be direct democracy where everybody participates in governmental decisions.

A theory or a model of e-democracy, however developed, will include new mechanisms for choosing and authorizing governments and, at the same time, describing a new kind of society, 'a whole complex of relations between individuals' (Macpherson, 1973, 51). The nature of human relations and their governance is intimately related. Governance and government, though, are not the same (Blomgren Bingham, Nabatchi and O'Leary, 2005; Kooiman, 1993; Lynn and Ingraham, 2004; March and Olsen, 1995; Peters, 1996; Rhodes, 1997; Rosenau and Czempiel, 1992). Government is about those with the legal and policing power who are able to execute and implement activities and policies.

> Governance refers to the creation, execution, and implementation of activities backed by the shared goals of citizens and organizations, who may or may not have formal authority and policing power. (Blomgren Bingham, Nabatchi and O'Leary, 2005)

E-governance. The involvement of citizens in policymaking and decision-making.

Governance seeks to share power in decision-making and encourage citizen autonomy and independence. It provides a process for developing the common good through civic engagement (Blomgren Bingham, Nabatchi and O'Leary, 2005). 'Public administration practitioners and scholars must reengage the public in governance, recognize the special duty we have to citizens, and move our research and teaching agendas in a direction that supports these new governance processes to address the fundamental imperatives of democracy' (2005). E-governance is an attempt to reflect ideas of new governance.

E-government versus e-governance

E-government. The provision of government services online.

The United Nations (UN) report on the uptake of Internet technology defines e-government as 'utilizing the Internet and the world-wide-web for delivering government information and services to citizens' (ASPA and UNDPEPA, 2002). The stages of e-government were classified by levels of sophistication in adoption of the Internet, including (1) 'emerging', an official government online presence is established; (2) 'enhanced', government sites increase: information becomes more dynamic; (3) 'transactional', users can actually pay for services and other transactions online; and (4) 'seamless', full integration of e-services across administrative boundaries.

The 2004 UN *Global E Government Survey* presents a comparative global ranking of 191 member states of the UN according to the state of e-government readiness and the extent of e-participation. The e-government index is based on website assessment, telecommunication infrastructure and human resource endowment. The e-participation index assesses whether or not governments provide online information and participatory tools and services to the people, for example allowing feedback on initiatives. Of 178 countries that maintained a government website, 43 had e-government policy statements encouraging people to participate in public policymaking and only 20 (11 per cent) had an actual provision for user feedback. Keep in mind, though, 'user feedback' to a website is not the same as participation in decision-making. Tables 10.1 and 10.2 give the ranking of leading countries based on an index of e-government and e-participation (as user feedback and attempts at consultation).

Table 10.1 Top 10 countries in the E-government Readiness Index

United States	0.9062
Denmark	0.9058
Sweden	0.8983
United Kingdom	0.8777
Republic of Korea	0.8727
Australia	0.8679
Singapore	0.8503
Canada	0.8425
Finland	0.8231
Norway	0.8228

Source: UNDESA (United Nations Department of Economic and Social Affairs) (2004). Accessed via UPAN (United Nations Online Network in Public Administration and Finance) (2004).

Table 10.2 Top 10 countries in the E-participation Index

United Kingdom	1.0000
Singapore	0.9841
United States	0.9048
Canada	0.8730
Republic of Korea	0.8730
New Zealand	0.7937
Denmark	0.7619
Mexico	0.7619
Australia	0.7143
Netherlands	0.6984

Source: UNDESA (United Nations Department of Economic and Social Affairs) (2004). Accessed via UPAN (United Nations Online Network in Public Administration and Finance) (2004).

Riley (2003) looked further at the differences between e-government and e-governance. Table 10.3 provides an overview of those differences by the different goals.

Table 10.3 Differences between government and governance

Government	Governance
superstructure	functionality
decisions	processes
rules	goals
roles	performance
implementation	coordination
outputs	outcomes
e-government	e-governance
electronic service delivery	electronic consultation
electronic workflow	electronic controllership
electronic voting	electronic engagement
electronic productivity	networked societal guidance

Source: Riley (2003).

Riley (2003) argues that government and governance both involve getting the consent and cooperation of the governed. E-government is the formal apparatus for this objective. E-governance is the 'outcome as experienced by those on the receiving end'. E-government, therefore, as superstructure, could clash with e-governance, as participatory process. The current feedback or transaction mechanisms built into government sites, for example, are not participation in decision-making mechanisms. Paying your driving licence online for example is 'interacting with the government' but not participating in decision-making. Even if millions of people could reply with comments through some of these portals, it would be beyond the means of the administrations to reply to them on an individual basis. Riley (2003) says that tensions will grow between e-government and e-governance as expectations about real participation increase and the mechanisms to provide real e-participation fail.

E-government therefore involves improved service delivery and can operate in a non-democratic state. It is the use of electronic media, such as email and databases, to enhance the administration of government. It also refers to use of media by government to disseminate information to citizens, corporate bodies, and so forth in a one-directional, top-down fashion. E-governance, at its best, is e-participation and that can go beyond simple feedback mechanisms and can only operate in a democratic state. It is the use of technology such as the Internet and interactive television to enhance citizen participation in government decision-making especially at the 'grassroots' community level.

Every modern democratic government now uses emails and databases to enhance its administration. This includes the use of electronic service delivery and electronic information infrastructures to coordinate organizational activity, and daily government and parliamentary work (Grönlund, 2002; Gibson, Ward and Rommele, 2004).

One United Nations report found that during 2001 there was a greater expansion in government online presence than in the previous five years combined. Between 1996 and 2001 the number of official government homepages grew from less than 50 to well over 50,000 official government websites. Those websites have also transformed from simple public affairs 'e-brochures' to virtual information centres where the interaction between citizen users and the public sector is continuous (ASPA and UNDPEPA, 2001, 5).

Directgov for example was the UK e-government initiative launched in 2004 that sought to offer citizens direct access to public information and services about topics ranging from employment, motoring and people through to problems with disability (http://ukonline.direct.gov.uk/). This site sits within a broader initiative, UK Online, which was launched in September 2000. Other more locally oriented websites offer services in which citizens can transact with government (for example lodging tax online) (Cross, 2004). A UK government White Paper established five baseline principles of e-government related to this type of activity:

1. Build services around citizens' choices

2. Make government and its services more accessible

3. Facilitate social inclusion

4. Provide information responsibly

5. Use government resources effectively and efficiently (White Paper cited in ASPA and UNDPEPA, 2001, 6).

A 2001 survey of 22 countries including Australia, Hong Kong, Ireland, Japan, Malaysia, New Zealand and Britain found that Canada, Singapore and the United States offered the most extensive online government services (Saywell, 2001). Much of the motivation for these web services is for more accessible, efficient and cheaper-per-unit transactions between government producers and citizen consumers, rather than any deep drive for e-democracy (Hobsbawn, 2003).

E-Seva centre in Andhra Pradesh State of India is an example of how the ideas of e-government have spread and how they are not western-centric. *E-Seva* provides utility bill payment systems, reservations for train tickets, ordering birth and death certificates, vehicle permits or driving licences. *Member Organized Resource Exchange (MORE)* in St Louis, Missouri was created as far back as 1983 and helps people to pull themselves out of poverty. It prepares community members for employment and runs an employment database to help low-income persons access information about jobs. *E-Seva* and *MORE* do not enable citizens to participate in policymaking or decision-making of the governments or jurisdictions in which they operate. They are, though, genuine services that assist local communities or marginalized groups.

The Internet and interactive television provide the potential to enhance citizen participation in government decision-making. The possibilities include anything ranging from citizen polling and consultation with government through to a more direct democratic model of participation based on the electronic town meeting (Abramson et al., 1988).

Brazil's city council of Porto Alegre, for example, uses email and websites to encourage citizen voting on issues (Hobsbawn, 2003). Minnesota E-Democracy hosts online public spaces for citizen interaction on public issues. The Netherlands' Minister for e-Democracy created online chat rooms in order to counter low voter turnout. The Australian New South Wales government sponsors the 'Community Builders' network of policy implementation (www.communitybuilders.nsw.gov.au). The *Citizenscape* website of the Western Australian government seeks to promote citizenship related activities (www.citizenscape.wa.gov.au). These projects are attempts at greater citizen engagement but do not represent changes in the way citizens are involved in actual decision-making.

At present most examples of e-participation are enhancements of dialogue rather than examples of direct participation in policymaking and decision-making. *Iperbole* (http://www.comune.bologna.it/) for example is a civic network in Bologna, Italy. Internet public places have been set up for local citizens with free access points, email and newsgroups. There is direct and remote Internet training, online healthcare support, online services for senior and disabled people and a time bank where citizens can exchange services. There is a range of discussion forums in *Iperbole* together with access to publications of local documents, including surveys of local populations. The ethos of the project is two-way communication. However, as Grossman (1995) long ago pointed out, how to get to the next stage – actual participation in local or state decision-making – is the key modelling problem.

Spot-polling in games shows on interactive television, popular in countries like the United Kingdom, also represents possible mechanisms for voting. The uptake of interactive television in countries such as the UK now exceeds that of the Internet. In the US digital TV can already be used to cast election ballots (Featherly, 2003).

All the above examples are based within the law. There are also those who seek e-participation by mobilizing public opinion for demonstrations, civil disobedience or hacking networks. These groups do so not for criminal and financial gain but as protest against perceived government or other injustices.

to recap...

E-participation in government processes and decision-making is not yet a reality in modern democratic e-government.
E-governance represents the participative component of e-government, but at present this primarily consists of feedback mechanisms through online sites. The provision of government services online is well advanced in democratic and non-democratic countries.

activity Make an inventory of e-services available through the two layers of government most apposite to your current situation. This may include a University system and a local Council; a residential board and a national government. Compare and contrast the kinds of services, the modes of interaction, and types of information provided.

Electronic civil disobedience

Countries are signing up to the Internet and computers because they think that technology will improve their economic position. This faith in new technology as a pathway to economic progress is much like the early simple media-economic development models. Singapore is a prime example of a country seeking to become an information or knowledge hub. According to Singapore's Minister of Information and Arts of the time, George Yeo, 'Geography will matter less in the future. We must therefore think of new ways to retain our position as a hub. Over the next 20 to 30 years, we must make sure that we have the new infrastructure to remain a junction for goods, services, people, information and ideas. If we succeed, we will be one of a number of great cities in the Pacific Century. If we fail, other hubs will displace us and we will be relegated to a backwater' (cited in Rodan, 2001).

Singapore quickly found that signing up to the Internet was not simply a matter of taking on a value-free technology that had no cultural or societal consequences. *soc. culture.singapore* was of one of the Internet newsgroups of most concern to the Singapore government when the Internet was first introduced. Over 10,000 messages were posted on it from mid-1994 to mid-1995 that, while not recording radical criticisms of the ruling PAP party, nevertheless were unmoderated. The PAP decided to engage with detractors rather than simply to block the site (Rodan, 2001). Singapore, despite dominance and political control by one political party, is a democracy. Political authority and legitimacy are interlinked. Mild criticism of a government, the PAP decided, is a long way from civil disobedience.

Civil disobedience was one of the first activist tools to be translated into an electronic context. The Electronic Disturbance Theater (EDT) is considered by many to be the first true *hacktivist* network. Hacktivism is a policy of hacking, *phreaking, phracking* or creating technology to achieve a political or social goal. A phreaker is someone who manipulates phones and a phracker is a combination of hacking computers and phones. Hackers do not necessarily like crackers. A *cracker* is someone who breaks security on a system for no 'ethical' purpose. It was created as a term to counter hacker concerns about journalistic use of the word 'hacker'.

The EDT coined the term electronic civil disobedience and, as far we know, is also responsible for the first major hacktivist act. The EDT supported the Zapatista movement in Chiapas, Mexico and provided the technical expertise for actions like SWARM. Traditional activists are now adopting the tools and techniques of the hackers. 'As a result, radical groups are discovering what hackers have always known: Traditional social institutions are more vulnerable in cyberspace than they are in the physical world. Likewise, some members of the famously sophomoric hacker underground are finding motivation in causes other than ego gratification' (Harmon, 1998). Table 10.4 highlights some prominent hacktivist activities.

Table 10.4 **Major hacktivist targets**

Target	International issues and tactics	Hacktivist
Balkan Press	Ethnic war: Black Hand, named after a historical clandestine Serbian military organization, attacked the site of the Croatian state-owned newspaper *Vjesnik*. Croation hackers retaliated with 'Read *Vjesnick* and not Serbian books'. Defacement is a common tactic. Attrition.org estimated in 2000 that there had been over 5,000 defacements, some just for fun.	Black Hand Kosovo Hackers Group Serbian Angel

Target	International issues and tactics	Hacktivist
China	Government censorship: Try to breach firewalls and infiltrate police and security networks to warn political targets of arrest.	Blondie Wong Hong Kong Blondes (Chinese dissidents)
France	Anti-nuclear protest: Denial of service attack directed at French government computers in 1995. 'Denial of service' involves creating massive volumes of requests that overwhelm a computer and can cause legitimate visitors to see error messages instead of content; can crash the server.	Strano Network
India/US	Independence for Indian controlled Kashmir: Defacement of Karachi Stock Exchange and US military and commercial sites.	Dr Nukor Hackerz Club Muslim Online Syndicate GFORCE
India	Protest nuclear bomb testing: Defacement of websites	Milworm & Ashtray Lumberjacks
Indonesia	Independence for East Timor and human rights abuses: Defacement of websites with phrases like 'We are groovy, we have power'.	Kaotik Team
Mexico	Independence for Chiapas: Denial of service attack using Floodnet utility	Electronic Disturbance Theater
Myanmar (Burma)	Political identity and human rights abuses: Defacement of websites	X-ORG
NASA	Anti-nuclear protest: Computer viruses and worms	Wank
Sri Lanka	Independent homeland for ethnic Tamils: Email bomb	Internet Black Tigers
World Trade Organization	Many agendas: Denial of service attacks	Electrohippies Collective and many others

Source: Adapted from Pearson (2000) and Balnaves, Shoesmith and Walsh (2006).

The hacker ethic

Hacktivists, as distinct from crackers, work from a quasi-codified ethic. Levy (1984) summarized the hacker ethic:

1. Information Wants to be Free
2. Mistrust Authority – Promote Decentralization
3. Hackers Should Be Judged By Their Hacking, Not Bogus Criteria Such As Degrees, Age, Race or Position
4. You Can Create Beauty and Art on a Computer
5. Computers Can Change Your Life for the Better.

Cult of the Dead Cow is one of the early and now famous hacking groups involved in organizing protests or creating hacking software to mock organizations. *BackOrifice*, for example, was created by the Cult to mock Microsoft. Cult of the Dead Cow is also an example of group members who started young in their interest in computers and graduated to a finer political sensibility. 'When the Cult of the Dead Cow was started in 1984, the average age was 14 and they spent their time hacking soda machines ... But the last couple of years has marked a turning point for us. Our members are older, politicized and extremely technically proficient' ('Oxblood Ruffian', group member, cited in McKay, 1998)

Hacktivism is not a shift of power to citizens. It is closer to traditional protest or acts of civil disobedience, using rights within democracy, even when protest bends the formal rules. The way democratic governments respond to electronic disobedience will shape the e-participation of the future. The lines of disagreement include problems of distinguishing interest groups and points of responsibility, for example:

- the thin line between commercial and national information – is the one subject to the other when a particular national industry is at stake?
- military and social information – in a situation of war, when a large part of the citizenry opposes the conflict in question, what would constitute treason?
- private versus public domains of information – who determines what belongs legally in the public sphere?
- digital identities – personae – in online and Internet worlds may well in the future be the means by which we protest and these personae might require legal protection.

Active and passive digital persona

Modern databases and digital depositories have the capacity to store vast amounts of information on individuals. In the case of normal everyday affairs, of course, there may be many databases and many organizations involved in collecting information on individuals. There are two types of digital persona possible in these environments – active persona and passive (Clarke, 1994). Many organizations collect information on people, ranging from health, justice, and social security through to education and finance. The current digital collection of information is primarily passive. In Figure 10.1 the Visa card company collects information through transactions about an individual. The aggregated information about an individual is, in turn, used by Visa to create a picture or profile of that individual.

Modern computers, however, also make possible active digital identities or digital personae. These identities are not simply the accumulation of data but active agents that can provide or seek information. In a digital context, an agent acts on behalf of the individual, and runs in the individual's workstation or elsewhere in the Internet. A simple example of this idea is the vacation feature in email servers. The vacation feature returns to senders of emails messages like 'I'm away on holidays until <date>' (Clarke, 1994). Artificial intelligence (AI) knowledge robots or avatars are more complex examples of active digital personae. Simple avatars may be a graphical representation of a person in an online or computer environment. However, the AI versions can be projected by the individual, or imposed by others; 'and it can be used for good or ill' (1994).

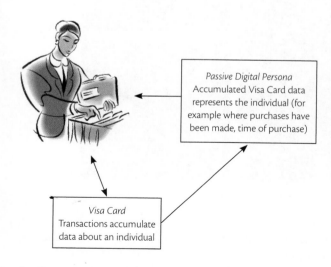

Passive Digital Persona
Accumulated Visa Card data
represents the individual (for
example where purchases have
been made, time of purchase)

Visa Card
Transactions accumulate
data about an individual

Figure 10.1 Passive digital persona

Source: Adapted from Clarke (1994).

The difference is in the power which the notion brings with it. It enables individuals to implement filters around themselves, whereby they can cope with the bombardment of data-flows that are increasingly apparent in the networked world. (Clarke, 1994)

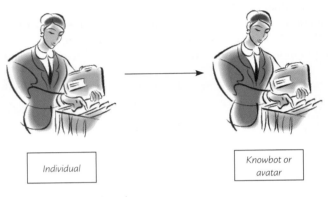

Individual

Knowbot or avatar

Figure 10.2 Active digital persona

Source: Adapted from Clarke (1994).

But a person's digital behaviour may also be monitored by active digital personae, for example their access to their mail and the location they accessed it from, and their usage of particular databases or records. In extreme cases, 'an active agent may be capable of autonomous behaviour. It may be unrecallable by its originator (as was the case with the Cornell worm). It may, by accident or design, be very difficult to trace to its originator. A familiar analogy is to short-duration nuisance telephone and fax calls' (1994). In Figure 10.2 the individual has created an active digital persona to represent him- or herself in an online world.

This process of creating avatars that represent identities in cyberspace is, of course, already happening. Figure 10.3 is a screenshot from *Second Life*, showing the avatar creation process.

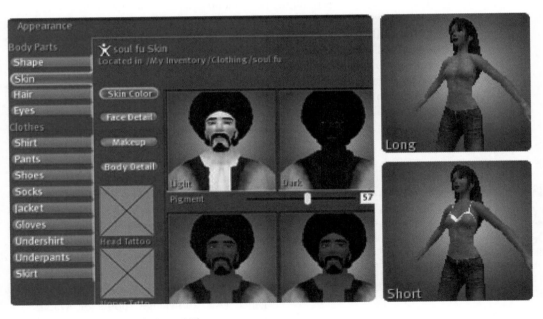

Figure 10.3 Creating avatars in *Second Life*

The idea that we could create active digital personae that run away from us and live their own lives in cyberspace sounds far-fetched, but the idea is not far from the future. Already, people can adopt identities in online environments and, indeed, invest emotional energy and time into those identities. Turkle in 1997 used the example of

Case to talk about gender identity and gender swapping on the Internet. Case was a 34-year-old male graphics designer who played a series of female characters in MUD (multi-user domain, dungeon or dimension). He described his identities in the MUDs as strong, dynamic, 'out there' women like Katharine Hepburn. He liked being a female identity because it made it easier for him to experiment with assertiveness both online and off (Turkle, 1997).

> There are aspects of my personality – the more assertive, administrative, bureaucratic ones – that I am able to work on in the MUDs. I've never been good at bureaucratic things, but I'm much better from practising on MUDs and playing a woman in charge. I am able to do things – in the real, that is – that I couldn't have before because I have played Katharine Hepburn characters. (Turkle, 1999)

Turkle (1999) says that online life selves are made and transformed by language and the notion of a de-centred identity. These identities are not necessarily related to multiple personality disorders (MPD). 'What I am saying is that the many manifestations of multiplicity in our culture, including the adoption of multiple on-line personae, are contributing to a general reconsideration of traditional, unitary notions of identity.' Online experiences with parallel lives are now part of the cultural context that supports new theorizations about multiple selves, what Turkle calls *nonpathological multiplicities*.

Turkle was herself surprised to find that someone in cyberspace had taken on her identity: 'One day on a MUD, I came across a reference to a character named Dr. Sherry, a cyberpsychologist with an office in the rambling house that constituted this MUD's virtual geography. There, I was informed, Dr. Sherry was administering questionnaires and conducting interviews about the psychology of MUDs. I suspected that the name Dr. Sherry referred to my long career as a student of the psychological impact of technology. But I didn't create this character' (1997, 15–16).

activity   Create a character based on a fictional character well known to you through any written medium. Do not make the character live online (this is unethical if the person were not fictional and it may in any case infringe IP – intellectual property – laws) but consider and note the implications for yourself if the same action should be taken with your name and features. What might be issues of security? Or ethical dilemmas? Or a sense of well-being?

to recap...

Active and passive digital personae represent the future of our identities online. How those personae are created and used represents a major challenge in democratic societies.

The world of cyberspace allows people to create identities and to invest their lives in those identities. However, organizations that collect data about us are also able to create our identity as passive and active personae. The lines of private and public seem to become blurred in the world of digital personae. Leaving aside issues of power and abuse by governments or corporations, there are important privacy issues that these new identities pose.

Privacy

Tavani and Grodzinsky (2002) give two examples from the United States of problems of privacy in cyberspace, one a case of cyberstalking and another of murder. In 1996

Randi Barber met Gary Dellapenta, a security guard. Dellapenta wanted a relationship but Barber did not. Barber, not long afterwards began to receive telephone calls from men she did not know and in one case a male lawyer looking for a relationship turned up on her doorstep.

> Barber had no idea how potentially dangerous her situation was. For example, she was not aware that Dellapenta had assumed her identity in various Internet chat rooms, when soliciting 'kinky sex'. Anonymity and pseudonymity tools, available to any Internet user, allowed Dellapenta to represent himself as Barber, via screen names such as a 'playfulkitty4U' and 'kinkygal30'. Having access to chat rooms and message boards, Dellapenta was able to disseminate information about Barber to Internet users around the globe. (Tavani and Grodzinsky, 2002)

Barber found out what was going on when she asked callers why they were phoning her. But in the case of Amy Boyer, a 20-year-old resident of Nashua, NH, in the US she was murdered in 1999 before she worked out what was going on. Liam Youens, her murderer, found her through the Internet, including where she lived, worked, and what kind of vehicle she drove. 'On one site, he posted personal information about Boyer, including a picture of her; and on another site, Youens described, in explicit detail, his plans to murder Boyer' (Tavani and Grodzinsky, 2002).

Tavani and Grodzinsky (2002) ask whether Amy Boyer's right to privacy was violated because of the personal information made available about her and whether Liam Youens had a right to set up a dedicated website about Amy Boyer without Boyer's knowledge and express consent; 'and did Youens have a right to post on that Web site any kind of information about Boyers?'

Privacy can be defined in terms of being let alone – a negative right – freedom from *intrusion* in one's physical space; freedom from *interference* in choices or decisions; and by extension *control* over the flow of personal information, including the transfer and exchange of information. Moor (1997) created a theory of privacy that incorporates elements of the non-intrusion, non-interference and control views of privacy. For Moor, an individual has privacy in a situation if the individual is protected from intrusion, interference, and information access by others. A situation can be an 'activity', a 'relationship' or a 'location' (for example storage and manipulation of data in a database).

Moor (1997) leaves the definition of a situation broad so that it can apply to a range of contexts or 'zones'. Some situations can be declared private in a *normative sense*.

Moor's distinction between *naturally private* and *normatively private* situations enables us to differentiate between the conditions required for having privacy and having a right to privacy. The former can involve loss of privacy; the latter a violation of privacy.

'Having privacy' may be protected by natural means such as physical boundaries in natural settings – walking in the woods free of intrusion from others. 'Having a right to privacy' involves protection by ethical and legal means. In a naturally private situation therefore privacy can be lost but not necessarily violated because there may be no convention or law that protects the person. A person has normative privacy for Moor only if the situation the individual is in is, in fact, protected from intrusion, interference, and information access by others (1997).

For example, if a person walks into a computer laboratory and sees you using a computer, then you have lost your privacy but it has not been violated. If a person uses binoculars to look through the window of your house while you are using a computer then your privacy has not only been lost but also violated.

to recap...

The new communicative spaces open us up to new kinds of intrusions that we do not necessarily want. Some of these intrusions can lead to terrible consequences, such as cyberbullying, stalking and even murder. The traditional conceptions of public and private get blurred. New privacy protections will be required to ensure that our identities are protected and the new intrusions limited in their effects.

Individuals in Moor's model do not have total control over all knowledge about them. It is the *choices* that the individual has over that knowledge that are important. Informed consent is about how those choices are played out in the public domain. Society may, for example, declare some situations normatively private. In a democracy individuals have the opportunity to debate whether or not some situations should be declared normatively private and others not. Moor's 'Publicity Principle' suggests that as much as possible 'private situations' that people want declared 'normatively private' need to be clarified in the public domain, openly. If the rules are rationally and publicly clear, then the way the situation will be dealt with will be clearer too.

Moor gives the example of salaries in a university in the United States. Some salary scales at some universities are declared normatively private situations and not accessible to the public. Other universities make the salary scales public. There is though no formal public rule that says one university is doing the right thing and the other university is doing the wrong thing.

Moor's idea of zones of privacy, of situations that may or may not be formally protected, is useful in the cases of Barber and Boyer. Modern society has to work out how digital identities are going to be protected and what the boundaries are, especially as digital identities become increasingly active digital personae.

Summary

People in democracies want to participate in decisions that are made about them. Even though traditional civic engagement is in decline in modern democracies, there is no lack of interest in the Internet as a participational medium. Modern democratic governments have developed sophisticated online services to their communities, with feedback mechanisms where possible. Representational government, as it stands, involves voting for members of government and those members make the decisions. Coleman and Gøtze (2001) point out there are still very few examples in any country of the Internet being used to involve citizens in policy deliberation: 'Almost all of the cases one finds are frustrated by the same two problems: too few people know about them; governments fail to integrate them into the policy process or respond to them effectively' (2001).

Nonetheless, developments in communications media are profoundly affecting communication between governments and citizens. This includes some of the trials mentioned above, but it also includes the rise of electronic disobedience. Hacktivism is an example where activists are competent in the new media and their potential for collaborative and peer-based networks in influencing decisions. Using new media for civil disobedience is an example of e-participation. Active and passive digital personae are examples where our identities can be represented in digital networks and act and react, like real people. These are also examples of e-participation, although not necessarily in government decision-making contexts.

E-government as the provision of government services online is now well established. E-participation in e-government is the next frontier. 'One thing's certain, though: e-government is as inevitable as the next generation of citizens who treat the free flow of digital information like oxygen' (Hobsbawn, 2003). Protection of our digital identities in this world of e-participation will, of course, also be a part of the new frontier.

At the conclusion of this chapter you should be able to:
- critically discuss the differences between e-government and e-participation;
- apply the concepts of active and passive digital personae to the operation of identity online;
- critically analyse the idea of privacy as it applies to digital identities.

Civic engagement and participation. Civic engagement intimately affects the performance of representative government. Civic engagement – participating in voluntary associations and helping your neighbour – and a healthy democracy are directly related. In his 20-year study of local governments in Italy Putnam found that while many of them seemed almost identical on paper, their effectiveness as local governments varied greatly. His research showed that the quality of governance was determined by longstanding traditions of civic engagement or its absence. Voter turnout, newspaper readership, membership in choral societies and football clubs were all the hallmarks of a successful region. Civic engagement is a precondition for socio-economic modernization, not a result of it. New media provide the possibilities for greater civic engagement as well as direct participation in the actual policy decisions made about us. They also provide the opportunity for protest outside traditional authority structures.

Digital persona. Modern databases and digital depositories have the capacity to store vast amounts of information on individuals. In the case of normal everyday affairs, of course, there may be many databases and many organizations involved in collecting information on individuals. There are two types of digital persona possible in these environments – active persona and passive. Many organizations collect information on people, ranging from health, justice, and social security through to education and finance. The current digital collection of information is primarily passive. Modern computers, however, also make possible active digital identities or digital personae. These identities are not simply the accumulation of data but active agents that can provide or seek information. If digital personae represent us as citizens in the digital world, then there is a range of issues associated with privacy and protection as well as how our identities might be used or abused by others, including corporations and governments.

1   How do you represent your identity online or in your mobile conversations? Bring to class examples of different representations of identity people use when going into cyberspace.

2   What are the limits of intrusion in the new communicative spaces? What are the boundaries of the public and the private in digital worlds? Discuss in class.

3   Bring to class examples of the active and passive digital persona. Do you know which organizations collect information about you?

4   Would you be 'electronically disobedient'? Discuss in class in what ways you might participate in online and real world protests.

Organization for Economic Co-operation and Development (OECD). *Promise and problems of e-democracy: Challenges of online citizen engagement.* Paris: OECD.

Bimber, B. (2003). *Information and American democracy: Technology in the evolution of political power.* Cambridge: Cambridge University Press.

Meikle, G. (2002). *Future active: Media activism and the internet.* Annandale: Pluto Press.

British Broadcasting Corporation (BBC). (2005). BBC Citizen Conference, November, http://www.bbc.co.uk/citizenship/text/agenda.html

Digital Persona: Roger Clarke's Dataveillance and Information Privacy Home-Page. http://www.anu.edu.au/people/Roger.Clarke/DV/

The Hansard Society: http://www.hansardsociety.org.uk/programmes/e-democracy

Oxford Internet Institute: http://www.oii.ox.ac.uk/

Steven Clift: http://www.publicus.net/e-government/

Minneapolis Issues Forum: http://forums.e-democracy.org/groups/mpls

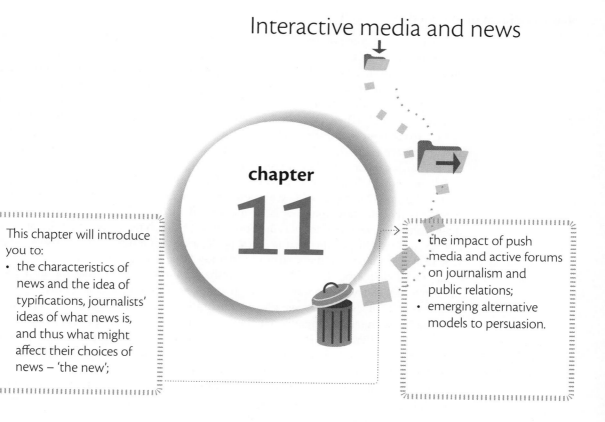

Interactive media and news

chapter

11

This chapter will introduce you to:
- the characteristics of news and the idea of typifications, journalists' ideas of what news is, and thus what might affect their choices of news – 'the new';

- the impact of push media and active forums on journalism and public relations;
- emerging alternative models to persuasion.

In Chapter 10 we investigated issues in modern propaganda. Here we discuss news. News reporting is, ideally, not propaganda. Public relations is similarly, ideally, not spin. This chapter will introduce you to:

- the characteristics of news and the idea of typifications, journalists' ideas of what news is, and thus what might affect their choices of news – 'the new';

- the impact of push media and active forums on journalism and public relations;

- emerging alternative models to persuasion.

Traditionally there has always been a distance between journalists and their readers and public relations practitioners and their publics. The news reporter would collect news, write it up, edit it, and submit it for publication. The public relations practitioner would conduct research and develop a media campaign that influenced the relevant publics towards the practitioner's organization's objectives. These two models of journalism and public relations still, for the most part, apply. If there is a corporate disaster, the odds are that a public relations campaign will try to minimize the responsibility of the organization involved. There are exceptions to the case, but these are rare.

But the media professions are changing. They are changing because of pressures from outside their professions and novel new models being developed within the professions. In this chapter we will look at some of the implications of those external and internal pressures on journalism and public relations.

News as a form of knowledge

Before looking at some of the effects of online and interactive media on journalism and public relations it is worthwhile examining what has traditionally been conceived as news. When Bernard C. Cohen was studying American journalists who specialized in covering foreign policy in the 1950s he found that although they spent their working days gathering and writing news, they had great difficulty in defining news in non-tautological terms. They gave him examples of events that reporters regarded as news or they trotted out tautologies such as 'a story is what is interesting, what is important' and 'There are no hard and fast rules about how news is selected. It is a spontaneous thing; things happen and they are reported' (1963, 54–5).

When Leon V. Sigal wrote his book on *The New York Times* and the *Washington Post* he began, 'One big trouble with news is that nobody knows what it is. The other trouble is that nobody knows what it means.' Like Cohen, he found that newsmen's definitions of news were not very helpful: 'When a dog bites a man, that is not news; but when a man bites a dog that is news', or 'News is something that will make people talk', or news is 'anything that makes a reader say, "Gee Whiz!"' (1973, 1).

James D. Halloran, Philip Elliott and Graham Murdock found that the insights of English journalists were no more fruitful than those of the Americans. In their study of the press and television coverage of a demonstration against the Vietnam War in 1968, they say, 'Newsmen are generally reluctant to try to explain their sense of news importance. They feel that trying to explain in words can never do justice to something which they themselves only feel on an intuitive basis. This reluctance to explain news sense is coupled with a genuine inability to do so' (1970, 191).

Ian Baker had similar problems in his Australian study of how journalists acquire and apply organizational news priorities. When he asked journalists, 'Could you please give us your definition of what is news?' he got such answers as 'News? I don't know how to answer that. It's odd that having worked with news for 14 odd years, I find it difficult to sort of say what news is', and 'God knows! I don't know'. Summing up the responses, Baker says, 'Taken individually, these definitions are generally imprecise, rambling, and vague. The conclusion can be put that journalists are uncomfortable when asked to explain news as a concept' (1980, 138–40).

Ray Brown (1976) had no more luck when he asked news consumers. Studying the satisfactions British viewers seek from television, he asked discussion panels, 'What is news?' and two or three hours later he was left with as many definitions as there were people on the panels. Although dictionaries defined news in such terms as 'recent and interesting events', 'fresh information' and 'reports of recent happenings', Brown found that his panel members showed scant respect for dictionary definitions. For some, news was what was in television news programmes, but others disagreed about what went into the programmes. For some, a battle in Vietnam was not news because they saw Vietnam on the news every day; for others even the first men on the moon were not news because the outcome of that expedition was predictable. Sport wasn't news because it wasn't serious enough; politics wasn't news because they could never get the 'true' facts. But some defined news as entertainment or as a release from boredom or loneliness. 'It's nice,' said one respondent, 'it's nice, when you're alone, to have those nice young men call in every night' (Brown, 1976).

Perhaps Bernard Roshco says it all when he begins his elegant chapter on the difficulty of defining news with the statement 'News is more easily pursued than defined, a characteristic it shares with such other enthralling abstractions as love and truth' (1975, 9).

Nevertheless, there have been some incisive attempts to analyse the nature of news. One of the best was by one of the USA's early muckraking reporters, Will Irwin, in a 15-part series on journalism in *Collier's* in 1911. Irwin (1988) saw that the nature of news had changed with the development of popular journalism and the decline of the old party press, which had been characterized by newspapers committed to political parties and their partisan views. 'This has come to be the age of the reporter,' he said. 'In even its simplest form, news is the nerves of the modern world. Because of the press in its news function ... democracy [is] possible in this immense country. Stated otherwise, the newspaper, in this simplest activity, furnishes the raw material for public opinion' (Irwin, 1988, 124). News, he said, had become both an intellectual craving and a commercial need in the modern world. Business people needed it to keep abreast of the thousand and one activities in the social structure that affected their businesses. Ordinary readers needed it as their 'principal outlook on the higher intelligence': for the views of the law, the university and the pulpit. News, he said, was a report of what had just occurred in the world – not everything that had just occurred, but of those things which represented a departure from the established order. John Smith, a virtuous man of well-conducted life going to his office and doing business honourably wasn't news but a surging crowd of 1,000 strikebreakers on the Canadian border certainly was.

A rich man who murdered his wife, crammed her body into a trunk and dropped it into Lake Como was definitely news, mainly because his actions departed from the established order but also because his deeds associated the upper class with crime. Even democracy could not cure the instinct for snobbery that made most people like to read about the doings of high society. 'Our interest in news increases in direct ratio to the general importance of the persons or activities which it affects,' he said (Irwin, 1988, 130).

Will Irwin had the reporter's instinct for what makes news and he explained his concepts mainly by example. Many journalism textbooks have attempted to define news by identifying certain qualities or characteristics to be found in it. Thus news is said to be about conflict, about people and about important or interesting events. Some say it is anything that happens in which people are interested; others admit that it's simply what's in the newspapers. A journalist who turned sociologist, Robert Ezra Park, in his 'News as a Form of Knowledge', noted that news has the following characteristics:

- it is timely – about current or recent events;
- it is unsystematic in that it deals with discrete events portrayed as unrelated happenings;
- it is perishable – today's news is often dead tomorrow;
- it is concerned with the unusual and the unexpected, even though they may also be unimportant;
- it is often tailored and chosen because journalists expect that it will be interesting to their audience;
- it is mainly a way of orienting people towards issues and events;
- it is often predictable in the sense that it is written according to traditional formats and expectations (Park, 1967).

As Galtung and Ruge (1970) found, news favours big events and important people, clear and unambiguous events which have happened recently and reports which are easy to gather and which fit audience expectations, particularly those which develop events already deemed newsworthy and which star elites and nations and negative occurrences. And it helps if the events and people fit into standard news categories, such as politics, sport, economics, education, culture, lifestyle and finance.

In his *The News in America* Frank Luther Mott argues that there is general agreement that the importance of news is commonly measured by at least four tests: its *timeliness*, the *prominence* of the people involved in it, the *proximity* of the events reported to the news medium's audience, and the *probable consequence* of the news for the audience (Mott, 1952). Others add that news may be unimportant but interesting, or another combination of those words or the opposites, that much news is about oddities and that a characteristic of most news is discontinuity in the way in which events are reported.

activity Choose a daily paper in your areas. List all the stories reported over a period of time on the front page and/or the inside page of the paper. Undertake a brief content analysis of your findings against the news 'criteria' given in the preceding section. Does the news make the front page according to those criteria? What problems do you encounter in clarifying what story fits which criterion (or many)? Do you detect local, cultural or other factors in the way news may be defined?

Timeliness

There is in most news media an emphasis on *timeliness* – that is, on news that is *recent*, *immediate* and *current*. But as Bernard Roshco points out, recency is a matter of recent disclosure rather than of recent occurrence. The Dead Sea Scrolls became news two millennia after they were written not because they were new but because they were recently discovered and deciphered (Roshco, 1975).

The competition to make these disclosures generally available is a competition for immediacy. Wire services compete with each other to have the news on their wires minutes before their rivals. Radio journalists would think they were remiss if they couldn't be more immediate than their colleagues in television and newspapers. Journalists in newspapers compete with each other to be first with new angles on the disclosures and news weeklies like to be first with new interpretations and perspectives.

In *The News in America* Frank Luther Mott gives an interesting account of what speed and immediacy meant to news in the United States:

> Pony expresses to the Far West, railway expresses in the East, frantic extension of telegraph systems as fast as workmen could stick poles in the ground to carry the inadequate wires – these were the signs of the opening of an era characterized by a new kind of news. Rush the news! Ten days from California! One week from Europe! By magnetic telegraph from Washington! (Mott, 1952, 22)

'Scoop', 'beat', 'flash', 'extra' were terms that came into the journalistic jargon to give names to the frenzy of competition in news speed. Then with the coming of the first successful Atlantic cable in 1866, the *New York Herald's* familiar heading 'One Week Later from Europe' gave place to 'Telegraphic News From All Over the World'.

But people want news to be not only immediate but also *current*, that is to say, relevant to their present concerns. A weather report contains an account of the most recent weather conditions and the most recent forecast, but even though its accuracy is frequently poor, it also contains the current long-term prediction. Newspapers and news bulletins also contain items about people of current interest – about celebrities, people known for their well-knownness – not because they have done anything of great importance but because other events or pseudo-events have made them of current interest.

Prominence

Clearly such people are people of prominence and the news is peppered with prominent people – some of them celebrities, some who wield genuine power and make decisions that have consequences for many. So prominence and possible consequences are characteristics of news that are often two sides of the one coin. Prominence relates to the importance of persons involved in an event. Names make news. A prime minister's cold is considered to be more important than a plumber's. When a president tweaks her dog's ears it's news. When you or I do it, it isn't. Roshco says if a cub reporter brought her editor that exemplary news story about man bites dog, she would inevitably be asked, 'Who was the man?' and might be asked, 'Who was the dog?' (Roshco, 1975, 9).

There is empirical support for this theory. Robert W. Janes studied local reporting in a midwestern American city of 70,000 people and found that newspaper references to individuals whose families were ranked in the highest social stratum were more than three times the proportion of these families in the population. This suggests that high social rank facilitates participation in newsworthy events. The study also suggests that high social standing facilitates holding a highly visible position in an active organization (Janes, 1958, 104–5).

In his sociological study of how US journalists decide what is news, Herbert Gans found that most news was about individuals and that these people could be divided into Knowns and Unknowns. The Knowns featured in 70–85 per cent of all domestic news and the Unknowns in about 20 per cent. The Knowns included the incumbent president; presidential candidates; leading federal officials, such as the leaders of the House of Representatives and the Senate, the heads of major committees and the secretaries of State and the Treasury; leading state and local officials such as governors and mayors; and alleged and actual violators of the laws and mores, such as the murderer Charles Manson, and Daniel Ellsberg, who leaked the Pentagon Papers. Knowns who were repeatedly in the news probably numbered fewer than fifty. Others who played important roles in the nation were rarely in the news. These included the heads of large corporations, the leaders of business organizations, generals, admirals, and the very wealthy. The Unknowns who occupied about 20 per cent of the news included protesters, rioters and strikers; victims of crimes, disasters and social disorders; alleged and actual violators of laws and mores; participants in unusual activities, such as bizarre fads and exotic cults; and voters, survey respondents and other aggregates. They were an unrepresentative lot. Gans says, 'most ordinary people never come into the news, except as statistics. How ordinary people work, what they do outside working hours, in their families, churches, clubs, and other organizations, and how they relate to government and public agencies hardly ever make the news' (Gans, 1979, 15).

Proximity

Mott argued that *proximity* was also an important factor in the choice of news. *Big* news that emanates from areas close to a newspaper's headquarters is usually judged to be of more consequence to its readers than similar news from elsewhere. A flash flood in New York is of greater importance to the *The New York Times* and its readers than a cyclone in China. 'A broken head in Cold Bath Fields produces a greater sensation among us than three pitched battles in India,' observed Lord Macaulay more than a century ago. This aspect of news has not changed in the intervening period.

Probable consequence

The news media tend to operate on the assumption that the axle of the earth revolves through their newsrooms. US American editors were playing up a war in Korea while they were playing down one in Indo-China between Asiatic communists and French soldiers. But when the Indo-China war became a conflict between North and South Vietnam that involved many US Americans it, too, became front-page news. This is because its *probable consequence* began to outweigh its remoteness. Probable conse-quence is the reason for running stories about possible tax increases, price rises, threats of contagious disease and the imminent collapse of governments. All such news is likely to influence the lives or fortunes of many people and so these stories are assessed as important.

Importance and interest

Henry Mayer and others have nominated importance as a characteristic of news. Mayer (1964) draws up a scale based on two qualities, importance and interest:

1. Important and interesting;
2. Unimportant and interesting;
3. Important and uninteresting;
4. Unimportant and uninteresting.

In discussing them, he stresses that assigning news events to any of these categories is a matter of subjective judgement. Some events – such as the threat of nuclear war – may be generally accepted as being important but most events are not so easily labelled nor are the judgements made about them so widely accepted (Mayer, 1964, 91–2).

activity 'Whose news?' Revisit your content analysis. How would you rate the stories that have made 'the news' against Mayer's scale. What ques-tions do you need to ask yourself in taking on this task? What are your own likes and dislikes? What is your area of interest and self-interest? Where do you live? As you try and come to objective conclusions against Mayer's standards, do you notice the problems that are built into any such evaluation? Test your findings and your list of questions against those of colleagues in your study group – if possible, test your findings against those of someone whose political outlook, social position, gender, ethnicity or residential location is different from your own.

Discontinuity

Henry Mayer (1964) notes yet another characteristic of news: discontinuity. Magazine articles, he observes, can give the background of particular events, present them in context, and interpret them. Much newspaper news, on the other hand, is discontinuous, and is reported only because someone notices it and decides it is worth reporting, or that only some aspects of it are worth reporting. 'The point is', says Walter Lippmann, 'that before a series of events become news they have usually to make themselves noticeable in some more or less overt act. Generally, too, in a crudely overt act' (Lippmann, 1922, 223).

By concentrating on people rather than processes, says W. Lance Bennett, journalists fragment the news. They produce stories of dramas, or melodramas, starring elite people who have sinned or transgressed or staged dramatic events but fail to make them clear (Bennett, 1988). Thus the news becomes an array of unrelated, self-contained events and stories – sketchy dramatic capsules that are easily consumed but lack explanatory power.

Bennett doesn't have much time for personalized, dramatized, fragmented and normalized news. He would prefer perspectives that are more institutional, analytical, historical and critical. This, he argues, would make people better equipped to understand the problems of society and prompt them to help solve them. Furthermore, discontinuous as it is, newspaper news also imposes a false order on the essential chaos of life because most news is collected from routine sources at regular office hours and is written in standard forms. It is also about discrete events often presented as being cut off from the rest of life and as being unrelated to similar events.

Acquaintance with, not knowledge about

Because news is so diverse, *because it is not an event but the report of one*, because news must obtrude itself on a reporter's attention and be judged to be within the range of a newspaper audience's interests, it tends to be about discrete events and to be cast in stereotyped forms. It gives you the facts about an event rather than the 'truth' about it. The US sociologist, Robert E. Park, argued that news is 'one of the earliest and most elementary forms of knowledge'. He said, 'News performs somewhat the same functions for the public that perception does for the individual; that is to say, it does not so much inform as orient the public, giving each and all notice of what is going on'. Using the distinction made by William James a half-century earlier, Park said there were two fundamental types of knowledge, namely, (1) 'acquaintance with' and (2) 'knowledge about'. Using this assumption, all news can be defined as timely acquaintance with. News tends to be concrete, personalized and descriptive. Knowledge about tends to be analytic and abstract. News, as Park said, 'is not systematic knowledge ... news remains news only until it has reached the persons for whom it has "news interest" ... this transient and ephemeral quality is of the very essence of news and is intimately connected with every other character that it exhibits'. It 'deals on the whole, with isolated events and does not seek to relate them to one another ... History not only describes events but seeks to put them in their proper place in historical succession' (Park, 1967).

News, then, is acquaintance with. It is rarely knowledge about. It is never 'the truth'. As Walter Lippmann said in *Public Opinion*, 'news and truth are not the same thing ... The functions of news is to signalize an event, the function of truth is to bring to light the hidden facts, to set them into relations with each other, and make a picture of reality on which men can act' (Lippmann, 1922, 226). For journalists, truth in reporting rarely amounts to much more than being accurate, fair and possibly objective. For scholars, truth might mean gathering all the available facts, analysing and weighing them, then putting them into perspective and proper context. It is not easy to discern trends or infer principles from the discrete facts and discontinuous accounts in the newspapers.

to recap...

News is a form of knowledge. The importance of news is commonly measured by at least four tests: its timeliness, the prominence of the people involved in it, the proximity of the events reported to the news medium's audience, and the probable consequence of the news for the audience.

Selection factors

Some of the characteristics of news, then, may be timeliness, prominence, proximity, probable consequence, importance, interest and discontinuity. Certainly there is a heavy emphasis on reports of events and a sporadic effort – when there is an effort – to set events in relation to each other. But how do events become news? This was a question Johan Galtung and Mari Holmboe Ruge asked when they made their famous analysis of the presentation of three international crises in four newspapers situated outside the USA (Galtung and Ruge, 1970, 259–98).

They suggested that the set of world events is like the cacophony of sound you get when you scan the dial of your radio on the short-wave or medium-wave band. The cacophony makes sense only when you tune in on a station. 'Since we cannot register everything, we have to select,' they said, 'and the question is what will strike our attention.' Galtung and Ruge argue that these hypotheses are culture-free in the sense that they cannot be expected to vary significantly with variations in human culture. They say, however, that there are four other hypotheses about the way events become news which are culture-bound:

1. The more an event concerns elite nations, the more probable that it will become news;

2. The more the event concerns elite people, the more probable that it will become news;

3. The more personalized it is – the more it is seen as the actions of specific individuals – the more likely it will become news;

4. The more negative the event's consequences, the more likely it will be news.

Galtung and Ruge see the elite as symbols for society. The actions of the elite, they say, are more consequential than the actions of others. Moreover, the elite 'can be used in a sense to tell about everybody ... Elite people are available to serve as objects of general identification' (1970). The news also tends to stress that events occur as a result of their actions as individuals, rather than as the outcome of social forces or the product of social structures. This is because it is easier for readers or viewers to identify with people, because people can act during a time span that fits the frequency of news, and because people are more concrete than 'forces' or 'structures'. Finally, personification reinforces the popular idea that people are the masters of their own destiny.

Good news is bad

Another aspect of the hypotheses of Galtung and Ruge may be summed up in the saying that good news is generally bad. Galtung and Ruge (1970) argue that negative news is more acceptable to the media because of the frequency criterion – negative events more easily unfold themselves between two issues of a newspaper than positive events; it takes a long time to build a dam but a short time to crash an aeroplane. Moreover, negative news is more likely to be *consensual* and *unambiguous* in the sense that there will be agreement about the interpretation of the event as negative and it is more likely to be *unexpected* than positive news and more *consonant* with at least some dominant pre-images of our time.

Certainly there have been few successful efforts to make the positive a basis of news selection. In 1970 the CBS network radio station in Seattle, KIRO, allocated $100,000 to publicize itself as the Good News station and so raise itself from the bottom of the ratings for the city's three network stations. After 18 months it was still

to recap...

There are selection factors involved with news. It helps if the news event concerns elite nations, institutions or people, if it can be seen as the consequence of the actions of individuals, and if it is negative.

where it started in the ratings, dead last. Listeners weren't turned on or tuned in to 'stories that accent the more positive aspects of our day-to-day living ... stories of success ... stories of people doing something for their neighbour, and so forth' (Doig and Doig, 1972, 14). Nor were all the readers happy when the Miami News decided to find out what would happen if a metropolitan daily eliminated all stories of violence for just one day. Even the comic strip character, *BC*, was axed for clubbing a snake. When one reader found *Orphan Annie* had been omitted he demanded that it be read to him over the phone.

Categories and typifications

So far the authors have discussed some of the characteristics of news such as timeliness, prominence, proximity and probable consequence. The authors have noted that news is generally acquaintance with, rather than knowledge about. It is generally concrete, personalized and descriptive. It often lacks continuity and perspective. It normally deals with obtrusive events made known by routine sources. Events tend to become news if their frequency coincides with that of the news media, if their amplitude is great, their ambiguity low, and their relationship to the audience's cultural framework is clear and conforms to its expectations. It helps if the event concerns elite nations (or we should add: the declared enemies or allies of those nations in times of conflict), institutions or people, if it can be seen as the consequence of the actions of individuals, and if it is negative. But in saying all this we have only identified some characteristics of news. We have not adequately defined it.

Another way of looking at news is to categorize it – and journalists are no better at doing this than they are at defining it. When the sociologist, Gaye Tuchman (1978), studied the ways in which news is 'made' she noted that, at work, reporters and editors referred to five categories of news: *hard, soft, spot, developing* and *continuing*. When she asked them to define these categories they were flustered. They gave examples rather than definitions. Their main distinction was between hard news and its antithesis, soft news. Hard news, they said, consisted of factual accounts of newsworthy events and gave accidents, murders and bank robberies as examples. Soft news referred to feature or human interest stories – a story about a lonely bear or a bus driver who always said a cheery 'good morning' to every passenger. Hard news, they said, concerned important matters; soft news, interesting matters. But as Tuchman says, it is frequently difficult to distinguish one from the other.

It was sometimes just as difficult to distinguish spot news from developing news. Spot news, they said, was a subclassification of hard news – example, a fire. Developing news was a story about which it took a longer time to learn 'the facts'. It remains developing news as long as 'facts' are still emerging. Continuing news, they said, was a series of stories on the same subject based upon events occurring over a period of time – the passage of a bill through the legislative maze, a trial, election campaign, or war.

Tuchman found these categories difficult to apply in practice. She suggested that they were not really categories (a classification of objects according to one or more relevant characteristics ruled salient by the classifiers) but typifications (a classification in which the relevant characteristics are central to the solution of practical tasks or problems at hand). She says that newspeople have devised these typifications because they draw on the synchronization of their work with the likely potential news occurrences. Thus hard news is an unscheduled or pre-scheduled event and its dissemination is urgent whereas soft news is a non-scheduled event and its dissemination is not urgent – its date of dissemination is determined by newsworkers.

Typifications. Classifications of news stories by newsworkers as a means of controlling the work flow.

She argues that newspeople use these typifications to impose order on the raw material of news and so reduce the variability or idiosyncrasy of the glut of events with which they are confronted daily. Knowing that a story is hard news or spot news helps a reporter to invoke the appropriate reportorial techniques. She also suggests another typification, 'What a story!', for events that erupt against all expectations, such as President Johnson's unexpected decision to resign or President Truman's unexpected victory over Dewey. In such a situation, she notes, reporters invoke a different routine. Instead of covering it in the normal way they cover it as if it were a hurricane or earthquake (Tuchman, 1978).

Tuchman's study brings us to the final, and perhaps the most fruitful way of looking at news. If news can be neither adequately defined nor easily categorized, perhaps the best way to understand it is to apply sociological analysis to the ways in which it is 'made'. This has been the approach in many of the most enlightening studies, such as those of David L. Altheide; Steve Chibnall; Bernard C. Cohen; Herbert J. Gans; Halloran, Elliott and Murdock; Gaye Tuchman; and Jeremy Tunstall.

Traditional characteristics of news are still relevant to our understanding about the nature of news. However, social media change the relationship between journalist and public relations practitioner and their audiences or publics. The news organizational typifications that guide journalists may also change as a result.

Journalism and push technology

Society is changing, and the news business along with it. But the very transformations that make reform so urgent also work against it. There is a tension between the demands of society and the habits of the industry. (Janeway, 2002)

The 'habits of the news industry' refers to the difficulty in engaging with modern readers in a complex social networking environment. Traditional newspaper readership has declined in most advanced industrial countries. In 1967 nearly three-quarters of US Americans over 30 read a daily newspaper and by the 1990s barely half did (Beckett, 1994). Media publishers assume that the lost youth market, inaccessible through traditional print sources, can be found on the Internet.

Online services allow media publishing companies to enhance brand. By entering into the new media and using basically the same content gathered for news stories – and sometimes the same staff – companies can increase their marketing power with added exposure and brand name extension. According to Miller (1998) the objective of tie-ins appears to be not only to increase online traffic, but to build the brand as well. Farhi (2000) argues that the most successful brands in cyberspace are those cloned from the old media and there is no secret why sites like MSNBC.com, usatoday.com and nytimes.com are among the most popular on the Web.

The Halifax Herald Ltd new media editor Paul Schneidereit is one of a number of commentators who describe electronic publishing as a marriage between low manufacturing costs and an expanding consumer market. Schneidereit argues that newspapers have been losing money and as there is an audience online there is also a market that will pay to get information online (Erlindson, 1995; Reddick and King, 1995, 10; Piller, 2000, 1). Of course, despite the potential for news organizations to build brand online, the youth market has not *paid* to get its news online.

An award-winning crime news site APBNews.com, for example, lost US$27.1 million in 18 months before firing all 140 seasoned writers and editors in June and filing for bankruptcy protection in July 2000 (Scheier, 2000a). Although it hired back 25 employees after filing for bankruptcy and continued to publish in cyberspace, APBNews.com was generally left for dead – despite its highly authoritative writers and editors and its extensive marketing budget and marketing campaigns (Scheier, 2000a). In September 2000, the troubled crime website was auctioned off to the highest and only bidder for US$575,000, a price less than the US$950,000 that SafetyTips.com originally said it would pay (Scheier, 2000b). SafetyTips.com, an online training and information site, announced it planned to continue publishing and said the site would operate under a newly named subsidiary of SafetyTips.com: New APB News. According to SafetyTips.com CEO, Yovette Mumford (in Scheier, 2000b), the quality of the content would continue to live on through New APB News, Inc. In January 2001, CNN (Cable News Network), the 24-hour cable news channel, cut 400 jobs, or nearly 10 per cent of it workforce, as part of its restructuring and one third of the job cuts came from CNN's interactive unit, including CNN.com and CNNfn.com (Beatty, 2001, 5; Rutenberg, 2001; Caney, 2001, 8; Barringer, 2001, 29).

Blogs as news

It is unlikely that the craft of journalism is responsible for the failure of media publishers to make substantial profits from online news. According to Pavlik (1997, 30–8) news content on the Internet has been evolving through three stages.

Stage One

Online journalists mostly repurpose content from their mother ship, the print newspaper. Such news content still dominates most news sites.

Stage Two

In most of the better news sites, online journalists create original news content and augment it with additives such as hyperlinks, interactive features and a degree of customization. SCMP is an excellent example (*South China Morning Post*).

Stage Three

This stage is characterized by original news content designed specifically for the Internet as a new medium of communication. An online journalist's willingness to experiment with new forms of storytelling allows the readers to enter and navigate through news report in ways different from just reading it and this is usually done through new technology.

activity   Find your own examples of each of these three stages. Be adventurous and seek out print and online sources that are not local to you or even from your own country. What are the key indicators of an innovative or autonomous stage three site? What are the advantages and drawbacks to the reader in the stage two example?

Pavlik argues that the potential to customize content means that readers might end up choosing only what appeals to their narrowest interests. But people also use media to connect to society (2001). They go online primarily to connect with the news of their community, whether this is a geographical community or one formed around some other common bond. Audiences use customization features to supplement their general news appetites, following their particular interests in finance, travel, education, the environment, or any number of things. So rather than fracturing society, new media with online journalism at its core can keep the audience bonded.

For Pavlik (2001), this process of bonding is still evolving. Weblogs or blogs, part of social media, provide insights into this evolution and how this bonding might occur and the journalism craft readjusted as a result. Blogs and their variations offer a much more intimate form of communication than the standard fare offered up by most print and broadcast publishers and, when handled properly by talented and experienced journalists, amount to high-quality journalism. Not all blogs are journalism, of course, and even defining blogs is difficult. In general, though, blogs are regularly updated online journals – websites where commentary, original reporting and links to other content on the web are sorted in reverse chronological order (newest items on top). Items posted to blogs typically are very short. Most blogs are a quick read.

Because of the more personal, less 'mass media' nature of blogs, they are a form of communication that tends to address one of the weaknesses of today's mass media – their inability to address a fragmenting market. Newspapers, and to a lesser extent broadcast publishers, have acknowledged the fragmentation of the mass market and the accompanying rise of niche market audiences by producing special editions, often based on geographic location, by sectionalizing their publications, by adding magazine 'inserts' most days of the week, and by promoting the talents of specific writers.

All these efforts, however, simply amount to more content passively received or ignored by the potential audience. A blog, on the other hand, can demand interactivity from audience members and at the very least is capable of involving a niche market segment of the audience.

If this were the sole level of interactivity, the advantages conferred by blogs would be only marginally more than those to be found in the offerings of popular columnists in 'traditional' media, where writer and audience members develop a rapport that can evolve into a devoted following. Blogs offer at least two other things, apart from their timeliness: the potential for content that would not find its way into 'traditional' publications and, in their ultimate form, an authoring partnership between journalist and audience members that takes interactivity to a new dimension.

All blogs offer audience members the opportunity to respond to what they read/see/hear and often the responses are incorporated into the blog. When this occurs, the blog often mutates into a collaborative blog, where the initiating journalist has only partial control over the content. In such cases, the roles of journalist and audience become blurred, with each taking on some of the roles and characteristics of the other. This high level of interactivity, between audience and writer, addresses one of the major problems the mass media are experiencing – low levels of engagement between publication and audience, resulting in at best static circulation figures. But the new relationship between writer and audience also raises structural and cultural problems for traditional media.

The problems are summarized in the question: who controls the content? Journalists are used to having their copy edited by a team of subeditors; even famous columnists submit to the process to a greater or lesser extent. But how does a collaborative blog get edited, who does the editing, and how much editing – if any – should be done? Traditional media tend to insist on their right to edit anything that appears in their publications; publishers particularly fear defamatory or otherwise legally dangerous content emanating from audience members who are not trained journalists. Yet part of the allure of blogs is the rawness – the 'candidness' – of the content and to heavily edit such content, with the aim of making it look and sound like the rest of a publication's stories, would be a sad misunderstanding of its strength.

According to Lasica (1997; 2000), push technology, like blogs, marked a seismic shift in the way content was delivered on the Internet. Push technology is the Internet's trend *du jour* that allows news sites to 'narrow-cast' personalized news directly to readers. This technological revolution redefines the relationship between online news operations and their readers. 'Push' refers to the concept of delivering content to Internet consumers rather than expecting them to seek out a website – the 'Pull' model. Push news has the potential to reshape the fundamentals of journalism in much the same way that television news has altered the rules of the profession.

Push news is more than simply a matter of dropping a publication's website on readers' digital doormats. Push news empowers readers by letting them specify what content they want delivered, as well as how often they want it. It allows consumers to customize and micro-tailor their news choices. As online editors know, it is difficult to rely on readers to come back to their sites day after day and even when visitors on the Web do stop by, it is often an anonymous, amorphous relationship.

Author and online media critic Jon Katz (1994) recognized in the early stages of the Internet that 'open' sites that carry news put users in touch with news and information elsewhere and that the conventional Web news approach, 'closed' media where journalists collect information, packaging it and selling it, was in trouble.

Since April 2001, Dow Jones & Co., the New York Times Co., the Washington Post Co. and Knight Ridder have set up portals. Portals provide local news, shopping, chat rooms and more services to the audience. *The New York Times*'s portal allows its audience to use the Internet to obtain high-quality information in a variety of content areas. New York Times Co. president and CEO, Russell T. Lewis says most web portals try to become a 'home' to users by offering at least four major services, including email, chat areas where users can exchange ideas, shopping, and directories of categorized links to other sites (Carlson, 1999).

Many newspapers, which are hoping to become the local portal of choice, are expanding their online offerings by creating regional portal sites, by aligning with local radio and television stations, and by adding some original content. Being local portals, they are hoping to compete on a regional basis with the huge mega portals, like *Google News*, that are the main entryways into cyberspace.

While organizations like Google become mega-news providers, the world of self-created, citizen-sourced, news through active forums has already become a part of the modern news-scape. Geert Lovink, a media and online activist theorist, sees the active forum as a quest for truth, but truth with a question mark. Electronic activists are becoming electronic pioneers. 'Through blogging, news is being transformed from a lecture into a conversation. Blogs echo rumours and gossip, conversations in cafes and bars, on squares and in corridors' (2007). Lovink also highlights the tension between traditional news reporting and perceptions of reliability of new media:

> Virtually everything is being taped and has the potential of becoming news. However, webcams hardly have any impact yet on the structure of news services. The opposite is more true. They fit in perfectly into the current media landscape. Alternative news that spreads like a bush fire over the Internet isn't picked up by the international press agencies. On the contrary. More and more the Internet is shunned as a reliable source of information. In an atmosphere of growing mutual

Push technology. Push technology is another term to describe the impact of participational media on modern society and is often used in the news context.

distrust, stirred up by hackers, trolls and quasi subversive ego artists, the Internet becomes a secondary shadow media. (Lovink, 2002)

Although many authors point out that the news story on the Internet has to follow a whole new set of writing style guidelines or formulae, no single formula for the perfect online story has yet been developed. Deuze (1998) says that a 'good' online journalist, professional or citizen, must realize that the Internet requires experiments with language and other style protocols. Active forums, in particular, require this type of flexibility.

The characteristics of news and the selection factors mentioned earlier do not necessarily change in a 'push' or active forum environment. News has always, ideally, been an 'active forum'; that is precisely why it has been called the Fourth Estate. However, the traditional mediated forum for news is changing.

activity Take a story that has been headlined in a national newspaper, on major television networks, and on radio bulletins. Now search for it online. Where do you find it? Is it still headlined in the attention of bloggers? Or are there other stories that seem more important? Are there particular interest groups and opinions in blogging communities that replicate the partiality in news selection experienced in other media outlets? Find an example and back it up by collecting examples of the bloggers' approach to a particular issue or event.

Public relations

Online and interactive media, the rise of social networking media, have also affected how public relations as a discipline engages with theory and practice. Social media have the potential to give individuals and groups a voice in a way that traditional media do not. Traditional public relations has been 'organization-centric' precisely because the assumption has been that it is organizations – corporate, government or community – that need to be persuaded.

Activists, however, do not always form a single organization and are capable of having a zealotry that mobilizes resources beyond the scope of the very corporations trying to influence them (Dozier and Lauzen, 2000). This point can also be applied to the active forum and its role in modern news and activism.

Two historical phenomena have affected statements about the nature of 'publics' within public relations; corporate responses to society on key disasters and activism. The corporate response may be concessions, but most often they are responses to a disaster. One famous corporate response to a disaster used as a classic case study in public relations is Exxon's response to its oil tanker *Exxon Valdez*'s oil spill.

In the case of the Exxon disaster, 11,000,000 gallons of crude oil were spilt by the *Exxon Valdez* into a Sound with almost 1,100 miles of the Alaskan shoreline contaminated. 'Exxon claimed to have treated most of it, the state of Alaska saying almost a thousand miles needed more cleaning' (Small, 1991, 10). An estimated 2,602,000 gallons of oil were recovered with the rest destroying wildlife and the environment. Once Exxon finally released an 'open letter to the public' stating their involvement in the environmental cleanup, the company still did not take responsibility for the accident. Their claims of moving swiftly and competently to minimize the damage of the spill on the environment were contradicted by the public knowledge that within the first three days little was done to contain the spill and beach cleanups had not yet started (Baker, 1993, 42).

Exxon's General Manager Otto Harrison said in a memo to company managers that 'Exxon will demobilise when it chooses, for safety reasons no winter operations occur, and there would be no commitments for future activity other than a survey of oil contaminated shores in the Spring of 1990' (Small, 1991, 14). Harrison added to this memo stating that these decisions were not negotiable nor was Exxon willing to discuss them. 'No longer would people blindly believe promises from corporations that their operations were completely safe' (Lundberg, 1999).

The media reaction to the Exxon crisis was to focus on the failure of its management to have senior presence. *The New York Times* said that 'the Exxon Valdez episode will become a textbook example of what not to do when an unexpected crisis thrusts a company into the limelight' and the 'biggest mistake was that Exxon's chairman, Lawrence G. Rawl, sent a succession of lower ranking executives to Alaska to deal with the spill instead of going there himself and taking control of the situation in a forceful, highly visible way' (21 April 1989 cited in Small, 1991, 18).

The US Supreme Court decided in 2008 that the US$2.5 billion in punitive damages awarded to 32,000 fishermen and property owners was excessive. In a 3–5 vote, judges ruled that Exxon Mobil only needed to pay US$507.5 million, the same figure as the compensation already awarded (Landers, 2008).

The Exxon problems were not simply a 'public relations error'; they highlighted more serious problems about credibility and trust. The biggest US corporate collapse of energy corporation Enron similarly was 'nothing to do with the amount of money involved, allegations that the highest levels of government received monetary rewards, or that a reputable accounting firm put money before good judgement. It has to do with credibility and trust' (Arbouw, 2002, 4).

Business Week (12 November 2001) said, 'Executives at high-flying Enron Corp. never seemed overly concerned with how the rest of the world viewed their business practices'. As a result of legal assistance the company responded to its crisis by pleading the Fifth Amendment and giving 'No Comment' to the media.

What has emerged from these corporate disasters is statements about 'trust', 'credibility', 'social responsibility', 'corporate responsibility' that have challenged what the philosopher Michel Foucault might call prescriptions about ways of talking about these phenomena. In management-speak there are now corporate statements about the 'triple bottom line' – economic, social and environmental intersections with profit – that signify modern corporate interest in responsibility and how that responsibility might impact on the sustainability of markets.

Being environmentally conscious, showing a social conscience and being a good corporate citizen are viewed in modern management theory as benefiting the bottom line. But this management-speak hides the growing focus in the media professions – the cultural boundary spanners – on genuine links between modern organizations and the different individuals and groups in society that deal with them. In the case of public relations, this has meant a shift from the idea of PR professionals as spin-doctors and 'outsourcers of trust' towards genuine symmetrical communication (Burton, 2001).

The language of 'asymmetrical' and 'symmetrical' communication comes from the normative theorist Grunig (1992, 347) who argued that the 'technician role' is more frequent in organizations practising traditional persuasive techniques. As 'technicians', public relations practitioners are responsible for delivering the message and other communication services but are excluded from key decision-making processes. The dominant form of public relations has been asymmetrical communication, or persuasion. In two-way symmetrical communication, the public relations practitioner is more likely be involved in the decision-making process. 'Manager role enactment is more frequent in organizations practicing the two-way symmetric ... models of communication' and the public has an equal opportunity of being able to change the attitude and behaviour of the organization (Grunig and Hunt, 1984, 23).

Not surprisingly, two-way symmetrical communication and 'public sphere' have many characteristics in common (that is to say, the requirement that argument takes place in an institutional context where there is no threat of force or coercion). Table 11.1 provides an overview of the different models of public relations that have developed over time. Traditional press agentry is promotions. Public information models are more sophisticated and include a broader purpose, including public campaigns designed to inform. Two-way asymmetrical models involve social science research into what is most likely to persuade audiences or publics and then campaigns are constructed as a result. Two-way symmetrical models, not common in the modern corporate world, involve genuine mutual communication where issues are negotiated. All parties might adjust their objectives as a result of this communication.

> **Two-way symmetrical communication.** A public relations theory term for participational decision-making between organizations and their publics.

> **Two-way asymmetrical communication.** A public relations theory term for persuasion.

Table 11.1 **Grunig's four models of public relations**

Press agentry:	When a communication programme strives for favourable publicity, especially in the mass media.
Public information:	Uses journalists in residence to disseminate relatively objective information through the mass media and controlled media such as newsletters, brochures and direct mail.
Two-way asymmetrical:	A more sophisticated approach that uses research, like surveys, to develop messages that are most likely to persuade strategic publics to behave as the organization wants.
Two-way symmetrical:	A public sphere model of public relations where conflicting parties negotiate outcomes and where persuasion is not used.

Activism as a phenomenon has also raised theoretical issues about powerless publics in the asymmetrical process, and how they come to be under-represented. Activist publics are not necessarily organizational in the traditional sense and annoy traditional public relations persuaders because they can mobilize significant resources to fight issues (Dozier and Lauzen, 2000). The reaction of some practitioners to *powerless publics* however has not been to see how the powerless can be persuaded and controlled, but rather how they can be brought into genuine communication processes, as Aldoory (2001) documents in the case of health communication for women.

The failure of persuasive, asymmetrical, campaigns in both corporate and activist contexts has been well documented by the practitioners. In the 1990s, for example, PR company Burson-Marsteller was commissioned by a group of multinational timber companies in Canada who were facing opposition to their logging practices. It put into place a programme identical to one it had run in the US, including setting up 'The Forest Alliance which could position itself as the "rational middle ground" on issues' (Guiniven, 2002).

Initially successful, at least in gaining what were deemed 'favourable media impressions' the coalition's true backers and true purpose were soon unveiled, much to the embarrassment of the timber companies. One of the reasons it failed was the inability of Canadians to adapt to the US-style persuasive campaign. One of the coalition's leaders, 'when shown an activist poster that read "In Canada 1 acre of forest falls every 12 seconds," quickly announced to the media: "That's not true. It's 1 acre every 12.9 seconds"' (Guiniven, 2002, 396–7).

The high-level theorizing about symmetrical communication in public relations and the need for genuine communication is cultural studies writ large (Jones, 2002; Kent and Taylor, 2002; Holtzhausen, 2002; Leeper, 1996; Toth, 2002). Indeed, if two-way symmetrical communication were genuinely adopted by organizations as a way of managing their communication with society then persuasion would have a very different role in the media professions.

case study

An example that illustrates blogs and the inability of a campaign of asymmetrical communication – or indeed traditional media – to satisfy the contemporary citizen or activist, is the media campaign surrounding the latest invasion of Iraq. President Bush and his advisers made clear from the start of the 2003 invasion of Iraq that the media would be much more tightly controlled. The delivery of information by the military generated a new generation of euphemisms for death and destruction (Miller, 2003) and the choice of language ensured that the otherness of the Iraqis, both political and private, was made clear to the coalition's audience. Journalists were either 'embeds' or 'unilaterals' and the military public relations operation relied on the competition between journalists (and their consequent need to have access to information) to help them keep control of the media. As one unilateral journalist noted:

> Think of it as the Disney Tour War. Almost daily, an air-conditioned tourist coach leaves Kuwait City, crammed with journalists fresh from their five-star hotels, for the 90-minute motorway drive to Iraq. Their destination is the latest propaganda opportunity laid on by the coalition: aid convoys, water supplies, power restored. The places they can visit are few – a couple of border towns deemed safe. The battles and dramas beyond are strictly off limits. (Mangan, 2003)

It was clear that for the unilaterals following the guidelines laid down by the military PR, there was

SALAM PAX AND BRING THEM HOME NOW

not much potential for analysis or background stories. Even for the embed, life was not much closer to the journalistic ideal of freedom of speech:

> Before the war started I was very limited in what I could say. Both my satellite and mobile phones, despite promises by the MoD that we would be allowed to use them, were confiscated before I got on board the ship … I was allowed to speak to the Guardian's foreign desk using the ship's secure telephone, but only with a minder listening in … the captain insisted on reading everything I wrote before I was allowed to file … For the Ministry of Defence … one of the great strengths of the embedding system [is that] it is undoubtedly much harder for journalists to be impartial when they are living with and have grown to like the people they are writing about. They treated me well and I guess that was always in the back of my mind when I was writing about them. (Mangan, 2003)

However, there was a major difference between the public discourse concerning this invasion and the last Iraq war: the advent of the blog. In September 2002 an Iraqi man, calling himself Salam Pax, began posting accounts of everyday life in Baghdad in a weblog. His was one of the few blogs in English and covered a range of topics, from his music preferences to criticisms of Saddam's regime.

> With blogs the web started talking to me in a much more personal way. Bits of news started having texture and most amazingly, these blogs talked with each other. That hyperlink to the next blog – I just couldn't stop clicking … I thought the

Arab world deserved a fair representation in the blogsphere, and decided that I would be the profane pervert Arab blogger just in case someone was looking. (Salam Pax, 2003)

Support quickly built for Salam Pax in the subculture of the blogosphere and his blog was linked to the popular Instapundit blog, a move that saw hits on his weblog increase from about 20 a day to 3,000.

With the attention came the fear that someone in Iraq might actually read the blog, since by now it had entered warblog territory ... Real trouble comes when big media takes notice and this happened when there was a mention of the blog and its URL in a Reuters piece. I totally flipped out ... Things got worse when the Reuters article got picked up by other news outlets. My brother saw my agitation and I had to tell him. He thought I was a fool to endanger the family, which was true. (Salam Pax, 2003)

By the end of January war was looming and the blog was being read by a huge number of people. Doubts were raised about whether Salam Pax was actually writing from Baghdad, whether he was a real person, whether he was a Ba'ath party official, or a CIA agent.

please stop sending emails asking if I were for real, don't believe it? then don't read it.

I am not anybody's propaganda ploy, well except my own.

2 more hours until the B52's get to Iraq.

:: salam 6:05 PM [+] ::

Another blog that provided a counterbalance to the asymmetrical flow of information about the invasion came from Bagdhad Burning (http:// riverbendblog.blogspot.com). She started blogging in August and her account provides a detailed account of daily life under the coalition occupation. One of her most poignant accounts is from 19 September 2003 when she recounts raids in neighbouring houses by the occupying troops.

The last family member out of the house was Reem, A.'s wife of only 4 months. She was being led firmly out into the street by two troops, one gripping each thin arm.

I'll never forget that scene. She stood, 22 years old, shivering in the warm, black night. The sleeveless nightgown that hung just below her knees exposed trembling limbs – you got the sense that the troops were holding her by the arms because if they let go for just a moment, she would fall senseless to the ground. I couldn't see her face because her head was bent and her hair fell down around it. It was the first time I had seen her hair ... under normal circumstances, she wore a hijab.

That moment I wanted to cry ... to scream ... to throw something at the chaos down the street. I could feel Reem's humiliation as she stood there, head hanging with shame – exposed to the world, in the middle of the night. (http://www.riverbend-blog.blogspot.com)

It is not just the Iraqis who use social media networking to find ways to have a voice. One group that is equally affected is the US troops themselves, and their families. When it became clear that the 'victory' in May signalled not the end of military operations but the start of a long and dangerous occupation, soldiers' wives in mainland USA started protesting and agitating for the troops to be brought home. The military moved quickly to quell these protests, blackmailing the women by telling them that they were endangering their loved ones by speaking out and in fact could be prolonging the occupation by presenting a dissident voice to the enemy.

However this group found a voice on the Internet through their website and the resulting activist movement 'BRING THEM HOME NOW!' which was a campaign by military families, veterans, active duty personnel, reservists and others opposed to the occupation of Iraq and 'galvanized to action by George W. Bush's inane and reckless challenge to armed Iraqis resisting occupation to "Bring 'em on!'" (www.bringthemhomenow.org).

Not surprisingly, public relations and journalism as disciplinary areas are in this environment seen by theorists to be converging. Audiences-as-publics and social media are having a direct impact on the media professions (Livingstone, 2005). Journalists and public relations practitioners have to address how credibility and trust are validated in a society with push technology, blogs and activist publics.

Summary

Journalists provide a system of selection, refinement and interpretation of news. Public relations professionals provide a bridge between corporate and non-corporate organizations and their publics. All these roles are legitimate. The underlying function of these media professions has not changed. However, the habits and behaviours of audiences-as-publics have changed. Interactivity and options provided by digital media generally and P2P (peer-to-peer) media in particular have enabled audiences to bypass traditional media. The P2P revolution enables audiences to gather news from sources other than the main news agencies, to bypass advertising and to mobilize public opinion for causes.

Push technology is a response to this fractionation of audiences, viewers, customers and readers. Personalization and customization of content will continue to evolve in an environment where traditional mass media meet only partly the information and media needs of modern industrial audiences. In the 1930s a family in the US, Australia or Britain might turn off the lights, turn on the radio, lie down on the floor of their home, and listen in the dark to the latest radio play and news reports. In the modern era there is a range of different media and a staggering number of information and entertainment options available to audiences. The business models associated with delivery of news and public relations are changing in response to the digital era and sophisticated and highly educated audiences. In news media, journalists cannot simply replicate print-based news in the online medium. In public relations, practitioners cannot simply sit back in corporate offices and develop persuasion campaigns without genuine engagement with the communities they serve.

At the conclusion of this chapter you should be able to:
- critically discuss the characteristics of news and news as a form of knowledge;
- analyse some of the key impacts of social media on journalism and public relations;
- recognize the role of active forums as news.

Key themes

News as a form of knowledge. News is a form of knowledge. News is a system for collecting information about what is happening that is shaped by news values and expectations about the characteristics of news. News, generally, has the characteristics of *timeliness*, the *prominence* of the people involved in it, the *proximity* of the events reported to the news medium's audience, the *probable consequence* of the news for the audience, *importance* and *interest* to the audience, *discontinuity* in the way in which events are reported, and *acquaintance with, not knowledge about*. Because news is so diverse, *because it is not an event but the report of one*, because news must obtrude itself on a reporter's attention and be judged to be within the range of an audience's interests, it tends to be about discrete events and to be cast in stereotyped forms. Even though news reporters themselves find it difficult to articulate what they mean by 'news', these characteristics of news tend to be global.

Changing models of public relations. Public relations, interestingly, does not occur in authoritarian countries – promotions might, but not public relations. This is because, ultimately, modern democracies expect information from governments or corporations to be honest and accurate. Modern publics know that this might not be the case in many of the events that are reported, especially corporate or governmental disasters, but at the heart of the public relations ethics code is accuracy of information. Even in the terminology of public relations it is 'publics' not 'customers' that practitioners are dealing with. Persuasion, in the past, has been the model adopted by public relations practitioners to influence publics to meet corporate objectives. However, major corporate disasters have demonstrated the weakness of pure persuasion as a method in public relations when people want openness and honesty. Two-way symmetrical communication is the term created by James Grunig, a public relations theorist, to describe this need for participation and honesty. Modern participational, social, media fit the model of two-way symmetrical communication in public relations. While examples of public relations practice based on this model are few and far between, it is interesting to see the emergence of these models as suggested practice in the media professions.

Discussion questions

1   What is an activist public and how does it differ (or not) from other media users?
2   Bring to class blogs that you think are examples of citizen reporting and citizen news. Also bring to class blogs that you think are the complete opposite. Discuss with the class the differences.
3   How do public relations professionals and journalists interact in online news making?
4   What is the role of trust in communications? Can you find examples of online news or public relations where trust and credibility played a key role? Bring them to class for discussion.
5   Are P2P media changing the definitions of news and public relations?
6   Do you think that public relations will always involve 'spin' and persuasion?

Further reading

Cottle, S. (ed.) (2003). *News, public relations and power.* London: Sage.
de Jong, W., Shaw, M. and Stammers, N. (2005). *Global activism, global media.* Pluto Press.
Flew, T. (2007). *Understanding global media.* London: Palgrave Macmillan.
Gunter, B. (2003). *News and the net.* Lawrence Erlbaum Associates.
Lovink, G. (2002). *Dark fiber: Tracking critical Internet culture.* Cambridge, MA: MIT.

Media economics

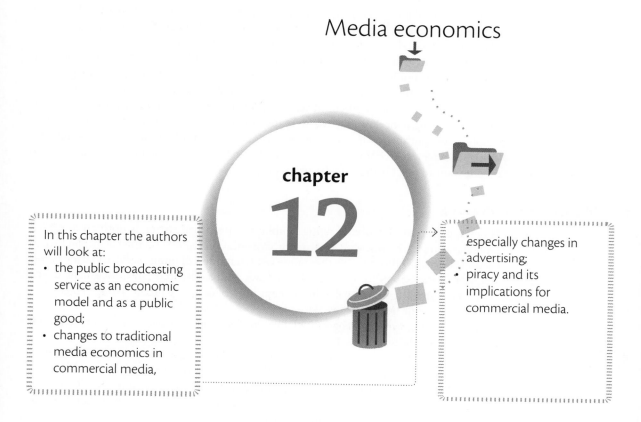

In this chapter the authors will look at:
- the public broadcasting service as an economic model and as a public good;
- changes to traditional media economics in commercial media,

especially changes in advertising; piracy and its implications for commercial media.

Chapter 11 discussed some of the changes underway for the media professions, especially the effect of participatory and social media on the professional structures and their organization. The national and global economic structures and organization of the media have also been affected by the rise of social media and increased competition. In this chapter the authors will look at:

- the public broadcasting service as an economic model and as a public good;
- changes to traditional media economics in commercial media, especially changes in advertising;
- piracy and its implications for commercial media.

Between 1983 and 1998 the European media and communications regime has changed dramatically. In the early 1980s it was (almost) universally presumed that efficient and reliable delivery of electronic media and communications services to the public required state intervention – telephone was usually provided by a state monopoly and broadcasting by a national public service broadcaster … By the end of the twentieth century, private broadcasting had become pervasive throughout the European Union (and Central and Eastern Europe). (Collins, 2002, 95)

Richard Collins's observations are basically correct. When you look around you, nationally and internationally, there can be little doubt that there is now a vast range of different options in media access, from the Internet through to interactive television (where it is available). Many of these media options are commercially run – they want to make money and to satisfy the needs of specific audiences. State-run broadcasting or media services do not dominate the landscape in the same way they used to.

However, this is not the full picture. As Collins and others recognize, the idea and the practice of public service broadcasting, or public service media, are not going to disappear. Indeed, the demand for independent media is growing, not declining. For example, in highly censored countries like Kuwait the audience demand for the state-run service might be low but the demand for an independent media is not. In this chapter, the authors will examine the principles behind public broadcasting and changes underway in commercial models. This includes the problem of audiences who do not want to pay for their media use – piracy.

Public service broadcasting

What is public service broadcasting? Public service broadcasting is both an ideal and an organization. The British Broadcasting Corporation (BBC) and the US Public Broadcasting Services (PBS) stand as the quintessential models of public service broadcasting. Michael Tracey (1998) draws on a UK Broadcasting Research Unit document developed in the 1980s to summarize the concept of public service broadcasting. Tracey was the unit's director from 1981 to 1988.

- *Universal accessibility (geographic):* Everyone should have access to a public broadcaster's signals, wherever they are located.
- *Universal appeal (general tastes and interests):* 'The principle of serving the diverse interests of the public is the basis then for the presence in the schedule of programmes which serve the young as well as the elderly, those interested in local affairs as well as the national political canvas, members of diverse subcultures as well as those in the mainstream' (Tracey, 1998, 27).
- *Particular attention to minorities:* This can include people of different colour, language and religious beliefs. Public broadcasting has a dual role: to give access to minority groups and provide them with opportunities to voice their issues as well as to provide to the broader community knowledge about their histories and cultures. There are in Britain and in the United States, for example, large numbers of Islamic migrants. Knowledge about this religion and culture is important to the broader community.
- *Contribution to a sense of national identity and community and a commitment to education:* Public broadcasters enable the nation to 'speak to itself', reflecting those things that are very different between us and those that are the same. A public broadcaster also has a role to inform and to educate (Tracey, 1998, 29).
- *Distance from vested interests:* This is the idea that public broadcasting programming works within a structure of independence. 'Programmes funded by advertising necessarily have their character influenced in some shape or form by the demand to maximize the garnering of consumers. Programmes directly funded by the government, and with no intervening structural heat shield, inevitably tend to utter the tones of their master's voice' (Tracey, 1998, 31).
- *Direct funding and universality of payment:* The forms of finance for public broadcasting are important to its retaining independence. If commercial sources of

revenue start to dominate a public service broadcaster's agenda then the principles of public service may suffer as a result.

- *Competition in good programming rather than for numbers:* Quality programming is expected from a public broadcaster regardless of the size of the audience or its potential to pay.

- *Guidelines that liberate rather than restrict programme makers:* This concept allows for experiment, innovation, quarrel and mistake in the programme making process or, as Tracey puts it, 'there should always be a place for the dissenting radical' (1998, 32).

Raboy (1999, 88) also reiterates these criteria when talking about the Asian context for the public broadcaster. While these characteristics might not be represented perfectly in all public broadcasting service systems worldwide, they are certainly the key criteria. Indeed it is not surprising to conclude, as Tracey does, that the public broadcasting system by its nature nurtures the public sphere (Tracey, 1998, 28).

It is worthwhile reading part of the charter of the US Public Broadcasting Service (PBS) to see how the concept of public service broadcasting is operationalized. PBS is a non-profit membership corporation whose members are licensees of non-commercial public television stations. It is governed by a board comprising representatives from member stations.

PBS

PBS operates in the public interest by serving the needs of its member stations. Four fundamental principles shape the content service that PBS provides to its member stations: editorial integrity, quality, diversity, and local station autonomy.

Editorial Integrity. PBS's reputation for quality reflects the public's trust in the editorial integrity of PBS content and the process by which it is produced and distributed. To maintain that trust, PBS and its member stations are responsible for shielding the creative and editorial processes from political pressure or improper influence from funders or other sources. PBS also must make every effort to ensure that the content it distributes satisfies those editorial standards designed to assure integrity.

Quality. In selecting programs and other content for its services, PBS seeks the highest quality available. Selection decisions require professional judgments about many different aspects of content quality, including but not limited to excellence, creativity, artistry, accuracy, balance, fairness, timeliness, innovation, boldness, thoroughness, credibility, and technical virtuosity. Similar judgments must be made about the content's ability to stimulate, enlighten, educate, inform, challenge, entertain, and amuse.

Diversity. To enhance each member station's ability to meet its local needs, PBS strives to offer a wide choice of quality content. Content diversity furthers the goals of a democratic society by enhancing public access to the full range of ideas, information, subject matter, and perspectives required to make informed judgments about the issues of our time. It also furthers public television's special mandate to serve many different and discrete audiences. The goal of diversity also requires continuing efforts to assure that PBS content fully reflects the pluralism of our society, including, for example, appropriate representation of women and minorities. The diversity of public television producers and funders helps to assure that content distributed by PBS is not dominated by any single point of view.

Local Station Autonomy. PBS believes that public broadcasting's greatest potential is realized when it serves the unique needs of the local community, and that there are wide variations in local needs and tastes. No one is better qualified to determine and respond to those local needs than the public television station licensed to that community.

Public service broadcasting can be funded directly by government, through licence fees and/or other supporters, as in the case of PBS. But public service broadcasting also has very important economic characteristics. Public service broadcasting has public good characteristics. For example, if I watch a television programme then the product is not lessened as a result of my watching, unlike traditional consumption. If I eat a pizza while watching the television programme, then the pizza is definitely 'consumed and gone' once I have finished. If I gave my partner my pizza while I was watching the television programme, then I would lose the pizza. However, an additional person watching television can happen at no additional cost and not diminish the product. Neither of us has lost the programme in its consumption. Indeed, if next day I talk to another person about the television programme then that person has the 'product' of our conversation as well, at no extra cost. The fixed costs of running the broadcasting and developing the television programmes, therefore, do not represent the actual potential of consumption and benefits that actually occur; unlike the consumption of the pizza.

The public good characteristics of communication, of course, extend beyond broadcasting. The idea of positive network externalities in telecommunications is based on the same principle of the public good. The fixed costs of setting up a telecommunications network and sending signals are different from the nature of the 'good' or 'product' that is consumed. Positive externalities are precisely those goods that benefit all of us. The telephone, for instance, gives us access to all our relatives and social support, as well as emergency services. The consequences of this 'consumption' are beneficial to the whole of society. Access to information, therefore, is a 'positive externality'. Other 'products' with positive externalities are clean air and functioning ecosystems.

Commercial media, of course, want to make a profit from the sales of their programmes. In Pay TV, for example, the programming is made scarce by limiting access to it by payment and by use of proprietary systems, like set top boxes, that isolate who can access the service. Free to air broadcasting is certainly not Pay TV, but advertising, that helps to fund the programming and affects what you end up seeing.

Public organizations like the BBC and PBS are needed, therefore, because they service the public sphere and the public good. 'The symbolic community projected by public service television also supports a sense of social cohesion and belonging. The groups most prone to social exclusion are old people, single parents, the unemployed and some ethnic minorities' (Curran, 2002, 207).

Both commercial network broadcasting and public service broadcasting have been affected by the diversification of media. But it would be misleading to say that public service broadcasting will disappear. Curran (2002) reported that in 2000, Britons spent

8/10ths of time looking at four channels, with 67 per cent of the British audience watching either BBC1 or ITV in prime time. Table 12.1 shows the percentage of time Britons spend on the major channels.

Table 12.1 **Share of TV viewing in Britain, 2000**

	BBC1	BBC2	ITV	CH4	CH5	Cable/satellite
All hours	27	11	30	11	6	16
Prime time (7–10.30pm)	28	10	37	8	6	11

Source: Adapted from Curran (2002).

By 2005 the BBC's share of total television viewing had fallen to about 35 per cent but its digital channels, interestingly, continue to grow. The average weekly reach for all BBC channels for 2005 was approximately 88 per cent. A BBC spokesman at the time said: 'BBC1 and BBC2 have held up incredibly well in such a competitive environment. As audiences fragment and consumption changes, reach and appreciation are absolutely critical. What is most important is that the BBC's portfolio of services and channels work as a whole to reach everybody – through radio, TV, online and interactive. It's not just about the performance of individual channels, and nor is it just about share; to take these in isolation tells you only part of the story' (Noah, 2005).

activity Conduct a piece of research among your peers, or family. Use the BBC/ITV chart above as an example for yourself of the kind of information you seek. Ask the research sample to log the hours spent watching television. Which channels are they watching, and for how long? What types of television provider operate in their/your zone? If there were alternative forms of provider or programming, would they change their preferences?

Even if people do not use public service broadcasters, they would soon notice if they – or the public sphere that they service – were gone. People are *citizens* in modern democracies and consumers. As citizens they have inbuilt expectations of the media system in which they live.

1. Citizens expect to be informed. Commercial media can generate news but those media attract paying audiences and a knowledge gap between elites and the general public can occur.

2. Citizens expect a rational democracy that encourages the transfer of relevant specialist knowledge to the political and public domains, and promotes balanced debate directed towards the public good.

3. Citizens expect a public culture of shared knowledge, values and points of reference. The idea that politicians can buy their votes and their power through the media, expensive campaigns or clever manipulation may occur, but it is not the expectation of a democratic citizenry. 'The argument that public service broadcasting fosters an informed, rational and fair democratic system is currently its single most important justification (though one that is being weakened by increased commercialization)' (Curran, 2002, 207).

The BBC

The British Broadcasting Corporation (BBC) is an example of a broadcasting service that exemplifies the model of a public service broadcaster, like PBS, but unlike many other national broadcasters it is loved and trusted by millions worldwide. In Bangladesh the BBC is revered. It produces the BBC Sanglap, which is a 'village hall' meeting type show that is produced from different locations within Bangladesh on topics of the day and then broadcast on Bangladesh Radio and the BBC World Service. It is extremely popular and considered the most reliable source of news in the country. The BBC's reputation for independence in news and its popularity also mean that it is often banned in authoritarian countries. In China, the BBC can normally only be found in 4 and 5 star hotels – through satellites from the Philippines.

The Second World War demonstrated the reputation of the BBC as an independent and trustworthy news source. The German generals and German citizens listened to the BBC for reliable information on what was happening, compared with Germany's own news sources or sources elsewhere. The BBC, despite its activities to support the resistance in Europe, never lost its position as an authoritative voice. This was, partly, because it announced British defeats as well as victories. The BBC though also broadcast more intimate news to German citizens.

> One of the Service's programmes would feature the names of German prisoners of war; and from 1943, a quarter of an hour each night was spent relaying messages recorded by PoWs to their families. On one occasion a family in Germany arranged a Requiem Mass for a soldier believed to have been killed. When they heard over the BBC that he was alive, their first thought was to cancel it – until they realised this would let the authorities know they had been listening to illegal broadcasts. The family went ahead with the service – but when they got to the church, nobody was there – because others had heard the broadcast too. (BBC, 2007)

How can an enemy broadcaster be trusted, with Nazi Generals and German citizens alike using it as the trusted source for news, despite threats of punishment from Nazi authorities?

There are two major reasons why the BBC has established its reputation for fairness and trustworthiness in news reporting. The first was people's experience of its reporting before and during the Second World War. The second is its formal structure as a 'public sphere' and the determination of BBC management to keep its independence (Briggs, 1995). The BBC was established under Royal Charter. The first Charter started on 1 January 1927 and ran to 31 December 1936. The Charters have a fixed length and provide the opportunity, approximately every ten years, to review the BBC's role, functions and structure. This review process has allowed the BBC self-reflexivity and an opportunity over time to adjust to new audiences and technologies, including entering into the digital era.

The Charter says that the BBC exists to service the public interest and its main objective is to promote its Public Purposes. The Public Purposes of the BBC are:

- sustaining citizenship and civil society;
- promoting education and learning;
- stimulating creativity and cultural excellence;
- representing the UK, its nations, regions and communities;
- bringing the UK to the world and the world to the UK

(see http://www.bbc.co.uk/bbctrust/assets/files/pdf/regulatory_framework/charter_agreement/royalchartersealed_sept06.txt).

However, the independence of the BBC was not 'a given' that was accepted without contest and without problems. Winston Churchill posed, in its early years, the first serious threat to the BBC's independence when he wanted it to toe the government line (DCMS, 2005; Briggs, 1995). John Reith, as General Manager, took seriously the BBC's role to 'inform, educate and entertain' and opposed Churchill. Reith's lobbying of the government of the day established the principle that the BBC was independent and provided impartial news.

The BBC lost its broadcasting monopoly in the 1950s but continued to adapt in a competitive environment. The BBC services listed in Table 12.2 show how it has expanded across media and internationally, at a time when there are over 300 broadcasting services in Britain.

Table 12.2 **BBC services**

Television	Radio	Other
BBC1	Radio 1	BBC online
BBC2	Radio 2	World Service
BBC3	Radio 3	BBC Scotland
BBC4	Radio 4	BBC Northern Ireland
CBeebies	Radio Five Live	BBC Wales
CBBC	Five Live Extra	BBC English regions
BBC News 24	1Xtra	
BBC Parliament	6 Music BBC 7 Asian Network 6 Nations services 40 local and regional services	

This capacity of the BBC to transform its activities across different media environments and to new audiences has been no accident. The ethos of public service broadcasting in Britain is matched by monetary support. Britain, interestingly, spends more on its television market, as a share of GDP (nearly 1 per cent), than any other country in the world. Like Germany, it is also a major supporter of its public broadcasting services. Figure 12.1 provides a profile of some of the countries with public service broadcasting.

The digital era poses problems of eroding broadcasting audiences as people move to different types of online media. A decline in traditional broadcasting services' audiences, however, does not mean the end of the BBC. As the latest review of its charter shows, the BBC is already planning for its presence in a digital culture (DCMS, 2005).

to recap...

The idea of a public broadcasting service and the public sphere are intimately linked. Public broadcasting services the public sphere. Its economics is based on the public good.

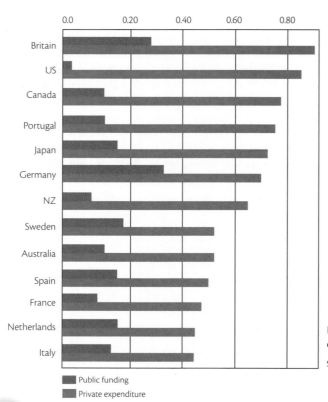

Figure 12.1 Expenditure on public and private funding of broadcasting services as a share of GDP

Source: Adapted from DCMS (2005).

Traditional media economics

Traditional media economics relies on relatively stable and identifiable audiences and especially audiences that will buy the products advertised. Advertising as a form of knowledge has a long pedigree. King Charles I used to have his dogs stolen regularly and just as regularly used to advertise his loss in a newspaper classified. George Washington sold lands he held along the Ohio River with want advertisements. Benjamin Franklin placed a classified advertisement when someone took his wife's prayer book from the family church pew. And Sir Ernest Shackleton ran classified advertisements to seek companions for his hazardous Polar expeditions.

Advertising, it has often been said, is the public language of modern capitalism. 'In this new world where almost anything can be true,' writes Daniel Boorstin in *The Image*, 'the socially rewarded art is that of making things seem true. It is the art not of discovery, but of invention. Finding a fact is easy; making a fact "believed" is slightly more difficult. The greatest effort goes into the realization not of dreams but of illusions. God makes our dreams come true. Skilful advertising men [sic] bring us our illusions, then make them seem true' (Boorstin, 1961, 212).

In *The Affluent Society* and other writings, the US economist J.K. Galbraith argues that the language of advertising is used to synthesize desires. People's wants, he says, are not independently determined but are a function of production. The task of advertising is to increase desires to keep pace with increases in production. A producer not only makes goods and services but also makes desires to consume them. Wants thus come to depend on output and so they produce what he calls the Dependence Effect (Galbraith, 1969, Ch. XI).

Advertisers want to communicate with those people who are most likely to buy the product they advertise. They seek the largest relevant target audience at the lowest possible price. In advertising cost efficiency may be expressed as cost-per-thousand readers or viewers or listeners. It may be determined by dividing the cost of advertising by the size of the audience. An advertising agency or media planners can work out the cost efficiency of the various media, or various programmes, or sections within the media and advise clients of the most efficient for their purpose.

When they read the results of such surveys some media executives are concerned with achieving maximum audience size, for example commercial television stations in prime time. Others are more interested in attracting audiences with particular demographic characteristics, such as heads of household or people within certain income bands. This is why a small industry of researchers earn their living analysing figures so that they can point to which magazines, which radio stations and which TV shows attract a certain demographic profile. Indeed, the big advertising agencies have their own research departments to test such things as commercials, advertising copy, locations, audience recall and brand and product segmentation.

Audience researchers are fond of dividing people up into value and lifestyle segments that they relate to goods and services. They talk of Achievers and Believers, Actualizers and Strivers and so on, producing stereotyped vignettes of each value system and lifestyle and advising advertisers that one group has a preference for, say, laptop computers and electronic organizers, while another group may make the major household purchasing decisions. All of this, of course, is directly related to the very basis of media economics, which is *delivering audiences to advertisers, preferably nicely targeted audiences.*

Generally, the big advertising agencies are called full-service firms. They liaise with the client, sort out their requirements, help define the market and the product, propose a campaign, draw up a budget, recommend appropriate media, create the advertisements, book media space and time and liaise with media advertising departments. Buying space goes back to the foundations of agencies. But these days, advertising, like much of the media, has been globalized and international full-service firms aim to provide more than buying services. Some can supply a full range of skills from their own resources but they may organize or buy-in associated promotions and public relations services. They usually employ campaign planners, media buyers, copywriters, artists, creative directors and art directors but may hire more for big campaigns. Big firms hire outside photographers and cine-photographers, specialist artists, printers, actors, models, celebrities, voice-over readers and special-effects people on a daily basis. They also hire props and properties for advertising shoots.

Generally, the agency will want to know the answers to five questions before it begins a campaign:

1. What is the product and what is distinctive about it?
2. What are the qualities of the rival products?
3. What group of people is most likely to be interested in the product?
4. What are the best media in which to advertise it?
5. What is the best strategy for reaching the target audience?

Results of readership surveys may not be publicly available from many newspapers, but marketing has become a magic word in many papers as they have tried to arrest declining circulations. When many proprietors are appointing editors today they are often seeking people who not only have a nose for news but also a feel for marketing.

In the 1990s Doug Underwood summed up this emerging attitude in a scathing critique of the new ethos, written from the perspective of a traditional journalist who believes that news and advertising are separate worlds.

> Welcome to the world of the editor of a modern daily newspaper, a person who, as likely as not, is going to be immersed in readership surveys, marketing plans, memos on management training, and budget planning goals. The daily newspaper business has undergone a remarkable transformation from the day when editors in green eyeshades made seat-of-the-pants news judgments and readers were noticed only when they wrote a letter to the newspaper. Today's market-savvy newspapers are planned and packaged to 'give readers what they want'; newspaper content is geared to the results of readership surveys, and newsroom organization has been reshaped by newspaper managers whose commitment to the marketing ethic is hardly distinguishable from their vision of what journalism is. (Underwood, 1993, xii)

activity In interviews with Chinese media professionals in March 2008, we spoke with a young writer who wants, eventually, to write novels that record the emotional experience of being Chinese in the current era. Meanwhile, in order to pay the rent, he writes advertising copy and stories that contain product placement for glossy magazines. Take some time to read and analyse magazine copy from the high-end glossies and also in the current affairs/gossip sectors of the magazine market. How would you recognize marketing-oriented copy? What are the types of stories or articles that are explicitly tied to commercial advantage?

There have been significant differences between print and broadcasting in how the *economic value of audiences* has been assessed. In print, newspapers and magazines may financially rely upon subscription alone, subscription and advertising, or advertising alone with the product going to the consumer 'free'. The audience or readers in a print environment were traditionally determined by circulation and there are audit circulation companies that independently assess the circulations of newspapers and magazines. This can include rule of thumb assessments, for example, that there are five readers for each purchase of a newspaper or a magazine. A print run from a small newspaper of 5,000 copies each week in Wheeling, West Virginia in the US might, technically have a readership of 25,000. As you might guess, such figures are rubbery at best. The newspaper might do some readership research and have a good idea about its readership, but the circulation estimates and the research only indirectly act as currency for the advertisers for the newspaper. The local newspaper would try to charge for its advertising space what the local market is likely to bear, against its production costs, rather than have a complex set of metrics for charging for advertising. The monetary value of advertising in print has not in the past been linked to survey technology and its results.

Because traditional mass media are sold to consumers for less than the cost of production, or in the case of radio and most television, provided 'free', advertisers effectively subsidize readers, listeners and viewers. A publication with little or no advertising is relatively expensive because it must depend for revenue mainly on subscriptions and news-stand sales, whereas one with high advertising volumes is relatively cheap.

The case study below provides an interesting insight into how media industry professionals in 2006 viewed some of the problems between the traditional economics of newspaper readership and advertising to the online consumer of news.

case study

This is a newspaper industry discussion on the advertiser and the online newspaper consumer, taken from a public online discussion on SunDog's website, http://www.sundog.net. SunDog is a marketing and new media company and represents advertisers.

1. Initial comment from Greg Ness at SunDog, 2006

As a company that represents advertisers, I did a doubletake when I saw … a story about a speech Vin Crosbie of Borrell Associates made to the World Newspaper Advertising Conference. In his speech, Crosbie was encouraging newspapers to move online faster because 'online advertising revenues are rising dramatically.' However, he said it will be a challenge because online advertising revenue produces 20 to 100 times less revenue per reader than traditional newspaper advertising. Doesn't this beg the question: 'Why would any advertiser want to pay 20 to 100 times more to reach an actual physical paper reader than an online reader?'

I believe in newspapers as a consumer. I believe in newspapers as a marketing company. At home, we have a paid subscription to our local newspaper's online addition. It is apparent the Web is changing everything from a marketing economics viewpoint. However, the figures cited in Crosbie's speech to a world gathering of the newspaper industry illustrate the tremendous challenge traditional media is facing when transitioning to a Web delivery model. My guess is these numbers would be similar for the magazine industry.

Gavin O'Reilly, President of the World Association of Newspapers, pointed out that one billion people read a newspaper every day. That is an impressive statistic, but we also have to remember there are now one billion people on the Internet. But, if I'm an advertiser, I still have to look at Crosbie's figures and go 'hmmmm.' In marketing, what really matters is not what something costs, but rather, what is the final return on investment. If traditional newspaper readers cost 20 to 100 times what online readers cost, that is a big gap to overcome.

2. Vin Crosbie's reply to Greg Ness

Just to note: Do remember the difference between just ad rates and overall organizational revenues. The advertiser doesn't pay 20 to 100 times more to reach a newspaper's printed edition reader than to reach a reader of its website. What I said in my speech was that the newspaper earns 20 to 100 times as much. Printed editions of newspapers earn two revenue streams: circulation revenues directly from subscribers and single-copy purchasers. And advertising revenues indirectly earned because readers exist.

The first is about $250 to $600 per year per consumer (depending upon the printed edition's subscription or newsstand costs). The second adds another $200 to $400 depending upon the size of the newspaper (divide its total advertising revenues by its circulation). The combined annual total is about $450 to $1,000 per consumer. However, most newspapers' websites aren't able to charge for access (akin to circulation revenues) and generate only advertising revenues. Moreover, they charge only for the actual number of online ads exposed, not an entire press-run circulation regardless of actual page readership. Nevertheless, the actual ad CPMs [cost per thousand] charged in print and online by newspapers aren't that much different,

ADVERTISERS AND ONLINE NEWSPAPER CONSUMERS

certainly not 20 to 100 different. The full text of the speech is at http://www.digitaldeliverance.com/MT/archives/000643.htm

3. Greg Ness's reply

Vin, Thank you for your comment and clarification. My main point is about the same issue you raised in your talk. It is difficult for traditional media economics to work when they are moved to the Web. An advertiser may not have to literally pay 20 to 100 times more per reader with traditional newspapers, but those advertisers still have to support a business model that brings in 20 to 100 times more revenue per reader. Also, according to our media buyers, traditional newspaper advertising still costs considerably more on a CPM basis than online newspaper advertising … at least 2 to 5 times as much by our calculations. Additionally, when somebody clicks on one of our advertiser's ads in the online edition, we know it and can analyze the effectiveness of the ad and the online campaign. Vin, as I said, we still believe in newspapers. They are a great way to get your message out to some demographic categories and to buy large reach quickly. However, the changing media landscape is not going to long support a model that has to bring in 20 to 100 times more revenue to be effective. Again, thanks for your response.

Periodically media commentators and others argue that we will never have a truly free press while newspapers and magazines rely on advertising for most of their income. However, there is little evidence that the majority of readers would prefer a newspaper or magazine without advertising, especially if the advertising subsidizes their access to the things that they want to read. The *Reader's Digest* used to publish without advertising but when it gave its readers a choice between a price rise and advertisements in 1955 the readers chose advertisements. The New York adless paper, *PM*, lost a fortune in the years after the Second World War and eventually had to run 'news stories' about the 'offers' being made each day by the city's department stores because those offers were being sorely missed by its readers. One adless paper that came close to being successful was Chicago's *The Day Book*, financed by the American newspaper baron E.W. Scripps, and published from 1911 to 1917. 'Oh, for the liberty to say in print what I think of the counter-jumping crowd (advertisers) and the ability to sell my thought for profit,' he sighed in a letter. He wanted to become 'a great public benefactor by founding and building a new generation of newspapers – not the old independence of politics and political pap, but independence of advertisers – newspapers that, while they will be commercial institutions, will still be free from the most debasing kind of commercialism.' He never achieved that ambition and, although *The Day Book's* circulation continued to increase until a price rise during the First World War caused it to decline, the paper was never an economic success (Knight, 1964).

The brief dialogue between Greg Ness and Vin Cosbie in the case study is a nice summary of some of the issues associated with assessing the economic value of audiences and/or readers in traditional versus new media environments. The monetary value of advertising is related to the identification of the right audiences and the cost of reaching those audiences. Traditional metrics – ways of measuring – for print-based advertising are different from new metrics for online audiences. Ness sets the scene with the question 'Why would any advertiser want to pay 20 to 100 times more to reach an actual physical paper reader than an online reader?'

Audience ratings

The monetary value of advertising in broadcasting is now intimately linked with survey technology and estimates of the size of audiences. The US company ACNielsen was established in the US in 1923 to measure radio audiences. After buying its opposition, CE Hooper, in 1950 it came to dominate the measurement of television audiences in the United States, although the major part of its business was checking supermarket and pharmacy shelves to measure the sales of clients' products. In this field it was a world leader. In radio days Nielsen had invested in a measurement device, the Audimeter, designed to measure the stations to which radios were tuned. This developed into a television Audimeter (or a people-meter) installed in more than a thousand homes and designed to send electrical impulses from all over the United States to the Nielsen computer in Dunedin, Florida. The Media Research Division of ACNielsen collected the data from the meters each day, tallied and classified it, then sent it out to television networks, programme suppliers, advertising agencies and advertisers around the country.

Thus the networks sent messages to audiences in the form of programmes, Neilsen measured the audiences and they returned messages to Neilsen via the Audimeters, showing the percentage of households with sets installed tuned to a particular programme at a particular time of day. Coupled with other demographic data and later linked to data gathered by supermarket wands, this became valuable information for advertisers and the advertising industry.

Television homes are now measured with Peoplemeters, a box that sits on the top of the television set and records the viewing of individuals in the household. This information is sent back to Nielsen and covers every minute of the day. The ratings results from television or diary viewing are sold by the audience research company to advertisers, media planners and others. This is called *syndicated research*. One television station alone could not afford to do research on its audiences on a continuous basis. The syndication reduces costs to the different organizations in the media industry chain. A television station, however, might do *customized research* on a local programme that it is developing. Syndicated research also has benefits beyond the economics of cost. The third-party and independent nature of the audience ratings results allows a level playing field in competitive broadcast planning. If media broadcasters were to hide their audience information from other competitors, then it would make it difficult for advertisers to rely on the truth of the private figures of one broadcaster alone. Broadcasters could potentially exaggerate or skew the results to their benefit. Even with third-party ratings, however, you will have noticed television stations or other broadcasters complaining about results, especially if those broadcasters have dropped in the ratings. Figures 12.2 and 12.3 give some basic guides to how ratings and share are calculated in audience ratings.

The television households are selected after an establishment survey is conducted by the audience research company. This establishment survey looks at all the demographics in the country and forms the basis for a random, statistical, selection of households for participation in the panel. These panels, consisting of thousands of households, are then able to represent millions of households. Figure 12.4 provides an example of the different panels that may operate in different countries. The panel figures provided by the authors are rough approximations as the actual panel sizes may differ slightly over time. The reason that the panels are not in the tens of thousands is statistical (as well as, of course, practical). In sampling, probability, theory there are levels of sampling error. The television panels chosen are at the optimum level with a set

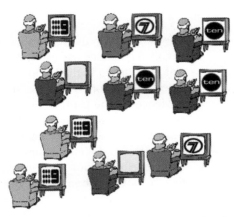

Share = Households viewing Channel 10 divided by people using television; 3/6 or 50 per cent. Channel 10 has a 50 per cent share. The blank screens in this example are those households without their television sets on.

Figure 12.2 Calculating share in audience ratings

Rating = Channel 10 households divided by the total TV households; 3/10 or 30 per cent. Channel 10 has a 30 per cent rating.

Figure 12.3 Calculating a rating

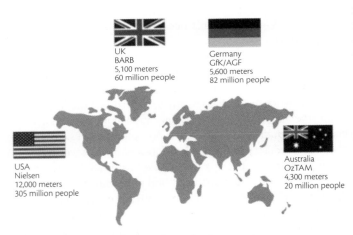

UK
BARB
5,100 meters
60 million people

Germany
GfK/AGF
5,600 meters
82 million people

USA
Nielsen
12,000 meters
305 million people

Australia
OzTAM
4,300 meters
20 million people

Figure 12.4 International comparison of ratings panels

margin of error, say 5 per cent. Pay TV channels are also using their subscriber bases to collect audience data, potentially rivalling traditional panels. In 2008, satellite television provider DirecTV partnered with measurement company TNS to create a panel of 100,000 participants from its 16 million customers. In Australia, Foxtel and regional Pay TV group Austar, in conjunction with MCN, announced the launch of AMS that would, the group argued, be the largest measurement system in Australia, providing viewing results from a panel of 10,000 Australian subscription homes (Bodey, 2008).

Many countries that previously lacked audience ratings regimes are now adopting them or planning to adopt them. National and international advertisers are a natural market for audience ratings because they pay hundreds of thousands of dollars to make a single commercial and hundreds of thousands more for a single insertion in a programme's commercial breaks. The audience ratings determined the fate of many a programme. Those with 'bad demographics' – an audience that had no significant purchasing power – would be excluded from decisions in programming.

There have been established assumptions in media planning about audience size, composition, and how often advertising might need to be repeated to reach an audience. Advertising gives us 'free' television and radio, but it also heavily influences the content we get. For instance, it makes the journalists who work for them 'market conscious' and leads to (often unconscious) self-censorship. It has influenced the general media orientation towards the advantages of capitalism and the importance of business. It has dominated radio and television programming, determining which programmes and which performers will survive in the ratings battle. It has influenced the choice of programmes, the times they are presented and the ways they are 'lined up'.

Exposure. A measure for audience ratings – who in the audience has been exposed to a programme and for how long.

to recap...

Traditional media economics relies on relatively stable and identifiable audiences and especially audiences that will buy the products advertised. Traditional print, newspaper or magazine, is funded by subscription, subscription with advertising, or advertising alone. The value of advertising in print is determined by audited circulations and estimates of readership demographics. In broadcasting, on the other hand, survey technology has been intimately tied to the value of advertising. Audience ratings act as currency for advertisers to make decisions on media space.

In broadcasting, the measurement of audiences exposed to the programme or advertisement has traditionally been seen as the key factor in making decisions on buying and selling media space. Exposure is, simply, that. Has the audience been exposed to the programme or the advertisement? And for how long? Over forty years ago, an Advertising Research Foundation (ARF) committee headed by Dr Seymour Banks, director of media research at Leo Burnett in the United States, created a model for evaluating media. That model was divided into six stages:

1. Distribution of the media advertising vehicle;

2. Audience exposure to the vehicle;

3. Audience exposure to a specific advertisement in the vehicle;

4. Audience members' perception of the advertisement;

5. Communication of the advertising message to the audience;

6. Eventual decision regarding whether to purchase the advertised item.

There have been attempts by the ARF to update this model (Phelps, 1989), but 'exposure' is still perceived as key to making decisions about buying and selling in advertising. Significant effort in modern advertising is directed towards maximizing exposure – to ensure that a broadcast audience is exposed to an optimum number of messages in a media planning schedule. But the new media environment has posed challenges to measurement of exposure and what, indeed, will count as currency in new business models.

New media economics

Interactivity as it is emerging in the current media environment is having a dramatic effect on traditional assumptions about frequency and reach in advertising. Frequency and reach in the language of media planning involve estimates about how many times the advertising message needs to be repeated and how extensively it needs to be exposed to the audience before it is effective. New media interactivity already allows the audience to bypass attempts by advertisers to expose them to their advertising. People can use their *time-shifting technology*, like the Personal Video Recorder, to programme-out advertisements or restrict Pop-ups on the Internet.

Audiences in an environment where they can personalize and customize a medium according to their preferences or become *prosumers* or 'producers' of content themselves will look for content and not only watch content designed for repetition in a mass medium. Interactive environments, like the Internet and interactive television, allow people to find out more and more about a topic that engages them. Attempts by advertisers to gain exposure to audiences through 30 second messages only make sense if there is an audience that is big enough or motivated enough to purchase the advertiser's products. There are various reasons for the shift to fragmentation of audiences and not all of them are related to ad avoidance.

- *Conduit multiplication:* There has been an increasing range of channels available for modern audiences in addition to new free-to-air networks. Conduit multiplication has diluted the broadcast network share of the audience because audiences have far more options available to them. Getting the attention of the audience has, as a result, become significantly more difficult.

- *Audience fragmentation:* It is much harder to gain a critical mass for audiences in a fragmented market. As more channels and Internet sites become available and more specialized audiences arise so the size of audience markets shrinks.
- *New uses for television:* There are new demands on viewer attention, from DVDs to game stations and, as a consequence, there is less time available for television viewing. There are countervailing trends. Game stations, for example, result in more televisions in the home with new televisions in kids' bedrooms.
- *Ambience:* Television like radio is shifting more to the background with people doing more and more tasks while watching television. Hence, there tends to be less attention when watching ads.
- *Erosion of metrics:* Faith in the power of audience ratings is slowly eroding. In an interactive climate there arise inefficiencies in audience ratings because simple exposure is not the only information that an advertiser might need.
- *Shift to below-the-line advertising:* There is a trend towards a more accountable media spend. Advertisers want to see that their audiences or consumers are reached and that their advertising was effective, not only that the audience was exposed to advertising.
- *Exposure loses value in this media environment:* Some exposure like advertisements during the Super Bowl – that still deliver critical mass – will increase significantly in value precisely because they represent greater scarcity. But this is premium advertising where only the very wealthy advertisers will be able to access mass audiences. How do other, less wealthy, legitimate advertisers gain access to and attention from their consumers or audiences in the new media environment? (See also Balnaves and Varan, 2002.)

There are several trends that are emerging to address these issues:

1. Use A2/M2, anytime anywhere media measurement;
2. Buy social media sites, like Facebook and YouTube, that deliver massive audiences;
3. Collaborate directly with audiences in the creation and selling of content, co-creation.

A2/M2 anytime anywhere media measurement

One way of getting around measuring exposure in one or two media is to measure absolutely everything that people do. In 2007, audience research company Nielsen used the term A2/M2 to describe its new strategy – anytime anywhere measurement. The aim of the strategy is to ask households to allow them to collect information about – everything. From Web surfing to mobile phone use, twenty-four hours a day, seven days a week. Nielsen recognizes the significant privacy issues. In 2008, Scott Springer, senior vice president for media product leadership, argued that multiple activities are more invasive and, therefore, you incur higher barriers psychologically for people to accept this. 'The ultimate research dream is to be able to measure everything in the universe. It's not realistic, obviously' (Story, 2008).

Traditionally, audience ratings have focused on exposure to television, radio and, more recently, the Internet. The new ratings regime, still in its experimental phase, involves companies like Nielsen tracking multiple activities of the same people. At present, for example, Nielsen maintains 17 panels of people who agree to have one or other aspect of their lives monitored. Table 12.3 shows how extensive this monitoring is within the United States and also internationally. Each household in the television panel, for example, can participate for two years and their identities remain secret. Panel members are rewarded with modest incentives, but the public interest side of participation – helping the society – is also an element.

In 2008 Nielsen cancelled its *Project Apollo*. Project Apollo monitored the buying and radio and television behaviour of 5,000 households. A joint venture with Arbitron, the project discovered that clients found the cost of purchasing the data was too high and that people were less likely to participate as the number of things monitored grew. However, as Table 12.3 shows, Nielsen already has a range of different panels covering different aspects of media and consumer behaviour, including its US Homescan panel of 125,000 people.

Nielsen is not the only audience measurement company in the US or in the world. TNS offers different types of ratings information, for example summarizing preferences of DirecTV's satellite subscribers. comScore competes with Nielsen on evaluating websites and M:Metrics competes with Nielsen on mobile phone tracking.

Table 12.3 **Nielsen panels**

	Year	Households in panel	Location
National Peoplemeter	1987	14,000	US
Local Peoplemeter	2002	600–800 in 13 markets	US
Set Metered Markets (Electronic boxes that track viewing but information about the view is in a diary)	1959	21,000	US
Hispanic People Meter Supplement	1994	270	US
Out of Home (Measures TV viewing at work, bars, airports, and so on, using sounds from the programmes that are recorded automatically by special mobile phones)	2008	4,700	US
Homescan Global (Purchasing behaviour)	1988	135,000	27 countries
Homescan US consumers	1988	125,000	US
Homescan Hispanic	2007	2,500	US/Latin America
FANLinks (Cross-references Homescan with their fan interests)	2005	50,000	US
Project Apollo (Multimedia consumption and purchasing – now cancelled)	2006	5,000	US
Nielsen BookScan (US book industry data)	2001	12,000 Booksellers	US
Your Voice (Online community for opinions)	2000	500,000+	Global
Nielsen Mobile Bill Panel (Activity on mobiles)	2005	20,000 Mobile bills	US
Hey! Nielsen (Website where users rate TV shows, movies, and so on)	2007	30,000	US
NetView Panel and MegaPanel (Offline and online audience and market research)	1997	475,000	US and 9 other countries
Pine Cone Research (Product and concept surveys)	1999	173,000	Global
The Hub (Former members of other panels who allow Nielsen to track them)	2008	1,000	US

Source: Story (2008).

There is not yet any agreed-upon metric that covers all media or a single currency that can be used by advertisers to cover all media and purchasing behaviour. However, as you can see, there are dramatic changes underway in the amount of information that advertisers and other companies want about their consumers. While audience measurement companies are experimenting with different ways of collecting information, without losing participants, companies like Google are looking at how to buy large audiences in a fragmented audience market.

Google Advertising and co-creation

Google bought YouTube in 2006 for $1.65 billion. YouTube was launched in February 2005 and by 2006 it had over 100 million videos viewed every day and over 72 million individual visitors each month. The sale made the YouTube owners rich men. But how does Google make money from YouTube? It still does not, at the time of writing this book.

The majority of Google's US$16.6 billion in revenue has been from small text advertisements that you see next to Google search results. But Google in future plans to sell advertisements to appear inside videos on sites across the Internet. In the US, advertising money spent on Internet video advertisements in 2008 was only in its infancy compared with the $20 billion spent overall on Internet advertisements. Google in buying YouTube took advantage of the explosion in online video, marked by YouTube. It also started purchasing smaller companies that provided different types of advertising services or software for use in an online video environment.

Google's new software program, AdSense for Video, for example, assists Internet publishers to make more money from their own videos. AdSense for Video provides advertisers a choice between video or text advertisement on a portion of the video viewer. But Google provided an interesting twist in its arrangements with video content providers. Those providers are called 'participating user-partners'. 'Participating user-partners will be treated as other content partners and will have the ability to control the monetization of the videos they create. Once they've selected a video to be monetized, we'll place advertising adjacent to their content so participating user-partners can reap the rewards from their work. Before you start fantasising about the hundreds of pennies you'll surely make from that video of Granny's teeth falling out, you should know that the program is not open to all, just a select invited few' (Google, 2007).

AdSense for Video will start with twenty partners. This includes video aggregator sites Revver and Blip.tv and video technology companies Brightcove and YuMe. These companies in turn deliver video content and advertisements to their own networks of Web publishers. What is interesting about the proposed partner program, however, is that in the long term the principle could apply to the individual user who wants to make money from the video that they produce for the Internet. Google is anticipating what has been called co-creation – a process where users and producers of media content become much closer in the new media economics.

The idea of co-creation emerged not as an abstract idea but as an actual activity in the world of digital games development. An important feature of the digital game culture is fan-created content, including extensions and additions to the game software (called 'mods' or 'add-ons'). Game development companies release software editing tools to fans that enable them to produce new material for the game. John Banks, who worked for Auran, a multimedia games company, reflected on the practice:

To assume that gamers and the corporation stand in an exterior relationship – on one side the producer and on the other side the consumer or audience – would be a

Co-creation. Companies involving audiences in the creation of their products; where fan programmers create their own programming content in addition to the game created.

mistake. For a start, many – if not most – of the designers, artists and programmers who work at Auran are also themselves game fans. Many of them participate actively in the fan networks that form around particular game titles and genres on the Internet. These gamer-employees bring with them skills, practices and cultures that are very much influenced by their activities as gamers. These practices in turn influence and impact upon Auran at the most basic level of work place practices. (Banks, 2002, 195)

Fan sites demonstrate this further. In 2007, for example, discussion boards filled with speculations on the backstory about Harry Potter's famous headmaster Professor Dumbledore's mysterious past relationships (it turns out, according to author J.K. Rowling, that he actually is gay). *Star Wars* fans create and distribute their own prequels and sequels; afficianados of hit game *Halo 3* film comedy skits based in the Halo world.

There are in the new media economics different ways of conceiving the modern audience-as-commodity. Google's approach is to buy massive audiences and to experiment with different ways of relating to content providers and the audience. Google does not need panels because it has either a record of what its users do, or a site like YouTube, where the audience gathers. That audience in itself has economic value. Nielsen's approach is to have panels that represent audiences and then sells research about those audiences to advertisers and others. In order to compete in the new media economics Nielsen's strategy is to find out everything about its audience.

The platforms that will be delivering advertising in the future are bringing together all the media, from mobile phones through to interactive television. It is worthwhile turning to digital television, an important convergence medium, to see how widespread these new media markets will be.

Digital television (DTV)

New media have always represented new potential for advertising. Newspapers and magazines offered advertisers the opportunity to intersperse advertisements with news, front page and back page, and to target specific audiences by readership demographic. Television enabled advertisers to interrupt programming and to advertise instantly to mass audiences. Digital television (DTV) provides the opportunity for enhanced viewing and enhanced access to information. But unlike print and traditional television broadcasting, DTV is an example of both 'technical convergence' and 'service level convergence' – improvements in technical delivery and improvements at the user level. The DTV environment provides an opportunity for both customization and high production values, at lower cost. It combines the capacities of television and the Internet.

Five countries (China, Russia, India, Japan, Brazil), all of which are outside western Europe and North America, will in 2010 account for over 50 per cent of global digital terrestrial television (DTT). Table 12.4 shows that penetration of digital television in China will not be as high as that of other industrialized countries by 2010 but as Table 12.5 demonstrates, China represents a key global market. It is not surprising therefore that News Corporation has invested significantly in delivering content to the Chinese and Asian television markets.

Adding value to advertising in a DTV world is the next step. Google's experiments with video on the Internet are a precursor to the broader digital developments like DTV. Adding value to advertising – Google's strategy – will become increasingly more important than measurement of exposure. Adding value to advertising, the authors argue, will become the basis of currency for advertising in the new media economics.

In the future audiences will advertise through new media their preferences – in processes like co-creation – rather than advertising being broadcast to mass audiences.

Table 12.4 **Global DTT homes as a percentage of TV households in 2010**

1	Italy	73.9
2	Greece	66.8
3	Australia	64.9
4	South Korea	57.8
5	New Zealand	57.8
6	France	57.5
7	Hong Kong	56.9
8	Singapore	54.1
9	Russia	53.6
10	Spain	53.3

Source: Baskerville Communications Corp. (now part of the Informa Telecoms group http://www.baskerville.telecoms.com/).

Table 12.5 **Global DTT homes rankings in 2010 (000s)**

1	China	100,064
2	Russia	28,569
3	India	22,294
4	Japan	19,314
5	Brazil	17,637
6	Italy	15,806
7	Indonesia	13,226
8	France	13,144
9	UK	12,449
10	USA	12,447

Source: Baskerville Communications Corp. (now part of the Informa Telecoms group http://www.baskerville.telecoms.com/).

While Nielsen, Google and others try to work out how to get the attention of audiences, research the audience or collaborate with them, there are forces at work in the new media economics that not only try to bypass advertising but also all try to bypass payment for media content.

Digital piracy

They tell me what I do is beautiful and ask why I am not more popular. Then they hand me a pirate disc to sign. (Carmen Paris, Spanish singer-songwriter)

Twenty billion music tracks were illegally swapped or downloaded on the Internet in 2005. This is the estimate of the International Federation of the Phonographic Industry (IFPI) that represents music producers. Internet download sales of music have continued to increase, as Table 12.6 demonstrates. However, as the illegal download figures suggest, P2P piracy continues on a large scale.

Table 12.6 **Internet download sales (units millions)**

		Q1 2005	Q1 2006
US	Single tracks	76.2	144.0
	Single tracks album equivalent	7.6	14.4
	Albums	3.0	7.4
UK	Single tracks	4.5	11.5
Japan	Internet downloads	1.1	5.9

Source: International Federation of the Phonographic Industry (IFPI) (2006).

In 2006 the International Federation of the Phonographic Industry (IFPI) tracked over ten weeks via the Internet the illegal distribution of Placebo's new album *Meds*.

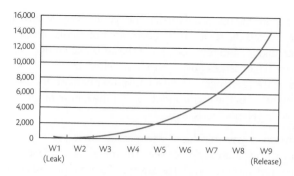

Figure 12.5 Pirating of Placebo's *Meds*

Source: International Federation of the Phonographic Industry (IFPI) (2006).

The first single from Placebo's *Meds* was leaked via a German website ten weeks prior to the official release of the album. A week later the entire album could be found on websites and then on P2P networks. Figure 12.5 shows the speed of diffusion of the pirated music.

More than one in three of all music discs purchased around the world is estimated to be an illegal copy. Almost 40 per cent of all CDs purchased in 2005 were pirated; 1.2 billion CDs in total. Piracy includes LAN file sharing, digital 'stream ripping' (the process of converting streamed music into stored files) and mobile music piracy. The music corporations are actively trying to stop music piracy. In September 2005 the Federal Court of Australia issued a ruling that file-sharing service Kazaa, one of the best-known brands in music piracy, was liable for copyright infringement and ordered to implement filtering. Kazaa had been the biggest single Internet piracy operation to that point with 2.4 million users.

Many members of the modern industrial audience, however defined, however conceived, or however theorized, are happy to download other people's music, without paying. The new media economics is faced, therefore, with audiences that have become more fragmented, more elusive and with the capacity to bypass payment.

There are two major economic models in modern media – public service and private competition. There are, internationally, variations on a theme when it comes to public service broadcasting. The BBC, for example, gains revenue from a variety of sources, but its Charter remains intact. The PBS in the US is very dependent on donations from sponsors, but its editorial independence is protected from undue influence. Table 12.7 provides a brief overview of the differences between public service broadcasting as a public good and competition in the private interest.

Table 12.7 Characteristics of public versus private media funding

Public Service Broadcasting	Competition
Public good	Private good
Owned by governments/public	Owned by private corporations/individuals
Services the public sphere	Services market demand
Public interest ethos	Profit ethos
Audiences as citizens	Audiences as commodities

Research into audiences serves different purposes in each model. In public service broadcasting *all* audiences are of interest and there is no desire to take advantage of particular segments of the population for profit. Audience research is designed to reflect the diversity of the population.

Audience research in the private model, however, is designed to find audiences and to work out ways of influencing them to spend money. Audience ratings systems in broadcasting provide an economic foundation for advertiser-supported media. The nature of the audience measurement process has in the past affected the structure and behaviour of media companies and regulators alike. When the techniques and technologies of the audience ratings change, these changes can, as Napoli (2003) observes, have 'a significant effect on the economics of media industries (because these changes can affect advertiser behaviour), the relative economic health of various segments of the media industry, and the nature of the content that media organizations provide' (Napoli, 2003, 65).

Although changes to the 'ratings convention' governing audience measurement can be disruptive, these changes are driven by the inevitable gap between the measured audience and the actual audience for a service or programmes. With the advent of a more diverse and fragmented media environment and fractionated audiences increasingly demographically defined, this gap has become even more evident with the validity of ratings as currency for buying and selling media being challenged in the US. Napoli (2003) suggests that this is leading to a decline in quality and value of the 'audience product' – data on who is watching when – because of changes in technology and audiences. The provision of reliable third-party syndicated and customized audience measurement technology for the production of audience ratings, however, remains essential to good media management nationally and internationally.

While measurement of audiences may be important to advertisers and the media industry generally, understanding media audiences does not stop there. Modern industrial audiences have taken up interactive console and online games on a massive scale. Audiences have recognized diversity and the opportunities to bypass traditional media sources. The new economics is not just about the opportunity for audiences to find out more about a topic but also for the audience to express its preferences more directly, as discussed in the concept of co-creation. Unlike traditional broadcasting the digital and online games in particular represent communities of play and communicative spaces where people can interact and share experiences as well as express their preferences to the makers of products. Young people, especially, are drawn to these games. In the next chapter we will look at the digital games phenomenon.

At the conclusion of this chapter you should be able to:

- critically discuss the differences between the public service and competitive models of media economics;
- distinguish between traditional and new media economics;
- apply the concept of co-creation to emerging new ways of linking audiences to media providers.

Key themes

Public service broadcasting. What is public service broadcasting? Public service broadcasting is both an ideal and an organization. The British Broadcasting Corporation (BBC) and the US Public Broadcasting Services (PBS) stand as the quintessential models of public service broadcasting. The principles of broadcasting, generally, entail:

- universal accessibility (geographic). Everyone should have access to a public broadcaster's signals, wherever they are located;
- universal appeal (general tastes and interests);
- particular attention to minorities;
- contribution to a sense of national identity and community and a commitment to education;
- distance from vested interests;
- direct funding and universality of payment;

• guidelines that liberate rather than restrict programme makers.

Most importantly, public broadcasting has public good characteristics. It attempts to represent the whole of a society and bring to it a sense of social cohesion and belonging. The ideal of public broadcasting is not going to disappear, even though its organizational formats may change over time.

New media economics. Traditional media economics assumes stable and identifiable audiences that can be sold to advertisers or other buyers. Audiences, however, have become increasing fractured by virtue of the number of media sources available to them and in how they might express their preferences for media content. This 'fractionization of audiences' does not mean that audiences have disappeared. Google bought YouTube for billions of dollars precisely because it is an audience of considerable size. However, how to measure those audiences and how to create a 'metric' that serves as currency for making decisions on the value of those audiences is a hot topic. Digital piracy is another signal to the media industries that the audience will bypass payment and advertisements, if that option is available. Creators of media content have a legitimate interest in protecting their rights to their works and to a living. The problem of the elusive audience is related to capacity not to pay.

Discussion questions

1   Bring to class for discussion examples of advertising that you think reflect audience research findings on particular demographics.
2   Is digital piracy strictly wrong? Or do you think that there are circumstances where downloading content, free, is acceptable, even when it breaches copyright or ownership rules? Discuss with the class.
3   Bring to class examples of file-sharing sites that you think are outside the law.
4   What are some of the problems of A2/M2 in terms of privacy?
5   Can you find examples of the benefits of public service broadcasting, in your own country and other countries?
6   Do you think that co-creation will succeed as a long-term media planning strategy? Or will corporations and businesses use it to take advantage of audiences at their cost?
7   Bring to class examples of advertisements in online environments. Which do you think are most successful at capturing your attention?
8   Does advertising corrupt the media? If so, then in what way and in which areas?
9   Can the ordering of the results from a Google search be paid for? (For example, can you pay Google to put your name first in a search for your name?)

Further reading

Balnaves, M., O'Regan, T. and Sternberg, J. (eds) (2002). *Mobilising the audience.* St Lucia: University of Queensland Press.
Banerjee, I. and Seneviratne, K. (eds) (2006). *Public service broadcasting in the age of globalization.* Asian Media Information and Communication Centre (AMIC).
Beville, H.M. (1985). *Audience ratings: Radio, television, cable.* Hillsdale, NJ: Lawrence Erlbaum.
Curran, J. (2002). *Media and power.* London: Routledge.
Livingstone, S. (2005). *Audiences and publics: when cultural engagement matters for the public sphere.* Bristol: Intellect.
Napoli, P.M. (2003). *Audience economics: Media institutions and the audience marketplace.* Columbia: Columbia University Press.
Webster, J.G., Phalen, P.F. and Lichty, L.W. (2000). *Ratings analysis: The theory and practice of audience research.* Hillsdale, NJ: Lawrence Erlbaum.

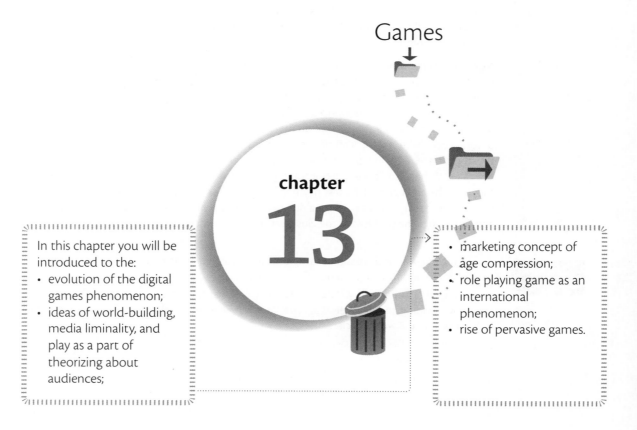

Games

chapter

13

In this chapter you will be introduced to the:
- evolution of the digital games phenomenon;
- ideas of world-building, media liminality, and play as a part of theorizing about audiences;

- marketing concept of age compression;
- role playing game as an international phenomenon;
- rise of pervasive games.

In Chapter 12 the authors argued that a new media economics that includes co-creation, and not only enhanced measures of exposure, will become important to understanding audiences and to calculations about audiences in media planning and the media industry. Digital games as a phenomenon highlight the potential of this new economic model as well as the development of new affinity communities. In this chapter you will be introduced to the:

- evolution of the digital games phenomenon;
- ideas of world-building, media liminality, and play as a part of theorizing about audiences;
- marketing concept of age compression;
- role playing game as an international phenomenon;
- rise of pervasive games.

> Well it's not just a game! It's a whole world. There's TV shows, comic books, little figures and card games …
>
> (10-year-old Scott Levine, cited in Peterson, 2003, 11)

I invoke Pokemon as an example of the kind of transformational multimedia phenomenon that students of media, culture, and society will be increasingly faced with in the twenty-first century. (Peterson, 2003, 14)

In their millions, young people and older people are taking up interactive games as world-building activities and those world-building games are making them smarter. But interactive and online games are also giving us an insight into the new media economics and changes in the nature of audiences. Audiences are already elusive and making a profit from them is now much more difficult. The games audience is a new type of audience and in this chapter the authors will introduce you to some of the major trends in digital games.

Media audiences

Audiences of course now have more options available to them than they did in the past. They do not have to watch the programming television networks put in front of them. They do not have to watch commercials. New media such as the Internet and mobile phones make audiences both more splintered and, potentially, more inaccessible to advertisers. According to Thomas Ryan, vice president of advertising at Gillette, 'There doesn't seem to be any question that the arrival of these new means of receiving information and entertainment in the home is going to cause a fractioning of viewing audiences' (Turow, 1997, 90).

The image tribes have, since the 1980s, developed more complex ways of 'signalling' to their audiences. Signalling is the way advertisers create media materials to indicate to certain types of people that they ought to be part of the audience. This is done by splitting audiences into different categories to establish appropriate emotional relationships and to establish an image of the advertisers and media as having the same values, activities and interests as the audience. 'Formats' and 'brands' guide this approach. A format is the layout and general approach to content that a specific media group, such as television, takes to its material. 'It is the format that creates what people think of the "personality" of a network, magazine, newspaper. When a company touts the distinctive identity of its format, that identity is known as a "brand". So, for example, CNN is a branded cable news format and *Ladies Home Journal* is a branded woman's magazine' (Turow, 1997, 91–2).

Not surprisingly, advertisers and programmers are in competition to get a share of the audience mind. This has involved the development of strategies such as versioning – creating entirely different campaigns for distinct audiences (Turow, 1997, 109). That was the idea behind an MCI ad campaign that aimed to speak to Generation X. The long-distance company's executives worried that their broad-based campaign aimed at baby boomers might not be connecting with the cohort that followed them. The company therefore decided to create a relatively inexpensive series of ads that would run on such GenX cable networks such as MTV and VH1.

To carry it out, the copywriter and art director of the project, GenXers themselves, chose three somewhat off-kilter incidents in the lives of young adults into which they expected people of their age cohort could project themselves or their friends: a couple getting married under water, a male Xer in a tattoo parlor, and a young man at a professional baseball game catching a foul ball with his popcorn cup. At the end of each vignette, a voiceover that reflected the age target asked, 'So what have *your* friends done since you last spoke to them? (Turow, 1997, 109)

This partitioning of audiences by category, and categories within categories, has encouraged the creation of formats and commercials that picture a society so split up that it is impossible to know all the parts. As Turow points out, the cumulative message 'might well be of a society so divided that it is impossible to know, or care about' (1997, 109). The move towards greater segmentation of audiences by advertisers and marketers is a local and global phenomenon and will continue.

The idea of audiences, however, also has theoretical issues attached to it. Images of audiences – perceptions of what the audience *is* and what it *wants* – are no doubt in the heads of individual professional communicators, whether television scriptwriters or journalists. Audience images, however, are not only in the individual work routines. They are also in the strategies of organizations. There are, as Ettema and Whitney (1994, 9) argue, institutionally constituted images of the audience. Audiences in media organizations only have influence if they are recognized as being real and reflecting real preferences and choices by individuals. Institutionally effective audiences that have social meaning and/or economic value within the media system include *measured audiences* that are generated by research services, sold by media channels, and bought by advertisers; *specialized or segmented audiences* whose particular interests are anticipated – or created – and then met by content producers; and *hypothesized audiences* whose interest, convenience and necessity are, presumably, protected by regulators (Ettema and Whitney, 1994, 5–6).

Webster and Phalen (1994, 19–37) argue that assumptions about audiences also affect decision-making in communication and media policy. They identify three main models that are used by policymakers:

1. *Effects model:* Audience members are easily exposed to programming that may not be in their own best interest. The media can cultivate an appetite for vulgar, hateful, or trivial programming. The public interest is served by a media system that limits exposure to undesirable programming and promotes exposure to meritorious content.

2. *Marketplace model:* Audience members are rational, well-informed individuals who will act in their own self-interest. Audience members come to the media with well-formed programme preferences that cause them to choose specific content. The public interest is served by a media system that is responsive to audience preferences as revealed in their viewing choices.

3. *Commodity model:* Audiences have an economic value that is expressed in measurements of their size and composition. Commercial media must be allowed to create and sell audiences if the media are to exist. The public interest is served by preserving the system of advertiser-supported identity.

Whether audiences are defined as victims, consumers or commodities, on Webster and Phalen's analysis, will depend upon institutional context. A community lobby group arguing for greater protection of citizen rights in media will use a very different model of the audience than would an advertising agency counterpart selling Sunlight Soap.

The difference between construing audiences as citizens and audiences as commodities is part of wider theoretical debates in literature about how data on audiences should be collected and for what purpose and, indeed, the very idea of the audience itself. Ang (1996) argues that any knowledge of the 'consumer', under what she terms behaviourist measurements like television ratings, will only lead to partial knowledge of the 'real consumer' of audiences. '[W]hat all this amounts to is the construction of a kind of streamline map of the "television audience", on which individual viewers are readable in terms of their resemblance to a "typical" consumer whose "viewing behaviour" can be objectively and unambiguously classified' (Ang, 1996, 57). Hartley (2005) makes a related point and calls television audiences *invisible fictions* that serve the needs of the imagining institutions. Audiences are only encountered as representations.

McQuail (1997) provides an overview of different audience analysis traditions. According to McQuail there are three main traditions of audience research:

1. *Structural:* Describes audiences using social-demographic and time use survey data.
2. *Behavioural:* Tries to predict audience choices and reactions using survey and experiment.
3. *Cultural:* Attempts to understand the meaning of content and the context of audience life by using ethnographic and qualitative methods (McQuail, 1997, 21). Buckingham (1993) in *Reading Audiences* provides a series of case studies showing how cultural studies scholars approach the study of audiences (see also Buckingham, 2006).

One phenomenon not mentioned in many models of the audience is the rise and importance of *play*. Audiences have indeed become fragmented and elusive for advertisers. Many have gone somewhere else. That somewhere else is games. In 2007 there were 217 million people playing online games worldwide. Many of the online games such as *World of Warcraft* have profits the equivalent of country GDPs. These new media audiences have implications for how we theorize audiences. The 2008 *Norton Online Living Report* provides a snapshot of the extent of the modern online and international audiences.

to recap...

Traditional models of the audience often do not include play. Much of audience activity is now online, globally, and a large proportion of online activity is itself play.

Global snapshot: The Norton Online Living Report, 2008

The Norton Online Living Report is a survey of the digital lifestyle habits of adults and children from eight countries – Britain, Australia, Brazil, China, France, Germany, Japan and the US. The report interviewed 4,687 adults and 2,717 children.

- online gaming in all surveyed countries is popular, with 97 per cent of online children and 65 per cent of online adults in Britain playing games online;
- email has overtaken the telephone as the major source of communication in the surveyed countries, with Chinese and British online users more likely to send an SMS than use a phone;
- in Britain, 40 per cent of children and 21 per cent of adults have created an online avatar. In China, by comparison, 72 per cent of adults and 88 per cent of (networked, that is, urban) children have created an online avatar;
- nearly one in five adults in the survey had spent time on their personal blog. In China, nearly 87 per cent of users have a personal blog compared with only 19 per cent Britons;
- half of adults in the survey had made friends online;
- British adults spend an average of 40 hours per month online, double that of their children who spend 24 hours online. The average Chinese adult spends almost 100 hours per month online;
- Britons are the largest users of online travel sites, with 81 per cent booking their travel online. Australia is second to the UK with 67 per cent;
- 19 per cent of British children say they do things online that they know their parents would disapprove of. That figure is even higher in China at 55 per cent.

activity   Play is a concept best understood by psychologists (Winnicott, 1953), theorists of fantasy and reality (that is, film studies), and children! Working in small groups, discuss the three major aspects of play in your experience. Is it functional? And if so, at what stages of life, and in what ways? What are the modes of play that you can list as relevant to your age group? Can you observe significant differences between how you play, and how those in the generation above you play, and what about the generation below you? Do you play alone or as a group?

Massively multiplayer

The console, online games and wireless games market will on some commercial estimates increase from US$27.1 billion in 2005 to US$46 billion in 2010 (PricewaterhouseCoopers, 2006). The global console game market is dominated by Nintendo, Sony and Microsoft, as Table 13.1 showing the evolution of games consoles suggests.

Table 13.1 **Games consoles 1970s onwards**

1975	Atari PONG	1991	SNES
1976	Coleco Telstar	1993	3DO
1977	Atari 2600	1993	Atari Jaguar
1978	Magnavox Odyssey 2	1994	Sega Saturn
1982	Atari 5200	1995	Sony PlayStation
1982	ColecoVision	1996	Nintendo 64
1982	Vectrex	1999	Sega Dreamcast
1983	SG-1000	2000	Sony PlayStation 2
1985	NES	2001	Nintendo Game Cube
1985	Sega Master System	2002	Microsoft Xbox
1986	Atari 7800	2005	Microsoft Xbox 360
1989	Turbo Grafx 16	2006	Nintendo Wii
1989	Sega Genesis	2006	Sony PlayStation 3
1990	Neo-Geo		

Online gaming began with MUDs (Multi User Domains, Dungeons or Dimensions). MUDS are text based and do not normally use a mouse. Everything is in writing and the MUDs allow player versus environment (PvE) or player versus player (PvP) modes. The majority of MUDs are run by amateurs and 200 players is considered a good player base (Mortensen, 2006).

In the 1990s as the technology of computers evolved, 3D games like *Quake* pioneered first-person shooters (FPS) and time strategy games (RTS) like *Dune II* set the scene for the massively multiplayer online role playing games (MMORPG) *Warcraft* and *StarCraft* and others.

Online computer games in 2006 have a very different position in culture from what they had in 1997, when I approached my first MUD. From being an obscure activity for geeks, they are now mainstream commercial entertainment. DragonRealms could have up to 200 players on an exceptionally good day, World of Warcraft had approximately 5 million players in December 2005 ... The economy of game development competes with the film and music industry (ies), and the medium is moving at full speed toward the mainstream of popular culture. The parent generation of today's children has their own computer gaming experiences, even if those were rare occurrences with arcade games. Personal computers even in workspaces come outfitted with some simple standard games, mainly solitaires, and the users are no longer total strangers to the concept of computer gaming the way their parent generation was. (Mortensen, 2006)

World of Warcraft is a three-dimensional world that simulates physical movement and where players control avatars. The game can be role play, PvP or PvE. The new role playing online games can be played through console, personal computers or wireless devices. The sophistication of the technology of the new games, of course, was not the only major change. The type of people playing role playing games has expanded from the narrow world of the computer geek to the wider population.

This means that the potential players of a game such as World of Warcraft are a much larger and diverse segment of the population than the players of MUDs. MUD users were much more heterogeneous, mainly represented by the early users of computers from the period when the net was dominated by young White males. (Mortensen, 2006)

Who plays games?

Everybody – well, almost. A British Broadcasting Corporation (BBC) study conducted in 2005 found that almost 60 per cent of 6–65 year olds in Britain played games; all 6–10 year olds, 97 per cent of 11–15 year olds, 82 per cent of 16–24 year olds, 65 per cent of 25–35 year olds, 51 per cent of 36–50 year olds, and 18 per cent of 51–65 year olds (Pratchett, 2005). Figure 13.1 shows that the gender breakdown is also interesting.

Britain and the US have similar demographic gaming profiles (Norton, 2008). If we look at Britain then we can get a sense of the size and reach of the console and online gaming phenomenon.

16–24 gamers
44 per cent   56 per cent

25–35 gamers
44 per cent   56 per cent

36–50 gamers
45 per cent   55 per cent

51–65 gamers
48 per cent   52 per cent

Britain's gamer profile

- 59 per cent of 6 to 65 year olds or 26.5 million people in Britain are gamers;
- 48 per cent or 21.6 million Britons aged 6 to 65 plays games at least once a week;
- all 6 to 10 year olds consider themselves to be gamers;
- one quarter of UK game players are aged 36 to 50;
- 18 per cent or 1.7 million gamers are aged between 51 and 65;
- the average age of UK gamer is approximately 28;
- 45 per cent of all gamers are female (Pratchet, 2005).

Figure 13.1 Gender and games

The games phenomenon, though, is not limited to western European or US demographics. Interactive games played by console or online are popular across national boundaries and across ages. Korean gamers are famously dedicated to their games schedules, and Table 13.2 shows how Chinese online gamers have taken to MMORPG (Wu et al., 2007).

Table 13.2 **Chinese online game players**

Online players (millions)	
2001	4.95
2002	9.50
2003	12.95
2004	19.76

Source: Wu et al. (2007).

Wu et al. (2007) document some of the interesting uses of MMORPG in China, including in-game marriage. They note the rise of MMORPG as one of the most popular activities among young urban Chinese.

Domestic MMORPG services, such as Netease.com and Kingsoft Corp., have developed massive resources through which millions of gamers will have access to play. With interactive gaming storytelling, upload screenshots, writing down personal feelings and gaming experiences in the Broad Bulletin System (BBS), gamers' particular Blogs, and semiofficial online journals, these extended spaces nurtured by MMORPG gaming activities create a relatively liberal communicative platform for young people to experience interactive entertainment with animated features and filmic story lines. Moreover, they offer possibilities for ongoing integration between the Internet and everyday life of the general public. (Wu et al., 2007)

Measuring these new audiences is not easy. comScore in 2007 provided one of the first attempts to provide a picture of the online games population, a snapshot in May 2007, taking into account all sites that provided online or downloadable games, excluding gambling sites. The methodology counts visits to gaming sites rather than user numbers. *Second Life* and *World of Warcraft* would attract a smaller share of the market in this methodology because many users or players would not regularly visit a central page but play directly from a desktop client. Table 13.3 provides an overview of the numbers by region.

Table 13.3 **Worldwide online gaming community**

Worldwide	Europe	North America	Latin America	Asia-Pacific	M. East-Africa
771,997	222,92	177,455	53,042	283,519	35,058

Source: comScore (www.comscore.com).

Table 13.4 provides an overview of video games console ownership, with greatest ownership concentrated in the highly industrialized countries.

These are sizeable 'digital communities' and audiences but they are not easily reachable by advertisers and indeed not easily identified by audience measurement companies that want to know lifestyles and demographics. Game players often have to pay game companies for the pleasure of using their software but the game players do not want to be exposed to advertising.

Table 13.4 **Possession of video games consoles per 100 households**

2005		2005	
Japan	31.1	Netherlands	13.4
USA	24.9	Mexico	12.5
Canada	24.3	Spain	11.5
France	19.6	Greece	10.5
Germany	19.0	Hungary	10.2
Malaysia	18.9	Czech Republic	9.5
South Korea	18.6	Thailand	9.1
Austria	17.3	Poland	7.9
Australia	17.2	Brazil	6.8
UK	17.2	Chile	6.7
Switzerland	17.0	South Africa	6.3
Belgium	16.9	Russia	3.5
Denmark	16.8	Romania	2.8
Taiwan	16.8	Philippines	2.1
Sweden	16.7	China	1.3
Italy	16.1	Egypt	1.0
Turkey	15.5	India	0.9
Argentina	14.1	Indonesia	0.3

Source: Euromonitor estimates (www.euromonitor.com/).

But game players definitely have an impact on the economics of media. When Blizzard Entertainment released *StarCraft* it was South Koreans who formed, in its first years, 3.5 million of the estimated 6 million players worldwide (Huhh, 2008). The demand for online gaming through PC bangs was also a catalyst for broadband development in South Korea.

Online gaming and PC bangs go together in modern South Korea. PC bangs are not simply Internet cafes. For Koreans the PC bang is a social space that traverses the online and offline (Huhh, 2008). South Korean Internet users considered broadband connection indispensable when playing *StarCraft*. A low monthly flat ISP pricing policy for broadband connection was developed in South Korea that led to opportunities for Internet cafes and game developers. Huhh (2008) uses the 1998 launched MMORPG Lineage by NCSoft as a key example:

It was the first generation of MMORPG online games that took advantage of high-speed Internet connection. The huge success of Lineage helped to forge a receptive environment for online gaming in general. Once the uncertainty about the business was lifted, a big rush to the MMORPG in Korea began in late 1999. It should be noted that these events had gained their momentum through the pivotal role of the PC bang ... the growth rate of PC bang businesses between 1998 and 1999 was remarkable. This growth was inevitably informed by the fact that in 1998 Internet cafés offered their visitors a more comfortable and conducive environment for gaming. At first, the ambience of the place altered from a quiet library style into an open, frenetic coin-operated setting, with most selling snacks and beverages. Food delivery was also allowed for customers. The pricing policy of PC bangs encouraged their visitors to play longer; the more you stayed on, the lower the hourly charge. It was not a coincidence that the Korean word 'Game bang' became interchangeable with PC bang. (Huhh, 2008)

activity

The next section is about genre. We have met that word in relation to other media.

Now we would like you to think about genres in games. Comparisons are not always possible between different media and cultural forms, but do your best to think about the narratives and designs of games that you know, and whether they bear any relation to, say, film genre or television genre, or to other kinds of online design and story telling. Make an argument for genre as a key concept in games research and evaluation.

New game genres

MMORPG is not the end of the story with games design. Pervasive games is the phrase used by Ian Bogost to describe the merging of digital gaming into the physical sphere (bogost.com). The *dance dance revolution* (DDR) video game mode is an example of these emerging genres (Behrenshausen, 2007). The Bemani version of DDR is a rhythm/music video game created by Konami. The games are located in public arcades and require players to dance, play the drums, or mimic disc jockey practices within a defined space and in conjunction with on-screen symbols or instructions. The machines turn players into performers by putting their bodies on display, but also allow users to take pleasure in kinetic activity (Behrenshausen, 2007).

As video games, Bemani machines also contain elements that emphasize discipline and competency. Players are rewarded for precise movement in time with machinic instructions; failure to fulfil the instructions of the game incurs a 'Game Over' and necessitates more quarters [money] from the pocket. In this way, Bemani machines emphasize the player's situation as both performer and audience, as the video games persistently rate player performances while they unfold and typically confer on players a grade indicating overall achievement at the end of each performance. (Behrenshausen, 2007)

Konami's DDR was released in Japan in 1998 and earned it US$173.6 billion in net revenues. After Konami released it in the US in 2005 cumulative worldwide sales of the DDR series exceeded 7.5 million units (Behrenshausen, 2007). But the new digital games are not limited to profit companies alone.

All of these types of games are specifically designed around radically different concepts than traditional digital games and, in some cases, blend the analog and the digital in a unique and intriguing way. … In each case, the player experience and community are placed first, and each game has affordances to adapt to the player as the game evolves. The focus is on humans rather than on code. As DeKoven would say, the game does not measure the value of the people, but the other way around. While the alternate-reality game I Love Bees … was originally developed as a marketing tool for Halo 2, it took on a life of its own during its limited run. The game propelled clues out into the real world via phones, Web pages, and other means. I Love Bees followed in the footsteps of The Beast, developed to promote the Stanley Kubrick and Stephen Spielberg film AI, and Majestic, the ill fated suspense thriller by Electronic Arts whose slogan was 'the game that plays you.' These games were designed to blur the boundary between game and reality, creating fissures in the 'magic circle' of the game. (Pearce et al., 2007)

In 2003 Nick Fortugno, Frank Lantz and Katie Salen from the University of Minnesota created 25 foot (7.6 metres) high inflatable chess pieces. The game (BUG) criss-crossed Minneapolis and St Paul on September 3 to 7. Three teams raced red, yellow, or blue game pieces over streets, bridges, parks, and rivers towards a finish line. Players registered online for a team and voted for the best route that the inflatable chess piece would take. 'This became a highly public event as teams carried the pieces through traffic from Point A to Point B. Participants at checkpoints greeted and cheered for their teams and rolled a pair of giant dice for a time advantage' (Pearce et al., 2007).

Pervasive games are many media and can intersect with physical activity and public spaces. They can be created for a variety of purposes and many of those purposes may be not for profit. Pervasive games also show us that affinity communities are a key trend in online and pervasive games. Affinity communities are lifestyle clusters based on common interests – such as cars, sport, fashion, or even helping others (Nichols et al., 2006, 48). MMORPG can be affinity communities along with traditional MUDs. Play is the activity that holds these affinity communities together.

World-building and age compression

There will be no attempt to give them serious consideration on aesthetic grounds, because they are simply not worth it. (Margaret Dalziel, Comics in New Zealand, *Landfall*, 1955)

The comics erode the most fundamental habits of humane, civilized living and they erode them in the most vulnerable element of our society, our children ... If we ban the comics we are reducing the chances of war and preventing the further perversion of the world's children. (Bill Pearson, Letter, *Landfall*, 1955)

Dalziel's and Pearson's condemnation in the 1950s of cartoons could be translated to the modern era and concerns about games. The condemnation is not, of course, appropriate. Cartoons did not destroy modern civilization. Indeed, many of the superheroes in the USA were created by Jewish émigré artists as a response to the Nazi suppression of free speech and to the murder of civilians from 1933 to 1944. There is though an important concept that underpins this condemnation – *play*. Whether reading comics or watching television or playing online games, play *can* transform society and affect behaviour. The MMORPGs have already transformed behaviour, for example.

World-building has always had a significant role in the nature of narrative and play. Tolkien describes the world-building process as sub-creation. The narrator creates a secondary world, a sub-creation, which a person can enter only with their minds. Once inside the sub-creation, or the world, what the narrator relates is 'true' and accords with the laws of that world. A reader or in our case player believes that world, while they are, as it were, inside. There is for Tolkien no higher process for humans than the sub-creation of a secondary world (Tolkien, 1977). *The Lord of the Rings* trilogy was revisited by millions through the film versions created by Peter Jackson's team in the early 21st century. In the 1990s, the phenomenon of Pokémon, a shape-shifter, dominated the entry of young media users into another equally complex secondary world.

So, too, modern digital and interactive games are world-building and have all the characteristics of Tolkien's secondary worlds. The Situationist movement of the late 1960s took world-building and play to be intimately linked to ethics and the meaning of life. Constant Nieuwenhuis's New Urbanism argued that our way of life will be determined in future not by profit but by play (Nieuwenhuis, 1966). The Situationists would be concerned at the extent of digital games as big business but equally pleasantly surprised at the rise of pervasive games.

Play for the Situationists and for play theorists like Johan Huizinga (1970) has recognizable characteristics:

- all play is a voluntary activity. Play to order is no longer play;
- play is not 'ordinary' or 'real' life. 'It is rather a stepping out of "real" life into a temporary sphere of activity with a disposition all of its own' (1970, 26). Not being 'ordinary life', play stands outside the immediate satisfaction of wants and appetites;
- play is distinct from 'ordinary' life both as to locality and duration. It is characterized by secludedness and limitedness. Games are 'played out' within certain limits of time and place. They contain their own course and meaning (1970, 28).

Children in particular are attracted to play and marketers are especially attracted to children. Nearly one-third of the world's population is made up of two billion young people under 18, making up half the population of the least developed nations and a quarter of the most industrialized countries.

Digital games have led marketers to the conclusion that children are learning faster in the new media environments than they did in older media environments. The expression 'age compression' has emerged to describe this phenomenon. The age compression phenomenon – also called the disappearance of childhood – is an example of how the media industry is taking advantage of techniques that enable younger children to learn faster, or what the industry calls KGOY – *Kids Grow Older Younger*.

The KGOY thesis argues that children are developing higher order cognitive skills faster and younger. As a consequence, toys and games normally created for older children are now being sold to younger children on the basis that they are smarter than earlier generations. The KGOY model involves introducing the world's 565 million urban population of 5–14 year olds to these products as soon as they can (McDougall and Chantrey, 2004).

It will surprise nobody that Tables 13.5, 13.6, 13.7 and 13.8 demonstrate the rise of the digital games market. Games have gone through at least three generations, since their introduction in the 1980s. The authors chose a snapshot of 2003 video games sales (not consoles) as a cultural marker for the era of age compression.

For children, Manga anime and its variations are at the forefront of much of the new digital games play. Companies like Konami, for example, produced YuGiOh as a many-media game and design their games to take advantage of myth and ritual symbol. In the first quarter of 2004 Konami sold 3.5 million copies of YuGiOh (Table 13.9 demonstrates sales in billion yen).

Table 13.5 Sales of video games by country, western Europe, US$ million 2003

Austria	236.9
Belgium	130.5
Denmark	94.5
Finland	117.7
France	1,363.8
Germany	2,580.6
Greece	106.1
Ireland	64.6
Italy	652.7
Netherlands	340.6
Norway	160.7
Portugal	127.6
Spain	959.4
Sweden	217.2
Switzerland	114.0
Turkey	18.7
UK	3,433.6
Other	35.3
	10,754.5

Table 13.6 Sales of video games by country, eastern Europe, US$ million 2003

Bulgaria	3.0
Czech Rep.	7.5
Hungary	7.3
Poland	38.7
Romania	5.0
Russia	72.2
Slovakia	3.1
Ukraine	8.6
Other	22.6
	168.1

Table 13.7 Sales of video games by country, Latin America, US$ million 2003

Argentina	14.6
Brazil	139.6
Chile	15.8
Colombia	144.5
Mexico	492.8
Venezuela	3.3
Other	118.4
	929.0

Table 13.8 Sales of video games by country, Australia, Canada, United States 2003

Australia	1,062.0	$AUmillion
Canada	1,004.4	$Cmillion
US	10,866.0	$USmillion

Sources: United States Department of Commerce, International Council of Toy Industries, Toy Industry Association, NPD Funworld, US Bancorp Piper Jaffray, Euromonitor estimates.

Table 13.9 Sales of YuGiOh and other card games, 2004

	Q1 2004 billion yen
YuGiOh Card Games (Japan, Asia)	9.5
YuGiOh Card Games (North America)	18.5
YuGiOh Card Games (Europe)	3.5
Other Cards	0.5

Boys in the 7–14 age group have been the prime target market for Manga games and comics over the past 20 years. The games targeting began with the development of Nintendo's Super Mario Bros games and the parallel but related development of the Teenage Mutant Ninja Turtles. Gaming subcultures began in the Manga children's comics and then gradually expanded to take advantage of multimedia. The comics generally road tested the popularity of the cartoons. YuGiOh is an example of the complex children's games genres that have gained popularity in western industrial culture, along with Pokémon, Digimon and DragonballZ.

Games like YuGiOh and Pokémon can and do lose popularity, but the Konami games phenomenon is successful precisely because of the formula to replicate a liminal-like space, much like the *ketai* lifestyle in Japan. Konami has intersected the games phenomenon with world-building. The liminal space in this type of world-building does not lead to a defined role or status, but it does allow people to explore and create and work in peer environments. Variations of this world-building are emerging in blogging and, indeed, in the coming together of smartmobs.

Manga anime, however, adds a worldview, its own aesthetic rules, an ethical framework, and a specific learning framework, to the process of world-building, distinguishing it from other types of digital games. The mathematics involved in games like YuGiOh alone distinguishes it from other games. YuGiOh involves children in difficult mental algorithms and a range of problem-solving strategies. According to one study, 82 per cent of children playing this game grew up to graduate from university. The study ruled out that this was due to IQ or to classroom behaviour (Chan, 1999).

Media-liminality

The authors argue that Manga anime and the world-building narrative framework embodied in games like those produced by Konami provide the liminal space required for creativity that has been lost via traditional means. Myths are intimately linked to 'rites of passage', from one status to another, in societies. There have been, normally, set physical and symbolic activities that mark a boy or a girl going from one phase of life to the next. There is a separation (divestiture) phase, a transition (liminality) phase and an incorporation (investiture) phase (Turner, 1995). During the separation phase, the person who is to be subjected to the passage becomes separated from their previous way of life. During the transition phase, the person separated from their previous environment experiences the liminal condition. During the incorporation phase they enter a new group and a new life. 'The ritual subjects pass through a period and an area of ambiguity, a sort of social limbo which has few … of the attributes of either the preceding or subsequent profane social statuses or cultural states' (Turner, 1982, 24).

Anthropologist Victor Turner created the term 'liminal' from the Latin limina for 'threshold', to describe the transitional phases in society that confirmed the identity of a person and their future role in society:

> Myth treats of origins but derives from transitions … Myths relate how one state of affairs became another; how an unpeopled world became populated; how chaos became cosmos; how immortals became mortal; how the seasons came to replace climate without seasons … and so on. Myths are liminal phenomena: they are frequently told at a time or in a site that is 'betwixt and between'. (Turner, 1979, 576)

The authors suggest that traditional myths and symbols that assist in rites of passage no longer exist for most western cultures. Boys do not go through elaborate ceremonies that mark their move to a different stage of life as part of society as a whole, although religions, of course, do have ceremonial events, as in Catholicism, where a different stage in the spiritual life is reached. The very idea of KGOY from a marketing point of view, of course, is to remove any idea of difference between adult and child. Indeed, Turner (1982) argued that traditional liminality did not exist in modern society and called the quasi-liminal states 'liminoid'.

The liminal condition also has its parallel in developmental psychology. Winnicott (1953) argued, for example, that children at certain stages in their development create substitutes for the mother–child relationship through 'transitional objects' like teddy bears. The transitional objects link the space between the psychic life of the child and the real social space – it is a space where identity is formed. Other authors have expanded on these ideas of liminality in the context of computers and learning (Weight, 2004).

The authors will call the modern liminal condition media-liminal space because it more accurately reflects what is happening with digital media and digital games and

Media-liminality. Play is not 'ordinary' or 'real' life. It is a stepping out of 'real' life into a temporary – liminal – sphere of activity with a disposition all its own.

the extensive many-media saturation (Balnaves and Tomlinson-Baillie, 2005). Conceptually, Turner is not alone in his idea that there are existential, structured, spaces in society that enhance creativity and community. Postmodern thinkers like Foucault (1998) called these spaces *heterotopia* and Deleuze and Guattari *territorialized [spaces]*. These are spaces where differences can be played out that could not be played out in normal social routines. The digital games phenomenon in modern society, it would seem, is an example of this produced subjectivity.

activity   Set up a debate in your study group on the pros and cons of learning through play. Seek out data on the ways in which educationalists, both traditional and alternative, have used play to help children learn. What role can many-media environments take in such a process?

Define knowledge, and then define play, using the ideas already developed in this chapter and your own conversations. How might media facilitate pathways between 'knowledge' and 'play' in modern society, businesses and education?

Digital gaming as a new form of knowledge

If digital games are potentially a different kind of structured subjective space, then they are also an example of a new kind of collective intelligence and form of knowledge that is required to build it. It takes software engineers, systems designers, hardware engineers, graphic artists, and many others to create a digital game. 'Modders' are a part of this professional system. They are fan programmers that signal a convergence of fan and producer (Postigo, 2007).

Fan programmers for profit and not-for-profit games form national and international knowledge communities. They work in a participatory culture where their ethos may be in direct opposition to the ethos of a profit driven media industry. But, as already discussed in this book, co-creation and consumer-created-content, participatory cultures, are now recognized by many media and online businesses as having economic value, including Google. Postigo's (2007) interesting research on 'modders' involved in games design provides an insight into the argot (local language) of the knowledge community and the nature of the knowledge being created. A brief definition of roles is needed first:

- *modders* make modifications, mods, to a game. Mods can be changes to the way a game physically works through to changes in the narrative;
- *mappers* design new levels for a game. These add-ons keep the same game characters and play but new virtual worlds are created by the fan programmers;
- *skinners* design new characters, weapons – all the tools inside the games.

Postigo (2007) estimates the cost of developing a digital game for commercial release at the time of his research at about US$10 million with about the same for marketing and promotions. He also estimated that the cost of supporting a 10 person development team for a digital game to be about US$520,000 per year with an average completion time of 6 to 18 months. Games companies would have had to pay out between US$10 million and US$30.4 million in salaries to create the equivalent fan programmer content made for fans of the top ranked FPS games. Fans themselves, believe it or not, rate the mods as a form of quality control:

> Many companies have openly acknowledged the value of the content that fans produce. Epic Games, Valve Software, and Id Software have all recognized the value of their gaming communities. Wagner James Au … in an article for Salon.com, has interviewed industry insiders on the role of fan communities in game design. In that article, Scott Miller of 3D Realms states that 'developers watched astounded as mods "actually helped extend the life of a game by providing free additional content for players to explore."' In the same article, Cliff Bleszinski of Epic Games (maker of the popular Unreal series) estimated that '5 to 10 percent of Unreal players have tinkered with the editing tools' and that at least half of the 2 million-plus players 'have downloaded and played mods or levels for the game.' No company has done as much as Id Software and Valve Software to incorporate fan add-ons into the development process. Id Software releases the source code for all of its games; it incorporated the most successful fan-developed game levels into one of its distributions of Doom and hired fan-programmer Robert Duffy to create the development kit, QERadiant, for Quake 3. (Postigo, 2007)

Textual poachers, fandom, transrating and cultural convergence

The idea that gamers can be within participatory cultures is not new. Henry Jenkins (1992) observed some time ago that a fan community of textual poachers could see itself in opposition to capitalist control of culture and create what he called meta stories. Meta stories for Jenkins are online stories developed by fans from television shows and movies. These stories represent an alternative form of ownership.

Jenkins's (2006) argument is that the very idea of 'audiences' is being reshaped because of the participatory cultures inherent in the textual poachers and in modern games. Games are not just any media but tied to what he terms cultural convergence. This convergence is not just national but global. Convergence for Jenkins does not occur through media appliances but within the brains of individual consumers and through their social interactions with each other (Jenkins, 2006, 3). This is one of Jenkins's examples of cultural convergence:

> In December 2004, a hotly anticipated Bollywood film, Rok Suka To Rok Lo was screened in its entirety to movie buffs in Delhi, Bangalore, Hyderabad, Mumbai, and other parts of India through EDGE-enabled mobile phones with live video streaming facility. This is believed to be the first time that a feature film had been fully accessible via mobile phones. It remains to be seen how this kind of distribution fits into people's lives. Will it substitute for going to the movies or will people simply use it to sample movies they may want to see at other venues? Who knows? (2006, 3)

The transactions across cultures are also complex. Jenkins interviewed Chris Kohler (2005) about his book *Power Up* and the cultural exchange in producing games. Kohler presented a miniature case study of a Nintendo DS music-action game designed by Keiichi Yano's company iNiS, called *Osu! Tatakae! Ouendan* or *Hey! Fight! Cheer Squad,* released in Japan in 2005. When the game was released the Nintendo DS had not yet made its mark and the game was not a major sales success. However, the Nintendo DS is region-free. This means that Japanese games can be played on the American DS system and vice versa. Kohler and a few fans of iNiS's previous game Gitaroo-Man imported the new game from Japan and loved it. They found it difficult to convince other players to import the game from Japan because of the extra expense and lobbied Nintendo of America to release it in the US.

Until the E3 expo in May 2006, Nintendo was silent on the subject. At the show, they revealed what they'd done. All of iNiS had been devoted to the creation of Elite Beat Agents, which took the Ouendan gameplay and swapped out the characters, scenarios, and songs for American ones. The main characters became sort of a cross between the Blues Brothers and the Men in Black. Songs like September by Earth, Wind, and Fire and Sk8r Boi by Avril Lavigne replaced the J-pop. What's interesting to note is that although certain Ouendan fans were angry that Nintendo was Americanizing the game, that's not really what happened. Yes, iNiS went back and re-tooled the game for Western audiences, but if you look at the final product it's still very much a crazy, manga-styled presentation that's going to appeal most strongly to the kind of gamer who reads manga, plays Katamari Damacy, etc. It's only Westernized enough to remove the sort of 'cultural odor' that would prevent it from doing well in the US, not the things that made it appealing in the first place. (Confessions of an Aca-Fan: the official weblog of Henry Jenkins. http://www.henryjenkins.org/2006/12/games_as_national_culture_the.html Dec. 1 2006)

The digital games industry is, therefore, a fascinating example of a profit driven environment that benefits from the non-profit activities of its fan programmers and writers – modders, mappers, skinners and textual poachers – and complex ways of satisfying player demands. It is not in the interests of big business to commodify the participatory cultures and knowledge communities that lay their golden eggs, but, as you can see, the temptation to control it and corporatize it must be immense.

Summary

The digital and online games phenomenon, play, is global. The games bring together players in affinity communities within the same culture and across national boundaries. These games are not, though, the utopia of Situationist thought. There is a dark side to the very idea of age compression and KGOY. In the United Kingdom government agencies have banned television advertising of junk foods while children are watching, but there is no such legal constraint on corporations in online game environments.

The reasons for KGOY in marketing, however, are understandable because the structured subjective spaces of digital and many-media games appear to enhance learning. World-building and play in the digital games environment also provide media-liminal spaces that enhance peer relations and create affinity communities. For additional studies on children and the media see Drotner and Livingstone (2008) and Donald (2000).

The games community influences the economy in various ways. In the case of South Korea, online gaming and PC bangs have sped up the demand for broadband, its introduction and expansion. The participatory subcultures of fan programmers have expanded the content and architecture of commercially produced games, with the knowledge and assent of the corporate owners.

The new digital games, like pervasive games, expand the idea of role playing outside the virtual world and spill it into public spaces and everyday, physical, life. These games will add another dimension to intercultural communication as well as to corporate efforts to make money from play.

Play above all is a voluntary activity. It is a temporary sphere of activity with a disposition all its own. In the digital and online world, though, it has taken on a life of its own and represents an economy and a way of life.

At the conclusion of this chapter you should be able to:
- critically discuss some of the major implications of modern digital games, including KGOY;
- identify some of the main types of digital games that have been developed and are emerging;
- apply the concept of world-building and liminality to the modern games phenomenon.

Key themes

Games as a form of knowledge. Modern digital games are an example of a new kind of collective intelligence and form of knowledge that has emerged to provide narratives, software and hardware to global audiences. It takes software engineers, systems designers, hardware engineers, graphic artists, and many others to create a digital game. But there is also a subculture of this knowledge that is not in the pay of corporations. 'Modders', 'skinners' and 'mappers', for example are a part of a participatory subculture that builds new narratives and software separate from the original games design.

World-building. Tolkien describes the world-building process as sub-creation. The narrator creates a secondary world, a sub-creation, which a person can enter only with their mind. Once inside the sub-creation, or the world, what the narrator relates is 'true' and accords with the laws of that world. A reader or in our case player believes that world, while they are, as it were, inside. There is for Tolkien no higher process for humans than the sub-creation of a secondary world. Modern digital and interactive games are world-building and have all the characteristics of Tolkien's secondary worlds. The Situationist movement of the late 1960s took world-building and play to be intimately linked to ethics and the meaning of life. Constant Nieuwenhuis's New Urbanism argued that our way of life will be determined in future not by profit but by play. The Situationists would be concerned at the extent of digital games as big business but equally pleasantly surprised at the rise of pervasive games and the participatory subcultures that maintain and enhance games.

Discussion questions

1. What digital games do you play? Discuss them in class.
2. Construct a multimedia presentation showing the difference between different types of console and online games, especially those that you think are problematic for children. Discuss in class.
3. Do you think that 'childhood' is an outdated concept? Is there a limit on how far marketers should have access to children? Find example of Internet games used by advertisers or corporations and bring them to class for discussion.
4. Do you see yourself as an elusive member of the online games audience, from a commercial perspective? Why? What have you done to be elusive?

Further reading

Castronova, E. (2005). *Synthetic worlds: The business and culture of online games.* Chicago: University of Chicago Press.

Jenkins, H. (2006). *Convergence culture: where old and new media collide.* New York: New York University Press.

Kerr, A. (2006). *The business and culture of digital games: gamework/gameplay.* London: Sage.

Nichols, D., Farrand, T., Rowley, T. and Avery, M. (2006). *Brands and gaming: The computer gaming phenomenon and its impact on brands and businesses.* Basingstoke: Palgrave Macmillan.

Ian Bogost's website: http://www.bogost.com/

Media research

The chapter will look at the:
- terminology of research and the differences between quantitative and qualitative research;
- interpretative paradigm in media studies research.

The media professions and the economics of media – structures and organizations – are changing. They have been affected by the new forms of audience and the new types of media to which those audiences respond, and which they use every day. This chapter will introduce you to media research, important to how audiences are conceived and analysed. The chapter will look at the:

- terminology of research and the differences between quantitative and qualitative research;

- interpretative paradigm in media studies research.

The administrative research and critical research divide, discussed in Chapters 1 and 2, represented real differences in how media researchers approached the study of media. Paul Lazarsfeld and Theodore Adorno represented the two sides of the research coin – quantitative and qualitative research. Lazarsfeld was a key founder of modern survey methods and statistics. Adorno was a key advocate for critique of the culture industry.

Globalization has not changed some of the key debates found in microcosm in Lazarsfeld's and Adorno's work. The media industries and governments still seek detailed information about audiences or consumers or citizens to try to meet their needs. Inequalities of power and influence also exist and require critique.

What has changed since Lazarsfeld's and Adorno's time is the emergence of sophisticated ways of collecting qualitative evidence about audiences and cultures, especially ethnographic techniques. Early behaviourist assumptions about cause and effect have also given way to more realistic assumptions about human behaviour. In this chapter the authors will introduce some of the terminology of media research, its conceptual foundations, and the rise of the interpretative paradigm as a way of doing media research.

Science and media research

At the beginning of the 20th century the idea that experimental social science could easily establish causes of audience behaviour was particularly appealing to the media industries involved in human persuasion. The advertising industry trade journals of the time made it clear that an understanding of the psychology of audiences and particular causes of mental conditions was essential for advertising success and that this is what their clients were paying for. In 1920, Professor Elton Mayo, chair of Psychology and Ethics at Queensland University, gave the major address at the Second Advertising Men's Conference:

> The ad. expert is an educator in the broadest and highest sense of the term. His task is the persuasion of the people to be civilized ... You must think for the housewife and if you do that for her and if she finds you are doing it, you will have her confidence ... It is necessary to understand the fear complexes that are disturbing our social serenity. It is not the slightest use meeting Satanism or Bolshevism by organized rage or hate. Your only chance of dealing with these things is by research, by discovering first and foremost of the cause of this mental condition. (cited in Braverman, 1974, 144–5)

The process of linking scientific experimental psychological research to commercial needs in the media industry was by 1920 well underway in the United States and elsewhere in the industrial world. For example, in 1922 J.B. Watson, the behavioural psychologist, was appointed vice president of advertising company J. Walter Thompson (JWT). JWT employed two psychologists, A.H. Martin and Rudolph Simmat, to investigate ways of collecting evidence about consumers of advertising. Martin used mental tests he developed at Columbia University to measure consumer attitudes towards advertising. In 1927 he established the Australian Institute of Industrial Psychology in Sydney with the support of University of Sydney's Psychology department and the Chamber of Manufacturers. In 1929, Simmat, as research manager for JWT in Sydney, standardized art production and research procedures. He also began some of the early research into the segmentation of audiences. Simmat divided Australian society into four market segments based on income and housewives. Classes A and B were high income housewives. Classes C and D were average or below average income housewives. Class D had 'barely sufficient or even insufficient income to provide itself with the necessities of life. Normally Class D is not greatly important except to the manufacturer of low price, necessary commodities' (Simmat, 1933, 12).

It is here that we can see why the Frankfurt School, discussed in Chapter 5, had a concern with quantification. For the Frankfurt School, scientific methods were not necessarily neutral when applied to the social and media world. The idea of cause and effect in itself embedded particular attitudes about the nature of humanity. In the example of Simmat there is also an issue of attitude towards gender. His 'scientific' evidence about women was not in fact scientific. Simmat's worldview affected the data he collected and the conclusions he made, dressed up in the words of science. But in Simmat you can also see how other groups or people could be excluded as part of an 'audience' or 'consumers'.

Simmat also standardized interviewing techniques because, he said, he had found that experience had shown that women were usually more effective as fieldworkers than men. 'Experiments have indicated that persons with a very high grade of intelligence are unsatisfactory for interviewing housewives ... usually a higher grade of intelligence is required to interview the higher class of housewife than is required to interview the lower grade housewife' (Simmat, 1933, 13). JWT had interviewed 32,000 Australian housewives by 1932. Advertising as a consequence of Simmat's research was then targeted to specific audiences, with sophistication 'definitely soft-pedalled' for Classes C and D. 'We believe that farce will be more popular with our *Rinso* [detergent] market than too much subtlety.' Soap was the major advertising market during the 1920s and, indeed, the 1930s because it crossed all market segments. In Australia, Lever, the largest soap manufacturer, was a leading supporter of 'scientific advertising'. Lever bought 183,000 inches of advertising space in 1933 in metropolitan dailies.

Psychologists were confident that they could establish 'cause and effect' in the psychology of advertising. That confidence continued well into the 20th century but expanded to other areas, including some populist versions of psychoanalysis. Dr Ernest Dichter of the Institute of Motivational Research lectured in the 1950s to packed halls of advertisers and their clients. Using a combination of psychoanalysis, folklore, mythology and anthropology, he gave his audiences case studies that he said demonstrated his capacity to determine cause and effect. There was the Case of the Nylon Bed Sheets. Women, he said, did not buy Dupont's nylon non-iron bed sheets even though they were of high quality and well priced. Dupont asked Dr Dichter to interview women and find out why:

> After exploring their answers and looking into the sexual and folk associations of bed sheets he discovered that the women were unconsciously jealous of the beautiful blonde lying on the sheets in the advertisements. (Actually, they said their husbands wouldn't like them.) When Grandma was substituted for the blonde, up went the sales. ('I'm surprised,' he said, 'that most of my theories work.') Then there was the Blood and Virility Case. Men had stopped giving blood to the Blood Bank. When consulted, Dr Dichter discovered they unconsciously feared castration or loss of masculinity. The Bank's name was changed to the Blood Lending Bank, advertisements of beautiful girls trailing masculine blood-donors were prepared, and all went well. (Coleman 1969, 23)

activity The authors are sceptical of Dr Dichter's assumptions and reasoning. Can you make a list of the assumptions built into his analysis that are predicated on (a) gender and (b) age. Offer alternative explanations for the results. Or, indicate where more information is required about the context of purchase and use to make a fair analysis.

Let us now contrast the behaviourist psychology work in advertising with Walter Benjamin (1970) the German cultural critic from the Frankfurt School (note that Benjamin died in 1942 but his works have been often re-published and translated). Benjamin argued that modern media and modern society everywhere produce in everyday life 'shocks to consciousness'. In his essay 'On Some Motifs in Baudelaire' Benjamin draws on Baudelaire's suggestion that people in the industrialized world have become 'kaleidoscopes equipped with consciousness'. 'Baudelaire speaks of a man who plunges into the crowd as into a reservoir of electric energy' (1970, 177). Nervous impulses flow through people as they in turn move through traffic, dangerous intersections, 'in rapid succession, like the energy from a battery' (1970, 177). Media like film, says Benjamin, have likewise subjected the human sensorium to a complex kind of training. Benjamin also drew on the work of Sigmund Freud (1938), the founder of psychoanalysis, with his notion of shock and said that citizens of the modern world need shields to help protect them from the constant overstimulation created by the external world. Consciousness, the main shield, protects the subconscious from the effects of shock. Echoes of Benjamin can be found in the more recent work on 'pure war' by Virilio and Lotringer (1997). Pure war, for Virilio and Lotringer (1997), is the psychological state that happens when people know that they live in a world where the potential for sudden and absolute destruction exists. It is not the capacity for destruction so much as it is the continual threat of sudden destruction that creates this psychology. Virilio and Lotringer are talking about nuclear destruction in their work. Arguably, the current mediated foci on risk as a main feature of the contemporary world: terror attacks, climate change, and flu epidemics, generate the same state of anxiety. This reinforces the idea that the media have a material as well as an ideological affect.

There is in Benjamin and Virilio a very different language from that of Simmat. Both have an interest in how humans act and how media affect them. But both also have very different ways of interpreting media and society and the relationship between them. In Chapter 5 the authors briefly discussed the idea of scientific positivism and the Frankfurt School's rejection of it. The Frankfurt School's concerns with causality and quantification – at the heart of scientific positivism – were also broadly and actively engaged by sociological theorists. Quantitative research dominated the first part of the 20th century. Qualitative research emerged as a counterpoint to the desire to measure human attitudes and behaviours.

But before proceeding to qualitative research, it is worthwhile looking at some of the terminology of research. In Simmat's and Benjamin's work there are various assumptions at work. These are:

1. theoretical assumptions;

2. methodological assumptions;

3. research methods;

4. evidence.

1. *Theory* is the explanatory framework that you are using. Theories are explanations of phenomena.

2. *Methodology* is the ontological or epistemic beliefs that give shape to the process of knowing (the science of method). *Do not panic.* You will, in fact, find the ideas of epistemology and ontology useful.

Quantitative research. Takes constructs or concepts and reduces them to variables – actual measurements.

Qualitative research. Focuses on the accounts of people or groups and tries to accurately reflect their attitudes, behaviours or culture.

Epistemology. Epistemology is ways of knowing – how knowledge is created.

Ontology. Ontology is what we take to be real – what is knowable.

Epistemology is ways of knowing – how knowledge is created. One ongoing debate, for example, is whether violence in media leads to violent behaviour; or whether representing thin women in the media leads to women being thin or anorexic. Different models of media effects come to different conclusions on the same evidence.

Psychologist Albert Bandura, for instance, challenged simple behaviouristic assumptions about cause and affect in aggression in adults (1977). He argued that environmental factors cause behaviour and behavioural factors cause the environment. He called this approach reciprocal determinism. His model is called observational learning or modelling.

Bandura's bobo doll studies, in particular, convinced him of the usefulness of his model. Bandura made a film of a woman beating up a bobo doll – an egg shaped balloon with a weight that made it rock back and forth when it was hit. The woman shouted 'sockeroo!' each time she hit the bobo doll.

Bandura then showed the film to young children. The children copied the behaviour of the young woman hitting the doll while shouting 'sockeroo!' The children's behaviour was not, in behaviouristic fashion, rewarded before or during or after the activity. Bandura concluded that we do, indeed, model the behaviour of others and not necessarily in a strict cause-effect-reinforcement way. What Bandura is doing is questioning the way of knowing proposed by the behaviouristic model; in short, behaviouristic epistemology.

Ontology is what we take to be real – what is knowable. Clearly, we want evidence that is real and that we can know. For example, we have little difficulty with Bandura talking about children watching a film and the film as counting as evidence. We would have significant difficulty if he said that he had done his study with ghosts. Every media discipline has its epistemology and ontology. Some communication and media research is more 'social science' oriented; some communication and research is more 'postmodern theory' oriented. Either way, theory, methodology and evidence will matter.

Ethnography. A method taken from anthropology that involves the researcher in direct participation with the people she or he is studying.

3. *Methods* are the actual techniques you use to collect evidence, such as surveys and experiments in quantitative research and ethnography and focus groups in qualitative research.

4. *Evidence* is the accounts that you will use as evidence to support your theories. In quantitative research this will most likely be statistics. In qualitative research it will be the actual accounts from people who you have interviewed.

Methodology and methods for someone like Walter Benjamin are going to be very different from Ralph Simmat. Benjamin is not employing fieldwork methods, like focus groups or surveys. His methodology and method are bound up in critical theory and psychoanalysis. Simmat is drawing on variable-analytic method and statistics.

Despite Simmat's thinking that human behaviour is law-like, it is important to realize that we do not have laws in social and media research, whether the research is applied or non-applied. We have conjectures and forecasts. Predictions like those of Dr Dichter though are more problematic. Predictions in the natural sciences are conditional statements about what will happen, assuming the validity of a relevant set of scientific laws and observations. Forecasts are unconditional statements and are not necessarily based on any notion of a causal structure; they tend to be based in projection or extrapolation from past observations or events. Conjectures are about possible futures; what we think may happen if certain conditions obtain.

What is the point of these notions to media research? Clearly if you have a particular frame of mind that is out to 'prove' things as though there are laws that govern human behaviour, then you are going to get back a certain kind of result. For example, if Simmat thinks that lower class, lower income women are inferior to higher class women, and with all due respect to Simmat the authors would argue that this is indeed his worldview, then your whole research design is going to work with that assumption.

Empirical research in media studies, therefore, is not a simple given and unproblematic. Empirical research is research based on observation and/or experiment but the epistemology and ontology of it affect what you see and what you get back. Empirical research is often divided into descriptive and explanatory research. Descriptive research tells us something about a phenomenon, but does not explain it. For example, the population census gives us data about different people but does not explain why they live in particular areas or why they have low incomes. Explanatory research seeks to explain why things are occurring. All explanatory research will, of course, have a descriptive aspect. Always remember that there is most likely going to be a general theoretical perspective that guides your work in communication and media research.

A uses and gratifications framework, for instance, will assume that people choose the content they want to watch. Those choices meet particular gratifications. You can see that much of research done in the uses and gratifications approach to media is 'psychological' in character, looking at specific gratifications. 'Diffusion of innovations', also falls partly into this category (and you will find this theoretical approach in public relations, marketing and various other disciplinary text books).

An agenda-setting framework would have a focus on how people use news and information and the emphasis that news sources place on particular stories. Information campaigns, for example, increase knowledge, but unequally (the knowledge gap hypothesis).

A critical theory framework is interested in how the media define what is legitimate and what is deviant. The media are controlled by capitalist enterprises and this has effects. Ideas of ideology are relevant here. Once again, while the authors are using 'media' as the focus, the ideas of power apply to a range of contexts (personal, inter group, organizational and mass).

Our point is straightforward, whatever your research design, it will be informed by conceptual definitions or ideas. Even if you use notions like 'power', you will need to conceptualize them properly.

to recap...

Theories of knowledge and assumptions about reality underlie modern media research methodologies. Strict law-like causal approaches to methodology dominated much of the early years of applied social science and media research. There are, though, no laws in modern media research to which our evidence should conform.

Interpretative paradigm

Statistical survey methodology is a creature of the 20th century. However, the desire to find out about what is happening to humans in quantitative form goes back much further. The British Bills of Mortality were a survey created in 1594 to record deaths from the plague and other sicknesses. The definitions of death included: 'Appoplex and suddenly', 'Bedrid', 'Blasted', 'Bloody Flux, Scowring and Flux', 'Drowned', 'Executed', 'Frighted', 'Griping in the Guts', 'Kings Evill', 'Lethargy', 'Spotted Fever and Purples', 'Teeth and Worm', among others. These statistics though had an interesting purpose –

to find out if there was a relationship between the type of death and God's intentions. Was there a correlation between a drop in baptisms and punishment by God? (David, 1962, cited in Balnaves and Caputi, 2001).

Karl Marx was the first to conduct a modern survey, asking people questions. He sent over 20,000 questionnaires to workers in factories asking about their relationships with their bosses (Marx cited in Bottomore and Rubel, 1956). Apparently Marx received no replies. Adorno and the Frankfurt School and other Marxist scholars were not worried about quantitative studies, per se. They were worried, however, about the use of quantification as an ideological tool.

Modern research methods have further developed since Marx's time. Figure 14.1 shows some of the different methods against the type of involvement of the research. A quantitative survey reduces concepts to questions that can be quantified. There is little personal involvement of the researcher with a participant because the survey itself is the data-gathering instrument. Structured and semi-structured interviews start to involve the researchers much more closely with participants. There are set questions that start to elicit information from close-ended or more open-ended approaches. Observation involves looking at human behaviour even though you might not be participating in it. This involves the emotions and views of the observer him- or herself. In-depth interviews allow the participant to talk at length about their experiences with the researcher having to develop rapport with the participant. Participant observation is where the researcher lives or participates directly in the lives of those she or he is studying. In anthropology students have tended to go and live with social groups in traditional societies, say for example the Amazon jungle, for an extended period of time. Sometimes these researchers do not return, or cannot adequately analyse their own findings, because they have 'gone native' (lost the capacity to be a participant-observer). In cultural anthropology there is also a requirement to spend extended time with the subjects of research, and in the conditions in which that subject experiences everyday life. Roger Silverstone's work with families and media is an example, whereby his emphasis on seeing media use *in place* exemplifies an appropriate and timely 'domestication' of research (Silverstone, 2005b). This kind of domestication does not rely on the same gendered and class-bound assumptions of earlier researchers.

> **Hypothesis.** A statement of relationship between two or more variables (statistical measurements of constructs).
>
> **Research question.** A statement that guides the research study.

Surveys tend to be deductive. Hypotheses and research questions are developed first, a survey constructed and the results analysed. Hypotheses in modern survey research are statements of relationship between two or more variables. For example, in the statement, 'Women watch more television than men' there are two variables – Gender (men and women) and Watching Television (number of hours as the measurement, perhaps). Participant observation tends to be inductive. The researcher goes and lives with the people she or he is studying and tries to find out what they are thinking and feel and returns a thick rich description of the encounter, often in narrative form. Figures 14.2 and 14.3 show graphically the differences in the steps of the two approaches. In Figure 14.2 a participant observer methodology and method is adopted and the evidence collected. In 14.3 the reverse is the case. A hypothesis or theory might guide the design of a questionnaire for a survey.

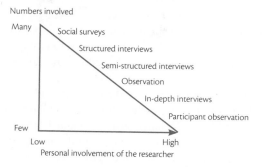

Figure 14.1 Methods of data collection and personal involvement

Source: Adapted from Worsley (1977).

Figure 14.2 Inductive approach

Figure 14.3 Deductive approach

Source: See also Balnaves and Caputi (2001).

The inductive model is a part of what researchers call the interpretative paradigm. A paradigm is a collection of theories that all have something in common. In Chapter 5 for instance it was possible to see that there was a range of different Marxist theories within the Marxist paradigm. In media studies research, similarly, there is a range of research approaches and methods that fall under the interpretative paradigm. One of the most prominent is ethnography. At the heart of the interpretative paradigm is its philosophy of human action. James Cary's statement, given in Chapter 5, is a good summary of not only cultural studies but the interpretative paradigm: 'It does not seek to reduce human action to underlying causes or structures but to interpret its significance. It does not attempt to predict human behaviour, but to diagnose human meanings.'

Ethnography

Ethnography has its origins in anthropology and is the paradigm example of participant observation. Peterson (2003, 8) gives a useful definition of ethnography:

> By ethnography I mean description based on intimate, long-term reflexive encounters between scholars and the peoples they are studying. Anthropological knowledge is largely situated knowledge, deriving from an intimate understanding of the structures of everyday life. The classic model of ethnography is participant-observation, which involves relatively long-term relationships between the ethnographer and his or her host community, in which researchers attempt to situate themselves within quotidian situations and events. (Peterson, 2003, 8)

Ethnography seeks to capture a way of life as it actually happens and not just as it is recounted by people in interviews, surveys, focus groups or quasi experimental situations. While ethnographic research in its strictest sense means living with people to discover their ways of life, ethnographic-like studies in media studies started to emerge in the early 1980s with the works of David Morley in the United Kingdom and Janice Radway in the United States.

Morley was fascinated by the work of Stuart Hall and others, and capturing evidence to show how Hall's ideas about codes worked in practice. Morley chose *Nationwide* as his focus. *Nationwide* was scheduled between the main national news from London and the peak viewing family entertainment times. It had a magazine format, talking to 'everyday people' about issues of the day. Morley recorded two *Nationwide* programmes, one broadcast in May 1976 and the other in March 1977. He then showed those two programmes to a range of different social and demographic groups. The first programme was shown to 18 groups. The second to 11 groups. The groups were from between five and ten people. After the viewing of the tape, Morley recorded the subsequent discussions. They lasted about 30 minutes in duration and the tapes were then transcribed. Morley explains his approach:

> My concern has been to examine the actual speech-forms, the working vocabulary, implicit conceptual frameworks, strategies of formulation and their underlying logics, through which interpretations, or decodings, are constructed – in short, the mechanisms of 'cultural competences'. (1980, 34)

Morley then tried to match what people said against the different codes. Was the audience employing the same code as that given by the 'transmitter' – the dominant ideology? The 'negotiated' version of the dominant ideology? Or an 'oppositional' code? The authors have taken some of the results from Morley's Group 26 as an example. Group 26 was a small group of male, mainly white, European management trainees, between the ages of 22 and 39, with a principally upper-middle-class background; predominantly Christian (1980, 122). For Morley this group was both part of the ruling class and its comments were representative of the ruling class; working within the dominant code. This is a comment by one of the participants in Group 26:

> An awful fact of Nationwide is that they're very subjective; the people are very pro-Labour … I watch them very often, they're always biased. If there's anybody, for example, who earns 10,000 pounds per annum they are sort of looking at them as if they were a rich bastard. That's what I've always found on Nationwide … They mentioned something, the person who has more than 20,000 pounds. Then they were saying, 'oh, yes, the bastard.' I find that extremely biased, saying something like that. (Morley, 1980, 123)

Interestingly, as Crouteau and Hoynes (2000, 272) point out, Morley in fact concluded that social class does not determine how people interpret media messages. While meaning is social class stratified, it is not altogether predictable or constant: 'If we reduce meaning-making to some simple formula focused on social class, we deny audiences the agency that the active audience theory has so usefully brought to our attention' (2000, 272).

Janice Radway's study also looked at how people interpret media, but in her case it was how US American women use romance novels as a means of resisting domestic systems of power. In a series of interviews with 44 women in 'Smithton' she found that the *act of reading* itself was important in our understanding of media use. It is worthwhile quoting her at length on her reaction to her findings:

> Ethnographic investigation, for instance, has led to the discovery that Dot and her customers see the act of reading as combative and compensatory. It is combative in the sense that it enables them to refuse the other directed role prescribed for them by their position within the institution of marriage. In picking up a book, as they have so eloquently told us, they refuse temporarily their family's otherwise constant demand that they attend to the wants of others even as they act deliberately to do something for their own pleasure. Their activity is compensatory, then, in that it permits them to focus on themselves and to carve out a solitary space within an arena where their self-interest is usually identified with the interests of others and where they are defined as a public resource to be mined at will by the family. For

them, romance reading addresses needs created in them but not met by patriarchal institutions and engendering practices. (Radway, 1991, 211)

It is also worthwhile presenting one of Radway's transcripts of her interviews with Dot and others to see why she came to the conclusions she did:

Dot: All right, there are pressures. Meeting your bills, meeting whatever standards or requirements your husband has for you or whatever your children have for you.

Ann: Or that you feel you should have. Like doing the housework just so.

Dot: And they do come to you with problems. Maybe they don't want you to – let's see – maybe they don't want you to solve it, but they certainly want to unload on you. You know. Or they say, 'Hey, I've got this problem.'

Ann: Those pressures build up.

Dot: Yeah, it's pressures.

Ann: You should be able to go to one of those good old – like the MGM musicals and just …

Dot: True.

Ann: Or one of those romantic stories and cry a little bit and relieve the pressure and – a legitimate excuse to cry and relieve some of the pressure build-up and not be laughed at.

Dot: That's true.

Ann: And you don't find that much anymore. I've had to go to books for it.

Dot: This is better than psychiatry.

Ann: Because I cry over books. I get wrapped up in them.

Dot: I do too. I sob in books! Oh yes. I think that's escape. Now I'm not gonna say I've got to escape my husband by reading. No.

Ann: No.

Dot: Or that I'm gonna escape my kids by getting my nose in a book. It isn't any one of those things. It's just – it's pressures that evolve from being what you are.

Kit: In this kind of society.

Dot: And people do pressure you. Inadvertently, maybe.

Ann: Yes, it's being more and more restrictive. You can't do this and you can't do that. (Radway, 1991, 95)

Jyoti Puri (1997), influenced by Radway's work, investigated how young, middle-class Indian women engaged with US and British romance novels. For the young Indian women the representations of western women in romance novels were examples of a potential progressive path compared with the inequalities facing them in their own society.

The days of strict behaviourist psychology have gone and psychologists like Kevin Durkin have used qualitative methods looking into the psychology of children and the media. Durkin's (1984) study on how young children interpret superheroes is a good example. Durkin's study is also a good example of a clear statement of a research question, as distinct from a hypothesis.

The aim of the research reported here is to explore young children's perception and comprehension of stereotyped sex roles in television … Children are often supposed to be particularly vulnerable to the deleterious consequences of biased sex-role portrayals, yet surprisingly little research has been conducted. A particularly important question that cannot be answered by experimental or correlational studies alone is whether children perceive the sex-role content of television as adults do. (Durkin, 1984, 341)

Durkin, after his literature review and presentation of methodology (qualitative), reports in the language of the participants. For example, this is Anna's reply to questions from the interviewer. Anna has just watched a short clip from *Superman* where Superman swoops down to save Lois Lane from a helicopter falling on her.

to recap...

The interpretative paradigm does not seek to reduce human action to underlying causes or structures but to interpret its significance. It does not attempt to predict human behaviour, but to diagnose human meaning. Ethnography as a method complements the interpretative methodology.

ANNA (aged 6 years, 11 months)

Interviewer: Do you think that ... ehm ... if there was a Superwoman, someone called Superwoman, would Superwoman be able to save somebody like that?

Anna (Shakes head)

Interviewer: Why not?

Anna: Because ehm ... she's not as strong.

Interviewer: Isn't she? But if she could fly like Superman can – she wouldn't be able to save a man in the helicopter, would she?

Anna: No, but only a child, if the child was very light.

Focus groups

Ethnography involves the collection of rich and thick descriptions of human behaviour through close participation with the people you are studying. There are other qualitative methods that are less intensive but that still yield important evidence or accounts. Focus groups, for example, have emerged as one of the main techniques used in the media industry to investigate attitudes and behaviour.

The focus group method originated from Paul Lazarsfeld's group at Columbia University. Robert Merton was invited by Lazarsfeld to sit in a session where audiences responses to radio programmes were tested for the war effort in the 1940s. The research was sponsored by the US Office for Facts and Figures, later the Voice of America.

Lazarsfeld had designed a way to record positive and negative responses to programs by having the audience press red and green buttons. The cumulative recordings from a session gave a measure of audience reaction, or overall program effect, but no clue as to why these effects came about. During the session Merton observed one of Lazarsfeld's assistants talking to participants about their reaction and then criticized Lazarsfeld for not being more systematic in his approach to interviews. Lazarsfeld then coopted Merton into developing better procedures. The result was the focused interview. The purpose of Merton's focused interviews at the time was to analyze and interpret reactions to an attempt of persuasion by a radio or film message. (Sorensen, 1991, 516)

Merton realized that focused interviews could be complemented with focus groups. Group responses can produce different kinds of accounts compared with individual accounts and both can be useful. Table 14.1 provides a summary of focus group method.

Table 14.1 **Elements of focus groups**

Format:	Group session
Size:	8–12 per session; but invite twice as many
Length:	1.5 to 2 hours
Number of sessions:	Enough to cover the topic or the demographics involved
Participants:	Have similar characteristics in each group
Forms of data:	Conversation, silences, words and issues, body language
Data collection:	Audio or videotape, later transcribed; observation and notes by a person who is not the moderator
Moderator:	Flexible but focused; uses guide that covers topics of interest
Formats for reporting results:	Selected quotations – verbatim accounts; analysis of common themes

Looking for love in cyberspace

It is worthwhile reporting briefly on one of the co-authors, Mark Balnaves's, students' work to exemplify focus groups. Laura Nelson was interested in Internet dating and motivations and experiences in using it. Internet dating is not limited to wealthy countries or to one type of country. It is now a worldwide phenomenon and Internet dating sites have attracted the big players in the media industry. Nelson's interest was in RSVP, one of Australia's major Internet dating websites.

John Fairfax Holdings Limited bought the privately owned RSVP.com.au Pty Ltd in 2005 for AU$38.92 million. Its expected earnings for that financial year were AU$4 million. Fairfax group executive Alan Revell said at the time that online dating had become a mainstream classifieds market, just like jobs, houses and cars. 'An important factor to us is that the RSVP demographic is similar to the strong AB reach that we enjoy today with our metro mastheads. The market growth has been driven by the increasing social acceptability of time-poor singles looking for better ways to meet people' (*Sydney Morning Herald*, 2005). RSVP had 600,000 members at the time of purchase. Jupiter Research's estimate is that online dating and personals will increase in the US alone from US$900 million in 2007 to US$1.9 billion in 2012.

Nelson's literature review found that early research into online communication and relationships mainly involved issues of identity and self-presentation within MUDs, and related to dedicated 'game' users only. Later research examined wider ranging Internet forums and modes of communication and these findings indicated a positive potential for developing interpersonal relationships (Hardey, 2004). There are, however, also arguments that lack of face-to-face verbal and non-verbal cues and nuances are detrimental to building interpersonal relations (Anderson and Emmers-Sommer, 2006; Gibbs, Ellison and Heino, 2006, 155).

Traditional theories of relationship formation in a face-to-face context emphasize the importance of spatial proximity and frequent interaction between potential partners (Altman and Taylor, 1973; Berger and Calabrese, 1975) in addition to physical attraction (Brehm, 1992). The Internet, with its relative anonymity, interestingly, produces what researchers call the hyperpersonal effect (Cooper and Sportolari, 1997; Walther, 1996). Instead of decreasing in an anonymous environment, candid self-disclosure is enhanced in an online setting and, indeed, may result in a heightened sense of intimacy and rapport. The role of self-disclosure online, the hyperpersonal effect, the differences in online relationships that become face-to-face relationships as opposed to those that are conceived and conducted in the 'real' world were the prime areas of Nelson's research. Her focus group participants were current members of RSVP, which, in 2007, had over 1,130,000 members. The site was chosen specifically because the stated intent of RSVP is to enable meeting new people for friendship and to facilitate the search for compatible romantic partners (RSVP site, 2007) as opposed to sites geared explicitly to sexual liaisons. Participants were given a verbal overview of the areas of interest namely:

- amount of contact (in various forms) resulting from having a profile on the RSVP site;
- relationships (romantic or friendship) that have formed as a result of being a member of RSVP;
- perception of personal satisfaction with the site over time;
- factors that prompted initial contact or response to another's contact;
- profile revision and any motivating factors.

The sample comprised four men and eight women who divided into two focus groups. An in-depth personal interview was conducted with another of the male participants and brief interviews were conducted with the remaining male and female respondents. The focus groups were conducted on separate evenings and ran for two and a half to three hours. They were conducted in the homes of three of the participants and the atmosphere was informal and relaxed with refreshments, so as to be conducive to ensuring a group dynamic of openness and contribution. The in-depth personal interview ran for 75 minutes and took place during the day at a coffee shop. The interviews with the remaining participants took place separately, in casual outdoor settings, and ran for 30 to 45 minutes.

Nelson used comments from the focus groups as subheadings to her research report. Selected excerpts are provided here.

'Is this all that's left in life, sitting in this apartment all on my lonesome?'

The common motivating factor behind all participants joining RSVP in Nelson's focus group was the desire for a significant, intimate romantic relationship. Despite varying relationship backgrounds, the lack of love and companionship in their lives was perceived to be affecting enough for participants to actively seek to enhance their prospects of meeting a potential partner through an online forum.

'I knew that I wanted more.'

'I would like a relationship.'

'My motivation for joining ... well, loneliness basically.'

Joining the site, particularly for the women, often came about through the urging of a friend who was themselves a member of the site, and the initial profile put up in several cases was a joint collaboration arising from a social gathering.

'A neighbour ... brought around a bottle of red one night and we sat down by the computer and she said "I'll make you sound wonderful!" and she did, then I had to go back and edit it all because it wasn't about me, it was all about her! But we had a lot of fun with that – like Helen said you start getting little hits and you go "ooh, he looks interesting" and before you know it, you're really addicted and you're up 'til midnight checking all the time.'

All participants had been on the site prior to becoming a member and had browsed profiles before they created theirs and were thus aware of common aspects of style and content. Although all participants aimed to create a profile that was an authentic representation of self, many also mentioned a desire to present themselves in the best possible light as they were aware of a certain 'marketplace' mentality intrinsic in the initial perusal of profiles by users of the site. This duality between truth and authenticity, and the ability and allure of selective self-representation, was a recurring theme in various guises throughout comments from Nelson's focus groups. Many of the participants construed this situation as having both positive and negative ramifications. Most participants likened creating the best profile possible as being reflective of a face-to-face meeting in that you 'put your best foot forward'. However, all participants were also absolutely aware of the potential, and actuality, of misrepresentation – both unintended and deliberate.

'The unfortunate thing with that of course, is that eventually you will meet face-to-face. I guess the logic is, on the part of the person that perhaps oversells themselves with a flattering photo, is they might think we get on well personality-wise and that may be enough or they just might not realize that they've fallen away a bit in the looks department but, yes, I've been disappointed a few times.'

'Put it this way, when you read the profiles it would be impossible to be everything that a lot of these people claim to be but, of course, everyone's putting their best foot forward so they say lots and lots of good stuff about themselves. Nothing negative, but life is not all positive, positive.'

'The other thing is they can spend so long working on that one e-mail, so they can carefully edit what they are presenting.'

'It's exciting ... you've got something to look forward to. I find the process quite enjoyable definitely.'

There was no consensus in Nelson's focus groups on what constituted acceptable embellishment. However, deliberate manipulation of self-presentation to be more appealing was seen as totally unacceptable, and almost contrary to the 'spirit' of openness inherent in the very act of making oneself accessible online.

'Once you put your profile on and you get a reaction, it gets addictive.'

Other factors that rated highly with participants were the ease of online dating and its appeal as an enjoyable activity in and of itself. All participants of the focus groups found the actual process of online dating to have many enjoyable, even compelling aspects.

'It's exciting. It's an ego boost. Everyone likes to be told that they're nice, that they're good, that they're accepted and it's one of the great "wants" of life, of people, that they are liked and accepted and this is one way in which that need can be fulfilled.'

'It could almost replace the TV.'

'It's flattering.'

'It's addictive.'

The convenience and ease of online dating was one of the most appealing aspects for participants. The time pressures endemic in modern life make the comparative efficiency of meeting many prospective partners through RSVP enticing.

'Well you could just go home and look on the computer and not have to think about where am I going to go, or how am I going to meet someone or having to get dressed up and all that. You just walk in, sit down and look'.

'I think it's convenient, you can do it in the comfort of your lounge chair. You don't have to be tired and busy and waste money going out and about'.

Although all participants had experienced negative responses, the ones that occurred only in an online environment were more easily dealt with emotionally and were perceived to be less hurtful than negative experiences that took place in face-to-face encounters. A rejection at an early stage, before meaningful exchange and disclosure occurred, and the lack of a physical reality, appeared to lessen the impact of these negative experiences. Nonetheless, there was still an element of rebuff although this appeared to become less so, the longer a participant was a member of the site. As participants became more selective about responding to contact and their filtering strategies became more evolved, there was a corresponding acceptance of others' decisions and an assumption of similar motives.

'It almost reverses the order of things ... it works backwards.'

Nelson found that the hyperpersonal effect, developing rapport online through self-disclosure, meant that the face-to-face encounter heightened tensions, especially on issues of compatibility.

'With RSVP you already know quite a lot about the person so it makes it a little bit easier in terms of finding common ground, things that you both want to talk about. The down-side to that is that you've often already covered those things. You've e-mailed back and forth a few times, you've had phone conversations, you've talked about the movies you both have in your profile, talked about the fact you both have a brother and a sister, they know about your work, you know about theirs, you've worked out you've got a couple of mutual friends because Perth's so small so its like ... and now what?'

'You don't want to get on well online and then meet them and think "my God, I'm so not attracted to you!" There's a level of disappointment if you're really building up to something so you just want to stave that off any which way you can'.

Nelson's study provides a small insight into the experiences of people using an Internet dating site. Her participants were within the same culture with a similar frame of reference. Many thousands of participants on Internet dating sites, of course, are making contact with partners in other cultures and nations. This form of international contact, and the scale of it, is new and made possible by both profit-making and non-profit-making Internet dating sites.

Research and impact: Global cyberbullying

Contemporary research, like Durkin's concern with stereotyping of women and Nelson's study of Internet dating site users, is often linked to specific issues, that are perceived as threats or problems or advantages within society, but which need to be researched and properly described, before solutions can be found. These may be new problems that arise within new media situations, although in fact they are actually *old problems* with *new formations* made possible through new media. An example of this is 'cyberbullying'. This term refers to bullying behaviours that are perpetrated on email, through mobile phones and on the Internet. They are 'old' in that bullying has always occurred, and that the tactics of humiliation, pain, personal attack, threatening behaviour, intentional exclusions and so on have always been used for intimidation. They are 'new' in that the new media facilitate particular forms of these behaviours.

Cyberbullying is a global trend. But the nature and impact of that bullying can vary, culture by culture. For Japanese children, for example, a mobile phone is a social lifeline 'but the anonymity it provides for perpetrators may have extra significance in Japan, where wariness of direct confrontation is a cultural norm' (Kubota, 2007).

Japanese high school student Makoto, not his real name, became anorexic and suicidal after constant harassment. 'Even when I stopped going to school and stayed at home, my cell phone kept ringing with harassing e-mails,' he told researchers at the International Project on Cyber Bullying at McGill University in Canada.

Makoto worked as a hair stylist after finishing high school. Fellow classmates posted photos of him along with insults on a website and emailed him constantly telling him to die. 'When people tell you your life is not worth living, you start to think that way. I couldn't believe in human beings anymore' he told the researchers (Kubota, 2007).

The cyberbully has various methods at hand:

- *Anonymity and aliases*, where the bullies send comments without giving their real names or use aliases, pseudonyms, to hide their identities or indeed pretend to be other people. This can include faking the development of a friendship;
- *Outing*, where the bully produces sensitive information, from mobile phone camera footage or text, in order to embarrass another person;
- *Flaming*, where the bully uses offensive language via emoticons or other means;
- *Repetition*, where the bully sends denigrating messages again and again;
- *Cyberstalking*, where the bully creates an environment of fear that there will be real harm visited upon the recipient.

activity Are there any other ways in which new media access might create new forms of cyberbullying? And how might cultural and subcultural differences be involved? Think about time, space and diffusion when preparing your answer.

The first stage in creating a bully-free environment is to be able to name a behaviour as bullying. If someone receives a text that says something demeaning, the receiver may not understand why they feel so hurt and possibly scared. Once they realize that they are being bullied there is more hope of seeking help, standing up against the perpetrator, and expecting redress or apology. In New South Wales in Australia, the Commission for Children and Young People has placed emphasis on identifying the causes and methods of bullying. In their report on children at work, they identified the following types of harassment, usually visited by an older or more senior or powerful person on a younger and less powerful person: shouting; making fun of; calling inappropriate names; making the butt of cruel or silly jokes; threats of harm; tricks (practical jokes); damage to possessions; unwanted physical attention.

If you think about how these behaviours might be transferred to a new or mobile media situation you can quickly surmise the extent of damage that could be done to a person's identity and sense of safety at work, at home or at school. New media diffuse messages and images to a great many receivers at one time.

Given the importance of mobile media and network media for communications and social interaction, it is a serious matter if a person, especially a young or otherwise vulnerable individual, becomes too scared or unsure of themselves to use a medium or remain in a group. Exclusion is often the intent of a bully, and when their victim withdraws they have won the first battle. The answer is not to tell all young people to 'not use email' or 'avoid social networking sites' or even ' use a landline'. That is very unlikely to work, and in any case why should the bullies push the victims or potential victims offline? There are many children and young people for whom new media are essential, as lifelines out of disturbing home situations, as access to schooling in rural and remote zones, as a way of overcoming the constraints of disability, and for exploring creative potential that may not find an outlet in their home or school environments. So, our challenge is not to shut down access to media, but to work systematically to discover the situation in which young people find themselves (of course bullying happens within other demographics as well), so as to create solutions.

group activity How might one go about researching the extent and intent of cyberbullying behaviour? How would you do it in an international context? What would be the most appropriate design for (a) gathering information on practices with new media, (b) assessing the level and scale of the problem and (c) analysing the circumstances and contexts in which the problem is prevalent in order to (d) make recommendations on how to eradicate or minimize the problem and its effects?

In designing your research methodology, make a list of the skills that you would need, or that you would need in your team. For instance, if you want to start by designing a representative survey you have to ask yourself: what kinds of statistical skills and programs do we need to make this worthwhile? How would you determine what is representative of a demographic group? What kinds of issues would you face in accessing your informants? If you decided that the survey would be followed by, say, intensive focus groups, you would again need to consider how that method would be approached. How would you choose or ask people to volunteer for such an activity? Would you use ethnography? What might be the ethical questions you face in this type of media research?

Having succeeded in your research, to whom would you communicate your findings? You need impact for the research to have lasting meaning. This means that you need to know who the stakeholders are in any given piece of work so that you can tailor your results in ways that will help them accept, or understand problems. Presumably in this case, you would need to include policy players (rule-makers), industry and young people and those who work alongside them. You might also find that a much wider strategy of communication is needed to educate people in general about what is and what is not experienced as bullying. 'It's just a joke' or 'He should just take it' are not excuses for making another person feel miserable.

Summary Media studies research at the level of methodology has embraced the interpretative paradigm as a way of getting rich accounts back from participants in order to explore phenomena of interest. David Morley did this in his study of interpretations from different groups of the programme *Nationwide*. Janice Radway did this in her study of romance novel readers. Nelson did this in her more modest study on Internet dating. In all cases, as you will have noticed, the researchers came up with research questions and related their evidence back to their original ideas. In the case of *Nationwide*, Morley was interested in Stuart Hall's theories of encoding and decoding. In the case of romance novels, Radway was interested in whether the act of reading had more to it than simply pleasure and found that it was related to domestic resistance. In the case of Nelson, she was interested in the hyperpersonal effect and gained accounts to expand on that concept.

Qualitative research methods are often combined with quantitative methods in modern media research. Focus groups may be combined with, for example, survey research. Qualitative research has been developed from a range of different disciplines, from sociology through to anthropology. Key to its approach is obtaining accounts from people or groups that as accurately as possible reflect their actual attitudes and behaviours. Participant observational research is one technique that tries to get as close as possible to participants (including living with them in the case of ethnography).

Focus groups were created by Robert Merton, a sociologist, during the 1940s in order to get a 'richer' sense of how people felt about particular topics. The idea of 'focus' is exactly that – a clear well-defined topic that people will have views on. Merton also created 'focused interviews' to deal with individual situations. Focus groups today are one of the most common qualitative methods used in communication and media research. The art is in conducting focus groups in a way that yields useful information for the researcher.

Future media studies research will increasingly become focused on each other's cultures and media and how we might better understand and interact with them. Intercultural communication theory and research have already uniformly shown that honesty and a sincere desire for mutual understanding are the cornerstones for successful relationships in an increasingly interconnected world. Research has an important and proactive role in informing media policy and international communication.

At the conclusion of this chapter you should be able to:
- distinguish between methodology and method;
- critically discuss the interpretative paradigm and the kinds of research in media studies that might be created in that paradigm;
- identify studies that use qualitative research methods.

Interpretative paradigm. Early media and social science research was dominated by a behaviourist or quasi-behaviourist methodology. The researcher on this view was a neutral observer trying to objectively divine laws of behaviour through quantitative methods. Often, however, this approach was neither neutral nor objective. In the latter half of the 20th century many social science researchers recognized the importance of a qualitative understanding of behaviour that was informed by involvement of the researcher with participants. Behaviouristic language like 'experimental subjects' is not used in the work of qualitative researchers. 'Subjects' in qualitative research are 'participants'. The methodology behind methods such as ethnography is one of diagnosing human meanings rather than seeking to reduce human action to underlying causes or structures. The interpretative paradigm is an overarching phrase to describe all those approaches that advocate this qualitative methodology. This does not mean, of course, that qualitative researchers do not use quantitative methods like survey or experiment, or vice versa. It does mean that the philosophy and methodology we adopt behind our methods are important to our understanding of the nature of evidence in media research.

Discussion questions

1   Provide key words that you think characterize the differences between quantitative and qualitative research.

Quantitative	Qualitative

2   Bring to class examples of refereed journal articles that you think have conducted empirical research into media studies. Find journal articles that have used:

- a survey method;
- a focus group method;
- an ethnographic or qualitative interview method.

3   See if you can identify the hypotheses or research questions in the studies that you have found and discuss them and the results with your class.

4   Go to the research ethics site of your university. University courses at undergraduate level that do applied research with humans often need unit licence approval. As you progress in your capacity, however, and do more complex research you will be required to submit an ethics application to your Faculty or University ethics committee. Discuss some of the issues of ethics in your class. What counts as unethical research? Can you find examples?

Further reading

Bertrand, I. and Hughes, P. (2004). *Media research methods: Audiences, institutions, texts.* London: Palgrave Macmillan.

Corner, J., Schlesinger, P. and Silverstone, R. (eds) (1997). *International media research: a critical survey.* London: Routledge.

Gunter, G. (2000). *Media research methods.* London: Sage.

Jensen, K.B. (ed.) (2002). *A handbook of media and communication research: Qualitative and quantitative methodologies.* London: Routledge.

Silverstone, R. (ed.) (2005). *Media, technology and everyday life in Europe.* Aldershot: Ashgate.

Research methods websites

University of Surrey provides a good overview of different research techniques and issues in data collection http://sru.soc.surrey.ac.uk/. There are also sites that take a particular philosophical approach, for example in phenomenology at http://webspace.ship.edu/cgboer/qualmeth.html. You can also practise your skills on http://www.surveymonkey.com!

Conclusion

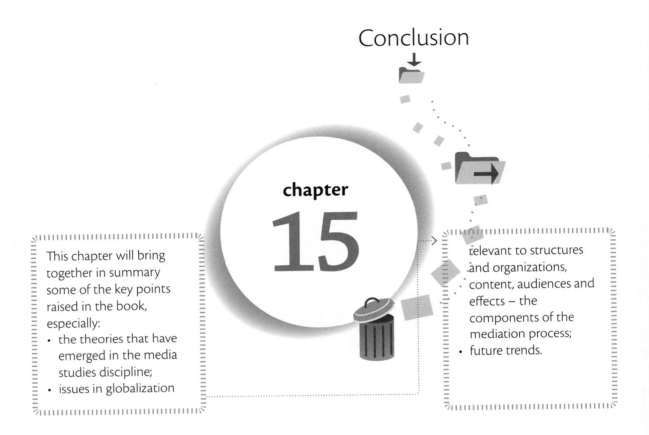

chapter

15

This chapter will bring together in summary some of the key points raised in the book, especially:
- the theories that have emerged in the media studies discipline;
- issues in globalization

relevant to structures and organizations, content, audiences and effects – the components of the mediation process;
- future trends.

At the time of writing this conclusion, Chinese television screens would intermittently go blank when it came to news on violence in Tibet. This literal blackout affected obvious targets such as the Tibetan leader-in-exile. The Chinese government was using force to crack down on protestors in Tibet and was also strongly managing the news on what was happening. Meanwhile, the international media were reporting on the protests and the Dalai Lama's responses to the situation. *The Hindu*, the online edition of India's national newspaper, quoted the Dalai Lama as saying 'This movement is beyond our control', and called on the 'international community to help us to cool down the situation' and probe the violence (*The Hindu*, 2008). At the same time, in a country far away, a small town editor of the *Yass Tribune* in Australia warned local residents as a matter of urgency that 'Tackling climate change is going to hit us in the hip pocket' (Sykes, 2008).

The authors started this book with the tragic story of the McCanns and how that story became part of the international news agenda. Indeed, as we write about the Chinese events, we also note that the McCanns have successfully sued two British newspapers for cumulative libel. Both the McCanns' struggle with media management in their search for their lost child, and China's focus on maintaining stability in its western regions at all cost represent a part of the international news agenda and local community agendas. In the case of China, while the world in theory respects national sovereignty, human rights are also a part of world interest and concern. In the case of global warming and climate change, even though there are debates about if, when and how, there is little doubt that the problem affects everyone. Each inch or centimetre of ice that melts at the North or South Pole now gets global attention. Every hurricane or tornado or tsunami, every strangely hot or strangely cold day, is reinterpreted as a possible signal of massive changes to our environment and our future.

Global media as a system of news agencies, television, radio, cinemas, games, Internet and mobile connections, and newspapers have a fundamental role in shaping what we take to be important and how we perceive others. But the study of the global media system, as we have seen in this book, is more than simply analysis of the media of communication. Media studies involves tracing the media through the ways in which they participate in contemporary social and cultural life. It deals with various components of that process, including structures and organization of media, content, audiences and effects. Globalization, as a focus of media studies, involves at the minimum networks – of media, goods, people – that cross national boundaries and can vary in their extent, intensity, tempo and influence.

In this book the authors have looked at both the positive and negative implications of globalization in the context of theories, structures and organizations, content, audience and effects within the media process. It is worthwhile summarizing some of these implications.

Theories

From its beginnings in the early 20th century theoretical development of the media studies discipline has been influenced by international events and intercultural influences. The distinction between administrative and critical research that emerged in the conversations and arguments between the German Theodore Adorno and the North American Paul Lazarsfeld are as relevant today as they were then. Administrative research was forged in the demand from governments and businesses for better knowledge about audiences and how to persuade them. Critical research, especially of the Frankfurt School kind, was forged in the shadow of extreme ideologies, Nazi and Soviet, and its focus was on the role of the culture industry; ideology and power in domination became a key focus.

As we discovered in Chapters 4 and 5, the theoretical approaches within these two broad 'schools' have in some ways converged, particularly in their understanding of audiences. Lazarsfeld and his colleagues discovered that the idea of a simple one-way powerful media effects model was wrong and that people were active interpreters. Critical theorists like Habermas and cultural studies researchers like Stuart Hall moved away from the idea of passive audiences completely subordinated to compact ideological messages. Oppositional readings and interpretative resistance are possible in people's interaction with media. The trends in media research associated with the development of media theories are:

- towards a more complex idea of media audiences, with audiences construed as active, not passive (a simple transmission model of communication – source–

message–receiver – has given way to complex psychological and cultural understandings of how media are used);

- greater recognition of the diversity of theoretical approaches associated with the audience (agenda setting as a model can be used to look at issues of power);
- towards more complex and sophisticated analysis of audiences, with a range of methods, quantitative and qualitative (ethnographic approaches emerged to understand better the complex relations between media and everyday life).

While there are similarities between the administrative and critical traditions, there are also significant differences in the way they conceptualize power. Table 15.1 provides a brief overview of the major differences.

Table 15.1 **Pluralist and hegemonic perspectives on media and power**

Pluralist perspective	Hegemonic perspective
Society is a complex set of competing groups and interests, none of them predominant all the time, in which alignments shift from issue to issue and from time to time.	Media are part of a powerful ideological apparatus within the class relationship of capitalist society. Socialist societies manage the media more closely but the hegemonic relationship still applies.
Media organizations are bounded organizational systems, enjoying an important degree of autonomy from the state, political parties and institutionalized pressure groups.	The media control much of the means of mental production, as their ownership is overwhelmingly in the private domain and is part of large-scale capitalist enterprise. They are controlled by people whose ideological dispositions are soundly conservative.
An autonomous managerial elite exists who allow a considerable degree of flexibility to media professionals.	Generally, the media reproduce their pictures of events within the field of meanings of the dominant ideology.

Empirical effects models like agenda setting, constructivism, diffusion of innovations, uses and gratifications, and the McLuhan and Innisian perspectives tend to be pluralistic in orientation. There are elites and powerful groups in society in a pluralistic perspective, but this power is not guaranteed and can change over time. Critical, neo-Marxist political economic, semiotic and cultural studies traditions tend to focus on issues associated with ideology, hegemony and power. The capitalist elites are part of an entrenched system that affects culture and economy.

As we found in Chapter 9 in the case studies of India and China it is impossible to exclude the role of ethnicity and social class as an important structure in any analysis of global media and power. Equally, however, India and China are examples of media development that are not solely tied to western influence even though there have been, over time, interconnections between east and west. At a global level, therefore, there can be competing explanations about what is happening with media. The cultural imperialism argument suggests that dominant, powerful, cultures are starting to erode or destroy weaker, indigenous, cultures or languages around the world. A contra-flow, and pluralist, perspective argues against a strong version of culture imperialism and suggests that cultures are adapting to the increased interconnections between nations and cultures.

Theories of information are also relevant to how global media operate now and in the future. In Chapter 6 two main positions were outlined that have very different orientations towards the future. Table 15.2 summarizes these positions.

Table 15.2 **Conceptions of information**

Information as a commodity	Informed citizen
In a second enclosure, individuals or corporations take knowledge – which is owned by the community – privatize it and close it off	The community owns knowledge, while authors are granted temporary rights to make money from their creations – temporary copyright or patent
All ideas are a resource and are commodities	Ideas are free
Private ownership, individual or corporate	Public domain, information commons, creative commons

Theorization about media or information is not just a mental exercise. How things are conceived and acted upon, like information, can often have real life consequences. The different conceptualizations about information can affect legal, political and democratic processes, not least in terms of the types of organizations we might end up with that govern us.

Structures and organizations

Media, political and social systems all affect the process of mediation of symbolic content. Ownership and control of the media, media economics, and of course the media professions themselves, are all part of the structures and organization of media. In Chapter 10, the authors examined how governments worldwide are making their services available on the Internet and introducing consultative and feedback mechanisms. Feedback mechanisms are not the same as participating in the policy decisions of the government. Modern democracies, at present, elect representative governments that make decisions for us. However, the modern citizen is increasingly interested in actual participation in decisions rather than relying solely on their representatives in government. There are, at present, no substantial examples of direct democracy even though there is significant interest from local municipal governments and some attempts by them to approximate it. Ironically, as we found, it is the Internet-savvy and politically motivated hacktivists who can sometimes actively influence the policy agenda. Often, though, these protests are illegal. The authors believe that the pressure for some form of direct democracy will be inevitable and, indeed, in the long term, global.

In Chapter 11, it became clear that social media are also influencing the shape and organization of modern public relations and news. Modern public relations theories have concepts like two-way symmetrical communication – participation – that complement the emergence of social networking media. Even though two-way asymmetrical communication – persuasion – currently dominates how corporations and big organizations intersect with modern publics through public relations, there can be no doubt that the shape of the public relations profession is going to change, radically.

Modern profit news organizations also have their social media counterparts in the rise of the citizen reporter and the active forum. News is a form of knowledge. Traditional news typifications have the journalist and news organization as news selector and agenda setter. The modern journalist is already part broadcast, part Internet, part print in operation. However, social media make news a conversation and news-as-conversation does not fit well into traditional news structures. News organizations, like many other organizations, are experimenting with ways of participating with their reading, viewing or listening publics. Those attempts, as the Nike example in Chapter 8 demonstrates, can fall flat.

Our digital identities are also strongly related to how our democracies and our rights will develop in the future. Digital media, as we discovered, can create active and passive digital personae. Our credit card records of all our transactions, where we were when we bought things and for how much, already give third parties significant information about our behaviour. Governments of course also hold significant information about us. There is a wide range of issues associated with how these digital personae, or identities, are protected and managed. Our digital persona will in future represent us as citizens and consumers and, indeed, in our relationships. People's avatars already do this. Our digital persona can already make decisions without our immediate presence. In Chapter 10 the example of a simple 'I am on holiday' reply to an email involves a digital persona. In future, though, your avatar will travel the digital world meeting other avatars and getting back information or messages for you. While this might sound like fun, the authors have tried to emphasize some of the real risks that are emerging.

Table 15.3 provides a comparison of some of the major trends in organization and their respective tension. E-government, for example, is not the same as e-democracy. A totalitarian government can put all its services online for its subjects, but those subjects do not necessarily have the freedom to protest or to comment.

Table 15.3 **Different dimensions of structures and organizations**

Persuasion and government	Public sphere and governance	Counter-culture and protest
E-government, propaganda, information warfare and perception management (asymmetrical communication)	E-participation, civic engagement, e-democracy (symmetrical communication)	Culture jamming, political jamming, activism
Privatization and monpolization of media; dominant flows	Public service broadcasting	Independent media and contra flows
Controlling digital personae/ identities (corporate and governmental management)	Protecting digital personae/ identities (privacy)	Hacktivism

Content

Communication and culture are intimately linked. Signs and symbols are communicated through language and through cultural artefacts. Each culture also has its own worldview or expectations about its cultural artefacts, human conduct and identity. The symbolic content is what lies behind the actual content, what we see, hear or read, whether today's news in a newspaper or an SMS message.

International cinema provides insights into how international audiences are adapting to or using content produced from cultures other than their own. In Chapter 9 we found Bollywood caters for a national and a diasporic audience but that it has also become extremely popular among non-Indian audiences, especially Germans. However, the audience interpretations and 'readings' of the films can vary. The Chinese film *Hero*, for example, reinforces the Chinese government's ideology of control. Chinese audiences would not miss the underlying message about state control – the Emperor unifying the nation for the people's good. Foreign audiences in comparison, as we know, focused primarily on the slick cinematography and the Jet Li martial arts action.

The content of the media has gone global in traditional media like film and in global interconnections through digital gaming. *World of Warcraft* and other massively multiplayer online role playing games are not as one might think mechanisms of social isolation. They build affinity communities – groups interested in lifestyle matters like cars, fashion, sport or, indeed, fantasy. Pervasive games go even further and bring together real people in real time as well as in digital environments.

Role playing and digital games have in their evolution brought with them an interesting trend called co-creation where the fans become a part of the creation of the content itself. While co-creation of content in the games community looks like a new phenomenon, early amateur radio, discussed briefly in Chapter 2, had the same characteristics before radio transmission was corporatized and the spectrum substantially closed off. Co-creation, though, is an important phenomenon and one that is still in its infancy.

It is important not to forget that traditional media are still essential for many of the world's citizens. The Berber were given as an example in Chapter 9 of a community that used both traditional and new media, over time, to protect their language and their heritage. It was not English or French or German or Spanish that was a threat to the survival of the language but Arabic. Arabic was the main language used in schools and media across North Africa. The Berbers through their music gained an international audience and put pressure on local governments to allow their language to be taught in schools and represented in the local cultures.

We also covered the dark arts of modern media. Information warfare and perception management involve no participation at all. They are designed to trick, deceive, cajole and persuade. They may use black, grey and white propaganda or PSYOPS and can be found in national and international campaigns or operations. Perception management, moreover, is not limited to warfare alone. Not all persuasion, of course, is unethical. In Chapter 7, Hugh Grant was used as an example of image restoration in public relations. Grant is certainly trying to persuade us but his process of persuasion was open. Rhetoric, similarly, can be used ethically or unethically.

Centralization and decentralization of the way media operate affect the nature of content in cultures. Information warfare and perception management are by their nature centralized. Sony and News Corporation are centralized. Google as a news aggregator is centrally controlled. Governments make decisions on languages, education and censorship. Shooting or arresting journalists, for example, affects what goes into the public domain. Table 15.4 provides an overview of some of the issues in centralization and decentralization in an interconnected world.

Table 15.4 **Broad differences between centralization and decentralization**

Centralization	Decentralization
Corporate creation of media content	Co-creation of media content
Uniformity of news agencies and news aggregator media content	Diversity of indigenous and local news media content
Standardization of language in media content	Diversity of ethnicity and languages in media content
Censorship of media	Freedom of the press and human rights

Audiences

Early media researchers had an intense interest in the behaviour of audiences or in fact what constituted 'an audience'. In Chapter 14 the authors showed how simplistic ideas about cause and effect and quantification in the study of media have given way to more sensitive means of understanding audiences, especially the rise of ethnography and qualitative research.

The modern media industry needs stable and reliable means of measuring and reporting on audiences in order to plan advertising and editorial. Traditional systems of measurement similarly treat the audience as identifiable and relatively stable. Measurement of exposure is used in broadcasting as the basis of advertising currency compared with circulation in newspapers and sales in cinema. Highly educated audiences, however, are increasingly recognizing their capacity to bypass advertising by programming it out and indeed bypass surveys of their behaviour. At the time of writing this book, the media industry is still experimenting on new ways to measure audiences, including anywhere and anytime measurement.

Audiences are not only commodities, to be bought and sold by media planners and advertisers. They are also publics and citizens. Public broadcasters enhance cultural democracy by trying to represent the cultural and ethnic interests of the whole community and not only those who can pay. The principles of broadcasting outlined in Chapter 12 will not disappear in a global context. Table 15.5 provides a brief overview of the differences between audience as commodity and audience as public.

Table 15.5 **Audiences as markets and publics**

Audiences as commodities	Audiences as a public
Syndicated and surveyed audiences – A2/M2 anywhere and anytime measurement of audiences that can pay	Cultural democracy – diverse audiences represented by virtue of citizenship
Audience preferences for media determined by estimates of exposure to media	Audience preferences elaborated upon by the audience itself
Stable identifiable audiences	Mobile, fractionated and anonymous audiences
Audiences intruded upon	Liberated, expressive and media-liminal audiences

Effects

The structures and organizations, content, audiences and effects of the mediation process are all interrelated. The rise of the entrepreneurial aspirational classes in China, for example, who want access to the Internet and to communicate freely, will, over time, affect the rigid control of the media under the current system. Even the current system in China, as we have seen, has changed significantly since the days of Mao. The Chinese government contradictions of introducing the Internet, a low context participational medium, into a high context authoritarian culture, give us a clue on what might happen into the future.

But the contradictions are not necessarily isolated to the Chinese government alone. In Chapters 1 and 2 the authors started with the ideas of technologization of the word, where the alphabet and writing emerged as one of the first revolutions in mediation, and convergence, where older media are transformed into new cultural forms. If we are looking at the extent, intensity, tempo and influence of our global media network then there appear to be several contradictions that emerge from the discussions in the previous chapters.

First, there is the contradiction of equality and inequality. Anthony Giddens, in his 1999 Reith lecture, pointed out that the share of the poorest fifth of the world's population in global income had dropped from 2.3 per cent to 1.4 per cent in the previous 10 years. The proportion taken by the richest fifth had risen from 70 per cent to 85 per cent. 'In Sub-Saharan Africa, 20 countries have lower incomes per head in real terms than they did two decades ago. In many less developed countries, safety and environmental regulations are low or virtually non-existent' (Giddens, 1999). The future could involve the emergence of supercultures that continue to dominate the wealth and the means of communication, whereas the media themselves often encourage supertribalism, bringing everyone closer together and more equal.

Second, there are contradictions in centralization and decentralization of media. International news, interestingly, is becoming increasingly monopolized while local audiences are increasingly taking advantage of reduced costs of media production and developing their own local or independent media.

Third, there are contradictions in regulation and deregulation of media. Deregulation of media is a major trend in modern industrialized countries but the demand for the public sphere is increasing, not decreasing. This expression for a public sphere is not only represented in the traditional demand for public broadcasting but in the use of new media for contact and news. It is still not clear how governments will protect the public sphere.

Fourth, there are contradictions in the private versus the public in the digital world. Ideas on what counts as public and private are being radically reshaped or taken advantage of in virtual communities. A cyberbully can use means of harassment not previously available. A government or a corporation can compile and survey digital identities. This increased surveillance by corporations or governments could lead to the life of panopticon. A panopticon is a prison design that allows the warder to see what all the prisoners are doing at anytime anywhere. Digital personae on the other hand also have a liberating potential by allowing people to explore their own identities and to develop affinity communities online or in mobile cultures.

Fifth, there are contradictions involved in preserving your own culture while importing cultural artefacts from other cultures. Cultural imperialism is the extreme form, where cultural deflation, loss of the original culture, might be a consequence. Cultural autonomy with possible adaptation is another possibility. Table 15.6 provides a brief overview of the major differences of effect of globalization identified by the authors.

Table 15.6 **Contradictions in globalization**

Supercultures	Supertribalism
Massification of content	Demassification of content
Panopticon and surveillance	Privacy and participation
Deregulation of media for private interests	Regulation of the media for the public good
Cultural imperialism and cultural deflation	Cultural autonomy and cultural saltation

Media capital

Finally, it is worthwhile concluding with a comment on the complexity of the media capitals that have emerged in this interconnected world. Some of the intercultural contact we have is seemingly innocuous, but there is much behind it. For example, the chances are that if you telephone your credit card company to make an enquiry you will end up speaking to someone in India, the Philippines or the Caribbean, depending on where you live. The process that creates this situation is known as outsourcing and is highly contentious in countries like England, the US and elsewhere because it seems that jobs are being exported like any other commodity. In very simple terms, this is modern capitalism taking advantage of the new networks and flows that convergence has created. It is much cheaper to employ well-educated young people in Galgoan, India, Manila, the Philippines or Bridgetown in Barbados than it is in London, New York or Sydney. Call centres are the ultimate global worksite and it is no accident that they are located in India, for example.

When you speak to Alan (Arjun) or Susie (Sushila) on the phone you are often talking to a highly educated, middle-class young Indian who possesses an MSc or MA, who works for US$400 per month compared with the US$3500 per month their Australian counterpart would earn. Call centres have become major employers of the vast number of graduates produced by the truly huge Indian higher education system. The graduates can speak English and they are grateful to get work in a highly competitive market. Convergence is not just about television and entertainment but also about employment and people's everyday lives. The computer and convergence have transformed India in the past two decades. The country has a large and efficient mobile phone network, cyber cafes are common in the smallest town, computer training bodies are also common and there are now millions of students studying computing at all levels.

One example of this transformation will suffice. Pollachi is a small city of approximately 150,000 in central Tamilnadu and by most criteria it is unprepossessing, and yet it is home to a modern, up-to-date technical institution that is supported by local business and produces well-trained and highly competent young graduates. The major computing firms also support the institution through the provision of equipment and staff; Mahalingam College of Engineering and Technology has become a convergence hub in an area where bullock carts are still a major means of transport. What is happening in Pollachi mirrors, in small way, what is happening in locations around the world.

In the popular imagination Banglaore is frequently linked with Silicon Valley. It is the home of hundreds of IT firms and is the Asian base for the world's biggest, Microsoft, which conducts product development there as do Unisys, Yahoo!, Phillips and Sun Microsystems, to mention a few. Bangalore has become branded as a global communication centre and has an annual economy in excess of US$60 billion. It has become a global city meeting the needs of global businesses, contributing to the flows of data and information that now dominate the global capital. And yet the brand is contested. Kannada linguistic nationalists have sought to change the name of the city to Bangalaru, arguing that Bangalore is the Anglicized version of this name and thus redolent of colonialism. The IT industry opposes the move, arguing that their effort to brand the city as a modern, highly competent and significant player in the global IT industry will be undone. To date the Indian government has supported the industry, but in many respects this struggle highlights the problematic nature of globalization and the ongoing competition between the global and the local.

In his work, Michael Curtin (2003) argues that media capitals are an important feature of understanding the geography of media. He means, briefly, that technological investment and know-how, creative talent, established institutional infrastructure, and investment, and a common media language combine to entice people and ideas to certain foci of production. London, Hollywood, Bollywood, Bangalore, Miami, Hong Kong, Lagos and Beijing are some key examples.

These 'capitals' function not alone, as there are many smaller media centres that support them in various ways, perhaps with post-production work, perhaps with special effects, or maybe with investment. But talent attracts talent and money attracts money, and when a media capital is strong, it tends to get stronger – as long as there is growth in its market that can sustain it effectively. We encourage you to read Curtin's work for yourself but the authors raise his arguments here as this allows us to make a few important points about studying local media, which you can take forward in your own studies.

First, the global media has more than one centre, the globe is not a single media market. So, shows in Spanish are made in Latin America, and in Spain, but also in Miami, a media capital because it has such good access to investment and audiences in the US. African films are usually distributed from Lagos. Chinese language media come from transnational hotspots such as Hong Kong, but other Chinese language sites are investing in their own media or creative futures as well (especially Singapore).

Beijing and London are unusual media capitals because they are also the seat of strong governments. US commentators like Curtin argue that government stifles media creativity just by being close by. However, within the PRC, Beijing still captures government investment, and some would say unfair protection regimes for the national broadcasters. Beijing bureaucrats and governments also stifle certain kinds of creativity but not always successfully. It is also helpful in China to be able to pop out to dinner with one of the Bureau officials to make a quick deal on a censorship issue. That is much harder to do from far away in Hong Kong, Chongqing or Guangzhou. Beijing has the advantage of a captive domestic market, strong government protectionism, and many talented people in one place. London has a long history of media production, and retains that 'cool' flavour against competition from smaller English rivals. Censorship is not an issue in London, but knowing the right people, going to the right clubs and, ideally, sending your children to the right schools (not necessarily private ones) is all part of building media capital.

Second, global media is a language-based economy. It is pointless to make Spanish language telenovellas and sell them in Australia, where Spanish is a minority language. It is however quite clever to sell them in eastern Europe, which is not an English language zone, but which has rejected Russian, and has yet no serious media capital of the region.

Third, by remembering that global media are dispersed across huge but differently configured markets, we remind ourselves of the diversity of taste and media cultures enjoyed by audiences. We would hope that this makes you feel both jealous of your freedoms, and optimistic about a world with options.

Further reading

Curtin, M. (2003). Media capital: Towards the study of spatial flows. *International Journal of Cultural Studies*, **6**(2), 202–28.

Webster, F. (1995). *Theories of the information society*. London: Routledge.

Glossary

Administrative research. This is a phrase used in early writings in media to characterize US research that was tied to commercial or governmental interests in audience behaviour and persuasion. Administrative research was characterized by experimental research in psychology and survey research.

Affective modulation. Brian Massumi's term to describe how, after 9/11, people have got used to alerts about fear and, as a consequence, how fear has become ingrained and routinized in all of us.

Agenda setting. Agenda setting, like diffusion, is interested in the individual psychological processes of selecting and deciding on media messages and the impact of the media and social organizational processes involved in the selection and emphasis of particular kinds of news. The simple version of the model assumes that people's ranking of news stories in their minds roughly matches the emphasis given by the news media on those stories. If, for example, a drunken movie star dominates news across a week, then people will have that story at the top of their minds, according to the model. Of course, more complex models have emerged because people's real interests may affect what they choose and many people may have no interest in movie stars and only focus on sports news. Framing and priming are a part of the agenda-setting model. The ability of news to activate emotions and schemata can have a dramatic effect on which stories gain attention.

Anchor. Anchors are what the propagandist targets. People are reluctant to change, and to convince them to do so the propagandist relates the change to something in which a person already believes. This is called an anchor because the appeal is to attitudes and behaviours already accepted by the person.

Art cinema. Used as a counterpoint to classic narrative and classic cinematic conventions where none of the conventional links of continuity occur.

Attitudes. Attitudes are mental states of readiness to respond based on experience and have an influence on behaviour. You can have more than one attitude towards a particular behaviour. You can have more than one attitude towards sex before marriage, for example. Attitudes and behaviour, however, are not the same thing. You can be anti-smoking and still smoke.

Auteur theory. Deals explicitly with the role of the author in the creative work.

Blogosphere. Online forums that allow conversation on any topic under the sun.

Broadcast media. Electronic systems such as traditional radio and television that provide information and entertainment one way.

Classic narrative system. This involves assumptions about structure, such as the linearity of cause and effect, a high degree of narrative closure, a fictional world governed by spatial and temporary verisimilitude (the appearance of being true) and the centrality of narrative agency of psychologically rounded characters.

Co-creation. Co-creation is a trend in the games industry where fan programmers create their own programming content in addition to the game created by a corporation (also discussed in Chapter 13). Games corporations involve these fans in the production of their products in a quasi-democratic fashion. Companies like Google have recognized this trend and are trying to take advantage of it. Co-creation is an example of participational cultures online intersecting with commercial interests.

Constructivism. The constructs people use to make decisions about the world form into schemata, much like Walter Lippmann assumed people created 'maps' of the world in order to simplify the complex of events around them. There are personal and social schemata and both affect how a person views the world.

Convergence. This is a term to describe a medium or media that bring together a range of other media into one place or activity. The Internet, for example, can combine video, audio and text. The term also refers to how audiences and cultures engage with media and other processes of convergence such as service level convergence (where different media services might combine) or corporate level convergence (where different types of media-related companies combine).

Copyright. Traditional copyright and patent laws hold that the community owns knowledge, while authors are granted temporary rights to make money from their creations.

Corantos. Primitive newsheets used on the streets written by intelligencers.

Creative commons. The creative commons movement is a response to the pressures of access and reward. It involves attempts to provide a licensing environment that strikes a balance between authors' rights and public access.

Creative industries. A name that evolved to describe the whole entertainment industry, from ballet dancer to movie producer.

Critical research. This is a phrase used in early writings in media to characterize European theorizing about media and is especially associated with the Frankfurt School, a group of 1940s–1960s scholars interested in ideology, power and the role of culture and media in reinforcing capitalism.

Cultural abrasion. Cultural abrasion is where media systems can act as cultural abrasive agents, producing in local cultures a fear of cultural domination.

Cultural deflation. From the Latin 'to blow away', where a local culture is carried off by an erosive cultural agent.

Cultural deposition. Cultural deposition is where people will adopt a foreign value, but it comes at the expense of another value.

Cultural imperialism. The idea that corporate influence pervades nearly every aspect of society, local and global: from simple things, like our daily diet and the clothes we wear, to matters of larger scale, like the way we communicate with each other. Cultural imperialism also involves the transfer of a dominant ideology to other cultures, potentially destroying the indigenous culture or making it dependent on the dominant culture.

Culture industry. The culture industry, the Frankfurt School argued, standardizes culture under the guise of individualization. The modern system is designed to commodify consumers and audiences and to control them.

Culture jamming. Culture jamming is an attempt to reverse and transgress the meaning of cultural codes whose primary aim is to persuade us to buy something or be someone.

Cultural saltation. Cultural saltation is similar to deposition, but foreign media systems help stimulate local cultural expression.

Diffusion of innovations. Rogers argued that diffusion was a special type of communication concerned with the spread of innovations (any new idea or thing). The innovation process is a mental process through which an individual passes. It consists of five stages:
1. knowledge (exposure to an innovation and some understanding about how it works)
2. persuasion (formation of an attitude towards the innovation)
3. decision (activity resulting in the choice to adopt or reject)
4. implementation (putting the innovation to use)
5. confirmation (reinforcement of the innovation decision made).

There are also types of 'adapter' in the process:
- Innovators (keen to try new ideas)
- Early adopters (highest degree of opinion leadership)
- Early majority (interact frequently with peers)
- Late majority (sceptical)
- Laggards (near isolates).

Rogers argued that most new ideas come through the media, but are mediated by individuals, like opinion leaders (people you trust – who could be different people for different things; such as the person you most trust on guidance on fashion).

Disintegrative function of the mass media. Argues that the mass media are contributing to the decay of primary relationships and the weakening of adherence to social norms and values.

Downplayer. A downplayer is a rhetorical device to make something seem less important than it really is. For example, adding 'quotation marks' to a word can downplay a person's achievement. Mark's 'theory' of the media is 'well known'. Adding the words 'so-called' might achieve the same effect: 'Mark's so-called theory of the media is well known'. Stereotypes, persuasive comparisons, persuasive explanations, and innuendo can all be a part of downplaying.

Dysphemisms. Dysphemisms replace one expression with another that carries with it negative associations. *'youde ren'* (some people), in certain circles in the PRC in the 1960s and 1970s, meant those who might be blamed for inappropriate politics, but not named explicitly by the speaker.

E-democracy. The ultimate form of e-democracy would be direct democracy where everybody participates in governmental decisions. There are, of course, variations of this theme. There is, at present, no formal system for e-democracy.

E-governance. E-governance in normal parlance would be what e-governments do. However, e-governance is an attempt to reflect ideas of new governance, especially the role of genuine participation in policymaking.

E-government. E-government is the provision of government services online. This can include feedback mechanisms but e-government and e-democracy are not necessarily the same thing.

Electronic civil disobedience. Social movements have emerged that use the new communicative structures made possible by new media to influence decision-making. This ranges from quasi-legitimate electronic protests through to hacktivism.

Empirical research. Empirical research involves observations about the world using systematic quantitative methods such as survey and experiment or qualitative methods such as ethnography and personal interview.

Ensemble of histories. When the printing press entered society it coexisted with scribal culture, the dominant form at the time. Ensemble of histories,

Braudel's term, refers to the capability of different economic and cultural phenomena to coexist, rather than one phenomenon completely displacing another when it occurs.

Epistemology. Epistemology is ways of knowing – how knowledge is created.

Ethnocentric. The tendency for us to see everything through our own cultural lens.

Ethnography. 'Mapping culture'. Ethnography is a method taken from anthropology that involves the researcher in direct participation with the people she or he is studying. For example, this might involve living with a remote community in the Amazon forests for many years in order to genuinely understand the community the anthropologist is interested in. Simple things like argot – the local language of groups – cannot be picked up by outsiders, just as your own family argot is not known to outsiders. Ethnographic-like methods have been adopted in media studies to try to map the cultures or subcultures of modern society. Ethnographic approaches are non-directive and designed to elicit accounts from participants without imposing the views of the researcher on them. David Morley's and Janice Radway's studies are early examples of this approach.

Ethos. In rhetoric, a persuasive argument that uses ethics or morality as the main appeal.

Euphemisms. Euphemisms replace one expression with another that carries with it positive associations. 'Special action' was a euphemism for 'killing' in Nazi Germany. Neutral language can function as euphemism or dysphemism. 'Negative income,' neutral as it sounds, is a euphemism for 'debt'.

Exposure. Measurement of broadcasting audiences has traditionally been by measurement of exposure in a few media. Audience ratings are a summation of this exposure and are used as the basis for making decisions on placement of advertising in different media. Exposure as a 'metric', a way of measuring, is unlikely to disappear altogether, but techniques of finding out preferences are changing, as the idea of co-creation suggests.

False consciousness. False consciousness is when people are dominated by others and take that domination to be legitimate. A slave who thinks that slavery is part of a natural order has taken on a false consciousness. Slavery is not a part of any natural order – it is imposed by humans on humans.

Film noir. A genre of cinema narrative, with highly stylized visual expression, a circular form of narration, and generally concerning a narrative of murder and deception in love.

First enclosure. In the feudal era the lords of the manor would invest in drainage, sheep purchases and crop rotation in the *commons* (land for the whole community) because they knew that there were social and economic benefits. The first enclosure movement involved privatizing the commons ('the tragedy of the commons') in order to enhance property rights over lands.

Fourth Estate. The three estates in Parliament were the nobles and clergy (House of Lords) and the House of Commons. The press is the Fourth Estate.

FPS. First person shooter.

Genre. Genres are recognizable repertoires of conventions running across visual imagery, plot, character, setting, modes of narrative development, music and stars.

Glocalization. A glocal media product involves media content and services being tailored to specific cultural consumers, not so much because of any particular regard for national cultures but because of commercial imperatives.

Greek alphabet. Theorists such as Walter Ong argue that the Greek phonetic alphabet was a revolution in how language was recorded and how thinking developed.

Habitats. The communicative spaces that we occupy.

Hegemony. Hegemony is the consensus of society given to the mode of life impressed on society in general by the ruling class. This consensus is achieved because of the prestige and trust the ruling class (or dominant group) enjoys due to its position (for example a queen or king). Gramsci said that hegemony exists when a ruling class is able not only to coerce a subordinate class to conform to its interests but also to exert a total social authority over the subordinate class and the whole society. Hegemony depends on both force and consent. Media, in Marxist and neo-Marxist thought, have a key role in ensuring the consensus.

High context communication. High context communication is ambiguous, indirect, maintaining harmony, understated and reserved.

Hyper-real. The idea that everything has become artificial where signs refer to nothing but themselves**.**

Hypothesis. In quantitative research, a hypothesis is a statement of relationship between two or more variables. Variables are a part of statistical measurement.

Ideology. Ideology is the means by which dominant economic classes, ruling classes, extend their control over others so that their rule is accepted as natural and inevitable. Adopting an ideology, therefore, is having a false consciousness.

Imagined communities. It is impossible whether we are North Americans or Australians or Indians or British or Chinese to physically know one another at any given time and yet we can all claim a relationship – we are North Americans, Australians or Indians. In short we inhabit an imagined community that is horizontal (we are all equal), bounded (this is the US or United Kingdom or India or China) and sovereign (we are in control of the territory we claim to be American or British or Chinese or Indian). In addition, as we claim a nationality we also claim an identity, often several identities all at once.

Information commons and the public domain. While the right to tangible expression of knowledge is called a property right, it is more precisely a right to reward to those who surrender their exclusive control of their own thoughts. Freedom of access to the public domain, to the totality of published works, refers to access to the tangible expressions of knowledge, such as documents, signals and data structures. The information commons is the public domain where the community's knowledge is accessible to all.

Information warfare. Information warfare refers to enemy attacks against information infrastructures in modern societies or your own military's attack on enemy information and communication infrastructures. However, the term has expanded to include 'hard' and 'soft' infrastructure (people). Information warfare can also be used by governments within their own countries to influence their own populations.

Integrative function of mass media. Argues that the media provide channels of information and symbolism required for integration and social solidarity in modern society.

Intelligencers. Forerunners of journalists.

Kinetoscope parlour. The first attempts at cinema.

Loaded questions. Loaded questions follow the logic of innuendo by suggesting something through the very existence of the question. 'Do you still hit your husband?' condemns the person who replies if they say 'yes' or 'no'.

Logos. In rhetoric, a persuasive argument that uses rational examples and logic as the main appeals.

Low context communication. Low context communication is precise, direct, open and based on explicit statements in text or in speech. On this view, the closer a relationship becomes and that a situation is understood, the less need there is for explicit statements (high context).

Many-to many-communication. A phrase developed in the 1990s to describe the difference between traditional broadcast technologies, like television and radio, and the emerging Internet and mobile technologies.

Mass communication and mass media. These terms are becoming less common because of the complexity of media networks in the modern world. Traditionally they refer to broadcast media such as radio and television, or print media such as newspapers.

Media-liminality. Play is not 'ordinary' or 'real' life. It is a stepping out of 'real' life into a temporary sphere of activity with a disposition all of its own. Modern digital games, especially many-media Manga anime and role playing games, are, the authors argue, a classic example of the creation of liminal space in a society. This type of world-building does not lead to a defined role or status, but it does allow people to explore and create and work in peer environments. The authors have used the expression media-liminal space to describe this phenomenon.

Mise en scène. Refers to the practice of stage direction in the theatre in which things are 'put into the scene' (arranged on the stage).

MMOFPS. Massively multiplayer online first person shooter.

MMORPG. Massively multiplayer online role playing game.

MMORTS. Massively multiplayer online real time strategy.

Modes of production. For Karl Marx, the modes of production comprise the substructure, *base* or economic foundation, of society and a great *superstructure* of political, legal, educational, spiritual and artistic institutions. The role of the superstructure is to reconcile members of society to the existing system by moulding their opinions, customs, moral and ethical values, expectations and behaviour patterns.

Monopolies of knowledge. Monopolies of knowledge is a theoretical term used to describe the role of communication and media in the distribution and control of knowledge. Space-biased media in Innisian terms potentially lead to less control over the social distribution of knowledge and a more secular society. Slower, time-biased, media by contrast may lead to more control and a more religious society. The slower the medium on this view the greater the potential for elites or rulers to control access to knowledge and the speed of news.

Narrative forms. The ways that stories and pictures are edited and presented.

News aggregator. The term 'news aggregator' emerged to described websites or search engines that select, retrieve and link news from anywhere on the Internet.

One-to-many communication. A term used to refer to traditional broadcasting where there is one communicator, for example a radio station that broadcasts to a large audience.

Ontology. Ontology is what we take to be real – what is knowable.

Pathos. In rhetoric, a persuasive argument that uses emotion as the main appeal.

Perception management and PSYOPS. Modern perception management involves actions by a government or the military to convey and/or deny selected information to foreign governments, intelligence systems, leaders or audiences in order to influence their emotions, motives, and objective reasoning. Modern perception management combines truth projection, operations security, cover and deception, and psychological operations (PSYOPS). PSYOPS can involve overt and covert psychological techniques to influence audiences.

Pluralism. Pluralists conceive of power as distributed across different groups in society, shifting over time and issues.

Preservation of knowledge. A phrase used to describe the advantages of the printing press in enabling the distribution and replacement of many copies of the same work, enhancing their longevity.

Proof surrogates. Proof surrogates refer to evidence without providing the details. 'Stephanie is obviously the best journalist in the city' or 'Most people agree that Stephanie is the best journalist in the city'.

Propaganda

• **Black propaganda.** Lies and manipulation. The source of information may be a complete fabrication as well as the information itself.

- **Grey propaganda.** Grey propaganda is when the nature of the source is not clear.
- **White propaganda.** The source of the information may be objective, independent and well known, but the use of information by the propagandist remains selective and designed to persuade not inform.

Public sphere. The ideal public sphere is an institutionally guaranteed space where people can communicate without their communication being distorted by threats or by force.

Push technology. Push technology is another term to describe the impact of participational media on modern society. Push technology is the Internet's trend *du jour* that allows news sites to 'narrow-cast' personalized news directly to readers. This technological revolution redefines the relationship between online news operations and their readers. 'Push' refers to the concept of delivering content to Internet consumers rather than expecting them to seek out a website – the 'Pull' model. Push news has the potential to reshape the fundamentals of journalism in much the same way that television news has altered the rules of the profession.

Qualitative research. Qualitative research focuses on the accounts of people or groups and tries to accurately reflect the attitudes, behaviours and cultures of the people studied.

Quantitative research. Quantitative research takes constructs or concepts and reduces them to variables – actual measurements. Surveys and experiments are variable-analytic and also try to accurately reflect the attitudes and behaviour of those studied.

Research question. A research question guides the research. Radway's study on women reading romance novels, for example, started with a very open research question – the role of romance novels in women's lives. She used an ethnographic method to get back accounts from female romance readers and concluded from emerging patterns that the women's act of reading novels was itself a form of combative resistance.

Rhetoric. Rhetor is from the same Latin root for orator, which means a public speaker. Rhetoric is the art of using public speaking for persuasion.

Rhetorical comparisons. Rhetorical comparisons link our feelings about something to something we are comparing it to: 'He had a smile like a bent street sign'.

Rhetorical definitions. Rhetorical definitions use loaded language. 'Abortion is the killing of innocent human life.'

Rhetorical explanations. These use loaded language while telling the reason for an event: 'Stephanie lost her job as a journalist because she lost her nerve'.

RTS. Real time strategy.

Semiotics/semiology. Semiotics is the study or science of signs and meaning. There is the *signified* – that to which a word or other signifier refers and the *signifier* – that which signifies. The immediate meaning of signs, though, is not necessarily the same as its metalanguage, where ideology may be embedded.

Slanters. Slanters are words or phrases or indeed grammatical structures that present a positive or negative slant. Ridicule, sarcasm, hyperbole and exaggeration are a part of the world of slanters.

Social engineering attack. The use of human failings to get access to information or to influence them. Calling someone up pretending to be their mother and asking them for their online banking password would be a social engineering attack.

Social media. Social media are those modern networks that make participatory forums possible, from blogs through to Facebook.

Space-biased media. Media that are light, portable and easily transported and disseminated, with a short lifespan unless preserved. They are associated with secular societies that occupy large territories.

Stereotypes. Popularly held, but often not evidence-based, images of a group: 'All women, as we know, are poor drivers'. This statement also includes, though, innuendo by implying what it does not say – that women are not smart. Rhetoric when used inappropriately can be very closely linked to tactics of bullying and discrimination.

Subaltern flows. Subaltern flows are a second layer of international media players and include private and state sponsored flows.

Technological determinism. A phrase used to describe theorists or writers who argue that technology is the primary cause of change in society. The difficulty with this position is that there are many influences on social change, even when new media like the printing press have a significant impact.

Technologization of the word. A phrase used by theorists to describe the move to media – such as writing and the alphabet – as major revolutions in human evolution.

Textual communities. A textual community revolves around an authoritative text and designated interpreters.

Time-biased media. Media that are durable and heavy and not easily transported. Their dissemination and spread is limited but they may have a long life. They are associated with hierarchical societies that are defined by sacred and moral precepts.

Two-way asymmetrical communication. Two-way asymmetrical communication is James Grunig's term for persuasion. Public relations has traditionally used persuasion to influence audiences or publics to see things the way that their employers, governments or organizations, want them to.

Two-way symmetrical communication. Two-way symmetrical communication is James Grunig's term for participational decision-making between organizations and their publics. It is the opposite of persuasion and is closer to Habermas's idea of the public sphere. As you might guess, participational decision-making is not an easy one for modern corporations. The Nike example in Chapter 8 shows what happens when participational media are used by corporations to give the impression of genuine participation, customization and personalization.

Typifications. Tuchman's study of how journalists selected news found that newsrooms did not use categories (a classification of objects according to one or more relevant characteristics ruled salient by the classifiers) but typifications (a classification in which the relevant characteristics are central to the solution of practical tasks or problems at hand). She found that news people have devised these typifications because they draw on the synchronization of their work with the likely potential news occurrences. Tuchman's study remains relevant today. Her ideas can be applied to the global news contexts.

Universal service. Legislative frameworks that ensure that people have access to society's basic communications and media.

Uses and gratifications model. Uses and gratifications deals with (1) the social and psychological origins of (2) needs, which generate (3) expectations of (4) the mass media or other sources, which lead to (5) differential patterns of media exposure (or engagement in other activities), resulting in (6) need gratifications and (7) other consequences, perhaps mostly unintended ones. The uses and gratifications approach proposes that people get out of the media what they want of it. Thus it avoids the deterministic theory of the hypodermic-effect, or stimulus–response, theory which holds that information transmitted by the mass media has a direct impact on how people view the world.

Weaslers. Weaslers are rhetorical devices, often legitimate, that allow the speaker to qualify what she or he says, shielding a claim from criticism. 'Possibly', 'as far as we know', are weasler words: 'As far as I know, Stephanie is the best journalist in the city'.

Worldview. Each culture also has its own worldview or expectations about its cultural artefacts, human conduct and identity.

Bibliography

Foreword

Briggs, A. and Burke, P. (2002). *A social history of the media: From Gutenberg to the internet.* Cambridge: Polity.

Prewitt, K., Alterman, E., Arato, A., Pyszczynski, T., Robin, C. and Stern, J. (2004). The politics of fear after 9/11. *Social Research,* **71**(4), 1129–47.

Chapter 1

Adams, P. (1998). Network topologies and virtual place. *Annals of the Association of American Geographers,* **88**(1), 88–106.

Brunn, S.D. and Leinbach, T.R. (1991). *Collapsing space and time: Geographic aspects of communication and information.* London: Routledge.

Castells, M. (1996). *The rise of the network society.* Oxford: Blackwell.

Castells, M. (1997). *The power of identity.* Oxford: Blackwell.

Castells, M. (1998). *The information age: Economy, society and culture.* Oxford: Blackwell.

Dicken, P. (1998). *Global shift: Transforming the world economy.* London: Paul Chapman Publishing.

Downing, J., McQuail, D., Schlesinger, P. and Wartella, E. (eds) (2004). *The Sage handbook of media studies.* London: Sage.

Economist (1996). The hitch-hiker's guide to cybernomics. **340**(7985), S3–7.

Friedland, L.A. and Webb, S. (1996). Incorporating online publishing into the curriculum. *Journalism and Mass Communication Educator,* **51**(3) autumn, 55–65.

Graham, S. (1998). *The end of geography or the explosion of place? Conceptualizing space, place and information technology.* London: Routledge.

Hjarvard, S. (2003). A mediated world: the globalization of society and the role of media. In S. Hjarvard (ed.) *Media in a globalized society.* København: Museum Tusculanum Press.

McBeth, J. (2002). Sea change. *Far Eastern Economic Review,* July, 51.

McLuhan, M. (1962). *The Gutenberg galaxy: The making of typographical man.* Toronto: University of Toronto Press.

Mittelman, J.H. (1996). The dynamics of globalization. In J.H. Mittelman (ed.) *Globalization: critical reflections.* London: Lynne Rienner.

Silverstone, R. (1999). *Why Study the Media?* London: Sage.

Soja, E. (1989). *Postmodern geographies. The re-assertion of space in critical social theory.* London: Verso.

Thompson, J.B. (1997). Mass communication and modern culture. In T. O'Sullivan, and Y. Jewkes (eds) *The media studies reader* (42–52). London: Arnold.

Valdivia, A.N. (ed.) (2003). *A companion to media studies.* Oxford: Blackwell.

Webster, F. (1995). *Theories of the information society.* London: Routledge.

Chapter 2

Albany Advertiser (1924). New picture theatre for Albany. September 3.

Barnouw, E. (1975). *The tube of plenty: The evolution of American television.* New York: Oxford.

Bektas, Y. (2000). The Sultan's messenger: Cultural constructions of Ottoman telegraphy, 1847–1880. *Technology and Culture,* **41**(4), 669–96.

Braudel, F. (1975). *Capitalism and material Life: 1400–1800.* London: Fontana.

Briggs, A. (1977). The pleasure telephone: A chapter in the prehistory of the media. In de Sola Pool, I. (ed.) *The social impact of the telephone* (40–65). Cambridge, MA: MIT Press.

Briggs, A. (1985). *The BBC: The first fifty years.* Oxford: Oxford University Press.

Briggs, A. and Burke, P. (2002). *A social history of the media: From Gutenberg to the internet.* Cambridge: Polity.

Carey, J.W. (1989). Technology and ideology: The case of the telegraph. In J.W. Carey (ed.) *Communication as culture: Essays in media and society* (210–30). London: Unwin Hyman.

Carlyle, T. (1904). *On heroes and hero worship and the heroic in history.* London: Oxford University Press.

Castells, M. (2001). *The Internet galaxy: Reflections on the Internet, business, and society.* New York: Oxford University Press.

Chapman, J. (2002). *Comparative media history.* Cambridge: Polity.

Cook, P. (1985). *The cinema book.* London: British Film Institute.

David Harvey, F. (1978). Greeks and Romans learn to write. In E.A. Havelock and J.P. Hershbell (eds) *Communication arts in the ancient world* (63–78). New York: Hastings House.

Douglas, S. (1987). *Inventing American broadcasting 1899–1922.* Baltimore: John Hopkins University Press.

Eisenstein, E.L. (1983). *The printing revolution in early modern Europe* (Vols 1–2). Cambridge: Cambridge University Press.

Emery, E. (1969). *The press and America.* New Jersey: Prentice Hall.

Febvre, L. and Martin, H-J. (1984). *The coming of the book. The impact of printing 1450–1800.* London: Verso.

Gates, B. (1995). *The road ahead.* London: Viking.

Headrick, D.R. (1981). *The tools of empire: Technology and European imperialism in the nineteenth century.* London: Oxford University Press.

Hilmes, M. (1997). *Radio voices: American broadcasting, 1922–1952.* Minneapolis: University of Minnesota Press.

James, L. (1976). *Print and the people 1819–1851.* London: Allen Lane.

Lazarsfeld, P.F. and Kendall, P.L. (1948). *Radio Listening in America: the people look at radio – again.* New York: Prentice Hall.

Marvin, C. (1988). *When old technologies were new: Thinking about electric communication in the late nineteenth century.* London: Oxford.

Mayhew, H. (1861). *London labour and the London poor.* London: Dover.

Negroponte, N. (1996). *Being digital.* Sydney: Hodder and Stoughton.

Neuman, R. (1991). *The future of the mass audience.* New York: Cambridge University Press.

Ong, W.J. (1988). *Orality and literacy: The technologizing of the word.* London: Routledge.

Rawlings, G.B. (1901). *The story of books.* London: George Newnes.

Chapter 3

Ang, I. (1996). *Living room wars.* London: Routledge.

Bell, D. (1965). *The end of ideology: On the exhaustion of political ideas in the fifties.* New York: Free Press.

Bell, D. (1973). *The coming of post-industrial society: A venture in social forecasting.* London: Heinemann.

Beniger, J. (1986). *The control revolution: Technological and economic origins of the information revolution.* New Haven: Harvard University Press.

Berland, J. (1999). Space at the margins: Critical theory and colonial space after Innis. In C. Acland, and W. Buxton (eds) *Harold Innis in the new century: Reflections and refractions* (281–308). Montreal: McGill-Queen's University Press.

British Broadcasting Corporation (2002). *Nigeria goes mad for mobiles.* Retrieved 10 March 2002, from http://news.bbc.co.uk/2/hi/business/1905744.stm.

Burke, P. (2000). *A social history of knowledge. From Gutenberg to Diderot.* Oxford: Polity.

Carey, J. (1989). *Communication and culture: Essays on media and society.* London: Unwin & Hyams.

Castells, M. (1996). *The rise of network society.* Oxford: Blackwell.

Castells, M. (2001). *The Internet galaxy: Reflections on the Internet, business and society.* London: Oxford.

Couldry, N. (2000). *The place of media power: Pilgrims and witnesses of the media age.* London: Routledge.

Crowley, D., and Heyer, P. (eds) (1991). *Communication in history: Technology, culture, society.* New York: Longman.

Dahrendorf, R. (1959). *Class and class conflict in an industrial society.* Stanford, CA: Stanford University Press.

Djilas, M. (1953). *The new class: An analysis of the communist regime.* New York: Praeger.

Drache, D. (ed.) (1995). *Staples, markets and cultural change: Selected essays of Harold Innis.* Montreal: McGill-Queen's University Press.

Gillard, P., Wale, K. and Bow, A. (1997). Prediction of future demand from current telecommunications uses in the home. *Telecommunications Policy,* **21**(4), 329–39.

Gore, A. (1994). *Building the information superhighway.* Speech delivered at the Information Superhighway Summit at UCLA January 11, 1994.

Green, N. (2002). Who's watching whom? Monitoring and accountability in mobile relations. In B. Brown, N. Green and R. Harper (eds) *Wireless world: Social and interactional aspects of the mobile age.* London: Springer.

Green, N. (2003). Outwardly mobile: Young people and mobile technologies. In Katz, J.E. (ed.) *Machines that become us: The social context of personal communication technology.* New Brunswick: Transaction Publishers.

Helvey, T.C. (1971). *The age of information: an interdisciplinary survey of cybernetics.* Englewood Cliffs, NJ: Educational Technology Publications.

Innis, H. (1951). *The bias of communication.* Toronto: University of Toronto Press.

Innis. H. (2007). *Empire and communication.* Lanham, MD: Rowman & Littlefield.

Innis, H. (1999). *The fur trade in Canada.* Toronto: University of Toronto Press.

Ito, M. (2003). Mobile phones, Japanese youth, and the re-placement of social contact. *Front stage – back stage: Mobile communication and the renegotiation of the social sphere in Grimstad,* Norway, June 22–24 (http://www.itofisher.com/PEOPLE/mito/mobileyouth.pdf).

Johnson, T.E. (2003). The social context of the mobile phone use of Norwegian teens. In Katz, J.E. (ed.) *Machines become us: The social context of personal communication technology.* London: Transaction Publishers.

Jones, S.G. (ed.). (1998). *Cybersociety 2.0: Revisiting computer-mediated communication and community*. London: Sage.

Lewontin, R., Rose, S., and Kamin, L. J. (1984). *Not in our genes: Biology, ideology and human nature*. New York: Pantheon Books.

Ling, R. and Yttri, B. (2002). Hyper-coordination via mobile phones in Norway. In J.E. Katz and Aakhus, M.A. *Perpetual contact: Mobile communication, private talk, public performance*. Cambridge: Cambridge University Press.

Ling, R. and Yttri, B. (2005). Control, emancipation and status: The mobile telephone in the teen's parental and peer group control relationships. In R. Kraut (ed.) *Information technology at home*. Oxford: Oxford University Press.

Livingstone, S.and Bovill, M. (eds) (2001). *Children and their changing media environment: A European comparative study*. Hillsdale, NJ: Lawrence Erlbaum Associates.

Lyotard, J.F. (1984). *The postmodern condition: A report on knowledge*. Minneapolis: University of Minnesota Press.

Martin, A. (1987). Media and social change – with special reference to television. *Pacific Islands Communication Journal*, **15**(1), 3–21.

Marvin, C. (1988). *When old technologies were new: Thinking about electric communication in the late nineteenth century*. London: Oxford.

Massey, D. (1993). Mapping the futures: Local cultures, global change. In J. Bird, J. Curtis, T. Putnam, G. Robertson (eds) *Power-geometry and a progressive sense of place*. London: Routledge.

McLuhan, M. (1964). *Understanding media*. London: APK Paperbacks.

Mittelman, J.H. (1996). The dynamics of globalization. In J.H. Mittelman (ed.) *Globalization: critical reflections*. London: Lynne Rienner.

Digital divide: beyond the infrastructure (2001). *MN Planning: critical issues*. August. St Paul, MN: Minnesota Department of Administration.

NTIA (National Telecommunications and Information Administration) (1995). *Falling through the net: A survey of the 'have nots' in rural and urban America*. Washington, DC: U.S. Department of Commerce.

NTIA (National Telecommunications and Information Administration) (1997). *Falling through the net II: New data on the digital divide*. Washington, DC: U.S. Department of Commerce.

NTIA (National Telecommunications and Information Administration) (1999). *Falling through the net: Defining the digital divide*. Washington, DC: U.S. Department of Commerce.

Norris, P. (2001). *Digital divide: Civic engagement, information poverty, and the Internet worldwide*. New York: Cambridge.

Ofcom (2006). *The international telecommunications market*.

Plant, S. (2001). *On the mobile: The effects of mobile telephones on social and individual life*. Motorola.

Porat, M.U. (1977). *The information economy: Definitions and measurement*. Washington, DC: U.S. Government Printing Office for U.S. Department of Commerce, Office of Telecommunications.

Rheingold, H. (1993). *The virtual community: Homesteading on the electronic frontier*. Reading, MA: Addison-Wesley.

Sassen, S. (ed.) (2002). *Global networks, linked cities*. New York: Routledge.

Skog, B. (2002). Mobiles and the Norweigian teen: identity, gender and class. In J.E. Katz and Aakhus, M.A. (eds) *Perpetual contact: Mobile communication, private talk, public performance*. Cambridge: Cambridge University Press.

Spry, D. (2007). East Asian youth mobile cultures. In U.M Rodrigues and B. Smaill (eds) (2008). *Youth, media and culture in the Asia Pacific region*. Cambridge: Scholars Press.

Stock, B. (1996). *Listening to the text: On the uses of the past.* Philadelphia: University of Pennsylvania Press.

Suoninen, A. (2001). The role of media in peer group relations. In S. Livingstone, and M. Bovill (eds) *Children and their changing media environment. A European comparative study* (201–219). London: Lawrence Erlbaum Associates.

Tingstad, V. (2003). Children's chat on the net: A study of social encounters in two Norwegian chatrooms. Unpublished PhD thesis: Norwegian University of Science and Technology.

Tofler, A. (1980). *The third wave.* New York: Bantam.

Tomita, H. (2005). Ketai and the intimate stranger. In M. Ito, D. Okabe and M. Matsuda (eds) *Personal, portable, pedestrian: Mobile phones in Japanese life.* Cambridge, MA: MIT Press.

Tunstall, J. (1977). *The media are American. Anglo-American media in the world.* London: Constable.

Tunstall, J. (2008). *The media were American. US mass media in decline.* New York: Oxford University Press.

UNESCO (United Nations Education Scientific and Cultural Organization) (2000). *IT revolution for developing countries (Bridging the digital divide).* Retrieved 1 October 2002, from http://www.mofa.go.jp/region/latin/fealac/it.html.

Wahyuni, S. (2007). Yogya mosque uses TV to reach the masses. *The Jakarta Post,* Saturday, October 6.

Warschauer, M. (2001). *Reconceptualizing the digital divide.* First Monday. Retrieved 9 September 2002, from http://www.firstmonday.dk/issues/issue7_7/waschauer/.

Weilemann, A. and Larsson, C. (2002). Local use and sharing of mobile phones. In B. Brown, Green, N. and Harper, R. (eds) *Wireless world: Social and interactional aspects of the mobile age.* London: Springer.

Young, M. (1958). *The rise of the meritocracy 1870–2033: An essay on education and equality.* Harmondsworth: Pelican.

Zachary, G.P. (2002). Ghana's digital dilemma. *Technology Review,* **105**(6), 66–72.

Chapter 4

Adorno, T., Frenkel-Brunswick, E., Levinson, D.J. and Nevitt Sanford, R. (1950). *The authoritarian personality.* New York: Harper and Brothers.

Ang, I. (1985). *Watching Dallas: Soap opera and the melodramatic imagination.* London: Routledge.

Bauer, R.A. (1971). The obstinate audience: the influence process from the point of view of social communication. In W. Schramm and D.F. Roberts. (eds) *The process and effects of mass communication* (326–46). Urbana: University of Illinois Press.

Beniger, J. (1986) *The control revolution: Technological and economic origins of the information society.* Cambridge, MA: Harvard University Press.

Berelson, B. (2004). What missing the newspaper means. In J.D. Peters and P. Simonson (eds) *Mass communication and American social thought: Key texts* (254–62). Lanham, MD: Rowman and Littlefield.

Berelson, B., Lazarsfeld, P.F. and McPhee, W.N. (1954). *Voting: A Study of opinion formation in a presidential campaign.*

Blumler, J.G. and McQuail, D. (1969). *Television in politics.* Chicago: University of Chicago Press.

Bogart, L. (1989). *Press and public: Who reads what and why.* Hillsdale, NJ: Lawrence Erlbaum.

Campbell, A., Converse, P.E., Miller, W.E. and Stokes, D. (1960). *The American voter.* New York: Wiley.

Cappella, J.N., and Jamieson, K.H. (1997). *Spiral of cynicism.* New York: Oxford University Press.

Chaffee, S.H. (1975). The diffusion of political information. In S.H. Chaffee (ed.) *Political communication: Issues and strategies for research*. Beverly Hills: Sage.

DeFleur, M.L. and Dennis, E.E. (1981). *Understanding mass communication*. Boston: Houghton Mifflin.

DeFleur, M.L. and Larsen, O. (1958). *The flow of information: An experiment in mass communication*. Boston: Houghton Mifflin.

Donald, S.H. (2005). *Little friends: Children's film and media culture in China*. Lanham, MD: Rowman and Littlefield.

Entman, R. (1993). Framing: Toward clarification of a fractured paradigm. *Journal of Communication, 43*(4), 51–8.

Entman, R. (2001). *The black image in the white mind: Media and race in America*. Chicago: University of Chicago Press.

Funkhouser, G.R. (1973). The issues of the sixties: An exploratory study in the dynamics of public opinion. *Public Opinion Quarterly, 37*, 62–75.

Gerbner, G. (1970). Cultural indicators: the case of violence in television drama. *The ANNALS of the American Academy of Political and Social Science, 388*(1), 69–81.

Graber, D.A. (1989). An information processing approach to public opinion analysis. In B. Dervin, L. Grossberg, B.J. O'Keefe and E. Wartella (eds) *Rethinking communication* (40–52). Newbury Park: Sage.

Hovland, C.I., Lumsdaine, A.A. and Sheffield, F.D. (1971). The effect of presenting 'one side' versus 'both sides' in changing opinions on a controversial subject. In W. Schramm, and D.F. Roberts. (eds) *The process and effects of mass communication* (467–84). Urbana: University of Illinois Press.

Innis, H. (1951). *The bias of communication*. Toronto: Toronto University Press.

Janowitz, M. (1952). *The community press in an urban setting*. New York: Free Press.

Kahn, J. (2003). Accidental hero. *Guardian*. January 10.

Katz, E., Blumler, J. and Gurevitch, M. (1974). Uses of mass communications by the indvidual. In W. Davison and F.T. Yu (eds) *Mass communication research*. New York: Praeger.

Katz, E., Gurevitch, M. and Haas, H. (1987). On the use of mass media for important things. *American Sociological Review, 38*, 164–81.

Kraus, S. and Davis, D. (1976). *The effects of mass communication on political behaviour*, University Park: Pennsylvania State University Press.

Lapiere, R.T. (1938). *Collective behaviour*. New York: McGraw Hill.

Lazarsfeld, P.F., Berelson, B. and Gaudet, H. (1944). *The people's choice*. New York: Duell, Sloan and Pearce.

Lippmann, W. (1922). *Public opinion*. New York: Free Press.

Lovgen, S. (2005). War of the Worlds: Behind the 1938 radio show panic. *National Geographic News*, June 17.

Mander, J. (1978). *Four arguments for the elimination of television*. New York: Morrow.

McLeod, J.M., Becker, L.B. and Byrnes, J.E. (1974). Another look at the agenda-setting function of the press. *Communication Research, 1*, 131–66.

McCombs, M.E. and Shaw, D.L. (1972). The agenda-setting function of mass media. *Public Opinion Quarterly, 36*, 176–87.

McCombs, M.E. (1981). The agenda-setting approach. In D.D. Nimmo and K.R. Sanders (eds) *Handbook of political communication* (121–40). Beverly Hills: Sage.

McCombs, M. E., and Zhu, J. (1995). Capacity, diversity and volatility of the public agenda: Trends from 1954 to 1994. *Public Opinion Quarterly, 59*, 495–525.

McLuhan, M. (1964) *Understanding media*. London: APK Paperbacks.

McQuail, D., Blumler, J.G. and Brown, J. (1972). The television audience: A revised perspective. In D. McQuail (ed.) *Sociology of mass communication*. Harmondsworth: Penguin.

McQuail, D. and Windahl, S. (1981). *Communication models for the study of mass communication*. London: Longman.

Mendelsohn, M. (1996). The media and interpersonal communications: The priming of issues, leaders, and party identification. *Journal of Politics*, **58**(1), 112–25.

Noelle-Neumann, E. (1977). Turbulences in the climate of opinion: Methodological applications of the spiral of silence theory. *Public Opinion Quarterly*, **41**, 143–58.

O'Keefe, G.J. and Mendelsohn, H. (1974). Voter selectivity, partisanship, and the challenge of Watergate. *Communication Research*, **1**(4), 345–67.

Pierce, J.C., Beatty, K.M. and Hagner, P.R. (1982). *The dynamics of American public opinion: Patterns and processes*. Glenview, IL: Scott, Foresman.

Rogers, E.M. (1983). *Diffusion of innovations*. New York: Free Press.

Severin, W.J. and Tankard, J.W. (1988). *Communication theories: Origins, methods and uses in the mass media*. New York: Longman.

Shaw, D.L. and McCombs, M.E. (1977). *The emergence of American political issues: The agenda-setting function of the press*. St Paul, MN: West Publishing.

Sheatsley, P. and Feldman, J.J. (1965). A national survey of public reactions and behaviour. In G. Bradley and E. Parker (eds) *The Kennedy assassination and the American public*. Stanford, CA: Stanford University Press.

Signorelli, N. and Gerbner, G. (1988). *Violence and terror in the mass media: an annotated bibliography*. Westport, CT: Greenwood.

Swanson, D.L. (1981). A constructivist approach to political communication. In D.D. Nimmo and K.R. Sanders (eds) *Handbook of political communication* (169–91). Beverly Hills: Sage.

United States Government (1982). *Television and behavior: Ten years of scientific progress and implications for the eighties*. Rockville, MD: National Institute of Health.

Walker, J.L. (1969). The diffusion of innovations among American states. *Political Science Review*, **63**, 880–89.

Weaver, D., Graber, D.A., McCombs, M.E. and Eyal, C.H. (1981). *Media agenda setting in a presidential election: Issues, images and interest*. New York: Praeger.

Winter, J.P. and Eyal, C.H. (1981). Agenda-setting for the civil rights issue. *Public Opinion Quarterly*, **45**, 376–83.

Winter, J.P., Eyal, C.H. and Rogers, A.H. (1980). Issues-specific agenda-setting: inflation, unemployment and national unity in Canada, 1977–1978. Paper presented to the Mass Communication Division, International Communication Association Annual Conference. Acapulco: Mexico.

Wright, C.R. (1975). *Mass communication: A sociological perspective*. New York: Random House.

Chapter 5

Adorno, T. and Horkheimer, M. (1979). *Dialectic of enlightenment*. London: Verso.

Althusser, L. (1970). *For Marx*. New York: Verso.

Althusser, L. and Balibar, E. (1970). *Reading capital*. New York: Verso.

Barthes, R. (1972). *Mythologies*. London: Cape.

Baudrillard, J. (1993). *Simulations*. New York: Semiotext(e).

Bauer, R.A. (1971). The obstinate audience: the influence process from the point of view of social communication. In W. Schramm and D.F. Roberts (eds) *The process and effects of mass communication* (326–46). Urbana: University of Illinois Press.

Bennett, T. (1982). Media, 'reality', signification. In M. Gurevitch, T. Bennett, J. Curran and J. Woollacott (eds) *Culture, society and the media* (287–308). London: Methuen.

Berger, P.L., and Luckmann, T. (1976). *The social construction of reality*. Harmondsworth: Penguin.

Blumler, J.G. and Ewbank, A.J. (1970). Trade unionists, the mass media and unofficial strikes. *British Journal of Industrial Relations*, **8**, March, 32–54.

Burgelin, O. (1972). Structuralist analysis and mass communication. In D. McQuail (ed.) *The sociology of mass communication*. Harmondsworth: Penguin.

Carey, J. (1977). Mass communication research and cultural studies: an American view. In J. Curran, M. Gurevitch and J. Woollacott (eds) *Mass communication and society* (409–26). Edward Arnold in association with Open University Press.

Chibnall, S. (1977). *Law and order news: An analysis of crime reporting in the British press*. London: Tavistock.

Cohen, S. and Young, J. (eds) (1973). *The manufacture of news: A reader*. London: Constable.

Ferment in the Field (1983). *Journal of Communication*, **33**(3).

Fitchen, R. (1981). European research. In D.D. Nimmo and K.R. Sanders (1981). *Handbook of political communication*. Beverly Hills: Sage.

Gitlin, T. (1980). *The whole world is watching: Mass media in the making and unmaking of the new left*. Berkeley, Los Angeles: University of California Press.

Gitlin, T. (1982). Television screens: Hegemony in transition. In M.W. Apple (ed.) *Cultural and economic reproduction in education*. London: Routledge and Kegan Paul.

Gitlin, T. (1983). *Inside prime time*. New York: Pantheon.

Glasgow University Media Group (1976). *Bad news*. London: Routledge and Kegan Paul.

Glasgow University Media Group (1980). *More bad news*. London: Routledge and Kegan Paul.

Glasgow University Media Group (1982). *Really bad news*. London: Writers and Readers.

Gramsci, A. (1968). *Prison notebooks*. London: Lawrence and Wishart.

Habermas, J. (1981). *Knowledge and human interests*. London: Heinemann.

Habermas, J. (1962). *The structural transformation of the public sphere*. Cambridge, MA: MIT Press.

Hall, S. (1977a). *Representation: Cultural representations and signifying practices*. London: Sage/ Open University.

Hall, S. (1977b). Culture, the media, and the 'ideological effect'. In J. Curran, Gurevitch, M. and Woollacott, J. (eds) *Mass communication and society*. London: Edward Arnold.

Hall, S. (1980). Encoding/decoding. In S. Hall, D. Hobson, A. Lowe and P. Willis (eds) *Culture, media, language*. Hutchinson: London.

Hall, S. (1989). Ideology and communication theory. In B. Dervin, L. Grossberg, B.J. O'Keefe and E. Wartella (eds) *Rethinking communication* (40–52). Newbury Park: Sage.

Halloran, J.D., Elliott, P. and Murdoch, G. (1970). *Demonstrations and communication: A case study*. Harmondsworth: Penguin.

Herman, E.S. and Chomsky, N. (2002). *Manufacturing consent: The political economy of the mass media*. New York: Pantheon.

Jaspers, K. (1951). *Way to wisdom*. London: Victor Gollancz.

King, A. (1992). What is postmodern rhetoric? In A. King (ed.) *Postmodern political communication* (1–12). Westport, CT: Praeger.

Lenin, V.I. (1918). The character of our newspapers. *Pravda*, 20 September, reprinted in Mattelart, A. and Siegelaub, S. (eds) (1983). *Communication and class struggle*. New York: International General.

Macey (1994). *The lives of Michel Foucault*. London: Vintage.

Marx, K. and Engels, E. (1972). *The German ideology*. New York: International Publishers.

Mattelart, A. (2003). *The information society*. New York: Sage.

Mattelart, A. and Siegelaub, S. (eds) (1983). *Communication and class struggle*. New York: International General.

Miliband, R. (1973). *The state in capitalist society*. London: Quartet.

Miller, T. (2001). *Sportsex*. Philadelphia: Temple University Press.

Morley, D. (1980). *The Nationwide Audience: structure and decoding*. London: British Film Institute.

Open University (1977) *The Audience*, Units 7 and 8, Walton Hall, Milton Keynes.

O'Sullivan, T., Hartley, J., Saunders, D. and Fiske, J. (1998). *Key concepts in communication and cultural studies*. London: Routledge.

O'Sullivan, T., Hartley, J. and Saunders, D. (1983). *Key concepts in communication*. New York: Methuen.

Real, M. (1984). The debate on critical theory and the study of communications. *Journal of Communication*, **34**(4).

Rees, L. (1992). *We have ways of making you think: Goebbels – master of propaganda*. BBC TV.

Reimer, R.C. (ed.) (2000). *Cultural history through a National Socialist lens: essays on the cinema of the Third Reich*. Boydell & Brewer.

Rogers, E.M. (1982). The Empirical and the Critical schools of communication research. In M. Burgoon (ed.) *Communication yearbook* 5 (124–44), New Brunswick: Transaction Books.

Schutz, A. (1962/1970). *Collected papers*. In A. Brodersen (ed.) The Hague: Martinus Nijhoff.

Trotsky, L. (1926). Radio: Don't lag behind! In A. Mattelart and S. Siegelaub (eds) (1983). *Communication and class struggle*. New York: International General.

Webster, F. (1995). *Theories of the information society*. London: Routledge.

Chapter 6

Balnaves, M., and Caputi, P. (2000). A theory of social action: why personal construct theory needs a superpattern corollary. *Journal of Constructivist Psychology*, **13**(2), 117–34.

Beniger, J.R. (1986). *The control revolution*. Cambridge: Harvard University Press.

Black, S.H. and Marchand, D.A. (1982). Assessing the value of information in organizations: a challenge for the 1980s. *The Information Society Journal*, **3**.

Bobrow, D.G. and Hayes, P.J. (1985). Artificial intelligence – where are we? *Artificial Intelligence*, **25**.

Bollier, D. and Watts, T. (2002). *Saving the information commons: A public interest agenda in digital media*. Washington, DC: Public Knowledge.

Boyle, J. (2003). The second enclosure movement: and the construction of the public domain. *Law and Contemporary Problems*, **66**(33), 33–74.

Briggs, W. (1906). *The law of international copyright*. London: Stevens and Haynes.

Campbell, J. (1982). *Grammatical man*. New York: Simon & Schuster.

Cohen, P.R. and Feigenbaum, E.A. (1982). *The handbook of artificial intelligence*, Vol. 3. Stanford, CA: Heuris Tech Press.

Coltoff, H. (1984). Transfer of information as seen by a user. In A. Van der Laan and A.A. Winters (eds) *The use of information*. New York: North-Holland.

Cronin, B. (1986). The information society. *Aslib Proceedings*, **38**(4) April.

Fox, C.J. (1983). *Information and misinformation: An investigation of the notions of information, misinformation, informing and misinforming*. Westport, CT: Greenwood Press.

Friedlander, S. (1997). *Nazi Germany and the Jews*. London: Weidenfeld and Nicolson.

Ghitis, F. (2006). Google's China web. *The Boston Globe*, January 26.

Habermas, J. (1984). *The theory of communicative action: Reason and the rationalization of society*. Vol. 1. Boston: Beacon Press.

Hacking, I. (1983). *Representing and intervening: Introductory topics in the philosophy of natural science.* New York: Cambridge University Press.

Hintikka, J. (1968). The varieties of information and scientific explanation. In B. Von Rootselaar and J.F. Staal (eds) *Logic, methodology and philosophy of science,* Vol. 3. Amsterdam: North-Holland.

Jonas, H. (1953). A critique of cybernetics. *Social Research,* **20**.

Kochen, M. (1983). Information and society. *Annual Review of Information Science and Technology,* **18**.

Krippendorf, K. (1984). Paradox and information. In B. Dervin and M.J. Voigt (eds) *Progress in communication sciences.* Norwood: Ablex.

Lamberton, D.M. (1975). *Who owns the unexpected? A perspective on the nation's information industry.* St Lucia: Queensland University Press.

Lancaster, F.W. (1968). *Information retrieval systems.* New York: John Wiley and Sons.

Lathi, B.P. (1983). *Modern digital and analog communication systems.* New York: Holt, Rinehart and Winston.

Lessig, L. (2002). The architecture of innovation. *Duke Law Journal,* **51**, 1783–8.

Levesque, H.J. (1986). Knowledge representation and reasoning. *Annual Review of Computing Science,* **1**.

Levitan, K.B. (1980). Applying a holistic framework to synthesise information science research. In B. Dervin and M.J. Voigt (eds) *Progress in communication sciences,* Vol. 2. Norwood: Ablex.

Lewis, C.T. and Short, C. (1900). *Latin dictionary.* Oxford: Oxford University Press.

Li Ming. (1985). On information. *Social Sciences in China,* **6**(2), June.

Lytle, R.H. (1986). Information resource management: 1981–1986. *Annual Review of Information Science and Technology,* **21**.

Mead, G.H. (1938). *Philosophy of the act.* Chicago: University of Chicago Press.

Metcalfe, J. (1959). *Subject classifying and indexing of libraries and literature.* London: Angus and Robertson.

Minsky, M.L. (1979). Computer science and the representation of knowledge. In M.L. Dertouzos, M.L. and J. Muses (eds) *The computer age.* Cambridge, MA: MIT Press.

Minsky, M.L. (1987). *The society of mind.* London: Heinemann.

Murdock, J.W. and Liston, D.M. (1967). A general model of information transfer. *American Documentation,* **18**.

NCLIS (National Commission on Libraries and Information Science) (1982). *Public Sector/Private Sector Interaction In Providing Information Services.* Washington, DC: NCLIS.

Paulsen, B.A. (1980). *Fundamental relationships of information, communication, and power with respect to organizations and automated information processing.* PhD Thesis: University of Colarado.

Pratt, A.D. (1977). The information of the image. *Libri,* **27**(3).

Rommetveit, R. (1968). *Words, meanings, and messages.* New York: Academic Press.

Sampson, J.R. (1976). *Adaptive information processing.* New York: Springer-Verlag.

Schramm, W (1963). Communication research in the United States.In W. Schramm (ed.) *The science of human communication.* New York: Basic Books.

Schramm, W. (1973). *Men, messages, and media.* New York: Harper and Row.

Shannon, C. and Weaver, W. (1964). *The mathematical theory of communication.* Urbana: University of Illinois Press.

Tell, B.V. (1974). The impact of technology on information transfer. *The Tell seminar: National information policy and the impact of social and technological change on national information planning.* 16–18 April. Canberra: National Library of Australia.

Tolkein, J.R.R. (1965). *The two towers*. New York: Ballantine Books.

Toobin, J. (2007). Google's moon shot: the quest for the universal library. *The New Yorker*, February 5.

Van Rijsbergen, C.J. (1975). *Information retrieval*. London: Butterworths.

Wicken, J.S. (1987). Entropy and information: suggestions for common language. *Philosophy of Science*, **54**, 176–93.

Wiener, N. (1950). *The human use of human beings*. New York: Avon Books.

Wiener, N. (1951). *Cybernetics*. New York: John Wiley.

Yovits, M.C. and Abilock, J.G. (1974). A semiotic framework for information science leading to the development of a quantitative measure of information. In P. Zunde (ed.) *Information utilities: Proceedings of the 37th ASIS annual meeting*, Washington: American Society for Information Science.

Chapter 7

Altheide, D.L. (2004). Consuming terrorism. *Symbolic Interaction*, **27**(3), 289–308.

Anderson, J.W. (1999). The Internet and Islam's new interpreters. In D.F. Eickelman and J.W. Anderson (eds) *New media in the Muslim world: The emerging public sphere*. Bloomington: Indiana University Press.

Arendt, H. (1958). *The Human Condition*. Chicago: University of Chicago Press.

Benoit, S.L. (1997). Hugh Grant's image restoration discourse: an actor apologizes. *Communication Quarterly*, **45**(3), 251–67.

Berelson, B. and Janowitz, M. (eds) (1966). *Public opinion and communication*. New York: The Free Press.

Childs, H.L. (1965). *Public opinion: Nature, formation and role*. Princeton, NJ: Van Nostrand.

Christenson, R.M. and McWilliams, R.O. (eds) (1967). *Voice of the people*. New York: McGraw-Hill.

Collins, S. (2007). *Mind games: An assessment of the Coalition's perception-management operations before, during and after Operation Iraqi Freedom and their implications for NATO*. Institute of Communications Studies: University of Leeds.

Crable, R., and Vibbert, S. (1985). Managing issues and influencing public policy. *Public Relations Review*, **11**(2), 3–15.

David, K. and Pavlik, J.V. (2003). Agenda setting and media coverage of SARS. *International Agenda Setting Conference*, Bonn, Germany.

Furedi, F. (2002). *Culture of fear*. Continuum International Publishing Group.

Grunig, J.E. (1979). A new measure of public opinion on corporate social responsibility. *Academy of Management Journal*, **22**(4), 238–64.

Hennessy, C. (1965). *Public opinion*. Belmont, CA: Wadsworth.

Hutchinson, W. (2006). Information warfare and deception. *Informing Science*, **9**, 211–23.

Hutchinson, W. and Warren, W. (2001). Principles of information warfare. *Journal of Information Warfare*, **1**(1), 1–11.

Jowett, G.S. and O'Donnell, V. (2006). *Propaganda and persuasion*. Sage: London.

Lee, A.M. and Lee, E.B. (1939). *The fine art of propaganda*. New York: Harcourt, Brace and Company.

Lee, J. (2007). Rise of the great green wash. *Sydney Morning Herald*, November 24.

MacArthur, J.R. (1992). *Second front: Censorship and propaganda in the Gulf War*. Berkeley, CA: University of California Press.

Massumi, B. (2005). Fear (The Spectrum Said). *Positions*, **13**(1), 31–48.

McAllister, I. (1992). *Political behaviour*. London: Longman Cheshire.

Nimmo, D. and Combs, J.E. (1983). *Mediated political realities*, New York: Praeger.

O'Carroll, A., Tryhorn, C. and Deans, J. (2008). War Watch: Claims and counter claims made during the media war over Iraq. *Guardian*, 11 April.

Petty, R.E. and Cacioppo, J.T. (1986). The elaboration likelihood model of persuasion. *Advanced Experimental Psychology*, **19**, 123–205.

Prewitt, K., Alterman, E., Arato, A., Pyszczynski, T., Robin, C. and Stern, J. (2004). Politics of fear after 9/11: Can the past inform the future? *Social Research*, **71**(4).

Reynolds, P. (2005). Nazis' exploding chocolate plans. BBC, 4 September.

Robin, C. (2004). *Fear: The History of a Political Idea*. New York: Oxford University Press.

Stauber, J. and Rampton, S. (1995). *Lies, damn lies and the public relations industry*. Monroe, Maine: Common Courage Press.

UNESCO (2003) http://www.uis.unesco.org.

Chapter 8

Almasude, A. (1999) The new mass media and the shaping of Amazigh identity. In J. Reyhner, G. Cantoni, R. N. St Clair, and E. Parsons-Yazzie, *Revitalizing indigenous languages* (117–28). Flagstaff, AZ: Northern Arizona University.

Altschull, J.H. (1984). *Agents of power*. New York: Longman.

Anheier, H. and Isar, Y.R. (eds) (2008). Introducing the cultures and globalization series and the cultural economy. In H. Anheier and Y.R. Isar (eds) Cultures and globalization: The cultural economy. London: Sage.

Bagdikian, B.H. (2004). *The new media monopoly*. Boston: Beacon Press.

Boler, M. (ed.) (2008). *Digital media and democracy: tactics in hard times*. Cambridge, MA: MIT.

Boyd-Barrett, O. and D.K. Thussu (1992). *Contra-flow in global news : international and regional news exchange mechanisms*. London: John Libbey.

Boyd-Barrett, O. (2007). *Communications media, globalization and empire*. Indiana University Press.

Cammaerts, B. (2007). Jamming the political: Beyond counter-hegemonic practices. *Continuum: Journal of Media and Cultural Studies*, **21**(1), 71–90.

Carlsson, C. (2003). *The rise and fall of NWICO – and then? From a vision of international regulation to a reality of multilevel governance*. NORDICOM.

Centeno, M.A. (2005). McDonalds, Wienerwald, and the Corner Deli. Unpublished paper, Department of Sociology, Princeton University.

Cozens, C. (2005). AFP sues Google over copyrighted content. *Guardian*, 21 March, accessed April 2006, http://media.guardian.co.uk/.

Dorfman, A. and Mattelart, A. (Trans. David Kunzle). (1975). *How to read Donald Duck: Imperialist ideology in the Disney comic*. New York: International General.

Global Press Freedom (2007). *Growing threats to media independence*. Freedom House.

Granzberg, G. (1985) Television as storyteller: The Algonkian Indians of central Canada. *Journal of Communication*, **32**(1), 43–52.

Hall, E.T. (1976). *Beyond culture*. New York: Doubleday/Anchor Press.

Hofstede, G. (1982). *Cultures consequences*. Beverly Hills, CA: Sage.

Jankowski, N.W. and Jansen, M. (2003). Indymedia: Exploration of an alternative Internet-based source of movement. *News Digital News, Social Change and Globalization*. Hong Kong Baptist University11–12 December http://www.hkbu.edu.hk/~jour/DN2003

Jordan, T. (2002). *Activism! Direct action, hacktivism and the future of society*. London: Reaktion Books.

Klein, N. (2000). *No logo*. Flamingo, London.

Kress, G. (1998) *Communication and culture*. Sydney: New South Wales University Press.

Lerner, D. (1958). *The passing of traditional society: modernizing the Middle East.* New York: Free Press.

McLaren, A. (2003). Targeting Chinese women: constructing a female cyberspace. *Women, Information and Communication Technology in India and China Forum.* 5–7 November. The Hawke Research Institute, University of South Australia, with the Institute of International Studies at the University of Technology Sydney, Melbourne Institute of Asian Languages and Societies, University of Melbourne.

Melvern, L. (2007). Missing the story: The media and the Rwanda genocide. In A. Thompson (ed.) *The media and the Rwanda genocide* (198–210). London: Pluto Press.

Miller, T., Nitin, G., McMurria, R. and Wang, T. (2005). *Global Hollywood 2.* London: British Film Institute.

Pallister, D. (2007). Junta tries to shut down internet and phone links. *Guardian*, Thursday, 27 September.

Paterson, C. (2006). *News agency dominance in international news on the Internet.* Centre for International Communications Research 01/06.

Schiller, H. (2000). *Living in the number one country: reflections from a critic of American empire.* Seven Stories Press.

Schiller, H.K. (1976). *Communications and cultural domination.* New York: International Arts and Science Press.

Siebert, F.S., Peterson T., and Schramm, W. (1963). *Four theories of the press.* Urbana, IL: University of Illinois Press.

Stevenson, R.L. (1994). *Global communication in the twenty-first century.* New York: Longman.

Thussu, D.K. (2006). *International communication: continuity and change.* London: Hodder Arnold.

Thussu, D.K. (ed.) (2007). *Media on the move: global flow and contra-flow.* New York: Routledge.

Tomlinson, J. (1992). *Globalization and culture.* Cambridge: Polity Press.

Tomlinson, J. (2001). *Cultural imperialism.* Continuum International Publishing Group.

UNESCO Work Plan for 1977–1978, 19C/5 Approved § 4155.

Varan, D. (1998). The cultural erosion metaphor and the transcultural impact of media systems. *Journal of Communication,* **48**(2).

Wallerstein, I. (1974). *The modern world system: Capitalist agriculture and the origins of the European world economy in the sixteenth century.* New York: Academic Press.

Williams, R. (1981). *Culture.* London: Fontana.

Chapter 9

Advani, M. (2008). Ballyhoo over Bollywood: Germany is proof the genre can travel. *Hollywood Reporter*, 12 February.

Anderson, B. (1991). *Imagined communities.* London: Verso.

Apter, D. and Saich, T. (1998). *Revolutionary discourse in Mao's republic.* Cambridge: Harvard University Press.

Bian, Y.J., Breiger, R., Davis, D. and J. Galaskiewicz, J. (2005). Occupation, class, and social networks in China. *Social Forces,* **83**(4), 1443–68.

Butcher, M. (2003). *Transnational television, cultural identity and change: When STAR came to India.* New Delhi: Sage.

CNNIC (2001). Semiannual Survey Report on the Development of China's Internet (Jan. 2001) China Internet Network Information Center http://www.cnnic.gov.cn/develst/e-cnnic200101.shtml.

Donald, S.H. (2008). Landscapes of class in contemporary Chinese film: from *Yellow Earth* to *Still Life*. In J. Malpas (ed.) *Problems of landscape*. Cambridge, MA: MIT Press.

Donald S.H. and Gammack, J.G. (2007). *Tourism and the branded city: Film and identity on the Pacific Rim*. Aldershot: Ashgate.

Donald, S.H. and Keane, M. (2002). Media in China: new convergences, new approaches. In S.H. Donald, M. Keane and Y. Hong (eds) *Media in China: Consumption, content and crisis* (3–17). London: Routledge Curzon.

Euromonitor. http://www.euromonitor.com/.

Fu, P. (2003). *Between Shanghai and Hong Kong: The politics of Chinese cinemas*. Stanford: Stanford University Press.

Gokulsing, K., and Dissanayake, W. (1998). *Indian Popular Cinema*. New Delhi, India: Orient Longman.

India Today (2007). 17 December.

Kapur, S. (2002, August 23). The Asians are coming. *Guardian*. Retrieved January 25, 2004, from http://www.guardian.co.uk/arts/fridayreview/story/ 0,12102,778838,00.html

Kavaratzis, M. and Ashworth, G.J. (2005). Partners in coffeeshops, canals and commerce: Marketing the city of Amsterdam. *Cities*, **24**(1), 16–25.

Mecklai, N. and Shoesmith, B. (2007). Religion as commodity images: Securing a Hindu Rashtra. In McGuire, J. and Copland, I. (eds) *Hindu nationalism and governance*. Oxford University Press.

Mishra, V. (2002). *Bollywood cinema: temples of desire*. London: Routledge.

Mishra, V. (2006). *Bollywood cinema: A critical genealogy*. Asia Studies Institute. Wellington, New Zealand: Victoria University of Wellington.

NUA Internet Surveys (1999). Chinese users to outnumber US users by 2010. 9 November.

NUA Internet Surveys (2000). India: Outlook positive for online banking. 15 December.

NUA Internet Surveys (2001a). The Net in India: A luxury few can afford. 8 January.

NUA Internet Surveys (2001b). US no longer dominates the Internet. 17 May.

Page, D. and Crawley, W. (2001). *Satellites over South Asia: Broadcasting culture and public interest*. New Delhi: Sage.

Prasad, R. (1999). Indian films show how the West can be won over. *Business Asia*, November 22.

Rajadhyaksha, A. (2003). The 'Bollywoodization' of the Indian cinema: Cultural nationalism in the global arena. *Inter-Asia Cultural Studies*, **4**(1), 25–39.

Rao, A.R. and Ruekert, R.W. (1994). Brand alliances as signals of product quality. *Sloan Management Review*, September, 87–97.

Said, E. (2003). *Orientalism*. New York: Penguin.

Singhal, A. and Rogers, E.M. (2001). *India's communication revolution: From bullock carts to cyber markets*. New Delhi: Sage.

Thomas, A.O. (2006). *Transnational media and contoured markets: Redefining Asian television and advertising*. New Delhi: Sage.

Tsering, L. (2003). Bollywood confidential. *Salon*. http://www.salon.com/ent/movies/feature/.

Wang, J. (2005). Youth culture, music and cell phone branding in China. *Global Media and Communication*, **1**(2), 185–201.

Wang, S. and Zhang, Z. (2005). The new retail economy of Shanghai. *Growth and Change*, **36**(1), 41–73.

World Bank. http://www.worldbank.org.

Chapter 10

Abramson, J.B., Christopher, F., Arterton, C. and Orren, G.R. (1988). *The electronic Common-wealth: The impact of new media technologies on democratic politics*. New York: Basic Books.

ASPA and UNDPEPA (2001). *Benchmarking e-government, a global perspective: Assessing the progress of the UN member states*. Report by the American Society for Public Administration (ASPA) and the United Nations Division for Public Economics and Public Administration (UNDPEPA), at http://216.149.125.141/about/pdfs/BenchmarkingEgov.pdf.

ASPA and UNDPEPA (2002). *Benchmarking e-government, a global perspective: Assessing the progress of the UN member states*. Report by the American Society for Public Administration (ASPA) and United Nations Division for Public Economics and Public Administration (UNDPEPA).

Balnaves, M., Shoesmith, B. and Walsh, L. (2006). E-democracy: Media-liminal space in the era of age compression. In J. Weiss, J. Nolan, J. Hunsinger and P. Trifonas (eds) *International handbook of virtual learning environments*. Springer.

Bimber, B. (2003). *Information and American democracy: Technology in the evolution of political power*. Cambridge: Cambridge University Press.

Blomgren Bingham, L., Nabatchi, T. and O'Leary, R. (2005). The new governance: Practices and processes for stakeholder and citizen participation in the work of government. *Public Administration Review*, **65**(5).

Briggs, A. (1965). *The history of broadcasting in the United Kingdom* (Vol. 2). Oxford: Oxford University Press.

Clarke, R. (1994). Digital persona: and its application to data surveillance. http://www.anu.edu.au/people/Roger.Clarke/DV/DigPersona.html.

Coleman, S. (1999). Can the new media invigorate democracy? *The Political Quarterly*, **70**(1), 16–22.

Coleman, S. and Gøtze, J. (2001). *Bowling together: Online public engagement in policy deliberation*. Hansard Society (http://bowlingtogether.net/).

Coleman, S., Taylor, W. and van de Donk, W. (1999). *Parliament in the age of the Internet*. New York: Oxford University Press.

Cross, M. (2004). Direct to your destination. *Guardian*, Thursday, 4 March 2004 at http://www.guardian.co.uk/online/story/0,3605,1161041,00.html.

Featherly, K. (2003). California firm prepares to test voting Vva Digital TV. *Newsbytes*, 29 November 2001, at http://www.politicsonline.com/coverage/newsbytes2/.

Foucault, M. (1998). *Aesthetics, method, and epistemology: essential works of Foucault 1954–1984*, Vol. 2, J. Faubion (ed.), London: Allen Lane, The Penguin Press, 175–85.

Gibson, R.K., Ward, S., and Rommele, A. (eds) (2004). *Electronic democracy: Mobilisation, participation and organisation via new ICTs*. London: Taylor & Francis.

Grönlund, Å. (2002). *Electronic government: Design, applications, and management*. Hershey, PA: Idea Group Publishing.

Grossman, L. (1995). *The electronic republic*. New York: Penguin.

Habermas, J. (1984). *The theory of communicative action: Reason and the rationalization of society*. Boston: Beacon Press.

Harmon, A. (1998). Hacktivists of all persuasions take their struggle to the Web. *New York Times Online*. 31 October.

Hobsbawn, A. (2003). Phone a foreigner. *Guardian*, Wednesday, 10 December, at http://society.guardian.co.uk/e-public/story/0,13927,1103283,00.html.

Kooiman, J. (ed.) (1993). *Modern governance: New government society interactions*. Thousand Oaks, CA: Sage Publications.

Levy, S. (1984). The hacker ethic. In *Hackers: Heroes of the computer revolution*. New York: Anchor Press/Doubleday.

Lewis, M. (2001). Why Wall Street hates this kid. *Australian Financial Review, The Weekend*, 10–11 March, 1.

Lynn, L.E. and Ingraham, P.W. (eds) (2004). Governance and public management: A symposium. *Journal of Policy Analysis and Management*, **23**(1), 3–96.

Macpherson, C.B. (1973). *Democractic theory: essays in retrieval*. Oxford: Clarendon Press.

March, J.G. and Olsen, J.P. (1995). *Democratic governance*. New York: Free Press.

McKay, N. (1998). The golden age of hacktivism. *Wired News* (http://www.wired.com/politics).

Meikle, G. (2002). *Future active: Media activism and the internet*. Annandale: Pluto Press.

Moor, J.H. (1997). Towards a theory of privacy in the Information Age. *Computers and Society*, **27**(3), 27–32.

Morris, D. (2000). *Vote.com*. Los Angeles: Renaissance Books.

Mueller, M. and Page, C. (2004). *Reinventing media activism: public interest advocacy in the making of US Communication-Information Policy, 1960–2002*. Syracuse: School of Information Studies, Syracuse University.

Pearson, E. (2000). The digital is political: are today's hackers, crackers and hacktivists leading the way to new forms of democracy? Murdoch University: Unpublished Honours Thesis.

Peters, B.G. (1996). *The future of governing: Four emerging models*. Lawrence: University Press of Kansas.

Putnam, R.D. (1995). Bowling alone: America's declining social capital. *Journal of Democracy*, **6**(1), January, 65–78.

Putnam, R.D. (2000). *Bowling alone: The collapse and revival of American community*. New York: Simon & Schuster.

Rhodes, R.A. (1997). *Understanding governance: Policy networks, governance, reflexivity, and accountability*. Open University Press.

Riley, T.B. (2003). Defining e-government and e-governance: Staying the course. *The Riley Report*, May.

Rodan, Garry. 2001. The Internet and political control in Singapore. http://unpan1.un.org/intradoc/groups/public/documents/apcity/unpan002726.pdf.

Rosenau, J.N. and Czempiel, E. (1992). *Governance without government: Order and change in world politics*. Cambridge: Cambridge University Press.

Saywell, T. (2001). Electronic bureaucracy: Governments in Asia are waking up to the importance of offering their citizens services on-line. In *Focus: Telecoms: E-Government*, Issue cover-dated June 21, 2001 at United Nations Online Network in Administration and Finance website (http://unpan1.un.org/intradoc/groups/public/documents/apcity/unpan001663.pdf).

Tavani, H.T. and Grodzinsky, F.X. (2002). Cyberstalking, personal privacy, and moral responsibility. *Ethics and Information Technology*, **4**, 123–32.

Turkle, S. (1995). *Life on the screen: Identity in the age of the Internet*. New York: Simon & Schuster.

Turkle, S. (1997). Computational technologies and images of the self. *Social Research*, **64**(3), 1093–1111.

Turkle, S. (1999). Looking toward cyberspace: Beyond grounded sociology. *Contemporary Sociology*, **28**(6), 643–53.

UNDESA (United Nations Department of Economic and Social Affairs) (2004). *United Nations global e-government readiness report 2004: Towards access for opportunity*. United Nations.

Chapter 11

Aldoory, L. (2001). Making health communications meaningful for women: factors that influence involvement. *Journal of Public Relations Research*, **13**(2),163–85.

Altheide, D.L. (1976). *Creating reality: How TV news distorts events*. Beverley Hills: Sage.

Arbouw, J. (2002). A personal view. *Company Directors*, February.

Baker, I. (1980). The gatekeeper chain: A two-step analysis of how journalists acquire and apply organizational news priorities. In P. Edgar, (ed.) *The news in focus: The journalism of exception*. Melbourne: Macmillan.

Baker, L. (1993). *The credibility factor: Putting ethics to work in public relations*. Illinois: Business One Irwin.

Barringer, F. (2001). Internet newspapers: News unplugged. *Sunday Times*, January, 28–9.

Beatty, S. (2001). CNN will lay off 400, broaden scope of jobs – one third of cuts to come from online staff. *The Asian Wall Street Journal*, January 19.

Beckett, A. (1994). From press to click. *Independent*, May 8, 106.

Bennett, W.L. (1988). *News: The politics of illusion*. New York: Longman.

Brown, R. (1976). So what is news? *Psychology Today*, **2**(12).

Burton, Bob (2001). When corporations want to cuddle: the corporate PR machine. In Evans, G., Goodman, J. and Lansbury, N. (eds) *Moving mountains: communities confront mining and globalisation*. Sydney: Contemporary Oxford Press/Mineral Policy Institute (MPI).

Business News (2001). The Enron debacle. 12 November, 106.

Caney, D. (2001). CNN cuts jobs as web merges with TV units: Top executive resigns: Restructuring means lopping 400 employees. *National Post*, 18 January.

Carlson, D. (1999). Media giants create web gateways. *American Journalism Review*, September, Newslink (Online) Available World Wide Web: http://ajr.newslink.org/ajrcarlsept99.html.

Chibnall, S. (1977). *Law-and-order news: An analysis of crime reporting in the British press*. London: Tavistock.

Cohen, B.C. (1963). *The press and foreign policy*. Princeton: Princeton University Press.

Deuze, M. (1998). The web communicators: Issues in research into online journalism and journalists. (Online) Available World Wide Web: http://www.firstmonday.dk/issues/issue3_12/deuze.

Doig, I. and Doig, C. (1972) *News: A consumer's guide*, Englewood Cliffs, NJ: Prentice Hall.

Dozier, D. and Lauzen, M. (2000). Liberating the intellectual domain from the practice: public relations, activism, and the role of the scholar. *Journal of Public Relations Research*, **12**(1), 3–22.

Erlindson, M. (1995). *Online newspaper: the newspaper industry dive into cyberspace*. Major research paper in journalism, graduate school of journalism, University of Western Ontario (Online). Available World Wide Web: http://www.interlog.com/~merlinds/paper/index.html.

Farhi, P. (2000). Surviving in cyberspace. *American Journalism Review*, 12–18 September, Newslink (Online) Available World Wide Web: http://ajr.newslink.org/ajrfarhiseptoo.html.

Galtung, J. and Ruge, M.H. (1970). The structure of foreign news. In J. Tunstall (ed.) *Media Sociology*. London: Constable.

Gans, H.J. (1979). *Deciding what's news: A study of CBS evening news, NBC nightly news, Newsweek and Time*. New York: Pantheon Books.

Grunig, J. (1992). *Excellence in public relations and communication management*. Hillsdale, NJ: Lawrence Erlbaum Associates.

Grunig, J. and Hunt, T. (1984). *Managing public relations*. New York: Holt, Rhinehart & Winston.

Guiniven, J. (2002). Dealing with activism in Canada: an ideal cultural fit for the two-way symmetrical public relations model. *Public Relations Review*, **28**(4), 393–402.

Halloran, J.D., Elliott, P. and Murdoch, G. (1970). *Demonstrations and communication: A case study.* Harmondsworth: Penguin.

Holtzhausen, Derina (2002). Towards a postmodern research agenda for public relations. *Public Relations Review*, **28**(3), 251–64.

Irwin, W. (1988). The American newspaper. In T. Goldstein (ed.) *Killing the messenger: 100 years of media criticism.* New York: Columbia University Press.

Janes, R.W. (1958). A technique for describing community structure through newspaper analysis. *Social Forces*, **37**.

Janeway, M. (2002). Rethinking the lessons of journalism school. *New York Times*, 17 August, 20.

Jones, R. (2002). Challenges to the notion of publics in public relations: implications of the risk society for the discipline. *Public Relations Review*, **28**(1), 49–62.

Katz, J. (1994). Online or not, newspapers still suck, *Wired*, September, 50–8.

Kent, M. and Taylor, M. (2002). Toward a dialogic theory of public relations. *Public Relations Review*, **28**(1), 21–37.

Landers, K. (2008). *Exxon Valdes $US2.5b oil spill ruling overturned.* ABC News. http://www.abc.net.au/news/stories/2008/06/26/2286105.htm.

Lasisca, J.D. (1997). When push comes to news. *American Journalism Review* (Online). Available World Wide Web: http://www.ajr.newslink.org.

Lasisca, J.D. (2000). Time to freshen up online newspapers. *American Journalism Review*, 8–14 August (Online).

Leeper, R. 1996). Moral objectivity. Jurgen Habermas's discourse ethics and public relations, *Public Relations Review*, **22**, 118–33.

Lippmann, W. (1922). *Public opinion.* New York: Harcourt Brace.

Lovink, G. (2002). Dark fiber: Tracking critical Internet culture. Cambridge, MA: MIT Press.

Livingstone, S. (2005). *Audiences and publics: when cultural engagement matters for the public sphere.* Bristol: Intellect.

Lovink, G. (2007). Blogging, the nihilst impulse. *Eurozine*, http://www.eurozine.com/articles/2007-01-02-lovink-en.html.

Lundberg, M. (1999). The Exxon Valdez oil spill disaster. *Explore North* (Online). http://www.explorenorth.com/library/weekly/aa032499.htm.

Mangan, L. (2003). Friend or Foe? *Guardian*, 7 April. Accessed 30/9/03 at: http://media.guardian.co.uk/mediaguardian/story/0,7558,930987,00.html.

Mayer, H. (1964). *The press in Australia.* Melbourne: Lansdowne Press.

Miller, S. (1998). TV networks on the web. *Online Journalism Review*, 14 July. http://ojr.usc.

Miller, S. (2003). The language of war. http://www.guardian.co.uk/Iraq/Story/0,2763,920643,00.html.

Mott, F.L. (1952). *The news in America.* Harvard: Harvard University Press.

Park, R.E. (1967). News as a form of knowledge. In R.H Turner (ed.) *Robert Park on social control and collective behavior.* Chicago: University of Chicago Press, Phoenix Books.

Pavlik, J.V. (1997). The future of online journalism: Bonanza or black hole? *Columbia Journalism Review*, **36**(2), July/August, 30–8.

Pavlik, J.V. (2001). *Journalism and new media.* Columbia: Columbia University Press.

Piller, C. (2000). Web news sites fail to click. *Los Angeles Times*, 18 August.

Reddick, R. and King, E. (1995) *The online journalist: Using the Internet and other electronic resources.* Fort Worth, TX: Harcourt Brace College.

Roshco, B. (1975). *Newsmaking.* Chicago: University of Chicago Press.

Rutenberg, J. (2001). CNN plans to lay off 400 as part of revamping. *New York Times*, 18 January.

Salam Pax (2003). I became the profane pervert Arab blogger. 9 September (http://media. guardian.co.uk/iraqandthemedia/story/0,12823,1038260,00.html).

Scheier, R. (2000a). Acclaimed crime news web site finds buyer. *Knight Ridder Tribune Business News*, 23 August (http://ptg.djnr.com).

Scheier, R. (2000b). Troubled crime web site auctioned off for $575,000. *Knight Ridder Tribune Business News*, 8 September (http://ptg.djnr.com).

Sigal, L.V. (1973). *Reporters and officials: The organization and politics of newsmaking.* Lexington, MA: Heath.

Small, W. (1991). Exxon Valdez: How to spend billions and still get a black eye. *Public Relations Review*, **17**(1), 9–25.

Toth, E. (2002). Postmodernism for modernist public relations: the cash value and application of critical research in public relations. *Public Relations Review*, **28**(3), 243–50.

Tuchman, G. (1978). *Making news: A study in the construction of reality.* New York: The Free Press.

Tunstall, J. (1970). *The Westminster lobby correspondents: A sociological study of national political journalism.* London: Routledge and Kegan Paul.

Tunstall, J. (1971). *Journalists at work. Specialist correspondents: their news organizations, news sources and competitor-colleagues.* London: Constable.

Chapter 12

Balnaves, M. and Varan, D. (2002). Beyond exposure: interactive television and the new media currency. *Media International Australia*, **105**, 95–104.

Banerjee, I. and Seneviratne, K. (eds) (2006). *Public service broadcasting in the age of globalization.* Asian Media Information and Communication Centre (AMIC).

Banks, J. (2002). Gamers as co-creators: enlisting the virtual audience – a report from the net face. In M. Balnaves, T. O'Regan and J. Sternberg (eds) *Mobilising the audience* (188–213). St Lucia: University of Queensland Press.

BBC (2007). http://www.bbc.co.uk/worldservice/history/story/2007/02/printable/070122_html_40s.shtml BBC World Service.com, 8 February.

Bodey, M. (2008). Ratings system for the future. *The Australian*, 20 March.

Boorstin, D.J. (1961). *The image: Or what happened to the American dream.* London, Weidenfeld and Nicolson.

Collins, R. (2002). *Media and identity in contemporary Europe: Consequences of global convergence.* Bristol: Intellect.

Curran, J. (2002). *Media and power.* London: Routledge.

Galbraith, J.K. (1969). *The affluent society.* London: Hamish Hamilton.

International Federation of the Phonographic Industry (IFPI) (2006). The recording industry 2006 Piracy Report.

Knight, O. (1964) Scripps and his adless newspaper, 'The Day Book'. *Journalism Quarterly*, Winter, **41**(1).

Livingstone, S. (2005). *Audiences and publics: when cultural engagement matters for the public sphere.* Bristol: Intellect.

Napoli, P.M. (2003). *Audience economics: Media institutions and the audience marketplace.* Columbia: Columbia University Press.

Noah, S. (2005). BBC1 and BBC2 report 6% decline in viewers. *Independent*, 23 November.

Phelps, S. (1989). A reconsideration of the ARF model. *Marketing & Media Decisions*, November, 98.

Rayboy, M. (1999). What is public service broadcasting? In *Public service broadcasting in Asia: Surviving the new information age* (1–24). AMIC.

Story, L. (2008). Nielsen looks beyond TV, and hits roadblocks. *New York Times*, 26 February.

Tracey, M. (1998). *The decline and fall of public service broadcasting*. Oxford: Oxford University Press.

Underwood, D. (1993). *When MBAs rule the newsroom: How the marketers and managers are reshaping today's media*. New York: Columbia University Press.

Chapter 13

Ang, I. (1996). *Living room wars*. London: Routledge.

Balnaves, M. and Tomlinson-Baillie, K. (2005). Yu-Gi-Oh: interactive games narratives in the era of age compression. *The Twelfth International Conference on Learning*, Faculty of Education at the University of Granada, 11–14 July 2005.

Behrenshausen, B.G. (2007). Toward a (kin)aesthetic of video gaming: The case of Dance Dance Revolution. *Games and Culture*, **2**(4), 335–54.

Buckingham, D. (1993). *Reading audiences: Young people and the media*. Manchester: Manchester University Press.

Buckingham, D. (2006). *Digital generations: Children, young people, and new media*. London: Routledge.

Castronova, E. (2005). *Synthetic worlds: The business and culture of online games*. Chicago: University of Chicago Press.

Chan, E.C. (1999). 'It's not just gaming': reflections on the nature of experience in learning through gaming. In C. Hoadley and J. Roschelle (eds) *Proceedings of the Conference on Computers for Supporting Collaborative Learning*, Stanford, California, December, 101–7.

Dalziel, J. (1955). Comics in New Zealand. *Landfall*, **9**(1), 52.

Donald, S.H. (2000). Seeing white: female whiteness and the purity of children in Australian, British and Chinese visual culture. *Social Semiotics*, **10**(2), 157–71.

Drotner, K. and Livingstone, S. (eds) (2008). *The international handbook of children's media culture*. London: Sage.

Ettema, J.S. and Whitney, D.C. (1994). The money arrow: An introduction to audiencemaking. In J.S. Ettema and D.C. Whitney (eds) *Audiencemaking: How the media create the audience*. Thousand Oaks: Sage.

Foucault, M. (1998). *Aesthetics, method, and epistemology: essential works of Foucault 1954–1984*, Vol. 2, J. Faubion (ed.), London: Allen Lane, The Penguin Press, 175–85.

Hartley, J. (2005). 'Read Thy Self.' Text, audience and method in cultural studies. In M. White, J. and Schwoch, J. (eds) *The question of method in cultural studies*. Oxford: Blackwell.

Huhh, J.S. (2008). Culture and business of PC bangs in Korea. *Games and Culture*, **3**(1), 26–37.

Huizinga, J. (1970). *Homo Ludens: a study of the play element in culture*. London: Temple Smith.

Jenkins, H. (1992). *Textual poachers: Television fans and participatory culture*. New York: Routledge, Chapman and Hall.

Jenkins, H. (2006). *Convergence culture: where old and new media collide*. New York: New York University Press.

Kerr, A. (2006). *The business and culture of digital games: gamework/gameplay*. London: Sage.

Kohler, C. (2005). *Power up: How Japanese video games gave the world an extra life*. Indianpolis: Brady Games.

McDougall, J. and Chantry, D. (2004). The making of tomorrow's consumer. *Young Consumers*, **5**(4).

McQuail, D. (1997). *Audience analysis*. Thousand Oaks: Sage.

Mortensen, T.E. (2006). WoW is the new MUD. Social gaming from text to video. *Games and Culture*, **1**(4), 397–413.

Nichols, D., Farrand, T., Rowley, T. and Avery, M. (2006). *Brands and gaming: The computer gaming phenomenon and its impact on brands and businesses*. Basingstoke: Palgrave Macmillan.

Nieuwenhuis, C. (1966). *Provo #9*. English translation published 1970 by The Friends of Malatesta. Buffalo, New York.

Norton (2008). The Norton Online Living Report (http://www.symantec.com/).

Pearce, C., Fullerton, T., Fron, J. and Jacquelyn Ford Morie, J.F. (2007). Sustainable play: Toward a new games movement for the digital age. *Games and Culture*, **2**(3), 261–78.

Pearson, B. (1955). Letter printed in *Landfall*, **9**(1), 95–7.

Peterson, M.A. (2003). *Anthropology and mass communication: Media and myth in the new millennium*. New York: Berghahn Books.

Postigo, H. (2007). Of mods and modders; Chasing down the value of fan-based digital game modifications. *Games and Culture*, **2**(4), 300–13.

Pratchet, R. (2005). *Games in the UK: Digital play, digital lifestyles*. BBC.

PricewaterhouseCoopers (2006). *Global entertainment and media outlook: 2006–2010* (http://www.pwc.com).

Tolkien, J.R.R. (1977). On fairy stories. In H. Carpenter (ed.) *J. R. R. Tolkien: a Biography*. London: Allen & Unwin.

Turner, V. (1979). Myth and symbol. In D. Sills (ed.) *The international encyclopedia of the social sciences*. New York: Macmillan Publishers, 576–82.

Turner, V. (1995). *The ritual process: structure and anti-structure*. New York: Aldine de Gruyter.

Turner, V. (1982). *From ritual to theatre: the human seriousness at play*. New York: Performing Arts Journal.

Turow, J. (1997) *Breaking up America: Advertisers and the new media world*. Chicago: University of Chicago Press.

Webster, J.G. and Phalen, P.F. (1994). Victim, consumer or commodity? Audience models in communication policy. In J.S. Ettema and D.C. Whitney (eds) *Audiencemaking: How the media create the audience*. Thousand Oaks: Sage.

Weight, J. (2004). Cyborg dreams: from ergodics to electracy. *On the Horizon*, **12**(1), 36–40.

Winnicott, D. (1953). Transitional objects and transitional phenomena. *International Journal of Psychoanalysis*, **34**, 89–97.

Wu, W., Fore, S., Wang, X. and Sik Ying Ho, P. (2007). Beyond virtual carnival and masquerade: In-game marriage on the Chinese internet. *Games and Culture*, **2**(1), 59–89.

Chapter 14

Altman, I. and Taylor, D. (1973). *Social penetration: The development of interpersonal relationships*. New York: Holt, Rinehart & Winston.

Anderson, T.L. and Emmers-Sommer, T.M. (2006). Predictors of relationship satisfaction in online romantic relationships. *Communication Studies*, **57**(2), 153–73.

Balnaves, M. and Caputi, P. (2001). *Introduction to quantitative research methods*. London: Sage.

Bandura, A. (1977). *Social learning theory*. New York: General Learning Press.

Benjamin, W. (1970). On some motifs in Baudelaire. *Illuminations* (ed. Hannah Arendt, trans. Harry Zohn). London: Jonathan Cape, 157–202.

Berger, C.R. and Calabrese, R.J. (1975). Some explorations in initial interaction and beyond: Toward a developmental theory of interpersonal communication. *Human Communication Research*, **1**, 99–112.

Bottomore, T.B. and Rubel, M. (eds) (1956). *Karl Marx: Selected writings in sociology and social philosophy.* New York: McGraw-Hill.

Braverman, H. (1974). *Labor and monopoly capital.* New York: Monthly Review Press.

Brehm, S. (1992). *Intimate relationships.* New York: McGraw-Hill.

Coleman, P. (1969). The coming war in advertising. *Observer*, **31**, 677–80.

Cooper, A. and Sportolari, L. (1997). Romance in cyberspace: Understanding online attraction. *Journal of Sex Education and Therapy*, **22**, 7–14.

Crouteau, D. and Hoynes, W. (2000). *Media society: industries, images and audiences.* Thousand Oaks, CA: Pine Forge Press.

Durkin, K. (1984). Children's accounts of sex-role stereotypes in television. *Communication research*, **11**(3), 341–62.

Freud, S. (1938). *An outline of psychoanalysis* (J. Strachey, Trans., 2001 edn, Vol. 23). London: Vintage.

Gibbs, J. L., Ellison, N. B. and Heino, R. D. (2006). Self-presentation in online personals: The role of anticipated future interaction, self-disclosure and perceived success in Internet dating. *Communication Research*, **33**, 152–77.

Gunter, G. (2000). *Media research methods.* London: Sage.

Hardey, M. (2004). Mediated relationships: Authenticity and the possibility of romance. *Information, Communication and Society*, **7**(2), 207–22.

Jensen, K.B. (ed.) (2002). *A handbook of media and communication research: Qualitative and quantitative methodologies.* London: Routledge.

Kubota, Y. (2007). Cyber bullying bedevils Japan. *International Business Times*, 12 November.

Morley, D. (1980). *The Nationwide audience: Structure and decoding.* London: British Film Institute.

Peterson, M.A. (2003). *Anthropology and mass communication: Media and myth in the new millennium.* New York: Berghahn Books.

Puri, J. (1997). Reading romance novels in postcolonial India. *Gender and Society*, **11**(4), 434–52.

Radway, J.A. (1991). *Reading the romance: women, patriarchy, and popular literature.* Chapel Hill: University of North Carolina Press.

Sydney Morning Herald (2005). Fairfax buys online dating service. 11 July.

Silverstone, R. (ed.) (2005a). *Media, technology and everyday life in Europe.* Aldershot: Ashgate.

Silverstone, R. (2005b). Domesticating domestication. Reflections on the life of concept. In T. Berker, M. Hartmann, Y. Punie and K. Ward (eds) *Domestication of media and technologies* (229–48). Maidenhead: Open University Press.

Silverstone, R. and L. Haddon (1996). Design and the domestication of information and communication technologies: Technical change and everyday life. In R. Silverstone and R. Mansell (eds) *Communication by design. The politics of information and communication technologies* (44–74). Oxford: Oxford University Press.

Silverstone, R. (1995). Media, communication, information and the 'revolution' of everyday life. In S. Emmott (ed.) *Information superhighways: Multimedia users and futures* (61–78). London: Academic Press.

Silverstone, R. (1994). *Television and everyday life.* London: Routledge.

Simmat, R. (1933). *The principles and practices of marketing.* Sir I. Pitman.

Sorenson, A.B. (1991). Merton and methodology. *Contemporary Sociology*, **20**(4), 516–19.

Virilio, P. and Lotringer, S. (1997). *Pure war.* New York: Semiotext(e).

Walther, J.B. (1996). Computer-mediated communication: Impersonal, interpersonal and hyperpersonal interaction. *Communication Research*, **23**, 3–43.

Worsley, P. (1977). *Introducing sociology.* Harmondsworth: Penguin.

Chapter 15

Curtin, M. (2003). Media capital: Towards the study of spatial flows. *International Journal of Cultural Studies*, **6**(2), 202–28.

Giddens, A. (1999). *The Reith Lectures*. BBC (http://news.bbc.co.uk/).

The Hindu (2008). Dalai Lama offers to quit as political head of movement. Staff Correspondent, Wednesday 19 March.

Sykes, R. (2008). Climate change to hit hip pocket nerve. *Yass Tribune*, 19 March.

Webster, F. (1995). *Theories of the information society*. London: Routledge.

Index